Foreign Trade and the National Economy

Mercantilist and Classical Perspectives

Leonard Gomes

St. Martin's Press   New York

© Leonard Gomes, 1987

All rights reserved. For information, write:
Scholarly & Reference Division,
St. Martin's Press, Inc., 175 Fifth Avenue, New York, NY 10010

First published in the United States of America in 1987

Printed in Hong Kong

ISBN 0–312–00765–5

Library of Congress Cataloging-in-Publication Data
Gomes, Leonard.
Foreign trade and the national economy.
Bibliography: p.
Includes index.
1. Commerce. 2. Mercantile system. 3. Classical school of economics. I. Title.
HF1008.G65 1987   382   87–4674
ISBN 0–312–00765–5

FOREIGN TRADE AND THE NATIONAL ECONOMY

By the same author

INTERNATIONAL ECONOMIC PROBLEMS

Contents

Preface   vii

PART I   REGULATED TRADE: MERCANTILISM

1 The Age of Mercantilism   3
    1.1 Interpreting the Mercantilist Literature   5
    1.2 Historical Background   12

2 Mercantilist Thought on Foreign Trade   38
    2.1 The Balance-of-trade Doctrine   38
    2.2 Trade, Employment and Growth   67
    2.3 Trade, Power and Plenty   78

3 The Decline of Mercantilist Trade Doctrines   94

PART II   CLASSICAL POLITICAL ECONOMY AND FOREIGN TRADE

4 Classical Trade Theory   129

5 The Economists, the Corn Laws and Commercial Policy   171
    5.1 The Economists and the Corn-Law Debate   171
    5.2 Commercial Policy   192
    5.3 The Export of Technology   211

6 Gold, Money and Trade   220

7 Free Trade and the National Economists   254

Notes and References   278

Index   314

Preface

This book is about international trade theory and policy seen in historical perspective. It covers the period from the mercantilists down to the classical economists and their critics. It deals in a comprehensive manner with doctrines relating to international economic relations during a period which saw the emergence and establishment of political economy as a distinct branch of the social sciences. These early writers were concerned with urgent and often complex matters relating to policy; and it was this intellectual involvement that produced the technical apparatus of reasoning about the international economy which in turn generated further controversy among economists – a process that continues today.

The book aims to convey the flavour of these early debates by way of tracing the development of analytical concepts and modes of reasoning. The historical context in doctrinal analysis means that one makes use of recent research in economic history and the history of ideas. It also means that one should take note, as far as possible, of the diversity of views expressed on any particular topic. This is done in the text – the aim being to give a stimulating and intellectually rewarding survey of doctrinal history.

Part I is concerned with the trade doctrines of the mercantilists. The historical background against which these ideas emerged is described. This leads to an account of the balance-of-trade and related doctrines, e.g. employment, growth and power. The focus is on the English mercantilists, but a summary is also given of the writings of other European mercantilists, including sections on French and Dutch mercantilist policies. This part ends with a survey of the important topic regarding the decline of mercantilist thought on foreign trade.

Part II deals with the classical economists. Chapter 4 traces the development of the theory of comparative advantage at the hands of Ricardo, Torrens and Mill. The revival of Ricardian scholarship (Sraffa, Hollander) has led to a reinterpretation of Ricardo's foreign-trade model based on his theory of profits – the policy implications of which are discussed in Chapter 5. There follows a critical assessment of the classical economists' discussions on free trade, the terms of trade and infant-industry argument for protection. Also included is the fascinating debate on the export of machinery – anticipating modern fears about loss of technological leadership. Chapter 6 is concerned with the origins of the gold standard – theoretical ideas and policy decisions. The discussion revolves around the Bullionist and Currency-Banking Schools controversy. The final chapter is devoted mainly to the writings of Friedrich List – sadly neglected in the English literature – who anticipated much of the later criticisms of the classical theory of international trade.

The book should appeal to students on undergraduate courses in history of economic thought, economic history and history of international relations. It should provide intellectual and historical breadth to a theoretical course in international economics. It also presents useful supplementary reading material for a variety of interdisciplinary courses, e.g. in connection with projects, extended essays, etc., in the topic-areas covered by the text. The book is fully annotated and contains ample references for further reading.

LEONARD GOMES

Part I
Regulated Trade: Mercantilism

1 The Age of Mercantilism

INTRODUCTION

'Bringing of forty ships filled with cedar logs. Shipbuilding of cedarwood, one ... ship, 100 cubits long. ... Making the doors of the royal palace of cedarwood.'[1]

Thus an entry from the annals of Pharaoh Sneferu, ruler of Egypt around 2650 B.C. This is our earliest written record of international trade. It relates to the import by Egypt of cedarwood from Lebanon for building purposes and the making of palace doors. International trade is as old as civilised man. From archaeological evidence and fragments of written records we know that there was a lively trade among the early peoples of the Near East which also extended to China and India. The earliest articles of trade were in stone, malachite and the black volcanic glass called 'obsidian', useful for knives and other cutting instruments. The Assyrians imported cotton from India and silver from Cilicia. The Mycenaeans obtained amber from the far Baltic region. The invention and use of bronze for tools and weapons provided a powerful stimulus to international trade in ancient times. The trade routes both by sea and donkey caravan spun a commercial network that involved practically all the great civilisations of the Old World, e.g. the Silk Road from China to Antioch. Among the Hittites, Egyptians and Mycenaean Greeks trade was officially controlled – an early form of state trading, whereas in ancient Iraq and Assyria foreign trade was largely in the hands of private entrepreneurs.

A succession of empires arose and fell, but trade continued regardless being based, as always, on differential resource endowments, tastes and the lure of profits. War and sometimes religion brought peoples of different lands into contact, but the most pervasive and enduring influence was that of international commerce.

Intelligent people in ancient times must have reflected on the nature and implications of foreign trade, but of what they thought little or nothing has survived. As regards what we consider to be economic analysis of international trade and finance this only emerges in the sixteenth century among the group of writers called 'mercantilists'.

The thinkers of Greece and Rome touched on economic matters and the medieval Schoolmen had much to say about questions of value and distribution. But they contributed little to the discussion of international trade and its relationship to the national economy. Perhaps this was due to the fact that the national economy as such did not then exist. Perceptions of such relationships, e.g. between trade and national economic structure, between the interests of the trader and the interests of the state, did not arise until the emergence of the nation state in the sixteenth century. Also discussions of these issues had to await for a climate of opinion more open to rational discourse. Indeed, it would have been surprising in an age of lively curiosity about the actual world if the writers of the sixteenth century had not engaged in discussions of trade and finance. For this was the age of the Renaissance and the great voyages of discovery and exploration which opened up the whole world to European shipping and commerce. In the realm of ideas, the invention of printing from movable type led to the secularisation of learning and the fragmentation of knowledge into specialised areas. No facet of experience was exempt from rational scrutiny. Medieval habits of thought persisted, of course, well into the eighteenth century, but what was new was the emergence of 'experts' or 'masters' in new domains of knowledge, of which 'statecraft' was the prime example. Initially allied to the new, 'empirical' science of political philosophy forcefully proclaimed by Machiavelli, the economic thinking pioneered by the mercantilists soon carved a niche for itself as the autonomous discipline of political economy.

The mercantilists had a rich experience on which to draw concerning the conduct and consequence of international trade. For instance, even before the opening of the New World the financing of foreign trade had reached a remarkable degree of sophistication. As early as the ninth century Venetian financiers had devised an arrangement known as the *commenda* which gave an enormous boost to foreign trade. This was a type of joint venture arrangement whereby capitalist investors would finance the purchase of goods by merchants or sea captains in return for three-quarters of the profit from the proceeds of the subsequent sale. The great fairs such as the Champagne Fairs became renowned centres of foreign-exchange transactions. Later, as trade boomed in the thirteenth- and early fourteenth-centuries the need to economize on specie encouraged the widespread use of letters of credit and bills of exchange. Here again, the Italians were pre-eminent. Merchant bankers in Florence and other Italian cities became specialists in various types of foreign-exchange transactions (including arbitrage on exchange rates) in addition to their regular business of deposit banking. Trade itself was the occasion for the initiation of national economic policies in the late Middle Ages. Kings and princes saw a valuable source of revenue in the traffic in goods into and out of their dominions and imposed duties on exports and imports – duties were levied upon wool exports in England as early as 1275. Exchange control came into being as under the office of England's Royal Exchanger. The control of foreign trade was seen as desirable for political purposes as well, e.g. embargoes on key exports could be imposed to force changes in other countries' attitude, e.g. to compel their neutrality or alliance. Trade policy was used in this way by English kings against the Flemings on at least three occasions during the late Middle Ages under the wool-staple system. Philip II imposed trade embargoes on English cloth exports in 1563–4 and 1568–73.

1.1 Interpreting the Mercantilist Literature

For our purpose it is convenient to adopt Jacob Viner's definition of mercantilism: the doctrine and practices of nation states from the fifteenth to the eighteenth centuries with respect to the nature and the appropriate regulation of international economic relations.[2] There are, of course, several competing definitions of the term and conflicting meanings have been attached to it. The term has been narrowed to mean the 'balance-of-trade' doctrine and broadened to encompass all the economic processes of state-building. The source of the confusion is partly due to the fact that mercantilism, as commonly understood, refers to a phase in the history of economic thought as well as the practical policies of governments during the relevant period. Practice is, however, seldom as perfect as precept. Some economic historians, perhaps most of them, see little point in using a term that suggests some sort of system or uniformity to what was in reality a hotchpotch of devices (administrative, legislative and regulatory) put together for diverse motives by a variety of states over three centuries. Specialists in the history of economics, however, have in general retained the use of the term as an organising category for the study of the economic literature of pre-industrial capitalism.

The basic elements of mercantilist doctrine, as contained in this literature, may be briefly summarised in terms of aims as follows:

1. A favourable trade balance for the maximum accumulation of the precious metals.
2. Economic policy, including foreign trade policy, must always be assessed with the above aim in mind, i.e. the effect such policies have on the national stock of gold and silver.

6　*Regulated Trade: Mercantilism*

3. National advantage must be the overriding objective of policy. Thus the regulation of foreign trade through the promotion of exports and restriction of imports or by other indirect means are justifiable as long as they produce a net inflow of specie, i.e. gold and silver bullion.
4. Promotion of industry through domestic subsidies to manufacturers, the development of cheap raw materials and low interest rates to increase investment and employment.
5. Rapid population growth and a large labour force so as to keep wages and prices low and thus encourage exports.

The term originated with Adam Smith, who devoted Book IV of the *Wealth of Nations* (more than 200 pages) to a wide-ranging criticism of what he called the 'commercial or mercantile system'. He attributed the various manifestations of mercantilist policy to the machinations of merchants and manufacturers, whose aim was the monopoly of the home market. The whole protectionist edifice was founded, he argued, on the fallacious ideas held by the mercantilists about money and the balance of payments. However effective mercantilist regulation was in promoting the interests of the commercial classes, it involved a massive misallocation of resources and was, moreover, in conflict with the 'obvious and simple system of natural liberty', i.e. *laissez-faire* capitalism.

The latter system – free enterprise capitalism – was, of course, what Smith proposed to erect on the ruins of the old, regulated economy. Free, competitive markets (both in foreign and domestic trades) guided by the 'invisible hand' would direct the employment of capital and enterprise to those trades and industries where they were likely to be most productive. This would ensure the maximum level of economic welfare and promote social harmony. Smith's powerful denunciation of mercantilist doctrine and policies, ably supported by the theoretical advances of Torrens, Ricardo and Mill, did not, however, go unchallenged for long. In the 1860s writers of the German Historical School, sympathetic to the economic and political philosophy of mercantilism revived the idea in opposition to the prevailing *laissez-faire* ideology of the English Classical School. For Gustav Schmoller, for example, 'merkantilismus' was an essential part of the process of state-building. Indeed, said Schmoller 'mercantilism in its innermost kernel is nothing but state-making'.[3] This interpretation of mercantilism was echoed in England in the 1890s in the work of Archdeacon William Cunningham, who went further than Schmoller in asserting that the rationale of mercantilism was 'the deliberate pursuit of national power'.[4]

The debate on the meaning of mercantilism was renewed with the appearance of Eli Heckscher's *Mercantilism*.[5] Writing from the standpoint of a free-trader in the neoclassical tradition, Heckscher obviously had little sympathy for the spirit of mercantilism in any form, but his analysis of it encompassed the widest possible range of meanings: it was treated as a system of national unification, a system of power, a monetary system and as a conception of society.

How do we deal with the mercantilist literature?

First, we consider some historiographical problems. What is the relationship between economic ideas and the circumstances of the time? Can we give an adequate account of the economic ideas held by people in the past without considering the context in which those ideas arose? No doubt we can, but would it be interesting, comprehensible or enlightening? Can one make sense of the medieval disquisitions on usury without some knowledge, however sketchy, of the historical context; or, for that matter, the preoccupation of mercantilist writers with the balance of trade without relating this to their circumstances (or their perception of the circumstance).

Obviously, we enhance, enrich, deepen our understanding of past economic literature when we read it in its contextual framework. The context that imparts meaning to a given body of economic literature includes such factors and bits of evidence as the writers' intentions, the social and intellectual concerns of the period, contemporary debates on economic policy, etc. This does not mean: *tout comprendre, c'est tout pardonner*; for we may still want to assess these writers' contribution to the discipline of economics. To do this, we naturally make use of our best theory, i.e. the current corpus of economic knowledge, techniques, conceptual apparatus and methodology. In so doing, we are bound to find analytical weaknesses, conceptual immaturity and theoretical inadequacies. Sometimes we are struck by the intellectual precocity of a writer of a bygone age. But what does all this mean? It simply means that, as in all scientific endeavour, there is secular development and refinement of techniques and concepts in economics. Development, if not progression. Only, perhaps, in the case of 'revealed truth', as in religion, is there no development of concepts; but this is patently not the case in science – to paraphrase Newton, in scientific work, every generation stands on the shoulders of its predecessors. Granted all this,

it is, however, not legitimate to interpret the evolution of economic ideas in a strictly teleological fashion; that is, to regard early writings as anticipations of more recent theories, or as a progression from error to truth. To go to the other extreme, on the other hand, would be to adopt a deterministic perspective, i.e. it would be to reduce economic thought to a species of economic history. Heckscher's interpretation of mercantilism is quite strongly antideterministic. He sees mercantilist policies as springing from economic ideas, many of which ideas he found fallacious. For him, mercantilist policies reflected mercantilist economic ideas, not circumstances or conditions of the time. Needless to say, Heckscher's absolutist position has been criticized by economic historians as being excessively unhistorical.[6] For historians of economic ideas the difficulty with the contextual approach (that which takes account of the actual circumstances of the time) to the understanding of earlier theories or policy recommendations is that it puts these ideas beyond reproach. That is to say, if the ideas and policy programmes (however naïve or unsound) can be explained as arising out of or based on circumstances, is there any sensible way we can say that they were wrong? Yes, there is, in terms of the effects of policy and the manifest contradictions that ensued when they were put into practice. And we have the historical record to tell us so.
'By their fruits ye shall know them.'

Joseph Schumpeter attempted to resolve or get around the problem, this tension between the contextual and strictly analytical approaches, by distinguishing between economic analysis (conceived as the hard core of formal analytical techniques, theorems, etc., that develops according to its own internal logic) and economic thought (which ultimately is ideological and comprises all other views on economic subjects, including policy proposals). For economic analysis, thus defined, he proposed a separate history which would chart the course of its scientific progress. Schumpeter's approach has been influential in providing a new orientation to writers on the history of economics, but it has not satisfied everyone. Recent books which provide alternatives to the Schumpeterian framework include H. W. Spiegel, *The Growth of Economic Thought* (1971); M. Berg, *The Machinery Question and the Making of Political Economy 1815–1848* (1980); E. K. Hunt, *History of Economic Thought: A Critical Perspective* (1979). With varying degrees of emphasis these books all attempt to integrate the history of economic ideas into the wider context of economic, social and political change. What books like these reflect are not merely the personal preferences of scholars, but fundamental differences of view about the nature and central objectives of economics itself.[7] Since these differences are well known, there is no need to dwell on them here. Turning now to the specific problems in interpreting the mercantilist literature, some remarks are called for on the general treatment of this literature by contemporary economists. The mercantilists are frequently referred to as 'men of commerce', merchants or businessmen with the implication that they were simply 'special pleaders' for their own particular interests which they cleverly disguised as being in the national interest. Second, it is sometimes asserted, one cannot talk about mercantilist theory only about mercantilist policy as there was little or no theory in these writings. The seventeenth- and eighteenth-century writers are alleged to be 'not very able' economic theorists, or that they were 'men of widely varying levels of intelligence and reasoning power'.[8] Adam Smith, as already noted, held much the same view of mercantilists and their writings. The mercantile system was animated by the 'spirit of monopoly'; monopolizing merchants successfully harnessed the power of the state to the pursuit of their own selfish goals to the detriment of overall economic development. Their writings were self-serving, for the most part mere 'sophistry' to justify government protection of their interests. Typical of Smith's point of view is the following:

> It cannot be very difficult to determine who have been the contrivers of this whole mercantile system; not the consumers, we may believe, whose interest has been entirely neglected; but the producers, whose interest has been so carefully attended to; and among this latter class our merchants and manufacturers have been by far the principal architects.[9]

This traditional impression of mercantilism has recently been endorsed by Robert Ekelund and Robert Tollison in their book *Mercantilism as a Rent-seeking Society* (1981). Adopting an *as if* methodology they use the new Stigler–Peltzman–Posner theory of regulation to show that mercantilism in all its manifestations can be explained in terms of 'rent-seeking' behaviour by monarchs who supplied monopolistic charters and regulations demanded by businessmen who bribed, lobbied and paid handsomely for these regulations and privileges in mercantile England and France. The process was entirely rational based as it was on wealth-maximising behaviour by the interested parties (monarchs and private entrepreneurs), but wasteful in terms of scarce resources and rested on the exploitation of other sections of society. The merchants gained monopoly rents from the system of regulation and the monarchs secured revenues, but the system was damaging to national economic welfare. In their opinion, previous authors (including Heckscher and Viner) have 'over-scholarised' the period by taking too seriously mercantilist notions like the 'balance of trade' or noble tenets such as the necessity for regulation in order to build a strong, unified national state.[10] The truth is, say the authors, the merchants were out for themselves; and thus the balance-of-trade objective, regulations of the trade sector and other goals claimed to be in the national interest were rationalisations designed to disguise the self-interested motives of the mercantilist authors. Ekelund and Tollison de-emphasise the importance of ideas in accounting for institutional change during the mercantilist era and stress the explanatory power of rent-seeking activity for a proper understanding of mercantilist economic policy. The rent-seeking hypothesis is both interesting and stimulating, but, as Hla Myint observes, 'it may fall between two schools' – it would neither satisfy the economic historians nor the historians of economic thought.[11] Economic historians take note of the power of vested interests, but they are also aware of the manifold interrelations of diverse motives, events and past economic policy. On the other hand, the rent-seeking hypothesis cannot be a substitute for intellectual history. Economic ideas, concepts, etc., however primitively expressed were fashioned by the mercantilists; and whatever the motivations behind the development of these ideas, the historian of economics must be concerned with their validity or formal structure as part of his study of the history of ideas. For as Schumpeter observes: 'The most stubborn class interest may induce true and valuable analysis, the most disinterested motive may lead to nothing but error and triviality.'[12] Thus Viner was quite entitled to make his judgment that mercantilist writers created 'an elaborate system of confused and self-contradictory argument' and at the same time to suggest that 'pleas for special interest, whether open or disguised, constituted the bulk of the mercantilist literature'. What Viner is doing here is to consider *both* ideas and motives.[13] Surely what the rent-seeking model has to offer to the understanding of the mercantilist economy is not a superior form of analysis, but an additional explanatory variable that is normally understood by the phrase 'circumstances of the time'. That is, given the form and distribution of political power in the early nation states, both kings and merchants behaved quite rationally by extracting and sharing in the monopoly rents from the regulation of internal and external trade.

Referring again to the stylised picture of the mercantilists and the quality of their works, there were certainly some prominent businessmen among them, but the mercantilists were very much a mixed bunch and included officials, pamphleteers, journalists, statesmen and philosophers. Of course, these writers did not reach the technical competence of modern neoclassical economists – there was no Samuelson amongst them – nevertheless as Blaug observes, they did grapple with the logical consequences of their basic premises, and in so doing 'displayed economic theory in its infancy'.[14] They were immature theorists, but this does not mean that they had no theory. Gottfried Haberler, in his well-known *Survey of International Trade Theory*, disputes the claim that the mercantilists had no theory. He recognises that pre-classical theory offers a great deal that is of interest and acknowledges that the mercantilists did much pioneering work for the classical writers.[15] Nevertheless, he began his survey with the classical economists because he felt it would do grave injustice to summarise the mercantilist material which embraced strongly divergent national groups and periods. No doubt for the same reason, John Chipman began his masterly three-part survey of the development of international trade theory with Ricardo, without mentioning the mercantilists or even Adam Smith. Textbook writers on international economics have, in general, followed this pattern of ignoring the contributions of the mercantilist writers. Among the exceptions P. T. Ellsworth's *The International Economy* is most notable, since he devotes 28 pages to an analysis of mercantilist thought and policy.[16]

The mercantilist literature is perhaps the best example in the history of economic thought of that wonderful combination of circumstances, theoretical development and policy recommendations, which constitutes scientific understanding in economics. That is to say, during three centuries of inquiry, we see developing (1) an interaction between theory and social-historical processes (circumstances) and (2) development in the internal structure of ideas. The early mercantilist economic ideas were attempts to explain the economic events and circumstances of the time.[17] Inevitably, these ideas reflected to a lesser or greater extent, depending on the perceptions of the various writers, the popular prejudices or preconceptions of contemporaries. The aim of the theorising (often crude and naïve) was to influence or shape these very circumstances and conditions (policy proposals). In some cases the theories were blatantly apologetic – rationalisations which sought to identify national goals with the ambitions of interest groups (overseas traders, notably). But, as economic ideas have their own internal logic, this logic began to impose its own peculiar discipline on the quality of subsequent economic thinking. The mercantilists were primarily interested in policy, and in response to perceptions of economic problems they forged analytical concepts that they required for the practical problems of policy they were discussing. The extensive English discussion on the foreign exchanges and the balance of payments in the early years of the seventeenth century is a case in point. The debate between Malynes and Misselden on the causes and consequences of the outflow of bullion during those years stimulated analytical clarity which led to the brilliant insights of Hume and the later mercantilists. In this foreign-exchange controversy Malynes not only developed a rudimentary form of the purchasing-power-parity theory; but, as Schumpeter claimed, he also 'saw nearly the whole' of the automatic mechanism of international adjustment. But, of course, the analyses of pressing policy problems have always been important vehicles for the refinement and elaboration of economic theories. Thus the debate between Keynes and Ohlin over German reparations stimulated theoretical advances in the study of the 'transfer problem'. By the middle of the eighteenth century almost all the basic conceptual building blocks of the classical system had been fashioned. All that was necessary was to assemble them into a new design that permitted, for the first time, an integrated view of the rapidly emerging market economy. That, of course, was the accomplishment of Adam Smith.

1.2 Historical Background[18]

Mercantilist ideas and policies developed against a background of intense national rivalries and conscious policies – economic, political and military – to enhance state power. Warfare was almost a normal relationship among the European superpowers – England, Spain, France and the Netherlands – as they engaged in geopolitical and dynastic struggles throughout most of the period. From 1494 to 1559 there were hostilities almost every year in some part of Europe. There was complete peace in only a single year during the period 1600 to 1667; and England was engaged in armed conflict for over half of the years between 1650 and 1815.

Commercial rivalry – 'jealousy of trade', as it was called – was a frequent cause of open conflict in sixteenth- and seventeenth-century Europe. Cold-war tactics, diplomatic and propagandist skirmishes were the usual preliminaries to open warfare that can only adequately

The Age of Mercantilism

be described as commercial wars. Such can be said of the First and Second Anglo-Dutch Wars and the French invasion of Holland, 1672. The motives here on the part of the British and the French were to oust the Dutch from their position as the leading commercial power of Europe. The English and the Dutch had much in common (Cromwell even offered the Dutch political union with England), but their interests clashed in matters of trade and colonies. Economic rivalry, particularly over the rewards of colonial trade fuelled hostility between Britain and France during the eighteenth century. In the Seven Years War the prize coveted by Britain was the fish, fur and timber of Canada and the French sugar islands in the West Indies.

With the expansion of European trade, shipping and colonisation outwards to the New World and the East, the interests of the mercantile powers clashed all along the newly opened trade routes. Armed conflicts were no longer confined to the European continent, but became miniature world wars. A decisive naval encounter in the West Indies or off the Malay peninsula was often enough to settle a dispute between Paris and London or between London and Amsterdam over purely European issues. Indeed, in the eighteenth century quarrels were fomented simply to provide a *casus belli* for the rich spoils of colonial territories, the slave trade, spices, sugar or whatever liable to fall in the hands of the victor. 'It was a period', says Professor Michael Howard, 'when war, discovery and trade were almost interchangeable terms.'[19]

Conflict overseas arose through attempts by some countries to enforce monopoly claims to trade with particular areas and the equally determined efforts by newcomers ('interlopers') to challenge such claims. As a result of their early start in exploration and conquest, Spain and Portugal claimed exclusive rights in their respective spheres of influence as agreed by the Treaty of Tordesillas (1494) between the two countries. Spain claimed all discoveries in the New World and Portugal the sea route to the East. Portugal ultimately also obtained Brazil, as the Treaty gave Portugal the right to explore as far as 370 leagues west of the Cape Verde Islands. By the earlier Treaty of Alcobaça (1479) between the two countries, Portugal's claim to a monopoly of trade with Africa was recognised by Spain.

During the next few years the Portuguese, having smashed the Muslim monopoly of trade in 1509, established a string of trading forts stretching from Moçambique to the Moluccas (Spice Islands). Lisbon replaced Venice as the leading spice market of Europe. Meanwhile, galleons began arriving at Seville with the treasures of the New World.

14 Regulated Trade: Mercantilism

The lucrative trade in spices and silver enjoyed by the Iberian powers inevitably aroused the jealousy of French, English and Dutch merchants. By the 1530s privateers from these countries, often with government blessing, preyed on the seaborne traffic of Spain and Portugal – in 1587 Drake captured a single Portuguese carrack with a cargo worth £114 000. The Spanish fleet reduced the risk of capture by sailing from the Americas in convoy. The Portuguese commercial empire in the East, which by the mid-1500s extended to Macao and Nagasaki (Japan), became administratively unwieldy and proved vulnerable to foreign encroachments. The first threat to Portugal's control of the Spice Islands arose in the wake of Magellan's round-the-world voyage which touched at the Philippines; but Portugal managed to keep Spain away from the Moluccas by the Treaty of Zaragossa (1529). However, Spain eventually founded a colony at Manila in 1571 in the face of only feeble protest from the Portuguese.

The far greater challenge to Portugal's monopoly of eastern trade came with the arrival of the Dutch, who first sailed to the Spice Islands in 1595. Ironically, the Dutch thrust to the East was triggered by Spain when Philip II closed the port of Lisbon to Dutch shipping in 1594. The blockade deprived Dutch merchants of access to a market and merchandise essential to their trading system: without the salt and spices from Lisbon both their North Sea fishing fleet and their Baltic trade in grain were crippled. The loss of supplies of Eastern spices was potentially serious as that commodity was becoming increasingly important in the Dutch distribution network based at Amsterdam. As nearly always with economic embargoes, the result was the opposite of that intended. Instead of ruining Dutch trade Philip's action merely propelled the Dutch into the East Indies to seek the spices at source. In an amazingly short period of time the Dutch succeeded in establishing their supremacy throughout the East Indies from their headquarters in Batavia (Jakarta).

That was the remarkable achievement of the United East India Company (*Vereenigde Oost-Indische Compagnie* or the VOC) established in 1602 when the Dutch realised that if they did not organise themselves effectively then the English, who had set up their own East India Company in 1600, would beat them to it. In the four years before the Dutch East India Company was set up, no fewer than ten independent companies (the *voorcompagnieën*) were involved in the scramble for the trade. Finding Portuguese resistance low and profits high, the rival companies launched as many as fifteen expeditions to the East in the space of those four years. Competition was chaotic and there was a danger of spoiling the European market through oversupply. Government prodding, in the person of the respected elder statesman Johan van Oldenbarnevelt, resulted in agreement to found a single joint-stock company. Its charter, under the seal of the States-General, conferred on it a monopoly in trade and navigation east of the Cape of Good Hope and west of the Strait of Magellan. It was an ambitious project for a small country yet to win its national independence. For the leaders of the merchant republic it was a splendid opportunity to harness the private pursuit of profit to the goal of national power and strategic advantage. National ambition was even more apparent in the formation of the Dutch West India Company (incorporated in 1620). It was intended to harass Spanish trade in the New World, prey on Spain's treasure fleets and to set up and protect profitable trading settlements. The Company obtained gold and ivory from West Africa, transported slaves to Brazil, the West Indies and Guiana and exported sugar to Europe. The two Dutch trading companies employed military personnel and were empowered to wage war, build forts and negotiate treaties with foreign potentates. This model of the armed trading company was adopted by other countries, e.g. France, Denmark. In an age of violence, political unrest and disputed territorial claims, long-distance commerce was a hazardous business and had to be pursued with vigorous ferocity. In an age such as this, the disruptive effect of war on international trade can easily be exaggerated. It is true whole areas or regions were often cut off from commercial contact with the outside world by the ravages of war, including civil war; but the same effect was produced by famines and plagues. Piracy, privateering and buccaneering increased the hazards and costs of seaborne commerce and reduced its level. Yet in all this turmoil, so inimical to commercial intercourse, there was a remarkable stability in the established channels of trade. For instance, despite the bitter eighty-year-long war between Holland and Spain, Dutch–Spanish trade was rarely interrupted; indeed, Dutch ships even carried the naval stores (from the Baltic) required by Spain which enabled the latter to continue the struggle. The merchants of Amsterdam traded with Spain as they did with England in the three Anglo-Dutch Wars. Even before the Netherlands was formally declared to be independent by the Peace of Westphalia (1648), the Dutch who were still technically enemies of Spain acted as financial agents for Spain's military disbursements in Flanders. Despite mutual antagonisms between England and Spain during most of the sixteenth and early seventeenth centuries, Spain remained England's most important customer for woollens. In 1709, although Holland was at war with France, Dutch grain shipments relieved a famine in France, and Dutch traders maintained their leading role in Bordeaux. In an earlier conflict with Spain, the Dutch found that their services as shippers of Baltic grain could not be dispensed with by Spain; hence they could freely obtain their usual supplies of salt from Cadiz and Portugal (1580–90).

Nor should we overlook the fact that wars were apt to benefit some merchants and capitalists. Blockades and embargoes, besides encouraging smuggling, provided opportunities for neutral traders to gain new markets or strengthen old ones. The Dutch East and West India companies did so well out of the war with Portugal that they were moved to petition the States-General against peace negotiations in 1640. In the age of Gunpowder Wars, the armament industry boomed, of course; and so did the fortunes of the arms dealers. The Amsterdam firms of de Geer and Tripp made a reputation for themselves as munitions merchants during the Thirty Years War, supplying both friend and foe alike.

The source of the national rivalry, so much a dominant motif in the mercantilist era undoubtedly stemmed from an assumption about international relations widely held by statesmen and merchants and regarded by them as axiomatic. It was the belief that the total wealth of the world was a fixed magnitude. In the nature of things this meant that various aspects of wealth – power, trade, treasure – were also fixed quantities. Merchant-authors of the seventeenth century, who should have known better, commonly thought about 'demand' as though it were a single magnitude, rather than a functional relationship which would have suggested the extensibility of demand. In this essentially static view of the world and its economic resources it followed that a nation could only increase its share of wealth and power at the expense of other countries. There was, for instance, a fixed pie of international commerce with the shares distributed among nations according to their ability to grab and hold their own portions. International economic relations (and international relations generally) was thus a 'zero-sum game'; one nation's gain was necessarily another's loss; prosperity was possible only at the expense of someone else's misery. As Adam Smith put it, under mercantilism 'nations have been taught that their interest consisted in beggaring all their neighbours'. In the domestic economic sphere this view was deeply rooted in medieval thinking which ultimately derived from Aristotle that in a 'just exchange' between private individuals everyone must come out without gain or loss. One party can only gain from a transaction if the other suffers a loss. Sixteenth- and seventeenth-century administrators and writers (including such enlightened thinkers as Montaigne and Francis Bacon) followed this tradition and extended it to trade between countries. Never far from the surface, however, was the knowledge that a country in possession of superior military force could ultimately, by conquest, win for itself the wealth of other nations. This was one of the two themes debated by the contending heralds of England and France in the mid-fifteenth-century work *Le Débat des Hérauts d'Armes de France et d'Angleterre*. But since, in most circumstances, conquest might prove too costly, the same objective could be achieved by engrossing the trade of commercial rivals. Trade thus took on the aspect of a species of warfare. It was seen as the most natural means to increase the wealth of a kingdom; but trade had to be wrested from others in the process. Therein lay the seeds of international conflict.

At a more basic level international conflict in all its manifestations reflected the conjunction of the interest of the rising merchant capitalist class and the emerging territorial (nation) states. The period as a whole was one of increasing economic activity as feudalism with its self-sufficient manor waned and trade horizons widened in the wake of the great geographical discoveries. These three events and circumstances: the rise of the commercial class, the appearance of national states and economic expansion interacted in a mutually reinforcing way to produce the lively, dynamic economies of pre-industrial Europe.

Economic growth during the period, although cumulatively quite impressive, was rather uneven. The early part of the period, 1450–1600, saw the most rapid expansion partly fed by inflationary pressure. The seventeenth century was generally one of stagnation accompanied by stable or falling prices. Some countries (Germany, Spain, Italy) suffered actual falls in output levels, while others (England, Holland and Sweden) less severely affected nevertheless went through periods of depression such as the 1620s and 1640s. A modest expansion, started in the early 1700s following the long decades of stagnation in the previous century, gathered momentum as the eighteenth century progressed. This latter phase, of course, heralded the Industrial Revolution, most notably in Britain. Population growth in western Europe broadly followed the movements in output – increasing by nearly one-third in the sixteenth century to stand at about 70 million in 1600. Between 1600 and the early eighteenth century population had declined in some countries (Spain, Portugal, Italy) and increased in others (France, England). Throughout the rest of the eighteenth century population increased steadily due to a moderate but sustained rise in the birth rate, particularly marked towards the end of the century.

A European population was steadily increasing its number in the New World, which by the 1770s had reached one million. Around this time about 5½ million black slaves had also crossed the Atlantic from West Africa. The period when mercantilism was at its height – the seventeenth century – was thus one of slow growth both of output and population. The experience of several decades of depression dampened expectations of continuing growth and out of which, no doubt, sprang the basic assumptions of contemporary economic writers that markets were static. The belief that markets were limited so that the expansion of commerce by one country could only be secured by displacing that of another was, no doubt, a reflection of mercantilist prejudice; but it also had some basis in fact, at least during the early years of the seventeenth century. It swayed the attitudes of merchants and administrators into the position that national markets and shares of particular trades could only be protected, maintained and augmented through the deliberate exercise of power. This means, of course, the power exerted by the state – diplomatic, regulatory and military.

Yet even in the depressed seventeenth-century trade (both regional and international) was still a dynamic element in many economies. For some, like England, France and the Dutch Republic, trade expanded and promoted innovations in ancillary industries and services such as shipbuilding, shipping, insurance and banking. It was also the century when the merchant capitalist class consolidated its power, wealth and influence in European society. Merchants and traders generally thrived in the previous century when the new oceanic trade routes to the East and the New World expanded trading opportunities beyond the confines of the existing Baltic and Mediterranean trades.

An increased volume of commodities, both old and new, passed through the busy ports. Among the imports from the New World not the least significant was bullion – gold and silver. Something like 180 tons of gold and 16 000 tons of silver flowed from the Americas between 1500 and 1660. The really large inflow of precious metals started in the 1550s; and although the precise effect of this influx is still a matter for debate among historians, there can be no doubt that it had a profound effect on the sixteenth-century European economy. Even if only in a marginal manner it (a) relieved an acute shortage of money (b) helped to finance the chronic Western European imbalance of trade

The Age of Mercantilism

with Asia and the Baltic region and (c) accelerated inflationary pressure in Spain, primarily, but also in other trading countries.

For two centuries before the late 1400s European gold and silver production had stagnated at a time when the money economy was expanding. The slow but steady disintegration of the self-sufficient manorial system brought about by increased trade, the gradual shift of land tenure to private ownership and money rental, population growth, urbanisation featuring division of labour and specialised craftsmen and artisans working for money incomes, and the increase in public expenditure (and revenues) called for increased quantities of money. Money, of course, consisted primarily of gold and silver coins (specie), and that was what was in short supply and caused the great fifteenth-century 'bullion famine'.

The debasement of the coinage in some states and an increase in the velocity of circulation through the use of bills of exchange were reactions to the problem of an inadequate money supply; but relief came only from about 1450. First, the Portuguese began extracting and shipping gold from Benin in the Gold Coast and, second, Europe's own silver production revived and increased fivefold between 1450 and 1530, e.g. from the mines at Joachimsthal in Bohemia (now Jachymov in Czechoslovakia). From the mid-sixteenth century the additions of large inflows of gold and silver from the Americas effectively turned a shortage into an over-supply of bullion relative to the overall volume of transactions, thus raising price levels. In the course of the sixteenth century the general level of prices roughly trebled – ranging from 400 per cent in Spain to 150 per cent in countries less severely affected. Some historians see a connection between the quickening of economic activity and the inflationary conditions of the time. The reasoning is that increases in money wage rates lagged behind the rate of inflation. The reduction of real wages implied a redistribution of income to merchants and capitalists in the form of swollen profits which provided the source for a large volume of investment. Investment from borrowed funds was further stimulated by the general reduction of interest rates resulting from the increased supply of money. Stock appreciation and the more rapid accumulation of capital increased the ability of merchants to finance the 'putting-out' industries.

In addition to the impetus provided by the growing number of traded commodities, foreign trade was further stimulated by the increase in international liquidity. The result of all this was a marked stimulus to economic growth. The historical evidence does, indeed, indicate that there was a disparity between wages and prices which persisted until late in the seventeenth century. However, food prices increased faster than the prices of manufactures during the 'price revolution'. This must have greatly contributed to the hardship and poverty suffered by the great mass of the population during this period and reflected in contemporary social tracts with their frequent complaint of 'dearth'. The erosion of the real income of workers obviously restricted the market for manufactured goods. Presumably the expansion of demand came from the beneficiaries of inflation – merchants, landowners and farmers. The best markets were located in the ports and towns which grew rapidly in the sixteenth century. Flourishing towns such as Bristol, Liverpool, Amsterdam, Lisbon, Seville, Genoa, Nantes, Bordeaux provided high-income customers for a wide range of manufactured goods (both basic and luxury). Together with the capital cities, these towns also provided profitable outlets for the investment of accumulated capital in money-lending, state financing and the finance of foreign trade.

The finance of foreign trade – particularly the Baltic and (from the seventeenth century), the Far Eastern trades – was considerably eased by increased gold and silver supplies. These trades were notorious for their famous 'drain of bullion' from Western Europe occasioned by adverse payments balances with these regions. Western European merchants (principally English and Dutch) found it impossible to sell enough fish, salt and cloth in the Baltic to pay for the huge imports of Polish grain, Swedish iron and timber, Russian hemp and Finnish pitch and tar. Many of these commodities were in inelastic demand in Western Europe (e.g. grain destined for towns like Lisbon and Amsterdam) and some were of 'strategic' importance (e.g. naval stores, timber and masts). Roughly half of these imports from the Baltic was not covered by corresponding Dutch and English exports basically because of low purchasing power and high duties in northern Europe. The trade imbalance was settled in bullion. An adequate supply of silver was therefore crucial for the maintenance of this trade, which was liable to periodic contraction when money supplies declined. From the 1540s an increasing quantity of Spanish silver came into the hands of English, Dutch and Italian merchants in exchange for the wide range of manufactured goods required by Spanish colonists in the New World – which Spain herself could not adequately provide; Spanish-made goods made up a mere 8 per cent of the total. Spain's military expenditure overseas and huge foreign-debt obligations created additional leakages of bullion to the rest of Europe. In this way, despite tight control over the export of bullion by the Spanish authorities, much of their treasure ultimately found its way through the Danish Sound to finance the Baltic trade.

From the early seventeenth century onwards the bullion constraint in this trade began to lift as a wider variety of goods was offered to Baltic customers, more services were sold to them and as multilateral settlements arose. The Dutch were particularly successful in overcoming the problems of their Baltic trade in this manner. Spanish bullion provided the international means of payment to lubricate the Far Eastern trade which was also subject to a bilateral constraint. The arrival of Spanish silver in the East soon after their presence was established in the Philippines greatly expanded European trade with the East initiated by the Portuguese. The Spanish connection reinforced a link between a region (China, India) where silver was in high demand with one where it was cheap and plentiful (the Americas). The Manila–Acapulco run was the axis of this trade, which consisted of the exchange of American silver for Asian silk, porcelain, jewellery and drugs brought to Manila by Chinese junks and Portuguese vessels from Macao. On arrival at Acapulco after a hazardous three-month voyage the exotic commodities were transhipped to Vera Cruz for sale in Mexico, other parts of Spanish America and for re-export to Europe.

The success of the various East India companies during the course of the seventeenth century would have been difficult, if not impossible, without the initial stimulus to trade with the East provided by gold and silver supplies from the Americas. Because of the relatively low prices of Indian and Chinese manufactures there was little demand for competing European wares. However, the habit of trading for Portuguese *cruzados* and Spanish *piasters* or pieces of eight became established among Eastern traders, who were thus willing to trade increasing quantities of spices, silks, calicoes and tea with the European trading companies for these coins or their equivalents.

Again, as happened in the case of the Baltic trade, Europeans were able, as time went on, to sell an increasing volume of shipping and mercantile services which helped to finance the deficit with the East. And here, as in the Baltic, the Dutch did better than the English. They soon dominated the intra-Asian carrying trade linking this with their entrepôt system based on Java (Batavia). In the 1640s the VOC (Dutch East India Company) maintained a fleet of some eighty vessels in Asiatic waters for this purpose. Besides being profitable, the sale of these services reduced the need to rely on the export of specie from Europe.

Whatever the precise contribution of American treasure and the sixteenth-century inflation to long-run economic growth, at all events, by the end of that century, substantial amounts of capital had accumulated in the hands of merchants. This increase in wealth provided the basis for further accumulation and cast these early entrepreneurs for a strategic role in the evolution of the new social and economic system, i.e. the transitional stage on the road that led to capitalism. The merchant capitalist became the dynamic element in society. The decisions they took with respect to investment, production, methods of manufacturing, distribution, etc., wrought subtle social changes that slowly but inexorably placed them in a dominant position at the top of the social and political hierarchy. As financiers to kings and princes they came increasingly to exercise a powerful influence directly or indirectly on the policies of governments.

The rise of the merchant class coincided with the emergence and growth of the territorial state. The nation states that exist today were forged out of the fire and passion of revolution over the past two hundred years or so (e.g. the American, French and Russian revolutions). Independent sovereign national states with defined territorial boundaries based on linguistic, ethnic and cultural ties constitute what has been called the modern 'Westphalian system'. This is an appropriate label to characterise the attributes of modern statehood, for the form of political organisation we call the state was established by the treaties known as the Peace of Westphalia (1648) which ended the Thirty Years War in Europe. By this Treaty the Holy Roman Emperor recognised the territorial sovereignty of the princes of the Empire and confirmed the independence of the Dutch Republic. It was a notable landmark in the evolution of the state, for it imparted international juridical recognition to a process that started at the dawn of the Renaissance with the centralisation and consolidation of power in the hands of the strong central governments of France, Spain and England. Certainly by the late sixteenth century in England and France the word 'state' or 'l'État' began to be used in the sense that we understand it today. These centralised states were the prototypes of others to follow in the next two centuries (e.g. the Dutch Republic, Sweden, Prussia). Whether it took the absolutist or constitutional form each state of early modern Europe wanted to enhance its power, to expand its frontiers or possessions and to increase its trade. The Westphalian system of territorial sovereignty was one where rulers, in Thomas Hobbes's words, 'because of their Independency, are in continual jealousies, and in the state and posture of Gladiators; having their weapons pointing

The Age of Mercantilism

and their eyes fixed on one another'.[20] Fortunately, as time went on, two mechanisms for regulating international relations emerged: (1) the development of what became known as the 'public law of Europe' and (2) the principle of the balance of power. The acts ratifying the Peace of Westphalia themselves, as well as every subsequent treaty which established a status quo in interstate political relations (e.g. the Treaty of Utrecht 1713 and the so-called American Treaty 1670) were contributions to the public law of Europe – the foundation of modern international law. As the guardians of that body of law the great powers, by the principle of the balance of power, were required to take vigorous action in the event of any infraction of the law. In this sense there was a certain community of interest among states; but powerful rulers were often the principal aggressors – thus force, or the threat of force remained the ultimate regulator of international relations. Domestically, the aim of every seventeenth- and eighteenth-century government was the promotion of national unity – political and economic – and the destruction of medieval localism. They all tried to remove local barriers to trade and industry and to concentrate regulatory power into their hands. Thus, often against the opposition of feudal lords, the guilds and other local vested interests, enlightened monarchs stood firmly for a unified coinage and monetary system, a standard system of weights and measures, a national system of taxation and tariffs and the elimination of purely local tolls on roads and rivers.

These centralising tendencies undermined the foundation of the privileges of regions, guilds and classes. That suited admirably the interests and aspirations of the rising commercial class in the towns and cities. It produced a fluid social environment and opened avenues of economic and social advancement for bourgeois energies and talents. Merchants and manufacturers benefited from the wider markets produced by the welding together of a national economy and the increased scope for standardisation and economies of scale.

Members of the new bourgeois class, merchants in particular, became the natural allies of the kings in their efforts to promote national unification and the centralisation of authority. Rulers came increasingly to rely on the new class and less on landlords and noblemen to help in the administration of their affairs. Everywhere merchants were brought into the counsels of princes, not least for the financial advice and help in financing state loans. The mutually beneficial relationship between ruler and merchant was particularly striking in the case of the maritime powers (Portugal, Holland and England). In the seventeenth century overseas trade was still largely speculative; and a risky business too. The merchant trading overseas looked to the state for protection and the furtherance of his interests. When required, it was the duty of the state to provide military, naval or diplomatic support to the nation's commerce. Such national support was the counterpart of the personal loyalty (and taxes) one owed to the state. Effective protection depended on the power of the state, which ultimately derived from its wealth and the profitability and volume of its foreign trade.

Rulers saw matters very much in the same light. In the king's eyes the activities of the overseas merchant were the very source and foundation of the nation's prosperity. A flourishing foreign trade provided him with a steady stream of tariff revenues in addition to the other sources of income derived from the sale of monopoly rights to trading companies. Less immediate and obvious, but equally important in a violent age, the activities of the overseas merchants constituted the very 'sinews of war'. The importance of hard cash, said the Florentine historian, Francesco Guicciardini, resided in the fact that it was easier to get soldiers with money than it was to obtain money with soldiers.[21] The resources used by traders had important strategic 'spin-offs'. The merchant navy was the nursery of fighting sailors: shipbuilding and ship supplies' industries produced the hardware for naval defence.

Other developments contributed to the rise of the state during this period. The use of gunpowder in cannons, muskets and rifles revolutionised the art of war and forcefully demonstrated the power of the Leviathan State extolled by Thomas Hobbes. The ambitions of overweening barons were effectively curbed by the new military technology which destroyed the impregnability of castle strongholds. Rulers, whether they read him or not, acted upon the advice of Machiavelli and replaced mercenaries by their own national, professional armies. The defeat of the Swiss pikemen by the army of Francis I of France at the Battle of Marignano (1515) marked the end of an epoch in European warfare. It demonstrated two things: the superiority of artillery even against the most formidable infantry force, and the efficiency of a disciplined national army led by professional commanders. The days of the mercenary captains – the *condottieri* – of Renaissance Italy were numbered and the age of the modern national army inaugurated. Such an army that impressed contemporaries was the Spanish infantry, reckoned the finest in Europe during the fifteenth and sixteenth centuries until their eclipse at the Battle of Rocroi (1643), when they suffered defeat at the hands of the French.

However, professional armies, artillery and other armaments cost money. The Spanish authorities had to find seven million guilders annually to pay for their garrison in Flanders alone; and at the end of the sixteenth century more than three quarters of Spanish national revenue was spent on defence – the bulk of the expenditure being on weapons. Other states probably incurred defence costs ranging between 60 to 70 per cent of state expenditure. Fernand Braudel observed: 'All States of Europe groaned under taxes in the late 16th century.'[22] The costs of maintaining standing armies, including their equipment with modern weaponry escalated beyond the normal revenues from crown lands and special war levies, so that rulers everywhere sought ways and means of extending the tax base so as to increase government revenues. The widening gap between public expenditures and revenues led, of course, to the creation of a national debt. In constitutional states, royal debt was eventually transformed into a liability funded on the credit of the nation as represented by legislative assemblies. This development in public finance was adopted in Britain during the 1690s when Parliament approved the public issue of government securities (e.g. annuities, exchequer bills, navy bills, etc.).

The burden of taxation was particularly heavy in the states that rose to prominence during the late seventeenth and early eighteenth centuries. Prussia under the Great Elector and Frederick the Great expanded on the strength of its superb military machine. The power and the glory were paid for by heavy taxation of the peasantry and the burgher class. Contemporaries, ill disposed towards what they regarded as an upstart state, referred to Frederick's Prussia as 'a large army with a small state attached'. But Frederick was a shrewd mercantilist who also knew his Machiavelli very well and ensured the financial viability of his state through a comprehensive system of taxation. In 1766, against opposition from his officials, he farmed out the inland revenue to a syndicate of French tax collectors known as the *Régie*. Yet, for the mass of the people, taxation was less onerous in Prussia than in the Austria of Maria Theresa or the France of Louis XV.

The birth of modern diplomacy in the late fifteenth century is in many ways comparable to the development in warfare, for it too reflected an altered conception of the state. The practice developed among the city states of northern Italy of using resident ambassadors to engage in diplomatic relations in neighbouring and other more distant states. The frequent internecine wars among the Italian city states during the late Middle Ages had resulted by the end of the fifteenth century in a situation of political and military equilibrium. The reduction of tension among them owed much to the Peace of Lodi (1454) between Milan, Florence and Venice and the diplomatic skill of Lorenzo de' Medici in maintaining the balance of power in northern Italy and fear of the destructive power of the new artillery. But political relations were still unstable and the conduct of international relations required reliable and prompt information about changes in policy and plans in other states. A representative on the spot could be more effective in strengthening alliances or preventing the outbreak of hostilities through diplomatic pressure and manoeuvre. The practice of diplomacy through the use of resident ambassadors was much advanced in Italy when this method of conducting international relations was adopted by the rising nation states of northern Europe during the early sixteenth century. Permanent diplomatic activity came to be associated with the very nature of the state as an independent entity. Diplomatic skill joined arms and trade as instruments in the furtherance of national interests.

The example of the Papacy and the Byzantine Empire no doubt played a part, but the perfection of the art and practice of diplomacy in Italy owed much to the development of trade. The extensive trading interests of the Venetians in the eastern Mediterranean and elsewhere involved them in the maintenance of agents in foreign ports to deal with trading matters – the most important of which was their *bailo* or bailiff in Constantinople. Similarly, the activities of the Medici bank were so important for the republic of Florence that the bank's representatives were often regarded by foreigners as honorary envoys of Florence. From its headquarters on the Via Larga the Medici bank controlled an international financial empire consisting of branches in Rome, Milan, Ancona, Pisa, Bruges, Geneva, London and Avignon.

In the age of mercantilism two great commercial empires held sway: first the Dutch in the seventeenth century and the British in the eighteenth century. They performed the commercial role and provided the financial services formerly done by Genoa, Venice and Antwerp.

The early success of the Dutch merchants in establishing Amsterdam as the leading commercial entrepôt was soon followed by equal success in the provision of financial and mercantile services. Eventually, commercial and financial leadership passed to Britain. The British commercial hegemony proved more durable because it became increasingly based on industrial prowess – something that the Dutch never managed to achieve. The success of these two maritime countries caused a marked and long-lasting shift in the balance of economic power in Europe, i.e. from the Mediterranean basin to the northwestern seaboard. The Atlantic economy that came into being reflected the relative decline of the older commercial and financial centres.

The Italian dominance of trade continued until the late Middle Ages. Their skill in banking, the finance of business and commercial organisation was unsurpassed until well into the sixteenth century. The merchants who controlled the city states of Genoa, Florence and Venice made their fortunes from buying wool cheaply (mainly from Spain and England), making it up into woollen goods and selling these all over Europe. Lucca specialised in silk, Venice traded in luxuries from the East: spices, sugar, wax, alum, lacquer as well as its own manufactured goods such as textiles, glassware, shipbuilding. Their expertise in banking and finance developed as a natural consequence of these trading activities. As mentioned earlier, these northern Italian merchants invented the modern system of double-entry bookkeeping, the company form of business organisation, the finance of companies through the issue of shares etc. The first great banks were founded in many of the major Italian cities during the sixteenth century following the example of the greatest, the Medici bank and the oldest, the Casa di San Giorgio of Genoa (founded 1407). Kings, princes and German emperors were counted among the clients of these Italian financial houses. The Fuggers of Augsburg were their only serious rivals for royal patronage, particularly after 1519 when the Tyrolean silver mines came under the control of these German merchant-bankers as security for substantial loans to the House of Habsburg.

THE GOLDEN AGE OF AMSTERDAM

The shift in the locus of economic and financial activity to northwestern Europe was signalled by the rise of Antwerp in the early years of the sixteenth century. It rivalled and soon surpassed Genoa as an emporium and leading centre for banking and finance. Antwerp's fortunes were linked with those of Spain and the Habsburg Empire. The decline of Spain and the internal problems of the Habsburgs undermined the basis of Antwerp's prosperity. The final blow came when the Netherlands revolted against Spanish rule (1572). Antwerp threw in its lot with the rebels, but eventually fell to the Spaniards in August 1585. The fall of the city sealed its commercial fate, but was the making of the Dutch commercial empire based on Amsterdam. With Spanish rule firmly re-established in Antwerp, the rebels were given four years to wind up their affairs and leave. The stream of refugees to the north became a flood. When the Dutch rebels – the 'Sea Beggars' as they were called – blockaded the Scheldt and cut off the city from the sea, business more or less came to a standstill, as even Catholic merchants and financiers made for Amsterdam and other Dutch towns.

The infusion into the Dutch economy of the capital, skill, talents and experience represented by these migrants from Antwerp was most salutary. As a consequence, the development of Amsterdam as a European entrepôt and financial centre was speeded up. The Exchange Bank of Amsterdam was founded in 1609 and the Stock Exchange, or *Beurs* was set up in 1611. Antwerp's reputation as a banking and financial centre rested on solid commercial advantages, as well as on its imperial connection. For instance, the Antwerp Exchange was open to citizens and aliens alike and tariffs and tolls were maintained at relatively low levels. These traditions found a fertile soil when transplanted to Amsterdam. The techniques of bill-discounting, deposit banking, ship-chartering, share-financing of companies used by the Antwerpers were by this time becoming fairly familiar in northern Europe. The Dutch adapted, developed and refined these practices to the circumstances and peculiar advantages of their own economy with striking success.

The seventeenth century was the Golden Age of Amsterdam. The prosperity of the Dutch rested on their skill as shipbuilders, their mastery of the sea, their efficiency in the gathering and processing of fish (North Sea herrings, Icelandic cod, Arctic whales) and their long experience as Baltic traders. The fisheries, often described as the 'Dutch Gold Mine' had important spin-off effects on other industries such as net-making, soap-making, shipbuilding, etc. Dutch sailors gained unrivalled seafaring experience from their employment as sea captains by Antwerp merchants, as pilots on Portuguese ships trading in the East as well as in the service of their own national merchants and in the fishing fleets. They owed their political independence to their prowess as fighting sailors. This experience, together with the common conviction that the sea was their life-line made an indelible mark on Dutch consciousness: the inhabitants turned their backs on the hinterland of Europe, faced the sea and conceived of their country as an island, dependent for their comfort and security on trade with the wider world.

The Baltic trade, which the Dutch fondly referred to as their *moeder commercie* ('mother trade'), was valued primarily because it involved the import of grain – the means of survival – against the export of more highly valued products. The control of the Baltic trade also swelled the capacity requirements of the carrying trade, i.e. it contributed to the

The Age of Mercantilism

efficiency of Dutch shipbuilding. The Dutch broke into the growing shipping trade by designing the low-cost, easily handled *fluitschip*, or flyboat. Its construction was cheap owing to the use of lighter timber such as fir and pine instead of the more expensive oak, bulk purchase of construction materials and large-scale standardised production methods. The operating costs were low, as the vessel could be manned with one-third less crew required for a conventional ship of comparable capacity – 18 hands as against a crew of 26–30 used on ships of other nations. The competitive advantages this innovation gave Dutch shipbuilders and shipping firms can be gauged by noting that Dutch freight rates were often half to two-thirds lower than those of their competitors, and that the Dutch merchant fleet accounted for perhaps three times English and more than half of European shipping tonnage in the 1670s. The percentage of Dutch-built ships was even greater. Dutch ships were reputedly safer, more durable and faster than foreign ships; they were also economical to maintain. Dutch shipowners also obtained lower insurance cover in Amsterdam because of economies of scale, specialised skills and availability of financial resources for underwriting purposes in that city. On the basis of these competitive advantages, allied with their domination of world markets, an enormous carrying trade grew up centring on the great Amsterdam staple market. But the biggest profits were made through marketing and stapling – a 'pay-off' based on the superiority of the Dutch form of commercial organisation. Just as in earlier times all roads led to Rome, so in the seventeenth century all trade routes converged on Amsterdam. Goods from all parts of the world passed into and out of the city – Europe's premier entrepôt. Even as late as 1728, Defoe could still describe the Dutch as

> the Carryers of the World, the middle Persons in Trade, the Factors and Brokers of Europe . . . they buy to sell again, take in to send out; and the Greatest Part of their vast Commerce consists in being supply'd from all parts of the World, that they may supply all the World again.[23]

As a result of its commercial dominance, Amsterdam performed another important function of great benefit to international trade – that of an 'information exchange', i.e. the city became a focal point for the gathering and dissemination of world-wide commercial information. Woodruff D. Smith has recently drawn attention to this important role of Amsterdam and considered it a significant factor in the modernisation of capitalism.[24]

Paralleling this spectacular dominance of trade and shipping services was the high reputation of the Dutch in the sphere of international finance. The 'bill on Amsterdam' became the normal form of international credit for European merchants able to make use of this facility. Commercial bills drawn on Amsterdam were easily obtained at competitive rates and subject to less risk and delay than at other centres such as London in the early seventeenth century. Unlike other mercantilist states, the Dutch Republic allowed the free export and import of the precious metals which made Amsterdam the bullion market of Europe. Building on Italian practices the Dutch developed a range of capital market facilities including speculation in bullion prices and share prices which complemented the active 'futures' trading on their commodity markets.

THE ENGLISH COMMERCIAL EMPIRE

From the last quarter of the seventeenth century, effectively after the Restoration, England rose to a position of commercial leadership based on a flourishing export trade in the cheaper, lighter new draperies – mixed fabrics and coloured cloth – mainly to Iberian and Mediterranean markets. To this was added a growing volume of trade in re-exports mainly of colonial goods promoted by the Navigation Acts and various protective measures. By the end of the seventeenth century London succeeded to the role of Amsterdam as the leading entrepôt.

Already at that time, re-exports, e.g. tobacco, coffee, sugar, Indian textiles and spices, accounted for one-third of total exports. Huge wharves and warehouses went up alongside the old London docks to handle the increased traffic that was now international in scope. The outports like Bristol and Liverpool shared in this expansion.

Although by the middle of the eighteenth century the bulk of British trade was still with Europe, the fastest-growing share was that with the American continent and India. This was significant, for it established a trend that was to continue and gather momentum over the next fifty years or so when Britain clearly stood out as the centre of an Atlantic economy firmly based on her leadership as the industrial giant of the age.

How Britain arrived at this position of economic pre-eminence is still a question of debate among economic historians. There is no doubt that by 1750 Britain was securely poised for take-off into self-sustaining

The Age of Mercantilism

industrial growth. She was the likeliest candidate among the European countries to make the first leap into the industrial age. Britain was the wealthiest country in Europe by the early 1700s. The average level of income (about £8 per annum) was sufficiently above subsistence level to sustain a large domestic market. After the mid-seventeenth century there was a significant increase in agricultural productivity which both released free labourers for work in the expanding new towns and increased the level of demand in the home market through the increase in real income resulting from cheaper basic foodstuffs. The integration of the national economy had proceeded far enough to create a national market free of internal customs barriers and served by a rapidly developing network of inland and coastwise transport. Urbanisation, the growth of agricultural productivity and increasing living standards led to a diversification of industrial output and the gradual process that ultimately resulted in the creation of mass markets. But however important these purely internal developments in the British economy were in quickening the pace of British economic growth, the role of foreign trade must be recognised as crucial. The growth of overseas trade and the expansion of foreign markets after 1650 provided a powerful stimulus to industrial investment and innovation at a time when the domestic market was still poor and fragmented. The foundations were therefore laid during the previous century of mercantilist rivalry for Britain's spectacular success in the early nineteenth century. But these foundations did not arise by accident, nor were they the result of any natural economic progression. They were erected by design, by conscious policy and determined competitive effort by Englishmen during the seventeenth and early eighteenth centuries – a period that has been characterised as the years of England's apprenticeship.[25]

In the early decades of the seventeenth century England burst into the international commercial arena when her merchants successfully penetrated the Mediterranean and broke the Venetian hegemony of trade and industry in that region. The Mediterranean and the Levant became the principal markets for English textiles of all kinds, but especially for the 'new draperies' the output of which increased 500 per cent between 1600 and 1640. Previously, English cloth travelled the short sea route across the North Sea to the Low Countries and Germany from whence they were distributed by foreign merchants to other parts of Europe. Now English merchants took their products to distant markets themselves using British ships.

This remarkable incursion into an established market was achieved by aggressive marketing, cut-throat competition and sharp commercial practices such as counterfeit branding and smuggling designed to ruin and then supplant the *Serenissima* as the dominant commercial and industrial power in the Mediterranean.[26] To be sure there were competitive advantages on the English side; for instance, access to low-cost raw material (e.g. wool) low labour costs and efficient and cheap transport facilities (e.g. shipping). But these cost-advantages, coupled with aggressive marketing, were exploited to the full in order to find outlets for the increased output of textiles and later a wider range of manufactured goods. In the next fifty years, with the acquisition of Menorca and Gibraltar, British dominion over the Mediterranean was complete, allowing British merchants to operate freely from their base in Livorno (Leghorn) under the protection of the Royal Navy.

The second stage in the progress of England towards her domination of world markets was initiated by the series of Navigation Acts designed to oust the Dutch from their leading role as sea-carriers and middlemen of Europe. This design was backed up by diplomatic and military aggression (e.g. the three Anglo-Dutch Wars) and by strenuous efforts to imitate Dutch commercial, shipping and financial practices.

For a while it seemed that there would be a great Dutch empire in South America following the successful VOC commercial venture in the East. The Dutch West India Company captured Pernambuco (Recife) and the sugar-producing region of north-eastern Brazil (between the Maranhão and the Rio São Francisco) from the Portuguese in 1637. They carried their aggression against the Portuguese across the Atlantic and took over the Portuguese slaving ports on the west African coast – the fortress of São Jorge da Mina on the Guinea Coast in 1637, São Paulo de Loanda in Angola and the sugar-producing island of São Tomé in the Gulf of Guinea during the next three years. The Dutch controlled the slave trade for some thirty years, supplying slaves not only to their newly acquired plantations in north-eastern Brazil (Pernambuco, Itamaraca and Paraiba), but also to the Spanish mainland and to the British and French West Indian islands. However, shortly after, when Portugal regained its independence from Spain (1 December 1640) a popular uprising by the settled Portuguese colonists ended with the eviction of the Dutch from Brazil.

By the time they were expelled from Brazil in 1654 the first English Navigation Act was in operation, England and Holland were at war and the French were expanding their Atlantic trade and colonisation. These factors severely circumscribed Dutch ambitions in the Americas. They retained their privateering and slaving depots on the West Indian islands of Saba, St Martin and Curaçao; and through these bases they continued supplying the region with slaves. And, of course, they still had their northern mainland settlement of Nieuw Amsterdam (New Amsterdam) on the Hudson River, which they proceeded to develop under the able leadership of Peter Stuyvesant, the governor of New Netherland.

By 1660 there were altogether about 10 000 Dutch settlers in the region stretching from the Hudson to the Delaware. The Dutch presence, however, created a loophole in the new navigation system and encouraged smuggling by the British colonists who wished to see the Dutch competing to carry their produce.[27]

If the Dutch were out of the way, the entire coast from Massachusetts to Virginia would be English territory; it would be easier to enforce the Navigation Act and the English could take over the profit the Dutch were making from the fur trade. These objectives were achieved without a shot being fired when on 29 April 1664 a small British fleet sailed up the Hudson River and seized Nieuw Amsterdam, which was promptly renamed New York. The Dutch retaliated by declaring war on Engand, which provided an opportunity for the English to harass Dutch trading posts in Africa. By the terms of the peace signed at Breda in July 1667 New York was officially turned over to the English. In return England recognised Holland's claim to Dutch Guiana (Surinam) on the South American mainland.

Bellicose mercantilism drove the Dutch from the Atlantic trade. They were kept away by further tightening of the Navigation Acts, the French ban on Dutch trade with their West Indian islands (1664) and the English take-over of the slave trade through the Royal Africa Company (founded in 1672). Excluded from their area of commercial activity, the Dutch West India Company failed to pay dividends for some years and finally became bankrupt in 1674.

In 1655 the English seized Jamaica and turned it into a centre for the contraband trade with Spanish America. It became a reliable source of silver – estimated at the end of the seventeenth century to be worth £200 000 annually. Spanish bullion via Jamaica helped finance the East India Company's trade.[28]

The final stage came when Britain began to reap the harvest of colonial expansion both in North America and in India when London replaced Amsterdam as the commercial entrepôt of Europe. The processing and re-export of colonial goods (sugar, tea, coffee, tobacco) became the fastest-growing sector of British trade. In addition the flood of Indian cottons (calicoes and muslins) brought into Britain by the

East India Company after 1660 (until 1721 when the sale of such goods on the home market was banned) challenged and stimulated the domestic textile industry to make the technical changes that heralded the Industrial Revolution. The colonial trades provided British industry with fresh sources of raw materials and opened up channels of demand for 'luxury' commodities like tea, coffee and tobacco. The demand for these commodities proved to be both income and price elastic in the long run as their consumption expanded down the social scale. As the colonists increased their exports to Britain they in turn were able to buy an increasing range of manufactured goods from Britain (metal-wares, hats, silks and leather goods) so that by the mid-eighteenth century the American colonists were Britain's best customers. The expansion of the British merchant fleet and the build-up of the Royal Navy witnessed at the time of England's commercial invasion of the Mediterranean continued under the regulated colonial trading system. The forests of New England provided timber for shipbuilding and stores (turpentine, especially) for the Royal Navy.

Indeed, despite higher labour costs, the ready supplies of first-class timber and excellent naval stores gave colonial shipbuilders a competitive advantage over English shipyards; and many ships were built in New England both for the Navy and the great trading companies. The growth of the North American and West Indian colonies also created a new interdependent trading system from which Britain benefited – in particular the merchants of Bristol and Liverpool and the financiers of London. This commerce is epitomised in the infamous triangular trade which involved Africa, the West Indies, America and England. The whole of American trade depended on an adequate supply of slaves to produce the sugar and tobacco sent to England. English merchants exchanged cottons, rum, knives, beads and other trinkets for slaves on the West African coast. The slaves were shipped by the 'middle passage' to the West Indies and Virginia; sugar, cotton and tobacco were then brought back to Liverpool and Bristol. The maintenance of the large African labour force on the plantations created a demand for food which provided the northern mainland colonies with an outlet for their surplus production. With the participation of the northern colonists, a more complex system of interlocking colonial trade triangles was developed. For instance, timber, fish, livestock and provisions would be shipped from the ports of New England, New York and Pennsylvania for rum, molasses and sugar of the West Indies. The rum was sent to the African coast to buy slaves, who were then brought to the ports of Richmond, Charleston and the West Indian islands of Jamaica, St

Kitts and Barbados. In another triangle, a ship might take a cargo from New England, exchange it in the West Indies for molasses, sugar and coffee, go on to England and trade for textiles and ironware and return to Newport, New York or Philadelphia. This Atlantic trade – the triangular trade, the direct trade with the colonies and the complex of re-exports to Europe – backed up by the Navigation Laws led to a great expansion in the size of the British merchant fleet. It also increased the volume of business handled by London bankers and specialist insurance brokers. By 1700 London financiers had picked up the techniques of banking, credit and investment so that from this time onwards the London money market was equipped to deal with the financial needs of the growing transatlantic trade. London financiers gained valuable experience and developed expertise in international credit and bills of exchange business from their role as government contractors for large military remittances overseas. In wartime, large sums of government money were remitted through these private contractors to various theatres of war. In normal times the same contractors handled regular remittances on behalf of the Admiralty and other official bodies for naval outfitting, fortification and the maintenance of troops in the West Indian and American stations.

The great colonial merchants of Boston, New York and Philadelphia established links with merchants in London who acted as their financial agents or correspondents. On behalf of their colonial principals, the English agents presented bills of exchange for payment, maintained and accounted for sterling balances, made remittances to English creditors and provided short-term credit (usually for a period of one year).

Multilateral exchange transactions also developed as the London agents improved their organisation. For instance, when they sold foodstuffs to the West Indies, the mainland American colonists accepted payment by bills of exchange drawn on the sugar planters' agents in London with which the northern colonists could pay for their own imports of European goods.

London began to catch up with Amsterdam; together these two centres cleared the bulk of international payments through the use of bills of exchange and the provision of facilities for short-term lending. Amsterdam remained an important international financial centre right up to the end of the eighteenth century long after that city ceased to function as the leading European entrepôt.

By the end of the seventeenth century the dealers (jobbers and stockbrokers) who met in Jonathan's Coffee House in 'Change Alley' formed an embryonic stock exchange. Active dealings took place in the stock of the East India Company, the Hudson's Bay Company and the Royal Africa Company and the industrial companies (notably mining companies) that proliferated in the 1690s. The market value of these joint-stock shares increased nearly fivefold between 1695 and 1716. Much of this reflected dubious promotions and speculation which ended with the South Sea Company fiasco and the passing of the Bubble Act of 1720. But it does indicate a buoyant supply of capital and a willingness to invest in assets other than land.

At this time the old fear of Dutch competition receded. British shipping and commercial facilities became competitive after fifty years of imitation, protection and state regulation. Dutch competition in the vital complex of Atlantic trades was virtually eliminated by military aggression. English mercantilist policies were incredibly successful in achieving the twin goals of strategic power and national wealth, both resting solidly on naval supremacy and colonial monopoly.

However, no sooner was the Dutch bogey laid to rest a new threat to England's power and prosperity appeared on the horizon – the France of Louis XIV. The commercial war between the two countries began with Colbert's tariffs of 1664 and 1667 and the English embargo of 1678 on French exports (linens, silks, soap, paper and glassware). British traders faced increased French competition in the Baltic, Mediterranean and Levantine markets. Woollen exports were particularly hard hit in the Mediterranean from competition by the Languedoc industry. France replaced the Netherlands as the principal purveyor of goods to Spain and, through Cadiz, dominated the export trade to Spanish America.

The growth of absolutism and religious intolerance in France (after the revocation of the Edict of Nantes, 1685) stirred anti-French opinion in England as did the generally expansionist policy of the Sun King. England's sea routes to her growing markets and colonies overseas seemed threatened by the build-up of the French fleet and mercantile marine. When to commercial rivalry between France and England was added conflicting colonial ambitions the conflict inevitably escalated from trade to arms. The struggle for empire and markets took four wars and more than seventy years to settle.

At the end of this long duel with France, Britain emerged with vastly increased territory in America, a secure foothold in India and the prospect of assured markets overseas. By the terms of peace signed in March 1763 (Treaty of Paris) Britain acquired Canada, Cape Breton, Louisiana east of the Mississippi; Tobago, St Vincent and the Grenadines in the West Indies; Senegal on the African coast and Menorca. The

Caribbean island of Guadeloupe was returned to France, although Pitt would have preferred the profitable sugar plantations there to the fur trade of Canada. Indeed, Pitt's aim in the war was not so much territorial expansion as the reduction of French foreign trade through the crippling of their naval power. He embarked on the war, he said, with the conviction that 'when trade is at stake it is your last retrenchment, you must defend it or perish'.[29]

The end of the Seven Years War was the turning-point in the history of mercantilism, at any rate of mercantilist imperialism. New, critical and challenging ideas of economic liberalism surfaced. The new economic thinking was even espoused by some merchants and manufacturers engaged in the newer trades who wanted freedom to expand their activities. Some influential politicians equally felt that Britain had too much to lose and little to gain from the continuation of a policy of belligerent mercantilism. Wars became more costly and the burden of taxation increased proportionately. War as an instrument of commercial policy worked well for Britain until now. It had destroyed the Dutch commercial empire, checked and reversed French expansionism. Britain now had command of the sea and 'captive' colonial markets. Doubtless Lord Shelburne was not alone when he expressed himself as preferring trade to dominion.

Mercantilist regulation and control failed to hold an essentially self-governing people that the American colonists were. With the coming of the American Revolution of 1776 the first crack appeared in the edifice of mercantilism. It was also the year that the *Wealth of Nations* was published. Behind the rallying cry of the revolutionaries: 'Taxation without representation is tyranny' lay economic interest, political ambitions and ideals inimical to mercantilism. The ideals were those of the Enlightenment which took root in America, political freedom, faith in Reason, renunciation of wars of aggression, improvement and reform. Later in the century, Pitt's plans for the expansion of trade through the rationalisation of duties and restrictions culminated in the Eden Treaty of 1785 which ended the long commercial war with France. He might have been influenced by Adam Smith, but of greater significance was the fact that the Industrial Revolution was well under way and Britain's cost advantages over foreign rivals were becoming daily more apparent. The coming of free trade remained in the future. Meanwhile, Britain's entrepreneurs set out on the road to industrialisation sheltered and protected behind tariff walls, bounties and restrictions – the average tariff rate on imports in 1704 stood at 20 per cent i.e. it quadrupled from the relatively moderate level of 1689.

2 Mercantilist Thought on Foreign Trade

2.1 The Balance-of-trade Doctrine

MONEY AND THE BALANCE OF TRADE

Students of international economics justly claim that their subject is the oldest branch of economics. Theorems, concepts and hypotheses still currently in use were developed during the infancy of the discipline. The concept of the balance of trade, the price-specie flow mechanism and comparative costs are examples of the ancient lineage of the concerns of international economics. In 1938 Samuelson observed: 'Historically, the development of economic theory owes much to the theory of international trade.'[1] More recently, in connection with a reference to Ohlin's contribution to the theory of international trade, Samuelson repeated that 'trade theory has always been the queen realm of economic theory'.[2] The economic historian Donald McCloskey noted in 1980: 'Since the inception of the discipline its best minds (many of them British) have put commercial policy at the centre of their thinking.'[3] This is so, primarily because problems of international trade and finance have always been among the most momentous and controversial of issues in economic debate. It all started with the writers we call mercantilist airing their views on pressing contemporary problems that happened to be those connected with foreign trade: monetary problems, the foreign exchanges and the balance of payments. Although they often differed in their perceptions of the problems, they shared a common assumption: namely, the necessity for regulating foreign trade by the state in the interests of national power, wealth and aggrandisement. The reconciliation of the pursuit of private profit through foreign trade with national security was thus a matter of primary concern for these writers. It is because the mass of writings on economic subjects during the seventeenth and early eighteenth centuries have these characteristics, we call them 'mercantilist'. Economic thinking in the age of mercantilism took it for granted that international economic relations were political relations, and since international economic interaction was in large part shaped by the policies of the emerging nation-state, much of the mercantilist writing was addressed to the new state bureaucracies. Indeed, some notable mercantilists were themselves bureaucrats who wrote for the instruction of their princes.

Mercantilists believed that wealth and power were intimately associated with possession of the precious metals; and since, for a country without gold and silver mines foreign trade was the only way to acquire treasure, the mercantilists emphasised international trade as a means of increasing the wealth and power of a nation. In particular they focused their attention on the balance of trade and the foreign exchanges as mechanisms which determine the net flow of precious metals.

According to Adam Smith the mercantilists entertained two fallacious ideas about money and the balance of payments which were expressed in their doctrine of the balance of trade. The first proposition was: that a country could only enrich itself by acquiring the precious metals. The second was, the way to acquire these monetary metals – for a country without gold and silver mines – was by measures of commercial policy (import substitution and export promotion) designed to achieve a favourable balance of trade.

Adam Smith exaggerated the extent to which the mercantilists identified money and wealth and underrated their percipience. But even so, modern economists aware of the ideological motive behind Smith's attack on mercantilism find it incredible that sensible men should have espoused such views. To the English classical economists this antedeluvian doctrine was the equivalent in political economy to pre-Copernican ideas in cosmology. In 1847 Richard Jones despite his misgivings about the abstract *a priori* methodology of the economics of his day felt obliged to label British economic writings before Adam Smith as 'primitive political economy'.[4] Primitive not only in a temporal sense, but also as being crude, naïve and unsophisticated in substance.

Keynes' defence of mercantilism in the form of a coda to his *General Theory* is, of course, well known to economists. To the chagrin of his teachers and the corps of orthodox economists Keynes protested that the classical economists had been unfair to the mercantilists who for two hundred years had seen 'a peculiar advantage' to their countries in a favourable balance of trade. Economists were therefore guilty of 'presumptuous error in treating as a puerile obsession what for centuries had been a prime object of practical statecraft'.[5] Earlier, Marx objected: 'it must not be thought that these mercantilists were as stupid as they were made out to be by the later Vulgar-Freetraders'.[6] But for economists wedded to the 'scientific' conclusions of modern international trade theory nothing can mitigate or condone the errors perpetrated by the mercantilist pamphleteers. Surely, these economists say, the self-defeating nature of a policy aimed at the achievement of a perpetual balance-of-trade surplus and the universal beneficiality of free trade should have been obvious if only at the intuitive level to these early writers on economic matters.

Why, then, did the mercantilists espouse these primitive ideas on money and the balance of payments which were no more than elements of a common 'folk doctrine' prevalent in the emerging nation states? Was mercantilist thought just a reflection of the economics of the man in the street? In a sense it was, if by the economics of the man in the street we mean the economics of the counting house. But to answer this question objectively, we need to trace the evolution of the balance-of-trade doctrine.

The balance-of-trade doctrine arose in the context of the widespread concern in Europe about the scarcity of coin towards the end of the sixteenth century. The prevailing view in many countries was that the drain of specie was caused by exchange-rate depreciation abroad resulting from debasement and other manipulations of foreign currencies. Economic distress was attributed to the scarcity of coin and the reaction of officials was to impose exchange controls and tighten regulation on the export of bullion. A critical literature arose which, while accepting that shortage of money was the cause of economic depression, challenged the official view that exchange or bullion export control was the appropriate remedy. The link between bullion flows and the balance of trade was, of course, recognised for a long time; but what was new was the awareness that the outpayments and inpayments of a country (which we know as the balance-of-payments position) were ultimately determined by economic conditions, such as the level and diversity of national production, the productivity and efficiency in the use of national resources.

Antonio Serra is usually credited with being the first to use the balance-of-trade concept in this sense appropriately and to link it with basic underlying economic factors.[7] He recognised the role of invisible items and used the idea very much the same as we do today when referring to the balance of payments. Writing in 1613 from a Papal prison in Naples he sought to refute the exchange-control views of de Santis, who had apparently argued that the shortage of money in Naples was due to the high exchange rate. Not so, claimed Serra. The rate of exchange was governed by the state of the balance of trade. A payments imbalance would be settled by gold flows and if the exchange rate is not regulated then a deficit would be reflected in a depreciating exchange rate. Regulation of the exchange rate and control over the export of bullion only struck ineffectually at the symptoms, not the cause of the payments imbalance. The real causes lie in such basic economic factors as the availability of natural resources, a thriving agriculture and the volume of manufactured exports. These conditions which produce a healthy balance of payments depend, in turn, on the size and quality of a country's population, the extent of its trade connections, favourable geographical location for engaging in entrepôt trade, etc.

The doctrine in a rudimentary and obvious form was, of course, an old one. It was the leading theme of several writers from at least the middle of the sixteenth century. Thus, the author of the *Discourse of the Common Weal* (Sir Thomas Smith?) warned in 1549 that 'we must alwaies take care that we bie no more of strangers than we sell them (for so we sholde empoverishe ourselves and enriche them'.[8] And Francis Bacon wrote in 1616: 'Let the foundation of profitable trade be thus laid that the exportation of home commodities be more in value than the importations of foreign, so we shall be sure that the stocks of the Kingdom shall increase, for the balance of trade must be returned in money or bullion.'[9]

In the previous year a compilation of England's balance of trade was made by two officials (Lionel Cranfield and John Wolstenholme) in connection with Cockayne's Project. The calculation was made on the basis of the customs revenue.

The idea of 'balance' in a country's international accounts was a direct application of double-entry bookkeeping practice which English merchants were then beginning to adopt. To writers of the time the nation was seen carrying on business in much the same way as an individual merchant. Its profit or loss over an accounting period could be determined from the state of the 'books'.

THE 1620s' ENGLISH DEBATE

The doctrine in its classic form arose in England out of the famous controversy during the early part of the seventeenth century between Malynes on one side and Mun and Misselden on the other, concerning the state of the foreign exchanges and the balance of payments.[10] The occasion was the economic and trade depression of 1619–22, and the issue under discussion was how to stop the outflow of the precious metals.

The depression was partly attributed by contemporaries to the effective reduction of the money supply resulting from the drain of silver abroad. For a period of six years from 1617 there occurred a series of currency manipulations and debasements in Germany, Poland and the Baltic states – the so-called *Kipper-und-Wipper Zeit*. Princes, magnates and mint-controllers in these areas attempted to protect themselves against inflation (and even to reap short-term profits) by lowering the nominal or actual silver content of their coins – measures which effectively devalued the local currencies. English exports (principally woollen cloth) to these areas fell drastically by as much as 50 per cent between 1618 and 1622 as sterling prices rose when expressed in local currencies. At the same time the relative cheapening of foreign goods (in terms of silver) resulted in increased English imports from the regions subject to monetary disorder; and since bullion was worth more abroad, merchants gained by exporting bullion, returning the proceeds in foreign goods. In addition, two years of bad harvests supervened which necessitated huge grain imports from abroad, paid for in specie. The result was a deficit in the English balance of payments and a slump in the main English industry, woollen textiles. Financial distress spread from merchants and clothiers to the families of weavers, spinners, carders and sorters (as well as the farmers who raised the sheep) resulting in massive unemployment in the principal clothing centres.

The problem of the depression engaged the attention of the Privy Council, which appointed a special commission to inquire into it. The Commission on Trade became the focus of the policy debates in which Gerard Malynes, Edward Misselden and Thomas Mun played prominent parts. The debate concerned the reasons for the loss of bullion and the depression in English foreign trade. Attention was focused on the foreign exchanges and the balance of payments; and the controversy turned on the question whether the exchange rate for sterling was a price like any other price determined by demand and supply.[11]

The traditional reaction to a crisis of foreign trade and bullion losses was to raise the valuation of English silver coins and impose controls over exchange transactions. This was the remedy proposed by Malynes.[12] Gerard de Malynes, who described himself as a merchant, was an 'interventionist' who believed in monetary control and regulation. He traced the roots of the crisis to the unregulated activities of European bankers who collectively had abused the foreign exchanges. Foreign-exchange dealers, he claimed, have used the foreign-exchange market as a vehicle for disguised usury and speculation. The results have been undesirable fluctuations in exchange rates and, in the case of sterling, a more or less permanent depreciation, i.e. English merchants, in exchange dealings, gave up more English coins per unit of foreign currency. This 'undervaluation of our moneys' has been the cause of the recent exportation of specie. The remedy was obvious: fix the exchange rate at par so that there would be no advantage to anyone from the movement of specie in one direction or the other. Exchange rates are at par – *pro pars pari* – when they are precisely equal to the ratios of the metallic content of currencies.[13] The strict maintenance of this parity relationship would eliminate the overvaluation and undervaluation of currencies which arise when the external and internal purchasing power of currencies diverge. For instance, a currency is said to be 'overvalued' on the foreign-exchange market when its external purchasing power (in terms of foreign commodities) is higher than its internal purchasing power (in terms of domestic commodities). The reason for this divergence is differences in rates of inflation among countries which Malynes attributed to differences in the metallic contents of national currencies.

In view of his advocacy of fixed exchange rates, did Malynes then believe that exchange rates were determined by supply and demand? There is no doubt that he did, although some of his critics have made out that he believed otherwise. His position is quite clear. In a free market, exchange rates are determined by the supply and demand for foreign currencies – 'according to scarcity and plenty of moneys to be taken and delivered', including amounts offered for speculative purposes. This is a positive statement. But Malynes's point is that the exchange rate is too important a price to be left to the free play of market forces. This is a normative statement – what *should* be the case. This he backed up with the observation that money is a medium of exchange and a measure of value. As a measure of value money itself must be invariant in price, i.e. the value of money must be grounded in the amount and purity of the precious metals each unit of the circulating medium contains. As he puts it: 'The yard doth measure the Cloth, but the Cloth doth not measure the yard.'[14] His complaint was that money, through foreign-exchange transactions had become an article of private commerce, with damaging consequences for the welfare of national economies. Since the exchange rate was nothing but the relative price of two national moneys, it has to be a matter of national concern and not one for private haggling. Malynes urged the restoration of the office of Royal Exchanger, combined with a comprehensive system of exchange control to fix and maintain the exchange rate for sterling *vis-à-vis* other currencies.[15] He further urged that periodic checks be made of the weight and fineness of all coins to discourage debasement and clipping. Malynes must have known, however, that two previous attempts to control money dealings and trade in bills of exchange (1546 and 1576) proved unsuccessful. The prime objective of the policy of regulation must be to prevent the undervaluation of sterling after the initial revaluation that Malynes thought was required.

Apart from stemming the outflow of bullion, such a policy had distinct advantages for Malynes, not the least important of which would be that it would reverse the deterioration of England's terms of trade. He took the view that the relative value of internationally traded commodities depends upon the value of the exchange rate and here his opinions clashed sharply with those of his fellow controversialists, Misselden and Mun. The latter attributed exchange-rate movements to autonomous real disturbances to particular components of the balance of payments (e.g. changes in the demand for and supply of exports and imports). The relative price of exports and imports would, on this view, then be determined by the basic supply/demand relationships in foreign trade rather than merely a reflection of the exchange rate. However, Malynes maintained that the exchanges 'overruled' commodities so that when sterling was undervalued (i.e. the exchange rate being below mint parity) the terms of trade turned against England, as English export prices fell relative to import prices. This was a real income loss suffered by England in addition to the loss from the export of specie. Indeed, the root cause of the 'overbalancing' (or balance-of-payments deficit) can be traced to the unfavourable terms of trade occasioned by the depreciated exchange rate.[16]

The argument that a depreciating exchange rate is likely to cause a deterioration in the terms of trade is consistent with the modern theory of the effects of a devaluation. But it is not a certain effect. With a devaluation, import and export prices will normally both rise in terms of home currency units. In foreign currency both are likely to fall. What is crucial for the movement of the terms of trade (when expressed in foreign currency) is whether export prices fall more than import prices. Although this is usually assumed to be the case, it does not always follow. If the foreign demand for exports and the home-country demand for imports are both highly elastic, and supplies of home exports and foreign imports highly inelastic with respect to price changes, a devaluation can actually bring about an improvement in the terms of trade (commodity or net barter terms of trade). The precise condition for the terms of trade to deteriorate with a devaluation is: when the product of demand elasticities for imports (in both countries) is less than the product of supply elasticities of exports (in both countries). Malynes assumed that the demand for English exports (mainly cloth) was inelastic; but while this is insufficient to establish his contention that England was selling cheap and buying dear, he made four additional observations which he felt supported his assertion about unfavourable terms of trade:

1. When sterling was below par, English merchants normally 'passed on' the whole of the increased worth of foreign currency by accepting a lower foreign currency price for English exports, which apparently fell to the full extent of the devaluation.
2. The loss of bullion consequent on the trade deficit reduced the domestic money supply and exerted downward pressure on the English price level, while the opposite occurred in England's trading partners. There the inflow of bullion increased the money supplies and increased foreign price levels.
3. The shortage of money at home and the high domestic interest rates forced 'young merchants' to seek trade credit abroad, through bills of exchange where interest rates were often lower who then 'dumped' English goods at low prices when their debts fell due. This often spoiled the market for others, who were forced to accept lower export prices.
4. Prices abroad had increased faster than English prices both because of the differential impact of American treasure on price levels in different countries and because of the enhancement and debasement of foreign coins. The result was disparate international prices that did not correspond with actual exchange rates.

Whether or not Malynes was correct in his observation of the factors which allegedly caused a steady deterioration of England's terms of trade, there is no doubt that he did hit on important elements of the later classical theory of international adjustment. What Malynes glimpsed in (1) and (4) above were aspects of what became known as the price-specie-flow mechanism and the PPP (purchasing-power-parity) theory of exchange rates respectively.

Both Schumpeter and Viner give high credit to Malynes for appreciating the workings of the international mechanism of adjustment, however vaguely the latter may have described it. Schumpeter claims that no other writer of the seventeenth century surpassed Malynes 'in clear and full understanding of the international mechanism'.[17] Viner, less effusively, notes that Malynes 'approached surprisingly close to a grasp of the self-regulating mechanism'.[18] And recently Malynes has been hailed as a forerunner of the purchasing-power-parity theory.[19] Briefly, this theory attributes movements in the exchange rate between two currencies to the differences in the rate of inflation between them. This is the reasoning behind (4) above where what he is claiming is that, for a variety of reasons, the PPP (purchasing-power-parity) relationship did not hold with the result that some currencies were overvalued while others were undervalued. To correct this disequilibrium and to restore the PPP relationship as far as England was concerned was Malynes's interest when he proposed the revaluation of sterling back to the mint parity level. The fixing of sterling's rate at par and its stabilisation by means of a comprehensive system of exchange control involved a substantial appreciation of the actual exchange rate. Malynes expected that this would (a) restore equilibrium to the balance of payments, (b) improve the terms of trade, and (c) stop the outflow of bullion. What were the grounds for this optimism? The belief that the foreign demand for English goods was inelastic. In his words: 'Our home commodities being also needful, and of continued request, that at all times they are most vendible.'[20] In statements he made elsewhere he indicated that the domestic demand for imports was also inelastic. In these circumstances an appreciation of the exchange rate would indeed be the appropriate policy. A modern theorist would endorse this, because with inelastic demands (i.e. the sum of the import and export demand elasticities less than one) the Marshall–Lerner condition would not be satisfied in which case the correct policy is one of appreciation rather than devaluation.

Malynes's modern critics doubt whether he really understood the price-specie-flow mechanism because if he did, why did he not accept its logic which would have suggested that balance-of-payments disequilibria are self-adjusting?[21] Malynes's insight into the automatic mechanism was indeed well in advance of his contemporaries, but it was a partial view. His understanding of it stopped short at the effect of gold flows on price levels at home and abroad. He did not carry the analysis forward from there to the further effect of these price changes on the demand for export and imports in both countries and the subsequent restoration of payments equilibrium.

Schumpter felt the reason Malynes did not pursue this line of thought was because he was more impressed with the shortcomings of the self-regulating mechanism than with the mechanism itself.[22] This seems to be the most plausible interpretation of Malynes's view. The free market (in foreign exchange most importantly) just does not work, or if it does only to produce disequilibria and disorder. Thus, a self-regulating mechanism cannot be relied upon. This attitude, in fact, explains Malynes's denunciation of the private exchange dealers, his complaint about unfavourable terms of trade and his long-standing advocacy of government intervention and control of the foreign-exchange market. Could it be that Malynes lost interest in pursuing the chain of reasoning further when he realised that it would have provided additional ammunition to his less far-sighted adversaries?

Malynes, as we have seen, believed that the demand for English exports was price-inelastic, and most modern commentators suggest that it was on the basis of this belief that Malynes rejected the automatic balancing mechanism.[23] But, as Allen points out, the inelasticity argument is insufficient ground for such a rejection. Allen's point is that *if* Malynes was aware of the Marshall–Lerner condition and better, *if* he knew the general-stability condition of the foreign-exchange market, then he would not have doubted the efficacy of the automatic adjustment mechanism merely because of the assumption of inelastic demand. In any case, says Allen, Malynes's assumption of demand inelasticity was an appropriate one to make, given the actual market conditions facing English cloth exporters in the early seventeenth century which was one of increasing competition (both in terms of price competition and competition from new suppliers) suggesting rather the opposite market characteristic, i.e. high export-demand elasticity.[24] This is true and Malynes was wrong on empirical grounds; but, perhaps we are imputing too much theoretical sophistication to Malynes's comments on this matter. He did not consciously use an empirically questionable assumption to cast doubt on what became known later as the 'price-specific-flow mechanism' (which he did not fully comprehend) neither was he aware of any exchange-market stability condition (which was only rigorously formulated in the 1930s).

What is more plausible is that Malynes genuinely believed that the demand for English goods abroad was inelastic; thus the country was forgoing an opportunity to profit from this situation by tolerating an unduly low exchange rate which caused England to buy dear and sell cheap. He therefore wanted to counter the argument of both those who recommended a policy of devaluation (Misselden) and those who argued for low export prices (Mun) as solutions to the problem of England's foreign trade. He saw an improvement in the terms of trade as the key to the whole problem, for not only would this reverse the flow of specie abroad, but would have additional beneficial effects on the level of employment at home.

He may have been misguided in his optimism and his empirical assessment hopelessly wrong – as Supple remarks: 'Few theories could have been less appropriate to the economic conditions of the early 1620s'.[25] But his reasoning and passionate advocacy provoked others to develop and refine the alternative and more characteristic mercantilist concept of the balance of trade.

Like Malynes, both Misselden and Mun agreed that 'the want of money... is the first cause of the decay of trade'.[26] They further agreed that the reduction of the money stock was linked to the export of specie; but they differed sharply from Malynes in their diagnosis of the ultimate cause of the efflux of treasure. Whereas Malynes located the bullion loss in an exchange rate below par, Misselden and Mun traced it to the state of the balance of payments (in particular, the state of the balance of trade).

Beside the exchange rate, various explanations for the shortage of money and trade slump were canvassed at the time including (1) the undervaluation of English coin relative to foreign moneys, (2) excessive imports of luxury goods, (3) defective enforcement of the regulations of the cloth trade, (4) disorderly marketing of English goods abroad, and (5) the trading activities of the East India Company which entailed a chronic drain of specie to the Orient.

Before they had formulated their distinctive 'balance-of-trade' doctrine, Misselden and Mun wrote tracts touching on these complaints and in addition felt obliged to defend their respective foreign trade organisations from the charge that their operations contributed to the crises. Thus, Misselden in his first work, *Free Trade: Or the Means to Make Trade Flourish* (1622) absolved the Merchant Adventurers (to which body he belonged) from any blame, and showed that it was the East India Company that was partly responsible for the loss of bullion. He accused the Company, in the first place, of being a monopolist (which indeed it was, as far as English trade with the East was concerned) and, in the second place, of exporting specie which did not return as payment for English goods. The Company's operations, additionally, increased the volume of imports into England.

In the previous year, 1621, Mun had written a tract of fifty pages in defence of the East India Company, of which he was a director. In it he repudiated the charge that the export of specie by the Company was disadvantageous to the kingdom. The true facts were, he claimed:

(1) That although the Company was licensed to export £30 000 in bullion per voyage it was required under its latters patent to

bring back an equivalent amount of silver; and in any case the Company did not normally export the maximum allowed.
(2) The Company cheapened the India trade by eliminating the Turkish middlemen and has provided employment for English ships, shipbuilding and ancillary trades.
(3) The goods brought in by the Company are essential commodities – goods that cannot be produced at home, or raw materials (e.g. raw silk, dyestuffs) which create industry and increase employment in the textile trades.
(4) If English merchants were not in this trade, then their keen rivals the Dutch would take over completely, dominate the trade and charge what prices they please.

Like Malynes, Mun concluded his tract with a condemnation of the tricks of the exchangers and the 'abuse of the exchange' – a common xenophobic complaint at the time, since the foreign-exchange market was almost wholly in the hands of foreigners. He also blamed currency manipulations for the loss of specie and, at this stage of the debate, this meant that he saw eye to eye with Misselden, at least on this point; for Misselden in his *Free Trade* had attributed the bullion export partly to currency manipulation on the continent which led to 'the undervaluation of his Majesty's coin, to that of our neighbour countries'.[27] He therefore proposed a lowering of the official mint ratio by raising the valuation of English silver coins. This was, in effect, a proposal for an English devaluation to counter depreciations abroad. Misselden recognised that this would inevitably result in domestic inflation (stemming from the increased monetary supplies), but he argued that was no bad thing because it would stimulate economic activity generally and lift England from the trade depression.

However, in 1623 or thereabouts, whether as a result of the fact that Misselden by then had a position with the East India Company, or that Misselden and Mun became better acquainted as neighbours in Hackney (East London) or that because they both further reflected on the East India Company and saw it as a microcosm of England's trading position, it appears that they made common cause and came up with essentially the same general balance-of-trade theory as an adequate and coherent doctrine for analysing and evaluating England's foreign trade.

In his second book, *The Circle of Commerce*, Misselden criticised Malynes's call for the restoration of exchange parity, referring to it as that 'old soil'd project'. Exchange rates are determined by the demand and supply of foreign exchange, which in turn depend on the demand

and supply of commodities. Misselden then proclaims the revolutionary doctrine that 'Exchange is a kind of Commerce exercised in money, in merchandize, in both, in either; of one man with another, of one country with another.'[28]

The view of precious metals as themselves articles of commerce struck at the root of traditional doctrine, for it attributed to mere merchants the power to set the value of coin – a right hitherto regarded as the prerogative of princes. He agreed with Malynes that there is an equilibrium exchange rate – 'whereunto all exchange have their naturall propension' – (i.e. the mint parity rate); but the actual exchange rate deviates from this equilibrium value (or real exchange rate) 'according to the occasion of both parties'.[29] The actual (or nominal) exchange rate is merely an indication of excess supply or demand in the foreign exchange market. In this sense it is passive; it does not determine the volume of exports and imports, neither does it regulate bullion flows. Both specie-flows and the exchange rate are determined by 'the abundance and scarcity of commodities', in other words, by the state of the balance of payments.

Although he did not use the expression 'balance of payments', this is what Misselden obviously meant; because in addition to the balance of trade, he referred to income from re-exports, the profits from fisheries and freight earnings. Thus, according to Misselden, England can avoid a loss of bullion only by securing a favourable balance of trade. The exchange rate would then reflect this fact, and there would be no need to worry about it. The balance of trade is therefore of critical importance to a country, for it is 'an excellent and politique Invention to shew us the difference of waight in the *Commerce* of one Kingdome with another'.[30] Misselden himself calculated balance-of-trade figures for 1622 and found a deficit of £298 878 – admittedly, he said, not a perfect estimate (assuming an average tariff rate of 5 per cent, he multiplied the customs revenue by a factor of twenty). Although disappointed with the negative balance, he pointed to the rational ('scientific') nature of the exercise: 'Wee see it to our griefe, that we are fallen into a great Underballance of Trade with other Nations. Wee felt it before in sense; but now we know it by science: wee found it before in operation; but now wee see it in speculation.'[31]

MUN ON THE BALANCE OF TRADE

During the course of the debates on trade and foreign exchanges Mun produced a series of papers and memoranda which formed the basis of his *England's Treasure by Forraign Trade*, published posthumously by his son in 1664. For later generations it became the *locus classicus* for mercantilist thought on the role of foreign trade in the national economy, as indeed it informed popular economic thinking for over a century afterwards. Foreign trade, through the balance of trade, is assigned a crucial role in the process of wealth-generation. The central theme is clearly stated at the beginning of the book:

> The ordinary means therefore to increase our wealth and treasure is by *Forraign Trade* wherein wee must ever observe this rule; to sell more to strangers yearly than wee consume of theirs in value. For suppose that when this Kingdom is plentifully served with the Cloth, Lead, Tinn, Iron, Fish and other native commodities, we doe yearly export the overplus to forraign countries to the value of twenty two hundred thousand pounds; by which means we are enabled beyond the Seas to buy and bring in forraign wares for our use and Consumptions, to the value of twenty hundred thousand pounds; By this order duly Kept in our trading, we may rest assured that the Kingdom shall be enriched yearly two hundred thousand pounds, which must be brought to us in so much Treasure; because that part of our stock which is not returned to us in wares must necessarily be brought home in treasure.[32]

The growth of wealth then depends on having an excess of exports over imports, and Mun lists twelve methods whereby this may be achieved: (1) Make full use of natural resources and cultivation of the fisheries so as to bring about a 'diversity of employment'; (2) curtail non-essential or luxury imports by means of higher duties; (3) a flexible pricing policy must be followed which maximises the value of exports at the best possible price (i.e. merchants should take into account foreign demand elasticities); (4) promote the use of English ships to avoid payments of freight and insurance to foreigners; (5) emulate the Dutch by developing an entrepôt trade, e.g. by the establishment of staple towns; (6) give encouragement to the long-distance trades; (7) import of raw materials for domestic processing should be admitted at low rates of duty, and for certain English exports bounties on their exportation would be desirable – the aim being to stimulate production and employment.

How these recommendations were to be implemented so as to achieve the ultimate desirable result – a more favourable trade balance – was not discussed in any detail. Some could be put into effect by merchants themselves, others would follow from the incentives provided by the market; but much of the programme obviously depended on prudent government regulation.

On the foreign exchanges Mun uses the same sort of argument as Misselden to attack Malynes's proposal for foreign-exchange control and the fixing of exchange rates by royal fiat so as to retain specie. Thus he claims:

> it is not the power of exchange that doth enforce the treasure where the rich prince will have it, but it is the money proceeding of wares in foreign trade that doth enforce the exchange, and rules the price thereof high or low, according to the plenty or scarcity of the said money. ...[33]

And again

> Let the meer Exchanger do his worst; Let Princes oppress, Lawyers extort, Usurers bite, Prodigals wast ... so much Treasure only will be brought in or carried out of a Commonwealth, as the Forraign Trade doth over or under ballance in value. And this must come to pass by a Necessity beyond all resistance.[34]

Foreign exchange plays only a passive role and responds to the flow of goods and services in trade. Money is the counterpart to the flow of goods and the exchange rate follows money. The exchange rate, therefore, has no necessary or causal relationship to specie-flows. What matters for specie-flows and the exchange rate is the balance of trade – the net debits or credits that remain from the annual flow of trade. Here Mun makes a distinction between 'particular' and 'general' balances of trade, and he argues that it is the general or total balance that counts. The East India trade is an example of a transaction which produces an excess of imports over exports; but, as Mun demonstrates more fully elsewhere, it contributes positively to the general balance through re-exports. He disdains the bullionist position, claiming that only the money earned from the surplus of the balance of trade is profitable: 'If we melt down our plate into Coyn ... it would cause Plenty of mony for a time, yet should we be none the richer.'[35]

The aim of policy must be the maximum accumulation of treasure or, more properly, earnings through a favourable balance of trade. Mun would nevertheless allow the export of money in certain cases. Indeed, he claims certain distinct advantages would follow from the exportation of money for purposes of trade. The country's stock of money or financial capital must be used as productively as possible. This means that money must not be left idle. In the form of financial capital, money must regularly be converted into goods and then subsequently exchanged for a larger quantity of money. This circuit, $M-C-M'$ (where M stands for money, C for commodities and $M' > M$), is, of course, Marx's well-known formula for describing the capitalist economy in the sphere of circulation, and is the central theme of Mun's book. For him, money is primarily esteemed because it functions as a medium of international exchange; it drives foreign trade and as he puts it succinctly: 'money begets trade and trade encreaseth money'. Here Mun echoes Misselden's idea of a commerce in money. By 'trading with its money' a country's foreign trade could be enlarged and diversified, resulting in a still higher level of earnings.

Mun discusses two additional reasons for desiring a constant turnover of money:

(1) The volume of available exports from England relative to the demand for them abroad sets a limit to the size of the favourable balance of trade and hence England's bullion accumulation. When this point is reached, further trade is only possible if part of the accumulated treasure is sent abroad in exchange for commodities that can subsequently be exported at a profit. Here again, Mun is obviously thinking of the East India trade and the re-export business in general.

(2) Since plenty of money raises prices, keeping the money at home merely serves to increase domestic prices, thus adversely affecting sales abroad and leading to a deterioration of the foreign balance. Mun thus recognises a crude quantity theory relationship between money and prices:

> If wee were once poor, and now having gained some store of mony by trade with resolutions to keep it still in the Realm; shall this cause other Nations to spend more of our commodities than formerly they have done, whereby we might say that our trade is Quickened and Enlarged? no verily, it will produce no such good effect ... ; for all men do consent that plenty of mony in a Kingdom doth make the native commodities dearer ... so it is directly against the benefit of the Publique in the quantity of the trade.[36]

And again

> plenty or scarcity of mony makes all things dear or good or cheap; and this mony is either gotten or lost in forraign trade by the over or under-ballancing of the same.[37]

Although generally myopic in his view of foreign trade, Mun showed evidence of some deeper thinking when he questions the desirability of an excessive imbalance in one's favour. For,

> how shall we than vent our commodities? What will become of our Ships, Mariners, Munitions, our poor Artificers and many others? doe we hope that other Countreys will afford us mony for All our wares without buying or bartering for Some of theirs?[38]

And, in an earlier discourse, referring to the role of treasure, he points out:

> It is not therefore the keeping of our Mony in the Kingdom which makes a quick and ample Trade, but the necessity and use of our Wares in Forreign Countreys, and our want of their Commodities which causeth the Vent and Consumption on all sides.[39]

Here he showed some understanding of the interdependence of exports and imports, i.e. that reduction of imports would have an adverse effect on exports and consequently on domestic employment.

Mun seems to have recognised the principle of price elasticity of demand, and discussed the factors affecting elasticity (e.g. necessities, substitutes, etc.). He believed that the demand for exports and imports was price elastic – he was not an 'elasticity pessimist' – and that domestic prices, through the exchange rate, were related to prices abroad. In a memorandum of April 1623 dealing with the effects on trade of exchange-rate changes, he estimated that a 10 per cent reduction in imports prices would increase the quantity demanded by 20 per cent and a 10 per cent increase in export price of English cloth would reduce export sales by something like 40 per cent.

MUN AND THE INTERNATIONAL ADJUSTMENT MECHANISM

Mun's book is a synthesis of the best economic ideas prevalent at the time; yet, for all his analytical clarity, Mun does not arrive at an understanding of the automatic mechanism of adjustment. All the elements of such a theory are there: the causal relationship between money and prices, the link between relative price levels at home and abroad and the value of exports and imports, the assumption that the demand for exports and imports is price elastic. Mun also explicitly recognises that only earnings in the form of money from the sale of English goods abroad would remain in the country, and repeats: 'Only so much will remain and abide with us as is gained and incorporated into the estate of the Kingdom by the overballance of the trade.'[40] He, however, fails to integrate these propositions into a coherent theory of the distribution of the world stock of specie among countries. Why? Of course, the enunciation of such a theory would have seriously undermined his otherwise logical system of the balance of trade. Even if Mun had intuitively arrived at the theory but had then dismissed it, unlike Malynes, he could not have rejected it on empirical grounds of demand inelasticity, since he assumes the opposite demand conditions and repeatedly stresses that high domestic prices reduce exports. One possibility is that Mun declined to embrace the self-regulation hypothesis because, as we have seen, he envisaged a situation where specie inflows (stemming from a payments surplus) would be used to finance a larger volume of trade. That is, as Blaug points out, what Mun (like other mercantilists) had in mind was not really the quantity theory but the equation of exchange (more properly, the identity of exchange) $MV = PT$.[41] This is the statement (true by definition) that the amount of money in an economy must be enough to finance the total volume of all economic activity. Thus Mun reasons if M increases then T would increase with no inflationary effect. Hence, a gold inflow induced by a payments surplus can stimulate domestic economic activity, including exports, without affecting their increased sales abroad because export prices would remain unchanged. Under certain conditions this might conceivably be the case, at any rate in the short run (e.g. the existence of unemployed resources); but it does not square with the rest of Mun's case for a favourable balance of trade based on long-run considerations. Mun's strategy to achieve this latter objective calls for a permanent 'export drive' or export-led growth policy based on the regular export of money which ultimately is the only means of sustaining an ever-increasing volume of exports and accumulation of treasure. But here is the dilemma and a basic contradiction in Mun's thinking: domestic prices will not remain unchanged with an accelerating inflow of specie; but in this case a permanent export surplus is unattainable and Mun's programme is in ruins. The only way Mun could have resolved this dilemma was to have recognised the logic of the automatic mechanism, but this would have been contrary to his mercantilist principles.[42] But perhaps there was a basis, however fragile, for Mun's mercantilist preconceptions. A hundred years after the publication of Mun's book, David Hume described a 'benign interval' between the influx of species and the subsequent price increase – a period when economic activity was stimulated. It was desirable to take advantage of that lag whenever money came in, for in that manner the economy could be periodically stimulated. What mattered was not the absolute quantity of money, but whether the level, whatever it happened to be, was increasing or decreasing. A decreasing monetary trend was to be avoided, since that spelled deflation, loss of output, unemployment and misery. A rising trend (through a payment surplus) must therefore be the aim of policy – although the beneficial effect would be checked from time to time as prices (including wages and material costs) reacted to monetary inflows.[43] Could it be that such a dynamic process was in Mun's mind when he called for a permanent export drive? Certainly, several mercantilists hinted at the effect of changes in the quantity of money over time, although they failed until Hume to analyse the sequence satisfactorily. Reverting to Mun's stated position on specie-flows, one way in which a payments surplus might be compatible with the maintenance of stable domestic prices is through a policy of 'neutralisation' or 'sterilisation' of specie inflows. But sterilisation is not viable in the long run and depends on the existence of an active securities market and the pursuit of 'open-market operations'. Neither condition obtained in Mun's day, but he does consider a substitute check on inflation resulting from specie inflows: the 'overplus' of the balance of payments can be drawn off in taxation, and if it remains inactivated in the king's treasury then domestic prices would not rise, and hence there would be no external loss of specie through an adverse balance of payments. If domestic prices are prevented from rising, then the automatic mechanism would not be set in motion.

When (in the chapter entitled 'The Spanish Treasure cannot be kept from other Kingdomes by any prohibition made by Spain') he discusses the diffusion of American treasure via Spain, he rightly stresses the importance of the balance of trade in this process. Spain lost treasure to her trading partners because of that country's adverse trade balance, plus net military expenditures abroad. The case of Spain, albeit not a typical example, could have afforded Mun an opportunity for seeing the process whereby the world's monetary stocks are distributed among countries through the price-specie-flow mechanism. He missed this opportunity because he ignored the changes in relative price levels that brought about the result he was describing.

In addition to what has been said above about Mun's failure to deal with the contradictions of his theory, other factors in this neglect include:

(1) A basic myopia on Mun's part (and other mercantilists as well). On matters of trade balances and specie flows, these were only

considered from the national viewpoint. Mun and other writers like him saw only one side of the coin, i.e. while they reflected on the possible inflationary impact on the domestic economy of large specie inflows, they were blind to the deflationary pressures on price levels abroad. Thus they did not conceive of any tendency towards equilibrium in the adjustment of balances of payments through specie-flows and relative price-level changes.

(2) The gains from foreign trade were conceived almost exclusively in terms of a favourable balance of trade and the accumulation of treasure with subsidiary beneficial effects on employment. They had no understanding of the world as an interdependent system and this relates to their view of international trade as a zero-sum game. Little thought was given to the real forces which determine the level and composition of a country's exports and imports.

(3) The experience of the important East India (and, to a lesser extent, the Baltic trade as well) did not inspire confidence in any automatic adjustment mechanism even if such a theory were hypothesised at the time. Specie sent to the Orient never seemed to return; much of it went out of monetary circulation (into hoards or jewellery). This seemed to have aborted the adjustment mechanism. Moreover, since the local inhabitants did not want very much of what the English produced, reciprocal trade appeared virtually impossible.

MUN'S MODEL OF TRADE AND GROWTH

Mun might not have comprehended the nature of the automatic adjustment mechanism, but he did perceive quite clearly the autonomy of the system of international exchange he was describing. The flow of goods and money across countries had its own self-sustaining momentum prompted by the ceaseless search for profit. Neither he nor anyone else in the early 1600s detected the actual or potential interdependencies implicit in the new market forces generated by expanded commercial relations; but Mun, at any rate, welcomed the lucrative opportunities provided by the new market economy. Since merchants would not be deterred from pursuing their profit, so it is futile (and harmful) to obstruct the natural flow of trade, for

by a course of trafficke (which changeth according to the accurrents of time) the particular members do accommodate each other, and all accomplish the whole body of the trade, which will ever languish if the harmony of her health be distempered by the diseases of excess at home, violence abroad, charges and restrictions at home or abroad.[44]

Besides his support for the new market economy, Mun provided his contemporaries with a model of economic growth based on foreign trade. Joyce Appleby writes: 'Mun created a paradigm. . . . He abstracted England's trade relations from their real context and built in that place an intellectual model.'[45] And William Barber observes: 'Mun's primary contribution was the formulation of an "official model" of economic growth in which the long-distance trades in general (and the East India trade in particular) could be seen to be crucial components.'[46]

In Mun's model, foreign trade was crucial: it was the source of economic 'surplus' – the sale of commodities above their purchase price (or values) – and therefore the activity that uniquely contributed to the accumulation of capital. Mun naturally envisaged this capital being reinvested in overseas trade. Mun was not consciously thinking of the principle of comparative advantage, but his model indicated a pattern of trade and development based on some such principle. Merchants would seek out domestic commodities that could profitably be sold abroad and fetch raw materials and essential commodities from foreign countries to be worked up and subsequently re-exported at increased value-added. For England, foreign trade thus afforded an opportunity to diversify export lines and break away from the relatively stagnant staples of wool and woollen cloths. A cumulative process of increased profits, greater accumulation, leading to larger diversified investments would thus be set in motion. Such was the path to economic growth.

But what is missing from Mun's model is the role of domestic production, consumption and the development of the internal market in the process of growth. The consumer remains very much in the background, referred to only by way of admonishment for excessive purchase of foreign luxuries. The end of economic activity is not domestic consumption, but foreign sales (i.e. foreign consumption). The role of production is recognised, but only as the means for delivering exportables. Consequently, the development of the domestic market was neglected in favour of foreign markets – the latter being regarded as dynamic and offering greater opportunities for profit-making. In this respect Mun's views partly reflected the prejudices of the merchant capitalist and the popular presuppositions of the time which regarded domestic exchange (or sales) as mere transfers of money – 'mere consumption' without enrichment, and partly the actual economic circumstances wherein enormous fortunes were being made in foreign trade. These factors combined, distracted the attention of economic thinkers like Mun from the sphere of production. Of course, in the realm of theory, this is the single most important difference between mercantilist thought and classical political economy – the major theme of the classical economists was the explanation of long-run capital accumulation through the generation of surplus within production. But even before Smith and the classical economists came on the scene there were writers who questioned the conventional wisdom inherited from Thomas Mun.

In Mun's trade model there is no recognition of the possibility of increased output from specialisation and trade. Exports can, indeed, generate growth; but the process is not automatic and self-evident. Mun emphasised one route towards growth via trade; but lacking an understanding of allocative mechanisms and a sensible view of the end of economic activity, he failed to notice some implications of his approach – the most important being the role of opportunity cost. For instance, Mun favoured the long-distance trades because these called for more expensive British ships and higher charges for insurance, freight, etc., as if the transport resources used in these trades were costless. The greater the utilisation of domestic resources, the higher the profit to the nation, according to Mun. In general there was no recognition of the sacrifice of resources involved in production for export – resources that alternatively could be used to produce domestic consumables. The view that exports are necessary only because they pay for imports, i.e. that the sacrifice of domestic labour and resources involved in exports is worth while only for the sake of the consumption of foreign output it permits, would have appeared strange and deplorable to Mun and his contemporaries.

EUROPEAN MERCANTILIST THOUGHT AND THE BALANCE-OF-TRADE DOCTRINE

By the time Mun's book was published the balance-of trade doctrine was already the economic orthodoxy of the age and remained so for the remainder of the seventeenth century and, indeed, persisted with elaborations and refinements until the mid-eighteenth century. In 1749 Matthew Decker could still repeat the argument that gold and silver were the ultimate objects of trade and that therefore, if the exports of Britain exceed its imports, Foreigners must pay the Balance in Treasure, and the Nation grow Rich. But if the Imports of Britain exceed its Exports, we must pay Foreigners the Balance in Treasure, and the Nation grow poor.[47]

Elsewhere in Europe typically mercantilist doctrines were enunciated by writers on economic matters; but the emphasis on the balance of trade was less than in England. Whereas in England the promotion of a favourable balance of trade became a cardinal tenet of economic thinking, in other parts of Europe the balance-of-trade theory was seen as only part of a more general programme of national self-sufficiency and economic development.

In France the mercantilist policies of Richelieu and Colbert had their roots in the writings of sixteenth-century economists and administrators, who presented arguments for a strategy of balanced economic development based on the diversity of resources possessed by France. Foreign trade had a role to play in this programme although writers differed in the importance they attached to it. There was agreement, however, that trade was advantageous when it resulted in a net inflow of bullion. Less clearly and emphatically than their English counterparts, several French writers mentioned a favourable balance of trade as the mechanism whereby this desirable result came about.

Three writers, Bodin, de Laffemas and Montchrétien, can be taken as fairly representative of French mercantilist thought in the late sixteenth and early seventeenth centuries. Bodin is, of course, well-known for his theory of sovereignty, his defence of absolute hereditary monarchy and the early formulation of the quantity theory of money. He was also a protectionist who recommended the replacement of the fiscal tariff with a protective one that would tax imported manufactures as well as raw material and staple exports. 'Wine, salt and wheat' are the inexhaustible springs of France, says Bodin, repeating a traditional eulogy on France's abundant natural resources.[48] He endorses export taxes on these staples on the grounds that, by so doing, not only would customs revenue be augmented but also because the increased supplies available for the domestic market would contribute to price-level stability. Although, of course, he does not use modern jargon, he assumes that, in respect of these staple commodities, France has a quasi-monopolistic position; and since the elasticity of demand for these products are relatively low, foreigners would pay the tax. Bodin estimates, for instance, that an export tax on salt which raises its price to foreign buyers by as much as 300 per cent would have barely noticeable effec on demand. It is therefore a rational policy to tax the export of commodities when the elasticity of demand is low and the exporting country is a major supplier in world markets. His support for import taxes on manufactured goods and export taxes on raw material is based on the premise that such taxes would increase employment in France and retain the value-added stages in France. Bodin was not, however, an economic nationalist. His protectionism was tempered by an enlightened cosmopolitan philosophical outlook. He was, in fact, one of the first important writers to stress the pacific influence of foreign trade on international relations, anticipating the views of classical free-traders like Cobden and Bright by some three hundred years. He doubts whether a country can ever be completely self-sufficient – in the sense that all its wants are met from domestic production. But even if that were in fact the case with France 'still . . . we ought always to trade, sell, buy, exchange, loan, give actually part of our goods to foreigners and indeed to our neighbours . . . if only to keep open friendly intercourse between them and us'.[49]

Barthélemy de Laffemas (1545–1611) was a royal household servant who became controller-general of commerce in 1602. Like Bodin, he was an advocate of protectionism who saw it both as a means whereby a favourable balance of trade could be achieved and industries (especially silk) established. From 1596 to 1604 he actively campaigned for royal encouragement and state regulation of industry through guilds. Laffemas's mercantilist programme was based on the conviction that France needed more gold and silver. To achieve this objective it was necessary to regulate foreign trade and encourage domestic manufacturing. 'To fill France with riches and wealth', writes Laffemas, 'keep her from seeking abroad what can be made and manufactured in France.'[50] This required the prohibition of all manufactured imports but the duty-free importation of raw materials. He denied that import substitution would raise prices on the domestic market, for with a large domestic market French producers would be able in a short time to produce as efficiently as foreigners.

Laffemas's ambitious plan for national industrial self-sufficiency came up against the opposition of vested interests. Laffemas backed the expansion of the native silk industry of Tours and obtained an edict banning the importation of Italian silks. This threatened the interests of the powerful merchants of Lyon who dealt in imported silks. After a few months, the ban was lifted following pressure from Lyon.

Antoyne de Montchrétien showed little interest in the balance of trade; indeed, apart from the colonial trades, he did not rate foreign trade very highly. It was valued simply as an outlet for domestic surplus goods. The colonial trades, particularly with America, were different. As sources of raw materials and potential markets for France's superfluities the colonies could serve to reduce the drain of bullion. For Montchrétien, gold and silver are important only in so far as they are necessary for the state's needs, i.e. the maintenance of the army, etc. What makes countries rich are 'the supply of things necessary for life'.[51] Such an abundance of commodities was within the reach of France, but to attain it fundamental changes in economic policy were required. National manufacture must be protected from foreign competition. That was the only way to secure the expansion of industry on a broad front – metal production, textiles, leather production, printing and glassware manufacture. The state had a role to play in this developmental programme by establishing manufactories, providing technical training to unemployed and unskilled workers and, of course, by the maintenance of a protectionist commercial policy. Montchrétien does not neglect agriculture. Unlike Laffemas, he considers the progress of agriculture as complementary to that of industry – it provides raw materials for production and the necessaries of life. Despite the secondary role he assigns to foreign trade Montchrétien was too much a mercantilist to ignore its role as a generator of bullion supplies: 'We live today by gold and silver ... they supply the needs of all men. ... Money is the sinews of war. ... One cannot make war without men, maintain them without pay, find pay without taxes, levy taxes without trade.'[52] He points to the example of Holland – a country that grew rich and powerful on the basis of its extensive commerce. France can increase its share of world commerce through the creation of a national merchant marine and the establishment of overseas trading companies. Thus equipped, the country would be able to exploit more advantageously the economic opportunities provided by the American settlements. Montchrétien's programme reflected the aspirations of the commercial and industrial bourgeoisie. They wanted state action to widen the scope and profitability of their activities, i.e. to forge a national economy and protect their interests.

When Colbert came on the scene with his unbounded energy, he took hold of the ideas and recommendations of his predecessors and codified them into a comprehensive system of industrial and commercial regulation. Colbert's system will be treated later. At this point we merely note that Colbert was essentially a bullionist who believed in the beneficial effect of adequate monetary supplies – not least because of the fact that the latter increased the taxable capacity of citizens and thereby augmented royal revenues. For him, therefore, foreign trade was of great importance, for it was the only way to attract bullion and keep it circulating in France. For this reason he cherished the trade with Spain through which bullion was earned, and watched closely the Marseille merchants who exported silver to the Levant and the East.

Seventeenth-century Spanish mercantilist writers were preoccupied with the problems posed by Spain's economic decline. The writers who dealt with the general crisis of the Spanish economy and society – usually legal consultants, accountants and officials – were known as *arbitristas*. The wealth and power of Spain in the sixteenth century rested on fragile foundations. Despite the overseas empire and a large commerce, the country was a virtual economic dependency of Europe. The bulk of Spanish exports were primary products – raw wool, salt, iron, olive oil and colonial products like cochineal, sugar and hides. These were exchanged for northern-European products (e.g. linen cloth, tin, textile fabrics, naval stores, fish and cereals), some of which were re-exported to the Indies. Spanish manufacturing was indeed stimulated by early colonial demand, assisted in the case of textiles by the imposition of moderate restriction on the import of foreign cloth. Thus, up to 1550 the textile industry of Valencia, Seville, Toledo, Segovia and Burgos still flourished. But domestic manufacturers could not obtain adequate supplies of high-quality raw wool owing to a combination of pressures from Crown, sheep-owners and merchants which permitted the export of up to two-thirds of Spanish wool. The *mesta* (wool producers' associations) and Burgos merchants found it more profitable to export raw wool than finished cloth. In addition the Crown relied on the export tax on raw wool at Burgos. These powerful interests prevailed over the manufacturers. National output of food, clothing and hardware was insufficient to meet the needs of Old Spain and the colonies. The result was that Spain had a large balance-of-payments deficit with the rest of Europe which was settled by export of silver. Half of the silver which arrived in Spain was used to pay for colonial requirements. The rest was used to pay interest on the Crown's past foreign debts and to finance current military expenditures abroad. The pressing financial needs of the government led to a series of debasements (e.g. the issue of bad copper currency) by the successors of Philip II, which accelerated the inflation in Spain. A wide and persistent price differential opened between Spanish manufactures and those of other European countries. Everyone wanted to sell to Spain, but few wanted to buy Spanish goods. The result was a rapid decline in Spanish agriculture, industry and commerce. By 1630, when shipments of

American treasure began to fall of sharply, there was very little viable industry left in Spain. For instance, in 1610 Segovia had 600 textile mills; by the end of the century the number had dropped to 159. Spain's population declined by one million during the seventeenth century. Symptomatic of the dereliction of industry and commerce – perhaps even a contributory factor in it – was the craze of *empleomanía*: everyone wanted a job in the civil service. Productive employment, even if it could be obtained, was shunned.[53]

The analyses of the *arbitristas* went unheeded and their recommendations were not implemented. The crisis of Spanish economy and society led to governmental apathy and bureaucratic immobility. It was only at the time of Uztáriz that some sporadic attempts were made to put right some of the more glaring failings of the Spanish economy. The literature is full of criticisms of official policy, in particular the prohibition on the illegal export of specie (for which the penalty was death in 1624). Treasure was regarded as desirable; but in the absence of a favourable balance of trade many Spanish writers doubted whether American treasure could either be retained or ensure economic prosperity, especially when the state was incurring vast foreign debts. A favourable balance of trade came to be viewed as the only sound guarantee of both the retention of treasure and national prosperity. The means for achieving this was through a protectionist policy of restrictions against the import of manufactured goods and the export of raw materials. Such a programme was outlined as early as 1558 by Luis Ortiz (a government accountant) in a petition which included a clear statement of the balance-of-trade doctrine.[54] The country's adverse balance of payments, responsible for the drain of specie, was due to the fact that Spain's exports consisted principally of low-value primary products while imports were of costly, processed articles. Ortiz estimated, on the basis of relative costs, that the value of imports was of the order of eight to ten times that of exports. Writing in the wake of the state bankruptcy of 1557, Ortiz outlined an ambitious four-year plan of industrial development, supported by a reform of the customs system. He recognized, however, that industrial self-sufficiency could not be achieved in such a short period. Hence his recommendation was for a gradual curtailment of non-essential manufactured imports, pending the build-up of industrial capacity. Pedro de Burgos dealt with the wool trade. He criticised the policies of the *mesta* and the merchants of Burgos which starved domestic woollen manufacturers of raw wool. The export of raw materials in general, he complained, hampered the expansion of Castilian industry. If the export of finest quality wool were banned, then 'I say that in the trade in cloth Castile ought to be Flanders ... so that the *alcabalas* [sales tax] and income of their highnesses would grow to a much greater quantity than they are today.'[55] The Spanish writers, in general, leaned towards protection rather than the manipulation of exchange rates as a method of retaining bullion, and frequently urged the reform of taxation, the encouragement of trading companies and the processing of native raw materials. One important objective of these measures was to make Spanish exports more competitive in terms of price and, hence a more favourable trade balance. The neglect of matters relating to exchange rates is perhaps understandable, since it was beyond the control of the authorities; yet it had serious consequences for Spanish trade. Although Spain had a chronic balance-of-payments deficit the exchange rate never really adjusted sufficiency to compensate for the difference between internal and world price levels. The reason for this was, of course, that the rest of Europe was awash with Spanish currency owing to illegal export of money and the sums legally remitted to settle debts contracted by the Crown. Since the supply of Spanish currency and bullion (international money) was elastic, the exchange rate only depreciated marginally. Spanish exports therefore suffered an extra disadvantage, and imports were excessively stimulated.

Sancho de Moncada, writing in 1619, pointed to the weakness of Spain's foreign trade as the source of the country's loss of bullion. He estimated that Spain lost annually 20 million ducats owing to the adverse trade balance with foreigners, accounted for by imports of cloth, fish and timber. The enforcement of the regulations governing the export of bullion was necessary, but the only effective remedy for redressing the adverse trade balance was low export prices for Spain's principal export products.[56]

Some of the *arbitristas* adopted the quantity-theory-of-money reasoning of the Salamanca School and argued that Spain could not indefinitely retain American treasure. Abundant treasure would raise the Spanish price level above the general European level, and so specie would flow out almost as fast as it came in to settle the country's inevitable balance-of-payments deficit. Writers such as Pedro de Valencia (1605), Fernández de Navarrete (1616) and Caxa de Leruela (1627) belonged to this group. Surveying the ruin of Spanish industry and commerce, labour, they claimed, was the true source of wealth. Tomás de Mercado followed this line of reasoning, and saw the economic value of the Indies less in terms of the gold and silver it brought Spain and more in terms of the additional demand it represented for the products of Spanish industry. The solution to the crisis was to use American treasure productively, i.e. use it to stimulate Spanish industry, agriculture and commerce. Perhaps the best-known Spanish mercantilist is Gerónimo de Uztáriz, whose book first appeared in 1724.[57] In it he argued the case for a balanced programme of industrial, agricultural and commercial development based on a policy of protection designed, in the end, to promote a favourable balance of trade. He criticised the futile attempts to enforce the specie-export prohibition. The measures he favoured comprised: (1) the removal of the 16 per cent tax on the export of manufactured goods, since export sales volume would increase at lower prices; (2) a ban on the export of industrial raw materials (wool, silk and potash); (3) the imposition of high duties on imported manufactured goods and, (4) the reduction or removal of the *alcabala* – the sales tax (really a turnover tax) of 15–20 per cent on the sale of raw materials, manufactured goods and general consumer goods. These taxes, besides being unnecessarily burdensome, increased the costs of production, and hence the prices of Spain's exports. The object of these tax changes, according to Uztáriz, was to increase exports and reduce imports and thus lead to a favourable trade balance. Uztáriz was an admirer of Colbert and desired a system of customs duties like the French tariffs of 1664 and 1667. He estimated that Spain lost something like $20 million a year because of the country's adverse balance of trade.

Surprisingly for a country that was then the dominant commercial power, the mercantilist literature produced in Holland is comparatively scant; and from what appeared in print there was a marked absence of concern with the balance of trade. Indeed, for the age, there was a considerable sentiment in favour of free trade both among leading writers like Grotius, Graswinckel and Salmasius and the oligarchy of merchants that controlled the Dutch Republic. Protectionism found adherents mainly in the manufacturing areas, e.g. among the woollen manufacturers of Leiden. But after all, it was the character of Dutch trade and the role of Amsterdam as the leading entrepôt and financial centre that explains this relatively benign neglect of the balance of trade. Bullionist arguments and balance-of-trade reasoning did not appear to have much relevance to the main business of the country which was entrepôt trading, bill-discounting, banking and insurance. However, the currency authorities were, from time to time, concerned about bullion flows, and Dutch economic policy was in times of stress often as mercantilist as that of their neighbouring countries.

Mercantilism (whether as doctrine or practice) was never dominant in the Italian city states and mercantilist writings – few in number –

Mercantilist Thought on Foreign Trade

reflected this moderate attitude. An early writer, Giovanni Botero (1589), for instance, was clear about the futility of accumulating gold and silver. Thus:

> But of what use is all the wealth of Croesus and Midas to a ruler who, when he is attacked by sea, has no timber to make ships and galleys, no artificers, sailors, navigators, no tackle nor any other essentials? ... He who has nothing to buy is as poor as he who has nothing to spend.[58]

In all cases he advised the prince to accumulate only as much money as corresponded with the balance-of-trade surplus. Should the balance of trade prove unfavourable, the appropriate response was to increase the efficiency of production. Botero wrote about the advantages of exporting labour in the form of processed goods – not only for balance-of-trade reasons, but also because such manufacture provided job opportunities for a larger population.

After Serra wrote his *Breve Trattato*, the next major literary output in the mercantilist tradition came in the mid-eighteenth century from writers such as Galiani, Genovesi and Bandini. The balance-of-trade concept featured in their writings; but they were basically empiricists and enlightened mercantilists who were conscious of the social and political constraints that circumscribed their recommendations.

Perhaps the clearest and most concise statement of the balance-of-trade doctrine and its corollaries outside of England is to be found in the work of the Austrian mercantilist, Philipp von Hornick (a civil administrator in the service of the prince-bishop of Passau). He laid down nine 'self-evident' rules for the development of Austria's economic potential in a programme strikingly similar to that of Mun's, twenty years earlier. All the ingredients of orthodox mercantilism are there: develop all the country's natural resources, process local raw materials, keep imports to the minimum and push exports as much as possible to develop a favourable balance of trade so that the maximum amount of bullion can be earned.[59]

2.2 Trade, Employment and Growth

A POLICY OF EMPLOYMENT

Adam Smith does not adequately explain why the mercantilists wanted a favourable balance of trade, nor indeed why the accumulation of bullion appeared so desirable to them. Apart from the exaggerated accusation that they confused money and wealth, he does mention one additional reason for wanting more bullion: the need to build a war chest of foreign-exchange reserves.

The mercantilists, however, had additional reasons for desiring the monetary inflows associated with balance-of-payments surpluses. Viner deals comprehensively with these further reasons, citing, among other functions, the role of bullion as a means of bringing about lower interest rates and generally acting as a stimulant to economic activity and higher levels of output and employment. Some mercantilist writers wrote as if the sole objective of a favourable balance of trade was the indefinite accumulation of the precious metals. In the minds of many others, however, there was a positive relationship between the quantity of money in circulation and levels of production, exports and employment. The balance of trade was, therefore, seen as being related in some certain but not yet fully understood way to the process of economic growth. Some writers perceived the growth-inducing consequence of a favourable balance of trade in terms of what we would now call the 'direct multiplier effect' of exports on the income flow and hence on production, employment and profits. Protective measures, in so far as they are successful in producing foreign balance work by directing aggregate demands towards domestic factors production. In this way greater resource use and production could be secured. Other mercantilists reasoned in terms of the direct liquidity influence of the positive foreign balance which draws in money to support higher levels of activity. The balance of trade was therefore a regulatory device and provided a substitute for what a later age called 'monetary policy'. Foreign trade and its regulation was the means to achieve full utilisation of resources. Increases in productive capacity and industrialisation would, in turn, lead to a more prosperous foreign trade which was the goal for many mercantilists. When Francis Brewster asserted in 1702: 'That the full employment of All Hands in the Nation is the surest way and means to bring Bullion into the Kingdom'[60] he was only repeating a widely held view. A number of writers, however, who measured national well-being in terms of a flourishing foreign trade and a favourable balance of trade related this condition to further indicators of national welfare such as the possibilities for greater employment for the poor and more profit for producers and merchants. Certainly among the later mercantilists there was a marked concern with remedying the endemic unemployment and underemployment of the times.

Misselden and Mun, among others, made explicit reference to the normal existence of unemployed labour and natural resources. Misselden, for instance, refers to:

> the exceeding great benefit ... which the employment [of the idle poor] in our Nature and Farraine Manufactures would purchase to the publique, if the same were orderly collected and prudently ordered for the Employment of the poor.[61]

To relieve unemployment Mun urged the export of manufactured goods: 'It were policie and profit for the State to suffer manufactures made of forraign Materials to be exported custome-free ... it would employ very many poor people.[62]

From the social investigation of Gregory King, John Graunt, Charles Davenant and William Petty the scale of the problem of unemployment was brought home to contemporaries. Late in the seventeenth century paupers and the labouring poor whose subsistence expenditures exceeded their incomes amounted to around 40 per cent of the active population. There is, of course, a striking parallel between the economic conditions of seventeenth- and early eighteenth-century economies and the present-day underdeveloped countries; and it is not surprising that protectionist arguments for employment and balance-of-payments reasons should have irresistible appeal for rational men at different times in similar conditions. Not many mercantilists seemed aware of the limitations of the employment argument for protection. Trade policies can increase employment in import-competing industries, but this gain is usually offset when exports fall either because foreigners retaliate by increasing their trade restrictions or because their ability to buy domestic goods declines as a consequence of the falling off of their exports to the domestic market. In addition, of course, the associated payments surplus will not be permanent. These policies might be effective only in so far as they result in a reduction of real wages which is again likely to be only temporary. Those who saw the alleviation of unemployment stemming from the monetary demand generated by a favourable balance of trade sometimes used the argument that increasing inflows would lower the rate of interest and increase the availability of credit. Reference was made to the prevailing low interest rates in Holland that gave the Dutch a competitive advantage in trade through a lowering of the interest cost of producing their exportables. At times of substantial unemployment of labour and idle resources the argument might be valid, but advocates of lower interest rates frequently overlooked the fact that as the economy approached full employment (or indeed long before then because of bottleneck problems and supply inelasticity of particular inputs) the rise in the price level would either leave the rate of interest unchanged or cause it to rise. In addition the availability of credit would contract because of the reduction of the real money stock.

Keynes claimed that mercantilism was no mere puerile obsession with treasure, but was primarily a policy of employment. Later W. D. Grampp produced evidence supporting the view that the most important economic objective of the mercantilists was the maintenance of a high level of employment.[63] Heckscher's criticism of Keynes's interpretation was not that he was wrong to suppose that unemployment was a matter of prime concern to the earlier thinkers, but that it was a mistake to apply Keynesian analysis to mercantilist economies. The employment problem in those early days was not one of aggregate demand deficiency such as characterised the developed industrialised economies in the 1930s, but rather (as mentioned before) the structural unemployment typically found in Third World countries today. In such countries with small industrial sectors, unemployment results primarily from supply constraints, shortage of capital and technology, low-productivity and high-dependency ratios.

In addition if we are to believe contemporary writers there was a good deal of voluntary unemployment and idleness in seventeenth-century England – pauperism, cheating, roaring, robbing, hanging, begging and perishing, as Mun describes it. Keynes was nevertheless justified in calling attention to an important element in mercantilist thought which the classical economists all too often ignored or explained away by appeal to Say's law of markets (that supply creates its own demand).

'It is therefore a general maxim, to discourage the importation of work, and to encourage the exportation of it.'[64] Thus Sir James Steuart summarises the essence of the employment argument for a favourable balance of trade held by a long line of mercantilist thinkers since Sir Thomàs Smith, which by that time had achieved the status of an economic nostrum.

Concern with employment was, of course, of long standing and stemmed from the medieval prince's duty to provide employment to the poor. Later, employment was related to the balance-of-trade objective which was thus given additional force. Exports represent a demand for domestic labour and therefore increase employment at home. Imports, on the other hand, being demand for foreign output displaces domestic labour. Hence, the larger the export surplus, the greater the employment of domestic labour. This was Mun's position, although it was employment in the export, or more precisely, the re-export industries that interested him. Those like Malynes and the French writer, Forbonnais, conceived of the employment-generating effect as stemming from the monetary inflow associated with a favourable trade balance. Malynes claimed that 'the more ready money ... that our merchants should make their return by ... the more employment would they make upon our home commodities, advancing the price thereof, which price would augment the quantity by setting more people on work.'[65]

Forbonnais regarded gold and silver as 'conventional wealth' which, 'by circulating domestically, will procure a comfortable existence for a greater number of citizens'.[66] Money was seen as active, the 'great wheel of commerce and industry'. It could arouse dormant, idle resources and initiate a cumulative process of economic expansion. Part of the product of domestic labour had to be given up to foreigners, for it was only through foreign sales that the production and sale of other commodities would be accomplished.

The maximisation of employment through foreign trade, therefore, led to the following policy recommendations:

(1) Encourage exports of manufactured or processed goods.
(2) Prohibit or restrict the export of native raw materials (raw wool, minerals, etc.).
(3) Prohibit or restrict the export of machinery, tools, etc., and the emigration of skilled artisans.
(4) Minimise imports, except in the case of essential foodstuffs and raw materials unavailable at home.

These measures were designed to enlarge the availability of raw materials, promote their further processing into fabricated manufactures and thereby increase the value-added by domestic labour.[67] From these considerations there arose the 'balance-of-labour' doctrine as a criterion of the social welfare benefits from foreign trade. Here a favourable balance was reckoned, not in monetary terms, but in terms of the aggregate excess of labour embodied in exports over the labour content of imports. Like its monetary counterpart, the balance-of-labour doctrine had its corollaries, such as the division of particular 'trades' into 'good' and 'bad' according to their actual or potential ability to stimulate or depress domestic employment.

Both Sir Josiah Child and the Bristol merchant John Cary were among those who modified the existing conception of the balance of trade and judged that those trades were beneficial which created most employment and helped solve the problem of poverty.[68] For Cary such trades could be increased by a policy of selling goods only after they had been 'encreased in their value by the labour of our people'. He claimed that the poverty of the Spanish people stemmed from the fact that they paid for their imports with treasure and raw materials with little value-added by productive labour. Child felt the monetary balance can sometimes be misleading as an indicator of national gains from trade; the only reliable way to measure it is by reference to the number of hands employed. In deciding on all matters of commercial policy, advises Josiah Tucker, the crucial question to ask is: 'Which scheme tends to find a constant employ for most hands at home, and to export most labour abroad?'[69]

Cantillon, for all his analytical brilliance, was also a partisan of this approach:

> It is by examining the results of each branch of commerce singly that Foreign trade can be usefully regulated. It cannot be distinctly apprehended by abstract reasons. It will always be found by examining particular cases that the exportation of all Manufactured articles is advantageous to the State, because in this case the Foreigner always pays and supports Workmen useful to the State: that the best returns or payments are specie, and in default of specie the produce of Foreign land into which there enters the least labour.[70]

John Newman, the Russian Consul in Hull, abandoned the conventional balance-of-trade test and argued that although Britain had a large trade deficit with Russia in 1785 (£800 000), Britain was the sole beneficiary of the trade between the two countries. Like Mun earlier, his explanation ran in terms of the profits of British shipping, the rise in value of the foreign imports, and increase in the re-export trade.[71]

Some of the enthusiasts for the new idea took their arguments to extreme, and some would say absurd lengths. Petty, for instance, noting that 'the labour of seamen is always of the nature of an exported commodity', goes on to say that the use of British ships by foreigners means that foreigners pay for the 'labour of seafaring men'. He was prepared to endorse a policy of practically giving away exports, provided it maintained employment and preserved skills. As he puts it, this, or burning the labour of a thousand men for a time is preferable to letting 'those thousand men by non-employment lose their faculty of labouring'.[72] For Mandeville, equally obsessed with the intractable problem of unemployment, a solution which involved the deliberate destruction of output had a certain compelling logic. Thus:

A Hundred Bales of Cloth that are burnt or sunk in the Mediterranean are as Beneficial to the Poor in England, as if they had safely arriv'd at Smyrna or Aleppo, and every yard of them had been Retail'd in the Grand Signior's Dominions.[73]

This theme of 'foreign-paid incomes' from the export of work was taken up by the Whig merchants who campaigned against the proposed commercial clauses (Articles 8 and 9) of the Peace of Utrecht, 1713.

If all that is asserted by the 'foreign-paid incomes' idea is that with unemployed resources at home, exports have the capacity to generate income then the propagandists of 1713 were not enunciating a novel proposition. But as a test of gainful trade it is, of course, of dubious validity, to say the least. The argument, naïve in substance yet powerfully persuasive, was that, since the consumer ultimately pays, the sale of British manufactured goods abroad meant that it was the foreigner who paid British wages, profits and rent incurred in the manufacture of the exported commodities. Thus if Britain had an unfavourable balance of labour with France then increased trade with France would simply increase British payments to French artisans, capitalists and farmers.

Viner denies that the balance-of-labour theory represented a refinement or improvement over the older balance-of-trade doctrine. In his opinion it is an absurd doctrine, but he regarded it 'as a stage of some importance in the evolution towards more sensible doctrine'.[74]

Underlying the balance-of-labour or 'export-of-work' view of foreign trade were three mercantilist assumptions:

(1) Unskilled labour was in such abundant supply that it was virtually a 'free' good.
(2) Manufacturing was a superior type of economic activity to agricultural and raw material production.
(3) The export of labour was the cheapest way to obtain treasure; moreover it was a means of getting foreigners to pay the wages of domestic workers.

A given trade flow under the balance-of-labour criterion might be judged 'favourable' but 'unfavourable' according to the balance-of-trade test. Later mercantilists do not appear to have been concerned about the terms of trade as Malynes was, for a favourable 'balance of labour' implies adverse terms of trade, i.e. a so-called 'beneficial balance of labour' means accepting fewer units of imported goods per unit of export commodity, *ceteris paribus*.

LABOUR AND WAGES

The views and policies of the mercantilists towards labour were shaped by their foreign trade theories, and it is useful to note what their views on labour and wages were.

Evidently, as Edgar Furniss notes, the mercantilists accorded labour 'a position of strategic importance'.[75] Statements conceding this importance to labour are common in the mercantilist literature. Thus:

> If labour is the true riches, and money only the sign or tally, is not that country the wealthiest which has the most labour?
> (JOSIAH TUCKER)

> The people are the riches and strength of the country.
> (NICHOLAS BARBON)

> People are ... in truth the chiefest, most fundamental, and precious commodity. (*Britannia Languens*)

Since real wealth was produced by labour, including its skill and industriousness, mercantilists favoured rapid population growth and a large labour force. But it was felt that the wealth represented by labour would not be realised unless trade and commerce were encouraged, so that producers and merchants could make profits.

William Petyt, the author of the influential *Britannia Languens* suggested that population growth depended critically on foreign trade (i.e. the state of the trade balance):

> a Forraign Trade (if managed to the best advantage) will yet further advance the values of Lands, by necessitating a vast increase of people, since it must maintain great multitudes of people in the very business of Trade, which could not otherwise be supported ...; All which having the Rewards of their Labours in their hands, will still enlarge the choice of Chapman to the Sellers, and there being so many more persons to be fed and cloathed, there must be a far greater home Consumption of all the products of Land.[76]

Undoubtedly, for many mercantilists, the desire for a large labouring population was motivated by the need, as they saw it, to keep wages and prices low so as to encourage exports. But it was not always clear how they reconciled this desire with their other objective of reducing unemployment.

The mercantilists were interested in aggregate output rather than output per man. They never bothered to inquire into the relationship between per capita and total output. Assuming that average output (or productivity) was virtually constant, they implicitly believed that total output was directly related to the size and degree of employment of the labour force.

Advocates of the low-wage doctrine generally held that while high profits spur economic activity on the part of entrepreneurs, high real wage-rates, far from inducing greater effort by workers simply lead to idleness. It was taken for granted that workers wants and aspirations were constant and limited. Implicitly they believed in what we now call a 'backward-bending supply curve of labour', i.e. once the minimum needs of workers were satisfied, the payment of higher wages induced workers to work less rather than buy more. A low-wage policy was justified, therefore, on the ground that that would bring about the maximum utilisation of the working population by forcing men to work hard and long as well as by inducing women and children to seek gainful employment in order to supplement family incomes. It was also good for the foreign balance, since a ceiling on workers' income (hence domestic absorption) would release more goods for export.

However, as Viner points out, this so-called 'mercantilist labour doctrine' was by no means a universally held dogma. Several prominent writers both in the seventeenth and eighteenth centuries, either denied the backward-sloping labour-supply hypothesis or else proposed social welfare measures as alternative remedies for dealing with voluntary idleness.[77]

Misselden, for instance, wrote in 1622 that 'for a small consideration, it would certainly give encouragement to the poore to labour'.[78] Josiah Child and Daniel Defoe were among those who did not believe that high wages had a deleterious effect on England's competitive position in world markets. Child inferred from the experience of the Dutch with their relatively high level of wages that

> wherever wages are high, universally throughout the whole world, it is an infallible evidence of the riches of that country; and whereever wages for labour run low it is proof of the poverty of that place.[79]

Defoe opposed any legislative lowering of wages, arguing on somewhat Keynesian lines that this would reduce total demand, output and employment at home. In foreign trade what matters is 'the value and goodness of the manufacture'. As long as England continues to produce high-quality export goods there was nothing to fear from the high wages of English workmen.[80]

John Cary, the Bristol sugar merchant, was another leading supporter of the high-wage argument. He also believed that low wages lead to poor-quality goods, but his emphasis on the virtues of high wages was somewhat different from that of Defoe's. His argument was that high wages would induce a substitution of capital for labour and stimulate technological improvements in production processes wherever feasible. The resulting increase in productivity would enable England to compete effectively in foreign trade despite high domestic wage-rates.[81]

Cary's analysis provides the basis for a rebuttal of one of the most enduring of mercantilist fallacies: the 'cheap foreign labour' argument for protection. Protectionists everywhere contend, as did the mercantilists, that high domestic wages make it impossible for home producers to compete with the products of cheap foreign labour under free-trade rules. The matter is complex, but one has to consider not only wage-rates but labour costs per unit of output which depend on labour productivity or labour efficiency. When skilled and industrious workers use capital equipment in proportions appropriate to the factor endowment of a country, then productivity will be high and costs per unit of output can be low even though wages are high.

The early mercantilist advocates of a low-wage economy can perhaps be forgiven for failure to perceive the full logic of the situation, which even today escapes many intelligent people.

NEGLECT OF THE HOME MARKET

In all of their discussions on production, employment and growth the mercantilists, at least until the closing decade of the seventeenth century neglected the role of the internal market and the aggregate expenditure generated by it as the key to increased output and employment. Indeed, the prevailing notions about 'thrift' (savings in the form of stored-up wealth), the balance of trade and actual economic circumstances led them to emphasise foreign trade as the dynamic element in demand – although Gregory King in 1688 had estimated that the home market was four times larger than the volume of exports and imports.[82] The domestic market was seen as a network of mere exchanges where one man gained at another's expense. An anonymous pamphleteer expressed the idea thus:

> Increase and Wealth of all States, is evermore made upon the

Forreigner for whatsoever is gained by one Native from another in one part of this Kingdom, must necessarily be lost in another part, and so the publick Stock nothing thereby Augmented.[83]

In support of this, Samuel Fortrey asserted:

the only way to be rich, is to have plenty of that commiditie to vent, that is of greatest value abroad; for what the price of anything is amongst ourselves, whether dear or cheap it matters not; for as we pay so we receive ... but the art is when we deal with strangers, to sell dear and to buy cheap and this will increase our wealth.[84]

Such views obscured the role of home consumption in sustaining higher levels of production, employment and growth. Indeed, except for the few exponents of high wages, excessive domestic consumption, especially of luxury goods was frowned upon. The undervaluation of domestic consumption in contemporary thinking was partly a reflection of demand conditions in pre-industrial economies, as D. C. Coleman points out.[85] Internal markets were stagnant due to several constraints (mainly incomes) which limited expansions in aggregate domestic consumption. These accounted for the frantic search for new markets abroad.

A more optimistic view of the potentialities of the internal market and the elasticity of domestic demand emerged towards the end of the seventeenth century as real incomes rose – evidenced in England, for example, by the high consumption of Indian fabrics and even earlier by the rebuilding of London after the Great Fire. Sir Humphrey Mackworth enthusiastically welcomed an increase in population on the ground that employment would be guaranteed by higher consumption power: 'I propose Employment, and there is no doubt, that the Consumption of the People is not so much, as the Product of their Labours, which is the real Riches and Strength of the Nation; And the more the merrier, like Bees in a Hive, and better cheer too.'[86] Finally, it may be doubted whether the mercantilists were genuinely interested in employment as an end in itself. Was there a real shift from the position taken by Brewster in 1702? With the possible exception of Cary, the mercantilists never consistently thought of the value of labour as being related to labour's productivity. Labour was regarded primarily as an instrument for the attainment of national goals – a favourable trade balance, social stability, national power. It is perhaps in this light we should see the arguments for full employment of 'our poor people'.

2.3 Trade, Power and Plenty

THE GOALS OF POLICY

When Francis Bacon accused Henry VII of 'bowing the ancient policy of this State from consideration of plenty to consideration of power' he was referring to one particular instance of fifteenth-century internaal economic diplomacy where the twin aims of state action (wealth and national security) got out of proper balance.[87] Heckscher went further and suggested, that as a general rule, mercantilist policy subordinated 'plenty' to 'power'. Viner disagreed with this judgment and contended that for the mercantilists 'power and plenty were regarded as coexisting ends of national policy which were fundamentally harmonious'.[88]

Adam Smith had no doubt that governments during the age of mercantilism genuinely tried to enrich their subjects. They followed policies which were intended to increase national wealth. He was entirely in favour of this end; what he objected to were the *means*.

Looking back from our own times to seventeenth- and eighteenth-century Europe with our experience of state trading, centrally planned economies, import-substitution policies, exchange control and suchlike devices, we do not find it difficult to recognise mercantilism as an early manifestation of economic nationalism. The politicians, merchants and publicists of the earlier age knew no other system of political economy. As far as they were concerned, economies had always been regulated. The greater involvement of merchants in economic activity and the desire of the new states to expand their wealth, population and territory called for new regulations or the adaptation of old ones to suit these needs. The doctrines they promoted reflected ordinary, common-sense notions about the nature of wealth, how an economy should function and the proper role of the state. Their thinking had an eminently practical orientation: how to use state power to achieve economic ends, and, just as importantly, how to use economic strength to achieve political goals. The mercantilist writers did not make any rigid distinction between economic and political objectives. What we would now normally regard as purely economic processes and events (business activity, consumer choice, the use of resources, etc.) were always thought of in relation to politics and strategy. Thus one of their prime concerns was to work out how exactly the merchant's gain from foreign trade was compatible with the national interest, including the security of the realm. In the 1620s Mun indicated how, through the pursuit of sound commercial policies, the king and the commonwealth would benefit as merchants increase their riches. Later in the century such a harmonious relationship was accepted as axiomatic. Sir Josiah Child, for one, had no doubt that the expansion of commerce produced a beneficent cycle. 'Foreign trade', he wrote in 1681 'produces riches, riches power, power preserves our trade and religion.'[89]

In the early modern period agriculture was, of course, the major source of income. The landed gentry gained wealth from the sale of grain and rising rents in the expanding home market. However, agricultural output increased only slowly and it was difficult to export. The low value relative to volume of agricultural produce meant high transport costs which made exports uncompetitive in foreign markets, except at times of famine prices. Mercantilists therefore looked to foreign trade as one of the few means of increasing wealth and power rapidly. The fact that the king could not effectively tax landed wealth added to the quest for other sources of royal revenue (customs and excise). The finances of the state – hence its power and ability to pursue foreign-policy objectives – came to depend critically on the state of its foreign trade. This was unpleasantly brought home to the French during the Seven Years War. The disruption of French trade (particularly the valuable colonial trades) reduced the government's ability to borrow, and with it the means of supporting allies and even the continued prosecution of the war itself. Choiseul, French Minister for Foreign Affairs, admitted in 1759: 'The disruption of commerce, followed by the loss of the colonies has destroyed credit, resulting in a kind of bankruptcy. It is not a question only of courage; one must have the means of sustaining it.'[90]

A further factor influencing the fulfilment of national ambitions in the sphere of international economic relations was the limitations to the attainment of military and diplomatic objectives set by small armies, diplomatic conventions, weak administrations, etc. No one state was able to exercise a permanent hegemony because power was nearly equally distributed and they all suffered to a lesser or greater degree from the same weaknesses. Thus foreign trade became the main area of competition and conflict. In the conditions of the times of mutual suspicion, rivalry and brutally competitive state-building (such as we described in Chapter 1) international economic relations were most definitely political relations. As regards the pursuit of power, what mattered was relative strength or, as Viner puts it, 'the ratio of power, not the terms of the ratio'. Relatively minor changes could alter the overall power position of states, so if a country lost out militarily on any particular occasion it sought compensation in the international economic sphere or vice versa. Commercial treaties and regulations affecting foreign trade, including shipping and the fisheries, were made with the expectation of gaining commercial advantages by applying the same criteria used in other negotiations where military, political, dynastic or religious advantages were sought.

TRADE AND THE BALANCE OF POWER

In mercantilist thought the balance-of-trade idea became part of the balance-of-power principle that supposedly regulated conduct in international relations. As Postlethwayt put it (1759): it was necessary 'to throw the balance of trade so effectually into the hands of Great Britain, as to put the constant balance of power in Europe into her hands'.[91] Both principles were founded on the maxim articulated by Francis Bacon: 'It is likewise to be remembered that, foreasmuch as the increase of any estate must be upon the foreigner (for whatsoever is somewhere gotten is somewhere lost). ...'[92] Market forces were acknowledged to have something to do with competition in international trade, but there was scant recognition of the role of an impersonal market as the arbiter of success or failure in international trade. Markets had to be won or captured from others, whether by naked force or diplomatic pressure. Conversely, markets, command of trade routes, shipping, etc., could be lost through political or military pusillanimity. There was little recognition of the possibility that nations could compete for trade by competing to create it. Trade matters were thus firmly located within the realm of statecraft. Adam Smith ridiculed this arrangement as a project which 'may at first sight appear ... fit only for a nation of shopkeepers. It is, however, a project altogether unfit for a nation of shopkeepers; but extremely fit for a nation whose government is influenced by shopkeepers.'[93] Smith's jibe, springing from a different conception of political economy, appears well-targeted; but if 'traders' were substituted for 'shopkeepers' in the above passage and notice taken of contemporary realities, Smith's remark loses much of its bite.

At any rate the political nature of trade, as it appeared to mercantilists, led to the conception of a symbiotic relationship between trade and power (with the exception, perhaps, of the later mercantilists in Prussia and Russia). Trade followed the flag; power was necessary to maintain and expand trade; trade ensured the means for the maintenance of power, etc. Numerous assertions to this effect can be quoted from contemporary sources. Are they merely the reflection of deficient theory or chronic paranoia, or both combined? In the early 1700s Defoe wrote:

> 'Tis for this, that these Nations keep up such a Military Force; such Fleets and such Armies to protect their Trade, to keep all the Back-doors open. ... Trading nations are obliged to defend their Commerce. ... If the Doors of our Commerce are shut, we must open them. ...[94]

Maritime power and trade were stressed by Lord Haversham in a speech to the House of Lords (1707):

> Your Fleet and your Trade have so near a relation, and such mutual influence upon each other, they cannot well be separated; your trade is the mother and nurse of your seamen; your seamen are the life of your fleet, and your fleet is the security and protection of your trade, and both together are the wealth, strength, security and glory of Britain.[95]

The English East India Company declared in a petition (1641):

> The safety of the Kingdom consists not only in its own strength and wealth but also in the laudable and lawful performance of those things which will weaken and impoverish such powerful Princes, as either are, or may become our Enemies.[96]

Some writers argued that the objectives of foreign policy, hegemony even, could be achieved solely through an ever-widening volume of trade, without recourse to armed conflict. Thus Andrew Yarranton, discussing how to deal with Dutch power and opulence, suggested 'beat them without fighting; that being the best and justest way to subdue our Enemies'.[97] Nicholas Barbon was of the same mind:

> Trade may be Assistant to the Inlarging of Empire; and if an Universal Empire, or Dominion of very Large Extent, can again be raised in the World, It seems more probable to be done by the Help of Trade; By the Increase of Ships at Sea, than by Arms at Land.[98]

At the domestic political level trade policy in modern states is a decision process that is obviously influenced by pressure groups, political alignments and changes in the international economic environment. Things were ordered no differently in the age of mercantilism, except that revenue considerations were prominent, and the debates were more openly political, accompanied by a good deal of patriotic fervour and balance-of-trade rhetoric.

D. C. Coleman concluded his penetrating study of the British political debate on the Anglo-French Trade Treaty of 1713 with the observation that the defeat of the commercial treaty (apart from pressure groups and political allegiances) owed much to the attitude of mind which viewed 'the nation's total commerce as an aggregation of separate, national quasi-political 'trades' all participating in a conflict over an international cake of a more or less fixed size'.[99] What is the difference between this attitude in early eighteenth-century Britain and the arguments used by the Americans during their debates on postbellum tariff policy, summarised as 'seemingly profound, but at bottom an almost classic case of economic nonsense'?[100]

In the eighteenth century the trade with France was a particularly sensitive ('quasi-political') one. Indeed, in general, all countries with whom Britain had unfavourable 'particular' trade balances were regarded virtually as enemies.[101] An anonymous author came out against peace with France in 1748 because, he declared, 'no peace can be solid to us which is not founded on the reduction, at least of the French commerce . . .'.[102] Supporting a Commons motion calling for a ban on French textiles, an alderman of the City of London said: 'I should rather chuse that the Germans should take £200,000 yearly from us for Dresden work, than that the French should take £100,000 yearly from us for cambrics and lawns. . . .'[103]

INSTRUMENTS OF POLICY

During the mercantilist age, as we have seen, 'wealth' and 'power' were intimately associated with possession of the precious metals. The way to gain treasure was through a favourable balance of trade. But the maintenance of a favourable balance could not be left to chance. Policy was required to assist in the process, and this took the form of (a) the 'twin engines' of the mercantile system, as Adam Smith called it – one working at full speed to promote exports, the other at import substitution, and (b) the encouragement of native shipping and control of colonial commerce. In England export promotion took the form of:

(i) remission of duties on goods re-exported ('drawbacks');
(ii) direct subsidies or 'bounties' on exports (e.g. on corn, salt pork, linen, silk, sailcloth etc.);
(iii) the retention of local raw materials through prohibitions or high duties on their exports, presumably on the ground that keeping

them at home they would be made abundant and cheap thereby increasing the rate of production of finished products. Wool, woollen yarn, and fuller's earth (used for cleaning raw wool) were the major items subject to export bans.

Import-substitution measures comprised tariffs, embargoes and prohibitions on the import of goods which could be produced at home.

In the early days of mercantilism, as we have seen, the chartering of trading companies was an important phase in English commercial expansion. The merchants that ran these companies gained monopoly privileges, but inevitably the politicians saw the far-flung enterprises as status symbols and instruments in the pursuit of power. They were agents through which the power of the state was indirectly felt overseas.

Bilateral commercial treaties were other weapons in the armoury of mercantilist practices. Since all European countries were pursuing broadly similar policies of self-sufficiency designed to foster the growth of the same range of industries and services, the basis for mutually beneficial trade negotiations was severely limited. Complementary trading patterns suited the interests of the major powers, but attempts to negotiate reciprocal agreements along these lines were only successful through the exercise of *force majeure* and often resulted in trade diversion. The political implications of trade (i.e. balance-of-power ramifications) were such that commercial clauses or agreements figured prominently in almost all major treaties ending international conflicts.

English woollen manufacturers pressed for the opening of the Portuguese market to British exports, which they obtained by the Methuen Treaty (1703) between England and Portugal. The result was that the Portuguese cloth industry was stifled at birth; but Portuguese wines were admitted at two-thirds of the duty imposed on French wines. The Methuen Treaty was a master stroke of English commercial diplomacy. Although the immediate object of the treaty was to draw Portugal away from its policy of neutrality to one of armed alliance on England's side during the War of the Spanish Succession, the agreement was long remembered for the two commercial clauses it contained. They formed the basis for England's commercial supremacy over its 'oldest ally'. The ground was prepared by a series of bilateral treaties (1642, 1654 and 1661) which opened Portuguese commerce to English merchants. The latter enjoyed special privileges, both in metropolitan Portugal and in its overseas possessions. By the end of the seventeenth century Portugal was a virtual commercial vassal of England; and what the treaty negotiated by John Methuen did was to confirm Portugal's dependency. Earlier, under the Duke of Ericeria, Portugal started its own cloth industry by means of a protective tariff, but efforts in that direction had to be abandoned; for under the 1703 treaty Portugal was for ever obliged to admit duty-free the products of the English woollen industry. The English cloth industry was saved, but it ruined Portuguese industry in general. Portugal's carrying trade came into English hands, and through the permanent trade surplus with its trading partner England obtained an annual inflow of between one-half to one million pounds sterling of Brazilian gold. Between 1703 and 1760 British exports to Portugal increased by just over 260 per cent.[104]

The other main pillar of British mercantile practice was enshrined in the so-called Navigation Code, comprising a series of Acts of Trade and Navigation passed between 1651 and 1733. The important ones were those of 1660, 1663, 1673 and 1696. In the minds of Sir George Downing and other architects of the Navigation Laws the legislation was clearly and directly aimed at the achievement of strategic power and wealth (relative to other states) through the control of native and colonial shipping and commerce. To understand these motives and ambitions it is important to consider them in the context of the growing importance of colonies in the mid-seventeenth century.

Between 1620 and 1650 the world economy entered a period of stagnation, even contraction, after a century of growth. England lost ground in its European trade during this period and the Dutch made inroads into English shipping during the Civil War of 1642–6. After 1650, however, there was a massive expansion of English overseas commerce and especially colonial trade. The prospect appeared quite favourable for the establishment of a discriminatory or preferential trading empire within England's own far-flung territorial orbit. The colonies, in particular those in North America and the West Indies, could become alternative, cheaper sources of supply of goods presently procured through foreigners (i.e. principally the Dutch) and provide markets for the products of English labour. In addition, despite the risks, there were monopoly profits to be reaped from the colonial trades in high-value commodities. As far as manufacturers and the gentry were concerned colonial produce at this time did not appear as a threat, since they were not competitive with domestic agriculture or native manufactures. Moreover, the much-sought-after complementary trading relationship could now be enforced at England's sovereign wish. But standing in the way of this grand design were the Dutch, who then controlled most of the sea trade of the world. The answer was Cromwell's Navigation Act of 1651, distinctly anti-Dutch in intent, designed to exclude the Dutch from the business of carrying freight to and from English and colonial ports.

Thomas Povey in 1657 wrote approvingly of this measure in the interests of the mercantile classes who felt aggrieved by supposed Dutch infringements of their commercial spheres, stressing the need for policy to provide: 'all possible encouragement and advantages for the adventurer, planter and English merchants, in order also to the shutting out all strangers from that trade, by making them not necessary to it, and by drawing it wholly ... into our ports here'.[105]

The initial blow intended to knock out Dutch shipping proved largely ineffectual. Administrative arrangements for inspection and control were wholly inadequate. Many ships in English ownership were in fact Dutch-built, and those that were English-owned were sometimes manned by Dutch crews. This made it difficult to prove the ownership and nationality of ships using English ports.

Since several of the leading Dutch merchant houses had branches in London, they were able to circumvent the regulations by simply assigning vessels to their London branches. In general it was impossible to enforce the Act in European trades, and in the colonial trade it came up against the opposition of the colonial planters who wished to see the Dutch competing to carry their produce. Subsequent Acts were tightened, and administrative mechanisms improved through the collaboration of the Navy with customs officials and colonial governors.

The 1660 Act provided for the registration of all Dutch-built ships in English ownership, and laid down that the captain and three-quarters of the crew of English-owned ships were to be English. The provisions of the Act were as follows:

(1) Most imports from Europe had to come into England in English ships or ships belonging to the country where the goods originated.
(2) All colonial trade was reserved to English or colonial ships.
(3) A list comprising the bulk of desired colonial products – the 'enumerated' commodities (sugar, tobacco, cotton wool, and dyes for the cloth industry) might only be exported to England in English or colonial ships. Other items were added to the enumerated list from time to time. Rice and molasses were added in 1704; naval stores in 1705 and furs and skins in 1721.

The 1663 Act for the Encouragement of Trade – the so-called Staple Act – forbade the colonists from buying nearly all the European goods they needed directly. Goods had to be imported into the colonies via

England and carried there in English-owned and English-manned ships. Exceptions were granted for direct shipment to America of commodities like salt and wine from ports south of Cape Finisterre. This allowed the American colonists to carry on a lively, direct trade with Portugal and Madeira – pitch and tar in exchange for Setubal salt and Madeira wine. Other enactments sought to discourage competitive colonial production by prohibiting the export of colonial wool, woollen yarn, finished wool products (1699), finished ironwares (1750) and hats made from beaver fur (1732). Colonial planters benefited, however. English sugar plantations in the West Indies and tobacco in Virginia developed under protection of the Navigation Acts and other trade regulations. Thus, under a tariff act of 1660, enumerated commodities such as tobacco and sugar obtained preferential customs treatment (and a virtual monopoly position) in the English market – duties on foreign tobacco and sugar were three times higher.

An instance where power (strategic considerations) yielded to the dictates of trade was the way in which the Whig ministry acquiesced in the flouting of the Molasses Act (1733) by the northern colonists. The Act imposed prohibitive duties on the import of molasses from the French West Indies into the American colonies. It threatened to cut off a profitable trade which the northern colonists conducted with the French islands, and also would have meant the ruin of the rum-distilling industry in New England. Strategic considerations and pressure from the British West Indian planters were behind the Act; but it was soon realised in London that if the northern colonists were deprived of this trade, their loss of income would force them to curtail their imports of British manufactured goods. Consequently, they would have been encouraged to set up their own industries. That had to be avoided at all costs, so that the northern colonists were passively allowed to trade with the enemy, and the Molasses Act was allowed to become a dead letter in New England.[106]

By the early eighteenth century, then, England had adopted a complex system of regulating trade, the keystone of which was the Navigation Laws. In conception and practical application these laws faithfully followed Josiah Child's injunction that 'Profit and Power ought jointly to be considered'.[107] They were the means for effectively controlling imports, keeping foreigners out of the colonial trades, undermining Dutch (and later, French) mercantile marines, ensuring the maintenance of a favourable balance of trade and the building up of naval power. Making the Navigation Acts an integral part of the Old

Colonial System exhibited a clear perception, too, of the interdependence of profit and power.[108]

As is well known, Adam Smith admired the Navigation Acts, calling them 'perhaps the wisest of all the commercial regulations of England'. But Smith makes it plain that he does not support them upon economic grounds, but because, in the last resort, 'defence is much more important than opulence'.[109] The English found that war as an instrument of policy could be both effective and profitable. When the Dutch refused Cromwell's offer of union, the Rump used naval action to enforce the Navigation Act, thus precipatating the first Dutch War. The war did not make the Dutch any more willing to accept Cromwell's improved offer (1653) to divide world trade between the two countries, but it did swell enormously the English mercantile fleet. Seventeen hundred enemy merchant vessels were seized as prizes. Practically overnight the English were equipped with carriers of bulk cargoes – the English merchant fleet almost doubled between 1660 and 1688.

The theme of 'power' and 'plenty' being mutally reinforcing joint goals of national policy echoes like a refrain throughout the mercantilist literature.[110] In the conditions of the time the two aims were never separated in men's minds. However, the pursuit of power and wealth varied according to time, place, and the ambitions of particular regimes. There were constraints set by resource endowments, levels of economic development, administrative machinery, tradition, etc. Opportunities were provided by favourable economic and political circumstances, extent and nature of involvement in trading relations, including colonial ties, etc. The emphasis accorded to one or the other twin goals naturally depended on these circumstances, and the instruments chosen for their attainment also varied according to what, in particular national contexts, were thought most suitable.

Professor Gerschenkron has proposed the hypothesis that the pursuit of mercantilist policies (as distinct from mercantilist theories) varied directly with the degree of economic backwardness of the European countries. Furthermore, the more backward the economy, the less was the concern with foreign economic policy and the greater the emphasis on power and economic development under state auspices. Gerschenkron has substantiated this proposition in regard to Russian mercantilism in the early eighteenth century, and the same interpretation could be given for the economic system of the *Aufklärung* under Frederick the Great's Prussia.[111] Central and Eastern Europe were the two areas of the continent largely untouched by the commercial revolution of the early modern period. The economies were feudal and backward. In both countries the aims of mercantilist rulers were the same: territorial unification, military strength and more state revenue. To achieve these ends they embarked on massive state-directed programmes of economic development and sought more efficient means of increasing the yield on taxation. Foreign trade and the balance of trade were subordinated to the goal of national power. The emphasis on wealth from foreign trade was less in Frederick's Prussia and Peter's Russia than it was elsewhere. But correspondingly, national power and economic development assumed far greater significance. To get a wider perspective on mercantilism in action, taking into account national differences as regards concrete policies, we conclude this chapter with a brief account of Colbert's mercantilism and the mercantilism of the Dutch Republic.

COLBERT'S MERCANTILISM

Jean-Baptiste Colbert, finance minister of Louis XIV for more than twenty years, is identified in the popular mind with French mercantilist thought and policy. He has been labelled as the arch-mercantilist, the quintessential economic planner, the bureaucrat par excellence. To Molière he was 'le grand Colbert' but Adam Smith denounced him as 'a laborious and plodding man of business'. Summarising Colbert's work, Viner said that he 'developed more elaborately than any other author the serviceability to power of economic warfare ... and the possibilities of substituting economic warfare for military warfare to attain national ends'.[112] Colbert's achievement was to put into practice the economic doctrines developed by a long line of French writers since the late Middle Ages (Bodin, de Laffemas, Montchrétien). Although he was a 'bullionist' who believed in the stimulating effect of a large monetary circulation in the kingdom, he was conscious of his country's weaknesses in industry, commerce and shipping. His great predecessor, Cardinal Richelieu, had resolutely pursued the goals of power and wealth through the formation of trading companies, colonial exploitation and the building up of naval strength. Earlier, Henri IV had established forty of the forty-seven manufactories which existed in 1610. When he came to power in 1661 Colbert continued these policies and, in addition, tried with the utmost vigour to extend and revitalise French industry. He had a low opinion of businessmen and their motives and did not believe that they promoted the national interest except within a framework of government direction, control and regulation. He believed that the state should take an active part in business when private enterprise was unable or unwilling to take the risk. This particularly applied to public works and other infrastructural projects such as roads, canals and river navigation which he also promoted in the interests of creating a national market (e.g. Canal du Midi).

He expanded the functions of the *Conseil de Commerce*, established by de Laffemas and turned it into an agent of industrial planning. Under its aegis, a whole range of industries were created subject to central control by a corps of local inspectors appointed from Paris. The industries Colbert sponsored were organised into national guilds and received subsidies and in some cases royal patronage. The aims of this programme were to stimulate industrial self-sufficiency, promote social stability and ensure the observance of strict quality control on the products for which France was famous and in great demand abroad – luxury products such as silks, linens, tapestries, furniture and wines. For such products Colbert believed, perhaps rightly, that quality rather than price was decisive in trade. Hence the necessity for the comprehensive system of uniform regulations promulgated in the Code of Commerce which incidentally through the Code Napoléon still forms the basis of modern French commercial law.

This policy of national self-sufficiency and industrial development was reinforced by protectionist trade measures. Steep tariffs were imposed in 1664 and 1667 aimed at sheltering the import-competing industries. Navigation laws were passed, in some respects even tougher than those recently put into operation in England – again obviously intended to weaken Dutch commercial strength. In 1659 all foreign ships using French ports were required to pay tonnage duty of fifty sous per register ton both on entry and exit. Three years later the burden was lightened when the duty was levied only on departure.

Colbert's view of international economic relations was typical of the age. It was a view that implied conflict and confrontation. He is remembered for his remark that commerce 'is a perpetual and peaceable war of wit and energy among all nations' equally as well as for his efforts at planning French industry. Colbert's attempts to foster French industry behind the high tariff wall erected in 1664 and 1667 naturally threatened the export industries of England and Holland. When England retaliated with tariff increases (in 1660 and 1670) and a three-year embargo on French imports in 1678 the commercial war between the two countries commenced. At the end of the seventeenth century, despite the absence of military hostilities, the level of duties on most French imports to England was over 50 per cent. Throughout the greater part of the eighteenth century Anglo-French trade was virtually at a standstill, so that by the time Smith came to write his *Wealth of Nations* he was moved to lament:

> Seventy-five per cent may be considered as the lowest duty to which the greater part of the goods of the growth, produce or manufacture of France were liable. But upon the greater part of goods, those duties are equivalent to a prohibition. The French in their turn have I believe treated our goods and manufactures just as hardly ... those mutual restraints have put an end to almost all fair commerce between the two nations, and smugglers are now the principal importers, either of British goods into France or of French goods into Great Britain.[113]

The French decision to invade the Dutch Republic in 1672 was partly motivated by the failure of Louis XIV and his minister to break the Dutch hold on their country's commerce by means of commercial and navigation policies. Even after the French navigation ordinances were introduced, the French had only about 600 ships compared to the Dutch with 3000. The newly established state-subsidised colonial trading companies, the French East and West India Companies met with some success, but a similar company, the Company of the North failed to dislodge the Dutch from the Baltic trade. What legitimate trade could not accomplish, war perhaps could. The French never managed to seize the Dutch entrepôt, but the prolonged wars against the Dutch (1672-8, 1689-97) coming after the two Anglo-Dutch maritime wars (1652-4, 1665-7) undermined Amsterdam's entrepôt function and diverted traffic to Hamburg. The attempt to make territorial gains at the expense of the Dutch cost the French dearly and in the process checked Colbert's programme of expansion.

Colbert's programme of industrial growth fell short of expectations. It was undertaken in a period of generally falling prices. Traders and contractors resented his system of control and he failed to attract sufficient capital for his enterprises, especially the overseas trading companies. The wars were a serious drain on the national revenues and aid to industry and commerce had to be curtailed. Some of his manufactures were hot-house developments, yet he raised manufacturing output and expanded trade. Some industries prospered under his revised tariff system, e.g. sugar refineries. By 1670 refined sugar ceased to be imported; indeed, France began to export refined sugar – refineries could claim a refund on the duties paid on raw sugar. It is also significant that the manufactories which survived were those given royal privileges or administered by the state, e.g. the Gobelins, the royal woollen manufactory at Abbeville, the Savonnerie, Aubusson, etc. In the long run, the shipbuilding programme was another success, for by the eighteenth century the French merchant fleet was a good second to England's.

DUTCH MERCANTILISM

From what has been said previously about the nature of the Dutch trading system – the deep involvement of Dutch merchants in staple-market trading and international money-market business – it can be assumed that Dutch mercantilism was of a different character to that of either French or English. A small country surrounded by powerful neighbours, the United Provinces of the Dutch Republic was militarily vulnerable. Professing a pacific and neutral foreign policy, the country was a haven for political and religious refugees (notable individuals included Bayle, Descartes, Spinoza and John Locke). The climate of toleration, the benefits of a free press and a policy of free immigration made the Republic open to new ideas and men with initiative, drive and capital. The Dutch clearly perceived the economic and social benefits of an 'open-door' policy. They encouraged and aided Huguenots to settle (exempting them from all taxation for twelve years). Flemish refugees from Hondschoote introduced the 'new draperies' in Leiden and revitalised the city's industry. Politically the country had a loose federal system of government and was also divided by religious and class differences. But what provided unity and strength to the people was their commitment to trade and shipping in which from the early seventeenth century they knew they excelled. A French traveller, Saint-Évremond, cynically remarked that if the inhabitants of Holland 'love the Republick, 'tis for the Benefit of their Trade, more than for any Satisfaction they find in being free'.[114] It was not an Amsterdam merchant, but the Leiden draper Pieter de la Court, who, in 1662, expressed the general opinion that the country's prosperity derived from the profits of commerce and adherence to a 'low-tariff' policy.

Certainly, at particular moments, the Dutch could pursue protectionist and power-oriented commercial policies, but as a general rule bellicose mercantilism found little favour with the merchants of Holland who had a preponderant influence on the affairs of the Republic and contributed two-thirds of its total revenue. Gold and silver coins could be freely imported and exported; hence there was little need for an apparatus of mercantilist control.

The mercantile interests of towns like Amsterdam, Delft and Rotterdam had no time for the reckless commercial policies pursued by their neighbours. Yet the Dutch burghers were not slow to defend themselves against the envy and sometimes malice of their rivals.[115] But the defensive measures were always tactical, adopted as bargaining counters in subsequent negotiations to cause withdrawal or moderation of the offending discrimination. Instinctively the Dutch felt they had more to lose than their competitors from open conflict. Wars could mean the disruption of trade and the loss of markets. If war was inevitable, then they would defend themselves and seek to contain or neutralise its harmful effect on their economy.

Dutch commercial policy, then, displayed a liberality unusual for this period. Low rates of duty were applied to exports and imports, and they were mainly for revenue purposes. The revenue from the customs duties was collected by the five Admiralties and used for the equipment and maintenance of the navy. Protectionist measures, usually in the form of prohibitions or embargoes, were adopted to safeguard the interests of the cloth industry, but were sparingly used and often adopted in retaliation for foreign action. Thus at the time of Alderman Cockayne's Project (1614) when James I issued a proclamation banning the export of unfinished cloth from England, the Estates General retaliated by prohibiting the import of dressed and dyed cloth. Although the English ban was lifted after two years following the failure of Cockayne's Project the Dutch maintained their prohibition and extended it to other countries' imports in 1651.

They were skilful, and often successful, in the use of commercial diplomacy to safeguard their economic interests. They managed to mitigate the rigours of the English Navigation Acts by securing the insertion of a clause in the Treaty of Breda (1667) which guaranteed the Dutch right to handle goods in transit from other countries which arrived into the Republic through the Rhine, Meuse and the Scheldt, e.g. German linens bleached in Haarlem. Another example: the Dutch were able to get reductions in Colbert's protectionist tariffs in exchange for the removal of their retaliatory measures after each of their wars with the French. By so doing they not only maintained their trade with France, but even extended it after the cessation of hostilities. It was natural for the Dutch to practise an 'open-door' policy in the period of their commercial hegemony, just as it was for Britain during the second half of the nineteenth century. The warehouses of Amsterdam and Rotterdam held the great bulk of the commodities traded across Europe and beyond. Combined with the control of credit facilities and shipping, this gave the Dutch a monopolistic position in commodity markets. They could create scarcity or glut to increase profits or stifle competition by regulating the flow of commodities through the staple market. In possession of such market power the Dutch could dispense with mercantilist devices; but rivals with no such advantages had to defend themselves as best they could. When from the 1730s onwards these competitors (primarily the British) were able to challenge Holland's leadership, Dutch commercial policy became less liberal. But moves in the protectionist direction were restrained by the powerful mercantile interests which continued to defend the traditional staple business. The result was that although the incidence of duties and imposts increased, it was not enough to protect Dutch industry from less-inhibited competitors. In 1749 the export of tools was prohibited, and two years later the emigration of skilled workers was banned. The herring fisheries were subsidised, and agricultural protection increased under the new tariff of 1725. Up to the end of the eighteenth century the Dutch tariff remained relatively low (5 per cent) – the lowest in Europe, except for Hamburg which was a 'free port'. Adam Smith remarked on this fact, though he added that Holland was 'still very remote' from a free-trade country.[116]

However pacific and cosmopolitan Dutch policy might have been in European waters, elsewhere, in the East and West Indies they were as ruthless and aggressive as any other. The Dutch jurist, Grotius (1609), formulated the Roman law idea of *mare liberum* (freedom of the seas) in order to undermine the legal basis of the Portuguese monopoly in the East Indies. Foreign critics pointed out, however, that the Dutch were all for *mare liberum*, except in their colonies where the 'closed sea' principle was strictly enforced.[117] In what became known in English history as the 'massacre of Amboyna' (1623) the Dutch, under their governor Herman Van Speult, arrested English traders on the spice island of Amboyna and publicly executed ten of them. The use of sea power was vigorously deployed to protect and extend their colonial trade, and under determined administrators like Jan Pieterzoon Coen (governor-general of the East Indies, 1618) even to found a territorial empire.

3 The Decline of Mercantilist Trade Doctrines

ECONOMIC AND INTELLECTUAL CHANGES

As the seventeenth century came to a close heterodox ideas appeared from many quarters containing statements normally associated with classical liberalism. To those imbued with the new spirit of inquiry and its successes typified by Newton's discovery of the laws of physics and Harvey's description of the circulation of the blood in the human body, mercantilist theory was vulnerable on two counts. First, protectionist policies might conceivably preserve trade for a while, but could not guarantee its expansion. The only sound basis for a thriving commerce is the accumulation and efficient utilisation of productive resources. And both commerce and the efficient employment of resources are best left to be carried on by individuals pursuing their own self-interest. Second, and reinforcing the first point, the indefinite accumulation of treasure must be self-defeating in the long run if the logic of the quantity theory was to be taken seriously.

The vulnerability of mercantilism on these points was noted before but the new criticism gathered force and added momentum when these views (a) were supported by the new philosophy with its gospel of individualism, and (b) appeared to be in harmony with changing economic circumstances.

In this chapter we are interested in tracing the decline of mercantilist foreign trade doctrines primarily through a consideration of the rise of free-trade ideas and the development of the international adjustment mechanism, but first we must briefly say something about the economic and philosophic background which were conducive to the propagation of non-interventionist ideas. First, the influence of changing economic circumstances. Defoe's England had changed considerably since the time of Thomas Mun. Changes in economic structure and institutions occurred which (a) made the old anxiety over the adequacy of bullion supplies if not otiose, at least less pressing; (b) strengthened attitudes antagonistic to the paternalistic view of the state and state regulation.

By the early 1700s trade was largely multilateral and an elaborate system of international settlements or clearing had developed through the widespread use of bills of exchange. The system appeared to have functioned with the minimum actual movement of specie; the specie-flows that actually took place were usually activated by exchange rates moving outside the specie export and import points. Trade routes multiplied and become more complex, replacing the earlier simpler patterns of trade. The range of commodities widened and new markets were exploited. As well as the old staples, the goods moving in international trade covered a broad variety of intermediate products. As was noted earlier, around this time the British re-export and entrepôt trades grew apace. Matching this growing complexity of trade was the equally marked growth in credit institutions, banking and insurance business. An important development was the growing use of paper substitutes for hard money in Britain; and although their circulation was mainly confined to the London area, by 1750 banknotes comprised something like one-third of the amount of silver and coin in circulation. In France, however, the early experiment with paper money inspired by John Law which involved the creation of note-issue by the Banque Royale in 1716 ended with the collapse of the 'Mississippi Bubble' in 1720 and the financial ruin of many members of the French upper classes. Yet such schemes indicated the possibility of providing a greater elasticity to the monetary system and, where successful, increased monetary supplies and allayed fears of 'shortage of money'.

These times, too, saw the rise of a new class of small businessmen who were increasingly coming to find that mercantile regulation was not in their best interest. These men typically arose from the ranks of the guild masters to become employers or capitalists and even moved into the fields of commerce and marketing. These entrepreneurs resented the monopolistic privileges granted a few big financiers and City merchants and complained about the taxes levied to maintain a system of power, unrelated, as they saw it, to their individual interests. The extension of capitalist control over the processes of production and commerce stemmed from the fact that it was becoming more difficult to make large profits simply from taking advantage of price differences between different regions and countries. The path to secure profits henceforth lay in the process of production and through attention to costs and productivity.

As the British economy became more diversified, the new entrepreneurs found their search for and exploitation of markets for their products obstructed by the corporate trading monopolies. The spreading dislike of regulation and commercial privilege met with some sympathetic response after the Glorious Revolution of 1688. In 1689 an Act allowed anyone to export cloth anywhere, and by 1700 English foreign trade was largely thrown open to individuals trading either on their own account or in partnership. Some were general exporters shipping anything that came their way; others concentrated on particular oversea markets or type of goods – all of them risking their own capital on trading voyages guided solely by expectations of profits. The development of capitalist relations in agriculture was greatly aided by the abolition of feudal tenures and wardships during the English Revolution. A much freer market in land resulted from the greater security of tenure accorded to landowners. Relations between landlords and tenants, and decisions about the disposition of land became market relations. Rents and leases, based on the cash nexus in a competitive market, became more common. In France, too, the rising class of small entrepreneurs felt hemmed in by Colbertian regulations. They resented the multiplicity of taxes and tolls and the privileges accorded to others. Feelings must have been deeply touched (and self-interest) for complaints to be voiced at meetings of the *Conseil de Commerce* by representatives of certain regions against monopolies and tariffs. Boisguillebert (1646–1714) called into question the preconceptions of the mercantilists. Money, for him, was a pledge for the handing over of real goods and other assets (i.e. for consumption). He stressed the importance of consumption in the circular flow of production, income and expenditure, and drew attention to the mutual interdependence of activities which linked buyers and sellers in the market. His exploration of the dynamics of domestic consumption enabled him to describe a process similar to that of the 'multiplier' in modern national-income analysis. Boisguillebert was in favour of an economy of high prices, especially for farm products. He asserted the primacy of agriculture over the two-hundred trades and professions in France – for the latter were all '*les enfants de la terre*'.[1] Long before the Physiocrats, he called for the removal of the export ban on grain because of its depressive effect on domestic prices and quantities supplied. He called for fiscal reform, including in this a plea for the diminution of customs duties or taxes on internal and external trade. Boisguillebert's thoughts (e.g. that a beneficent equilibrium only results when '*on laisse faire la nature*') echoed the protest of many small French producers, farmers and traders.[2]

The very expression 'laissez faire' apparently originated in these merchants' complaints, later to be endowed with the status of an

The Decline of Mercantilist Trade Doctrines

economic principle by the government inspector of trademarks, Vincent de Gourney (1712–59), who, disenchanted with mercantilist regulation, extended this cry into the classic liberal phrase 'laissez faire, laissez passez' – 'free enterprise, free trade'. The origin of the classical liberal slogan, in fact, epitomises the transition to economic liberalism. The grievances of the early capitalists could easily have been dismissed as mere special pleading by vested interests (of a particular industry, region, town or port). What gave added merit to these demands, however, was the supportive voice of philosophy. The thinkers of the Enlightenment threw their weight behind the men of business who clamoured for freedom from detailed regulation by the state. Thus an ideology was born.

The ideas, attitudes and programmes of the *philosophes* and *illuminati* of the Age of Reason presented the first real intellectual challenge to mercantilism. The ideas of the men of the Enlightenment were not wholly new; some of their theories were aired during the preceding century and others can be traced back to the Renaissance. But they were zealots for the cause of freedom, reason and the new science. They took hold of age-old concepts like Reason, Law, Nature, Liberty, Humanity, Perfectibiliby, invested them with new meanings and then applied them to social phenomena. Condorcet said of himself and his friends that they were 'a class of men less concerned with discovering truth than with propagating it ... [who] find their glory rather in destroying popular error than in pushing back the frontiers of knowledge'.[3] They were greatly impressed with the mathematical and experimental methods used by Newton in his *Principia* and *Opticks*, which had shed so much light on the nature of physical reality. The discovery of the universal laws of motion and gravitation suggested to the *philosophes* the existence of similar orderly, predictable laws in society. Newton discovered the marvellous properties of light simply by playing about with a prism. Using reason as their prism, the *philosophes* felt they could discover equally wonderful truths about human society. 'What we can do for bees and beavers', said Condorcet, 'we ought to do for man.'[4] Following this injunction, thinkers set about laying the foundations of systematic work in the social sciences by writing the classics. They confidently believed that rational criticism (the 'light of reason') could free the world from myth, superstition and ignorance. Oliver Goldsmith called them 'cosmopolites', citizens of the world. And indeed, it was this frame of mind – at once pacific and cosmopolitan – that confronted the chauvinism and bellicosity of the mercantilists. Voltaire's call 'Ecrasez l'infâme' was meant to encompass all this as well as the injustice and iniquities that constricted the individual in society. Earlier, the spokesman for the Whig oligarchy in England and staunch defender of property, John Locke, gained wide acceptance for his views on political liberty and toleration. He inspired belief in the inalienable rights of the human individual in society based on the 'natural' and 'original' liberties of man. Eighteenth-century thinkers interpreted this as a plea for limited government: on the whole, things, if left to themselves, were more likely to work together for good than if regulated by interfering governments. Governments cannot change the basic nature of individuals motivated as they are by egoistic or selfish motives. Laws and institutions walk properly with Nature when they provide an orderly social framework for the pursuit of self-interest, which is the only avenue for advancing towards national prosperity.

DEVELOPMENT OF FREE-TRADE IDEAS

In the economic sphere this sort of reasoning led naturally to *laissez faire*. Just as David Hume hoped that politics might be reduced to a science, so some of these thinkers believed that the laws of economy could be discovered by the same methods that enlightened mankind about the laws of physics. The first step in this direction was to get a proper understanding of the *motivation* rather than the *ethics* of economic behaviour, i.e. to apply cause-and-effect analysis to economic activity. Here, perhaps more than in other fields of social activity, the eighteenth-century thinkers found what they expected: selfish, egoistic motives were the primary, if not the only, ones that moved men to economic endeavour. Somehow, it was believed, the pursuit of private, selfish interests would tend to promote the social and economic good. This social vision was admirably put by one of the finest poets of the age, Alexander Pope in his *Essay on Man*:

> That REASON, PASSION answer one great aim;
> That true SELF-LOVE and SOCIETY are the same.

Earlier, the same idea was expressed in rather more controversial tones by Bernard de Mandeville in his long doggerel poem *The Fable of the Bees* (1714) and succinctly affirmed by Nicholas Barbon in 1690 thus: 'Prodigality is a vice that is prejudicial to the man, but not to trade.'[5] Mandeville's shocking paradox – 'private vices are often public benefits' – caused a bit of a stir among his contemporaries in the early eighteenth century, and his book achieved an immediate *succès de scandale*. Mandeville's paradox outraged the sensibilities of the moralists by exposing the hypocrisy of their praise of frugality and contentment, but it was merely stating an obvious economic fact; and this latter fact was not lost on the liberal-minded writers on economics. Mandeville's argument is simply that individuals, by indulging in vices, pursuing self-love or self-interest contribute to social welfare and economic prosperity.

Turning now to the rise of free trade ideas, we find ourselves dealing with the application by writers of the same basic principle of the self-regulatory nature of the economy to the conduct of foreign trade. The writers who pioneered various aspects of the free-trade approach to international trade before Adam Smith include North, Davenant and the anonymous author (Henry Martin?) of *Some Considerations on the East India Trade*.

For these writers, foreign trade was in essence not different from domestic trade; businessmen engaged in them for the same reason – the prospect of making a profit. Unlike most of their contemporaries, they saw the profit motive as the regulator of orderly economic activity. There are no 'good' and 'bad' trades, only profitable and unprofitable ones; and whatever was profitable to private businessmen in free bargains was socially beneficial. They did not, however, like Cantillon, press the logic of the profit motive to reach a theory of the allocation of resources among alternative uses through the phenomena of market exchanges. Neither did they consistently think, like Cantillon, of the economy as an automatically adjusting mechanism, but what they glimpsed of it convinced them of the futility of mercantilist regulation.

Starting with the axiom that all men are motivated by self-interest, Dudley North (1641–1691) develops an uncompromising case for free trade in his book *Discourses Upon Trade* (1691). The profit motive, he maintains, must be the sole arbiter of what goods to export and import, from which sources supplies are to be obtained and to which markets goods are to be consigned. He declares 'there can be no trade unprofitable to the public; for if any prove so, men leave it off; and wherever the traders thrive, the public, of which they are a part, thrives also'. And again, 'no people ever grew rich by policies; but it is peace, industry, and freedom that brings trade and wealth and nothing else'. North went on to attack the assumption that a favourable balance of trade was necessarily desirable. The supply of money adjusts itself automatically among countries according to the needs of trade; but he did not develop this argument since evidently he did not quite grasp the quantity theory of money. He firmly denied, however, another mercantilist maxim, namely, that in trade one nation's loss was another's gain. No, says North, it was the loss of all; 'for all is combined together'.[6]

Charles Davenant, who held the post of Inspector-General of Imports and Exports from 1703 to 1714 held much the same opinions. In his 1696 *Essays on the East India Trade* he asserts: 'Trade is in its nature free, finds its own channel and best directeth its own course; and all laws to give it rules and directions, and to limit and circumscribe it may serve the particular ends of private men, but are seldom advantageous to the public' and further: 'They say few laws in a state are an indication of wisdom in a people; but it may be more truly said that few laws relating to trade are the mark of a nation that thrives by traffic.'[7]

In one of his official reports (1712) Davenant wrote: 'It is utterly impossible exactly to state the balance between our country and another, all traffic have a mutual dependence one upon the other.'[8] The early mercantilists either ignored opportunity costs or had no conception of it. This neglect or ignorance of the alternative use of money and resources might have been partly due to the fact that the economy they lived in was characterised by widespread unemployment and underemployment of labour – then a key factor of production. This fact, however, meant that men's minds did not turn in the direction that would have led to the discovery of the law of comparative advantage. They therefore were bereft of any substantial theory of the gains from trade. For them, there was a profit in foreign trade, but this profit was only realised as a consequence of a favourable balance of trade. Mun was quite explicit that the gain or loss to the nation from foreign trade could only be measured by reference to the state of the balance of trade. The classical economists' case for free trade based on comparative advantage, by contrast, relied on the principle of specialisation and division of labour to promote the accumulation and efficient utilisation of resources which alone can make a country rich.

It was these advantages of international specialisation that writers like North, Davenant and in particular the anonymous author of the remarkable pamphlet *Considerations on the East India Trade* dimly saw as the source of mutually beneficial trade. In this pamphlet Henry Martin, its probable author who succeeded to Davenant's job, mounted an attack on the textile manufacturers who clamoured for protection against Indian imports. He pointed to the advantages (increases in productivity) resulting from the use of machinery and the practice of division of labour. The latter concept he referred to as 'order and regularity' and applied it to international trade. Bullion is exchanged for Indian finished textiles, he declares, because it is a cheaper way of getting textiles than by producing them at home. He illustrates this argument by an example to show the saving in labour costs (or labour time) that results when certain goods are obtained through trade rather than by self-sufficient production at home:

> If nine cannot produce above three bushels of wheat in England, if by equal labour they might procure nine bushels from another country, to employ these in agriculture at home, is to employ nine to do no more work than might be done as well by three; ... is the loss of six bushels of wheat; is therefore the loss of so much value.[9]

Martin implies that the benefits of specialisation or division of labour can best be reaped under a regime of relatively free trade, for trade is nothing more than a voluntary exchange of marketable assets and commodities. Martin likened the effects of free trade to the benefits of technical progress and the division of labour. Imports of cheap Indian fabrics would exert a downward competitive pressure on the prices of British textiles, and workers would be thrown out of employment as high-cost producers contracted their output. But the real-income gain to consumers would increase spending on other efficiently produced English products. These industries would expand, both because of the increased demand for their output and lower manufacturing costs brought about by the lower level of wages consequent upon the increased labour supply. Eventually he envisaged a situation where the surplus labour would be absorbed by output expansions of the remaining efficient English industries.

Both North and Davenant also made references to the international division of labour. Davenant argued against the promotion of industry in a country which is unsuitable to it either by reason of climate or availability of resources, i.e. an industry should only be encouraged if it has natural advantages in a particular region.

It is not clear what influence these works had on contemporaries – apparently not much. North's book was published anonymously in the year of his death. Martin's pamphlet also came out anonymously, and both were virtually ignored at the time. Only Davenant's work was known, and a few years before the *Wealth of Nations* came out a five-volume edition of his collected works was published.

The Victorian liberals were full of praise for these writers, who they regarded as pioneers of *laissez-faire* and free-trade doctrines. However, the truth is that these writers' statements of general liberal principles were often at variance with their recommendations on specific issues. They were very much men of their time, political animals, and in the case of Davenant and Martin senior public servants who had careers to safeguard and political masters to humour. Davenant and North were Tories and Martin a Whig. Despite his liberal free-trade utterances, Martin for instance, was bitterly opposed to freer trade with France and was a notable contributor to the *British Merchant*, the news-sheet which campaigned against the 1713 commercial treaty with France. Referring to the economic writings of Child, Barbon, Davenant and North, E. A. Johnson commented: 'the liberal theories of trade espoused by the Tory pamphleteer were perhaps more the result of circumstances and political sympathy than evidence of superior enlightenment'.[10] And Leslie Stephen, the late-Victorian historian, said of them: 'For one moment they reach an elevation from which they can contemplate the planet as a whole, and at the next moment their vision is confined to the horizon visible from an English shop window.'[11]

Schumpeter's opinion was that excepting North, none of the others were thoroughgoing free-traders – 'North alone was'. He had a high opinion, though, of Martin's analytical accomplishment, referring to it as 'a technically superior formulation of the benefits from territorial division of labour' and hailed the author as 'a predecessor of Ricardo, though possibly a quite uninfluential one'.[12]

However, the fact remains that economic sentiments of a distinctively 'liberal' flavour – opposed to mercantilist reasoning – did surface in the early years of the eighteenth century. But, perhaps, more important than this for the early development of the theory of the gains from trade was the explicit recognition of the essence of opportunity costs and its relevance to an understanding of the benefits of international trade in a competitive market context.

Stemming from this acceptance of the principle of opportunity costs joined with the equally relevant notion of division of labour, there grew up a doctrine standing in uneasy rivalry with the balance-of-trade dogma—the doctrine referred to by Viner as the '18th-century rule'. The 'rule' stated that trade was beneficial to a country when it provided commodities 'which could not be produced at home at all or could be produced at home only at costs absolutely greater than those at which they could be produced abroad'.[13] It is, of course, a statement of the case for free trade based on *absolute advantages* in production and was in essence the argument put forward in the 1701 *Considerations Upon the East India Trade* in favour of the free importation of Indian calicoes. In effect, the 'rule' states that the opportunity cost of importing goods from abroad is the quantity of real resources devoted to the production of the required exports given in exchange. Whenever the resource cost of obtaining say commodity X (imports) in terms of commodity *Y* (exports) is lower when obtained through trade than when produced domestically, then trade is clearly beneficial. The advantage from trading then exists in the amount of goods that can be produced with the resources saved. Even Adam Smith did not advance the argument beyond this point, for the eighteenth-century rule, while not inconsistent with the notion of *comparative* advantage is not identical with it. What remained to be further explained was how trade (in two goods, for example) could take place between two countries to the advantage of each when one country was absolutely more efficient in the production of both goods. In terms of the 'rule', that is, it has to be shown that it might still be profitable to import commodity *X*.

However what later generations of free-traders applauded was that, at any rate, the eighteenth-century rule wrecked the notion that trade was a zero-sum game. Perhaps Schumpeter had in mind this contribution of Martin, as well as those of the other Restoration liberals, when he suggested that there was no need for any spectacular break between mercantilists and classical liberals as far as economic analysis was concerned. But he stuck his neck out a bit when he continued by further surmising that if Smith and his followers had refined and developed the mercantilist hypotheses instead of throwing them away, 'a much truer and much richer theory of international economic relations could have been developed by 1848'.[14] This generalisation has not pleased some mainstream neoclassical economists, but surely Schumpeter's point was both reasonable and defensible, one that is fully endorsed by modern development economists. The mercantilist trade propositions were embedded in a total paradigm which included a concern with international inequalities, national power, growth and development. The trade theory which became associated with the classical economists – rightly or wrongly – abstracted from these real-world concerns, and this default impoverished the utility and relevance of classical theory. It triggered the repudiation of classical trade theory by the national economists of the nineteenth century; and that was what Schumpeter deplored. It need not have happened, since some of the classical economists themselves were forced to recognise legitimate exceptions to the anaytical core of their doctrine.

THE QUANTITY THEORY OF MONEY AND INTERNATIONAL ADJUSTMENT MECHANISMS

The relationship between the quantity of money and the general level of prices must have been apparent to thoughtful people who experienced the 'price revolution' in the second half of the eighteenth century after the relative price stability of the Middle Ages. Jean Bodin, for one, recognised the quantity-theory relationship and helped to popularise the idea in France, Spain and England, where his works were read by jurists and political thinkers.

Bodin formulated his explanation in reply to the views of a contemporary writer, M. de Malestroit, who denied that inflation even existed, or else that if it did, it was due to the recoinages and debasement of the period. According to Malestroit, prices have not risen during the past three hundred years. Admittedly, he says, one has to pay out more in *livres* now for the same article than formerly. But this is only because the *livre* now contains less grammes of silver owing to the recent debasements. In terms of silver (or gold), however, prices have remained relatively stable. Bodin argued that it was misleading to relate price levels simply to the silver or gold content of coins. The principal reason for the contemporary world inflation was, he indicated, the increase in the quantity of gold and silver from America 'which today in this realm is greater than it has been for four hundred years'. He enunciated the general proposition that: 'The principal reason which raises the price of everything wherever one may be, is the abundance which governs the appraisal and price of things. ... It [is] the abundance of gold and silver.'[15]

Bodin's explanation thus runs in terms of a direct causal relationship between an exogenous increase in the world money supply and the increase in world prices. Bodin himself admitted that he was not the first to notice this relationship; and, indeed, there is evidence that several writers came to the same conclusion at about this time, most notably the Salamanca jurist Martin de Azpilcueta (1493–1587) – also known as Navarro, Francisco Lopez de Gomara (the biographer of Cortes and Charles V), Luis de Molina, the Portuguese Jesuit and the Italian Bernardo Davanzati. Even earlier, in 1526, none other than Copernicus expressed the dictum: 'Money usually depreciates when it becomes too abundant.'[16]

It is no accident that the quantity theory emerged out of the observations and reflections of the jurists and theologians of the School of Salamanca. Sixteenth-century Spain was the ideal laboratory for observing connections between money and prices. The Spanish writers were also well-equipped for making fruitful deductions about the inflation phenomenon, for they were accustomed to thinking of exchange value in terms of a relationship between wants or utility in the ordinary sense of capacity to satisfy some practical need on the one hand and scarcity on the other. That is, they explained exchange value or price in terms of what we understand by the forces of supply and demand. The quantity theory of money is, of course, merely a particular application of supply-and-demand analysis; and it was this model of reasoning, given the objective phenomenon of rising prices, that led the Salamanca writers to their monetary theories. Navarro (1556) thus explains the relative value of two moneys:

> money is worth more when and where it is scarce than where it is abundant... in countries where there is a great scarcity of money, all other saleable goods and even the hands and labour of men are given for less money than where it is abundant. Thus we see by experience that in France, where money is scarcer than in Spain, bread, wine, cloth and labour are worth much less.[17]

Following this line of reasoning, Navarro grasped the essence of the PPP doctrine and the existence of commodity arbitrage (buying commodities cheap in one country and reselling in another at a risk-free profit) because of international differences in purchasing power. As a result of such arbitrage, exchange rates would be adjusted to reflect differences in the value of two national moneys. Navarro's version of the PPP doctrine, based on quantity-theory reasoning is almost as sophisticated as any produced in the nineteenth century by Ricardo or Wheatley, for example. Navarro's opinion was held in high esteem by jurists in the sixteenth and seventeenth centuries and his works were translated into Latin and Italian. In the early seventeenth century the eminent writer Sancho de Moncada did much to popularise the views of Navarro as well as those of Bodin. By the time of Malynes, Misselden and Mun, then, the simple quantity-theory explanation was clearly well-established, and Mun indicates that the causality relationship running from money to prices was well-known in his day: 'It is a common saying that plenty or scarcity of money makes all things dear or good or cheap.'[18]

At this stage, however, the money–price causality relationship was understood more as an empirical statement than an analytical proposition; and despite the monetary insights already noted of Malynes and Mun the quantity-theory relationship was not properly integrated into current thought. Such integration would have undermined the feasibility of attaining the paramount objective of permanent balance-of-trade surpluses. Indeed, as we have seen (perhaps because of the assumption of unemployed resources), the orthodox position emphasised the effect of increases in the money supply on wealth and trade through the stimulus provided to mercantile and productive activities. Here we have an example of a phenomenon that was to be repeated in the history of economics – the proclivity of economic theorists to either ignore or deny propositions that sit incongruously with the rest of their doctrines, particularly when these touch on policy matters.

At all events, by the end of the seventeenth century, the essential components of the monetary model of a closed economy were in place, including the proportionality relationship between goods and money and the neutrality concept, i.e. the idea that money-supply changes have no permanent effect on real economic activity. These developments were too important to be ignored, and it was the political philosopher John Locke who, in 1692, brought these elements together in a clear and emphatic statement of the quantity theory as it pertains to a closed economy.[19] He carefully analysed the determinants of the income velocity of money, for instance; but maintained that in the long run, the value or purchasing power of the domestic monetary unit varied inversely with the quantity of money. Locke forms a link with writers like Vanderlint, Cantillon, Gervaise and Hume, who, in the first half of the eighteenth century developed the theory of international monetary equilibrium which was to shatter the intellectual credibility of mercantilist doctrine. However refined Locke's monetary model was, it was not adequately tied up with the balance-of-trade doctrine. He points out that in the open economy, domestic prices must adjust to world prices and therefore presumably would have agreed with his contemporary Dudley North, who declared that, in a trading world, the total money stock would be automatically distributed among countries 'without any aid of Politicians'.[20] Locke recognised this difference between a closed and an open economy, and implicitly admitted the existence of what is now called the 'law of one price' (or the PPP equilibrium condition). He noted that the PPP equilibrium condition (the equality of silver prices in different countries) could be disturbed by risk factors, transfer costs and capital movements. He had other interesting things to say about exchange rates; for instance, that domestic monetary contraction need not induce specie inflows if the exchange rate remains within the 'silver points' – determined by transfer costs. But he does not go further and describe the mechanism which supposedly provides for the natural distribution of specie (and hence the linkage of domestic and world prices) through changes in commodity balances and specie-flows.

Despite some sophisticated monetary analyses, Locke did not draw the appropriate policy conclusions – indeed, he did the opposite. He continued to adhere to balance-of-trade doctrine and policies; in particular, he saw advantages in the maintenance of a large national stock of money. The high prices associated with such accumulation were not only a sign of prosperity (fully employed resources), but were also the means whereby more gold was attracted to a country – a policy position far removed from his otherwise subtle analysis of international money. As a member of the Board of Trade he helped to frame the new policy of industrial protection during the 1690s. He repeated the old mercantilist slogans: that wealth consisted in having more gold and silver, that only war and foreign trade could secure them for a country without mines –

> In a country not furnished with Mines there are but two ways of growing Rich, either Conquest, or Commerce ... Commerce therefore is the only way left to us, either for Riches or Subsistence. ... Trade then is necessary to the producing of Riches, and Money necessary to the carrying on of Trade.[21]

Among Hume's contemporaries who probed the links between the quantity theory and the preconceptions of mercantilism, Vanderlint, Gervaise and Cantillon deserve more than passing mention.

Economists immediately think of Hume at any mention of the classical price-specie-flow mechanism and, indeed, he is often claimed to be the forerunner of the modern monetary approach to the balance of payments. He was a synthesiser of the already existing material; but as so often happens in the case of brilliant and original minds that cannot help but implanting, stamping or marking contemporary thought with their own originality, so Hume contributed part of his own genius to the theory of the monetary mechanism of international trade.

Writing in 1734 Jacob Vanderlint alluded to various aspects of the price-specie-flow mechanism in several places of his book *Money Answers All Things*.[22] Using a quantity theory of money framework, he explains how an increase in the money supply would stimulate aggregate expenditure, and hence raise domestic prices. This would, in turn, lead to a balance-of-trade deficit as exports fall and imports increase. The accompanying specie outflow would then restore the domestic money supply to its original level. Vanderlint, however, believed in the circulation function of money – increased money supplies stimulate trade – and felt that the key to a favourable trade balance lay in relatively lower domestic prices. He therefore advocated a policy of 'sterilization' of gold inflows to prevent domestic prices from rising when the country enjoys a favourable balance of payments. There is thus an inconsistency between Vanderlint's theoretical reasoning and his policy recommendations.

The same is true of Cantillon, although to a lesser extent. Richard Cantillon wrote his remarkable *Essai sur la Nature du Commerce en Général* between 1730 and his murder in May 1734.[23] His originality is manifest in various parts of this work including Part II, where he treats of monetary matters. Here he gives a sophisticated account of the quantity theory of money and the income approach to monetary theory. He emphasises that changes in velocity of circulation are equivalent to changes in the money stock, and traces the channels whereby changes in money supply impinge on prices, including a consideration of 'real-balance' effects. He carefully distinguishes between open and closed economies and between traded and non-traded goods and implicitly recognises that for traded goods there is a single world market which constrains their prices.[24] He describes the basic processes involved in the self-regulating specie-flow mechanism when he analyses the effects of increases in the money supply resulting from balance-of-payments surpluses. Yet for all his analytical insight, Cantillon could not quite escape from mercantilist habits of thought. In a passage describing the economic decline of states he writes: 'I assume always that the comparative wealth of states consists principally in the respective quantities of money which they possess.'[25] He admits that a country cannot permanently enjoy a favourable balance of trade, but believes that the day when the surplus turns into a deficit can be indefinitely postponed if the country follows a policy of 'sterilization' (i.e. withdrawing the payments surplus from circulation and hoarding it as emergency reserves). Alternatively a stable equilibrium is possible with a balance-of-payments surplus if the country has an efficient merchant navy, since low freight charges can partially, at any rate, offset high domestic prices thus enabling the country to remain internationally competitive. But Cantillon was not so much interested in long-run equilibrium states as he was with the analysis of the short-run dynamics of disequilibrium. It is in this light that his supposedly mercantilist leanings and his failure to perceive the concept of the international distribution of species must be seen.

Isaac Gervaise, the last notable monetary theorist before Hume, wrote in 1720 a pamphlet of thirty-four pages containing all the main ingredients of the modern monetary approach to the balance of payments.[26] Written in an obscure style, Gervaise's work went unnoticed by contemporaries, and only saw the light of day fifty years ago; and since then its high merits have been praised by many economists. Harry Johnson writes of Gervaise that he gave 'a statement of the relevant monetary theory clearer in some ways than Hume's',[27] and Frank Fetter acknowledged that 'the first extended (and in depth) analysis of the process of international adjustment came from Isaac Gervaise'.[28] Jacob Viner, by clarifying some of the obscurities of Gervaise's terminology, did much to secure Gervaise's work the recognition it amply deserves.

Gervaise starts with a well-rounded treatment of the natural distribution of specie hypothesis and explains that the existing world stock of money is shared out among countries according to their relative levels of real income or production (the 'produce of their labour'). From the context, and with the help of Viner's interpretation, the relevant passage reads as follows:

> A nation can naturally draw and keep unto itself, but such a proportion of the real money stock of the world as is proportioned to the quantity of its inhabitants, because the money stock can be attracted but by its production only. A nation cannot retain more than its natural proportion of what is in the world; and the balance of trade must run against it.[29]

This natural distribution of specie comes about through the linkage of the money supply to the balance of payments. Starting from a position of equilibrium where the world money stock is distributed among countries in strict proportion to their respective levels of real economic activity, an autonomous increase in the money supply of one country results in a temporary rise in residents' cash balances. This induces additional expenditure (including spending on imports) which results in a trade deficit and an outflow of precious metals, thereby removing the excess cash balances. He notes explicitly that persistent payments deficits mean that the domestic money supply is excessive. Thus:

> When the balance of trade runs, and continues running against a Nation, we may conclude its money stock exceeds its natural proportion.[30]

Gervaise concludes his analysis of the adjustment process with the observation that

> all the profit a nation gains, by unnaturally swelling its denominator (stock of precious metals), consists only in its inhabitants living for a time in proportion to that swelling, so as to make a greater figure than the rest of the world, but always at the cost of their coin, or of their store of real and exportable labour.[31]

When Hume came to write his economic essays in 1752, then, he had a rich body of monetary theory before him. He was certainly familiar with Locke's work and, as von Hayek suspects, must have seen Cantillon's *Essay* in manuscript which although not published until 1755 was widely circulated before then. And if we are to believe Marx and Engels, Hume made use of Vanderlint's ideas.[32] There is no evidence, however, that Hume had ever heard of Gervaise or his pamphlet. Hume endorsed the following propositions associated with the monetary approach to international payments equilibrium: (1) natural distribution of specie; (2) purchasing-power parity or law of one price; (3) self-adjusting specie-flow mechanism.

World money would be distributed among countries in proportion to countries' demand for money as determined by value of transactions, real incomes and population, i.e. all the factors that modern monetarists include in the catch-all of V and Q in the $MV = PQ$ equation of exchange. He used the analogy of water seeking its own level to make the point:

> It does not seem that money any more than water can be raised or lowered anywhere much beyond the level it has in places where communication is open (i.e. where international trade takes place).[33]

An implication of the natural distribution hypothesis is the equalisation of prices in a trading world, or the maintenance of purchasing-power parity, or the equalisation of the value of money across countries. Hume was quite insistent on the 'law of one price' in long-run equilibrium. In a letter to Turgot he wrote: 'there cannot be two prices for the same species of labour'.[34] Similarly, as between the various regions within a country, we observe a process at work which tends to keep the competitive prices of the same good virtually the same, and hence the maintenance of a uniform value of money. 'How', asks Hume, 'is the balance kept (internally) in the provinces of every kingdom among themselves, but by the force of this principle, which makes it impossible for money to lose its level, and either to rise or sink beyond the proportion of labour and commodities which are in each province?'[35] In the same way, transactions between cheap and dear markets in different parts of the world lead to worldwide price equalisation for similar goods. On the self-regulating mechanism, Hume placed the emphasis on divergent movements in national money price levels as the adjustment mechanism following a monetary disturbance. But Hume also accepted the assumption of integrated world commodity markets and common world commodity prices, which would seem to rule out variation in relative prices as the adjustment mechanism. Hence, Hume has been criticised for inconsistency. In correspondence with his friend and critic, James Oswald of Dunnikier, he agreed that precisely because his example referred to an open trading economy, prices in one country would never rise in direct proportion to an exogenous increase in the (gold) money supply. Since (except for transport costs) the same good must always sell for the same competitive price everywhere in the world.[36] Viner defended Hume's adjustment mechanism against the objection that the adjustment process does not work because, with integrated world commodity markets, British prices would not go down by four-fifths as Hume assumed following a sudden loss of four-fifths of all the money in Great Britain. And if it is impossible for British prices to fall by this proportion, then the British money supply would not be restored – hence, no stable equilibrium.

Viner maintained that there is no inconsistency between the assumption of perfect commodity arbitrage and an adjustment mechanism that works through relative price changes. The relevant price variable emphasised by Viner is the terms of trade, i.e. 'relative variations in the prices of different commodities in the same market, and primarily [on] ... variations in prices as between export and import commodities'.[37] But this is not a satisfactory explanation, since Viner elsewhere recognises that the restoration of stable equilibrium may come about through changes in money wage-rates (or factor prices generally) induced by gold flows which change *all* prices and costs the same way in any market – relative changes in the supply schedules of identical commodities. Another way of resolving the seeming inconsistency in Hume's account of the self-correcting international trade mechanism is by recognising the equilibrating role of differential movements in the prices of non-traded goods relative to traded goods as between the deficit and surplus countries. But Hume explicitly denied that changes in the ratio of non-traded goods' prices could play a part in the adjustment process. Thus he writes: 'Even were there some commodities of which no part is exported, the price of Labour employ'd in them cou'd not rise; for this high Price wou'd tempt so many hands to go into that Species of Industry as must immediately bring down the Prices.'[38] As one would put it today: domestic prices are linked to world prices through substitutions in consumption and production.

Recently, however, Paul Samuelson has shown that the confusion stems from a defect in Hume's model. He calls this model 'both wrong and incomplete'. It was, however, a 'beautiful mistake' which, because of its brilliant simplicity, so beguiled successive generations of economists that they failed to offer correct alternative explanations.[39] Hume's fundamental mistake, Samuelson points out, was to make the balance of trade a function of prices at home relative to prices abroad, i.e. $B = f(P/\overset{*}{P})$ and $dB/d(P/\overset{*}{P}) < 0$. For, as we have seen, Hume was adamant that P and $\overset{*}{P}$ must be identical. If this is indeed the case, then the rest of Hume's syllogism is false. In Samuelson's corrected version of Hume's model, the unity of price for freely transportable goods is recognised, and results derived which are consistent with what Hume sought – a stable and self-correcting mechanism. In this amended version, equilibration is achieved not via relative price-level changes at home and abroad, but through the *direct* contractionary or expansionary effect on *spending* (on both exportables and importables) induced by changes in the money supply. When the excess money is all spent, gold losses cease; exports, imports and relative money supplies return to their equilibrium levels – i.e. long-run normal values. Along these lines, Samuelson's reconstituted Humean model is both stable and self-correcting even when, at home and abroad, there are no changes (1) between tradable and non-tradable prices; (2) in absolute price levels; and (3) in the terms of trade, i.e. between export and import prices.[40]

There is, however, an alternative interpretation of the Humean model – admittedly descriptive rather than analytical – which, like Samuelson's version, resolves the inconsistency problem. This view relies on Hume's well-known distinction between transitory adjustment processes and the long-run equilibrium position involved in balance-of-payments adjustment. Also, the law of one price need not hold continuously throughout the process of adjustment, since arbitrage takes time, i.e. $P(t)$ and $\overset{*}{P}(t)$ need not be identical at every moment. Uniformity of sales price is a static equilibrium condition that prevails following the adjustment of the system after an initial perturbation. But in the short-run transition stage to this new equilibrium, prices may deviate from unity as trading takes place at disequilibrium prices.[41] A sequential (rather than an instantaneous) approach to equilibrium is envisaged, during which price differentials are gradually narrowed and then eliminated as specie gets fully redistributed. Thus, if there takes place an autonomous increase of the money stock in Great Britain, British prices would rise temporarily, but the increased British expenditure induced by more money would lead to a trade deficit and specie outflow. Equilibrium would then be restored through commodity and money flows, with the changes in relative prices playing only a passive and temporary, but none the less essential role in the process of adjustment to equilibrium. In a perceptive footnote, Hume recognises an additional, though less significant corrective mechanism – the variation of the exchange rate within the 'specie points' set by the positive costs of shipping gold. For a deficit country the depreciation of its exchange rate down to the export gold-point has an equilibrating effect on trade flows.[42] Hume, however, does not integrate exchange-rate theory into the main adjustment process. Like Gervaise, Hume also shows that as far as the adjustment process is concerned, it makes no difference whether part of the money stock consists of paper credit. Hume seems to have ignored the certainty that an exogenous increase in the money supply of a large country would result in a higher world price level after the completion of all international adjustments.

Whether the *modus operandi* of Hume's adjustment mechanism should properly be interpreted in terms of divergent movements in national price levels or as operating via money flows and real balance effects, there is no doubt that 'it sounded the death-knell of mercantilism', as Mark Blaug puts it.[43] He applied his sceptical and empiricist mind to the grosser contradictions of mercantilist dogma. Free international trade will not drain a country of its money. One-way gold losses are ruled out because of the specie-flow mechanism. Hence, it is futile to maintain trade controls designed to amass precious metals and to prevent their loss since 'it is impossible to heap up money, more than any fluid, beyond its proper level'.[44] His immediate predecessors or contemporaries like Locke, Vanderlint and Gervaise were content to expound the novel monetary doctrine and make the occasional critical asides. Hume, however, pointedly and effectively deployed the quantity theory and the self-regulating mechanism in a deliberate attack on mercantilist prejudices. He was successful in this effort, inasmuch as through Adam Smith it was his insights that were absorbed into the later dominant classical tradition of economic thought.

But those who claim the sceptical philosopher and man of independent mind as the progenitor of modern monetarist orthodoxy must obviously do so with some reservation. While Hume stoutly refuted the mercantilist identification of money with wealth, declaring that '[money] is none of the wheels of trade: It is the oil which renders the motion of the wheels more smooth and easy', he shared none of the modern monetarist strong opposition to inflation. On the contrary, he believed in the benign influence of moderate inflation and supported increases in the money-supply that help to further monetise the economy in the interests of economic development.

> It is of no manner of consequence ... whether money be in a greater or less quantity. The good policy of the magistrate consists only in keeping it, if possible, still increasing; because by that means he keeps alive a spirit of industry in the nation, and increases the stock of labour in which consists all real power and riches. A nation, whose money decreases, is actually at that time weaker and more miserable than another nation which possesses no more money, but is on the increasing hand.[45]

As for his classical credentials, Keynes was surely right when he declared that 'Hume had a foot and a half in the classical world'. Hume's analysis indicated that a country does not suffer a permanent loss of specie by importing goods because the very loss of money serves to lower domestic prices, reduce further imports and may even stimulate increased exports. Equally, mercantilist policies designed to reduce unemployment through a favourable balance of trade are doomed to failure since in the long run increases in the stock of money simply raise prices with little or no impact on levels of output and employment. Yet he was a protectionist, even if only a mild one, and he made invidious distinctions between productive and unproductive occupations. Thus despite Hume's general anti-interventionist stance, Viner cautions against placing him unreservedly in the classical camp: 'in Hume's economic writings the *laissez-faire* doctrine is to be found only by implication if at all'.[46] Hume's affinity with the classical school was perhaps most marked in his analytical emphasis on the long run, but as Keynes observed, Hume did not neglect the vital short-run dynamic processes:

> Hume began the practice amongst economists of stressing the importance of the equilibrium position as compared with the ever-shifting transition towards it, though he was still enough of a mercantilist not to overlook the fact that it is in the transition that we actually have our being.[47]

Hume's thinking on foreign trade is a curious mixture of divergent doctrinal ingredients, classical and mercantilist. He took part as a relay runner in the marathon from mercantilism to classical liberalism. He never reached the finishing-post, but played a key role in the transition (by anticipating the classical position). There are inconsistencies in his foreign-trade ideas which he fails to resolve (a) owing to his unsuccessful attempts to combine the two distinct perspectives – long-run growth and short-run disequilibrium – noted by Keynes; and (b) his sceptical, flexible philosophical stance which cautioned him against going all the way with any single theoretical schema which can easily degenerate into dogmatism.

Hence we find Hume approving of specie inflows and gradual increases in the money supply that stimulate economic growth and the 'spirit of industry itself', while he repudiates the balance-of-trade doctrine. He is in favour of free trade, yet on social and political grounds he approves of moderate tariffs to protect certain domestic industries, to maintain colonial preferences and for the stimulation of employment: 'a tax on German linen encourages home manufactures, and thereby multiplies our people and industry. A tax on brandy encreases the sale of rum, and supports our southern colonists.'[48]

Yet for all these inconsistencies (from some of which even Adam Smith was not entirely free) Hume's economic essays amount to a powerful and impressive plea for freedom in foreign trade based on the inestimable benefits that spring from allowing 'the natural course of things'. In his essay 'Of the Jealousy of Trade' Hume makes the point that diversity among countries, i.e. different 'soils, climates and geniuses [skills]' was clearly intended by the 'Author of the World' so that nations would be forced to exchange their goods with one another.[49] This circumstance ensured that all countries would have (as later writers were to put it) comparative advantage in some goods. If France can produce wine cheaper than Great Britain then let France increase her vineyards to supply the British market with wines. The purchase of French wines by British consumers necessarily implies that the French would have to accept British products (wheat, barley, etc.) as counterpart payment. Thus both countries trade to their mutual benefit. Each country contributes to the prosperity of the world when it concentrates on what it can produce best.

The 'jealousy of trade' to which European statesmen were so long emotionally attached is shown to be both absurd and inhumane. 'I shall therefore venture to acknowledge' says Hume in an expansive gesture 'that, not only as a man, but as a BRITISH subject, I pray for the flourishing commerce of GERMANY, SPAIN, ITALY and even FRANCE itself. I am at least certain, that GREAT BRITAIN, and all those nations, would flourish more, did their sovereigns and ministers adopt such enlarged and benevolent sentiments towards each other.'[50]

In an argument that prefigures the classical case for free trade Hume sanctions free trade on the grounds that it increases real income by bringing about a more efficient use of resources. Under free trade all countries gain. Trade 'furnishes materials for new manufactures ... increases the stock of labour in the nation' and by means of exports it permits the employment of labour in particular commodities which cannot all be consumed at home. Foreign competition stimulates domestic industry to increase its efficiency and leads to the full utilisation of resources. 'In short', says Hume, 'a kingdom that has a large import and export must abound more with industry ... than a kingdom which rests contented with its own commodities.'[51]

THE PHYSIOCRATS AND FOREIGN TRADE

In France the most notable critics of mercantilist regulation in all its forms – guilds, state monopolies, restrictions on trade, special privileges – were the *Économistes*, better known as the Physiocrats. François Quesnay ('the guru of Versailles') was the intellectual leader of the school which included Pierre Paul Mercier de la Rivière, Pierre Samuel du Pont de Nemours and the brilliant but non-doctrinaire Anne-Robert-Jacques Turgot, who served Louis XVI as comptroller-general.

The Physiocrats were mainly, indeed exclusively concerned with the problems of the French economy, the sources of its weaknesses and the conditions necessary for economic development and regeneration. They explored novel methods for analysing the structure of the economy (the 1757–8 'zigzag' tableau and the 1766 *précis* version of the 'Tableau économique'); and from these quantitative exercises on the interrelationships of the French economy they developed further concepts and ideas that were to have an important influence on subsequent economic thought.

They conceived the economy as consisting of an intricately built mechanism (system, or machine) consisting of interdependent parts functioning in a regular and orderly manner. They introduced the concept of social reproduction and showed how this exhibited unplanned regularities through the 'circular flow' process from one year to the next. Indeed, they were the discoverers of macroeconomics – 'the general system of expenditure, work, gain and consumption' as Quesnay defined it in his 1756 article on 'grain' in Diderot's *Encyclopédie*.

The Physiocrats traced the source of economic surplus – the *produit net* – to the agricultural sector. This net product was looked upon as the true source of real wealth, since all other incomes depended on it. It was their basic assumption that agriculture is the one and only source of productivity that separated them from the mercantilists. Trade and industry yield no disposable surplus over necessary cost; although necessary activities, they are 'sterile' in this sense. Whereas the mercantilists had located the economic surplus in the profits of foreign trade (measured by a favourable balance of trade) the Physiocrats found it in the net gains from domestic agricultural production. The means to prosperity lay not in exchange but in *production*. To the Physiocrats it was folly to indulge in an exchange of real goods for specie, as the mercantilist system dictated.

The path to economic development lay rather in the growth of employment and prosperity in the rural sector – the most dynamic sector of the economy. The 'ripple effects' from agricultural growth would stimulate trade and industry and lead, in turn, to higher rents and tax revenues. The home market must take precedence over the foreign market if the aim of mass consumption was to be achieved. Mercantilists everywhere were wrong to believe that the wealth of a nation could be increased by destroying one's neighbours' trade. Not only was it futile, it was dangerous as well since the natural order suggested co-operation among nations. The obstacles to economic growth were thus clearly identified as residing in the mercantilist policies regulating domestic and foreign trade which favoured and protected such trades and, particularly, the iniquitous tax system associated with these policies. The old system only served the interests of powerful groups, i.e. the *société d'ordres*. The Physiocrats wanted to do away with all this including the guilds, state monopolies, the uneconomic industries fostered by mercantilism and policies of market intervention. If Quesnay's maxim: 'Pauvres paysans, pauvre royaume' was to be taken seriously it implied the demotion of the oversea merchant and the industrialist from the centre of the economic stage in favour of the '*laboureurs*' – the substantial peasant class.

For all their fervent belief in '*laissez faire, laissez passer*' the Physiocrats (with the exception of Turgot) made no notable contributions to the development of international trade theory. Their arguments certainly challenged the assumptions on which the mercantilism of the *ancien régime* rested. For the Physiocrats, foreign trade was largely exploitative in nature and the benefits derived from it merely ephemeral, stemming as they do from monopoly and other temporary advantages which tend to be eroded over time. Trade in industrial products (particularly luxury goods) is also uncertain in another respect, since, when times are bad, demand falls off substantially. In any case, trade is merely transactions is the sphere of exchange and therefore adds nothing to real value. Moreover, foreign trade often causes a diversion of scarce investment funds away from more socially productive uses in the agricultural sector – after all, the subsidies which sustain certain high-cost export industries come directly out of the net product of agriculture. Foreign trade was valued only in so far as it contributed to increased agricultural production. It was on this ground that the Physiocrats mounted their attack against the prohibition on the export of grain. The Corn Laws, they argued, prevented a *bon prix* being obtained for farm products by keeping down the domestic price of grain. The export ban (designed to provide cheap food for the cities so as to lower manufacturing costs) therefore constituted an obstacle to rural development. The Physiocrats therefore advocated *laissez-faire* or internal and external free trade in farm products which would allow agricultural prices to find their natural level. Increased profits, improved incentives and more favourable marketing conditions would, according to their reasoning, lead to large-scale capitalist agriculture, expansion of farm output and faster economic growth through an increase in the size of the circular flow over time.

Quesnay estimated that free trade in agricultural products would increase the rate of return on annual agricultural advances (working capital) from 30 per cent to about 50 per cent consequent upon the prospect of more stable and higher prices. Agriculture, as the generator of general incomes, would become the leading sector of the economy by raising the prosperity of manufacturing. Quesnay confidently predicted:

> Given free trade, France could bring forth an abundance of produce of primary necessity, which would be sufficient both for a large consumption and a large internal trade, and which could maintain in the kingdom a large trade in manufactured goods.[52]

It was in this manner that trade in agricultural products was crucial for the physiocrat programme. There was no special need to rely on foreign demand to raise the level of total expenditure on industrial goods. But in regard to agriculture, trade was absolutely essential for its prosperity. The worldwide market secured by free trade would support agricultural prices at a high, profitable level. Without this support, as Quesnay recognised, there was a danger of glut and stagnation resulting from the fall in the value of agricultural produce. This prompts us to ask, why, if foreign trade was necessary to maintain demand in the one case (agriculture), it was deemed unnecessary in the other (industry and services)? Quesnay does, indeed, discuss the potential benefit of free trade in manufactured goods. But it is a qualified argument based on absolute cost differences – the qualification being that each country must have the necessary raw materials and suitable labour skills. Thus he writes:

> A nation ought to devote itself only to those manufactured commodities for which it possesses the raw materials; and which it can make at less expense than other countries and it should purchase from abroad such manufactured commodities as can be bought at a price lower than the cost which would be involved if the nation makes them itself.[53]

This argument certainly reflected the Physiocrats' concern with efficiency and the optimal allocation of resources; but it never went beyond this, since in their conception, commerce was not a wealth-creating or productive activity subject to the 'economising' principle. They had little confidence in the capacity of foreign trade in industrial products to enhance the rate of economic growth – which objective was, of course, their prime concern. Quesnay and his associates outlined a legitimate (and fruitful) developmental strategy. Although it was firmly based on agricultural surplus as the lynchpin of the system, it could be interpreted as leading on to a more diversified economy as resource endowments change over time. The programme came under attack by the nineteenth-century 'national economists', but countries which followed the physiocratic path did experience substantial growth.

The Physiocrats' attitude reflected the parlous state of the French economy in the latter half of the eighteenth century. The Colbertian industrial edifice was crumbling, commerce was ruined by the Seven Years War and many colonies were lost. The promised gain from foreign trade did not materialise; and, unlike Great Britain, trade was not playing a dynamic role in French economic growth. Agriculture appeared more promising and full of potential;[54] all that was necessary was to raise the level of its technology and investment. The assignment of such an exclusive role to agriculture in physiocratic thought was not, therefore, such an absurd notion as it appears to us today – especially when we consider that the Physiocrats reasoned in terms of *physical* productivity, not value productivity.

As a product of the French Enlightenment, the physiocratic school shared the philosophical and ideological bias of that intellectual movement. They believed in the existence of a natural harmony between public and private interests which prevails when the 'natural order' ordained by Providence corresponds with the actual 'civil' order. But this correspondence will not occur as a matter of course. It requires the establishment of a new political order (under the tutelage of a 'legal' or 'enlightened' despot) which would guarantee the rights of property and personal liberty and support 'correct' economic policies, i.e. physiocracy. This would free the beneficial forces of the natural order and allow free competition and self-interest to flourish. Until the reform programme had been carried out the state had a duty to encourage productive activities and trade in raw produce. Free trade itself might even be undesirable, should world-market conditions cause a drastic fall of agricultural prices in France.

Thus although the radical programme sprung from exasperation with government intervention in economic affairs the Physiocrats still had an important place for the state within it; hence they did not espouse a *laissez-faire* doctrine. Their economic proposals were not, however, fully shared by leading Enlightenment figures such as Voltaire, Galiani and Hume. Their opinions (e.g. on tax reform, free trade, the role of agriculture, etc.) were regarded as either doctrinaire or muddled or both. Turgot was, however, one member of the school who was neither doctrinaire nor woolly-minded. As Minister of Finance for two years (1774–6) he introduced a number of physiocratic reforms on the eve of the Revolution (e.g. the abolition of internal customs dues, elimination of guild regulation and consolidation of tax rates) which foundered on the rock of vested interests. His achievements in the field of economic analysis were more durable and memorable. Recently he has been hailed as 'one of the leading theoretical economists of the eighteenth century ... one of the major contributors to the rise of economic liberalism in Europe ...'.[55] On international trade theory, he endorsed the 'eighteenth-century rule' in connection with the case he made for opposing protection to the iron industry:

> To persist in opposing ... the advantages of free trade from a narrowminded political viewpoint which thinks it is possible to grow everything at home, would be to act just like the proprietors of Brie who thought themselves thrifty by drinking bad wine from their own vineyards, which really cost them more in the sacrifice of land suitable for good wheat than they would have paid for the best Burgundy, which they could have bought from the proceeds of their wheat.[56]

In the elaboration of his case for free trade he placed particular emphasis on the gains to the domestic consumer and the stimulus to competition provided by a regime of unrestricted trade. Thus 'the general freedom of buying and selling will assure the consumer of the best merchandise at the lowest price', and there is 'no means of stipulating any trade or industry than that of giving it the greatest freedom'.[57]

Turgot further argues that protection involves a welfare loss to the community, since it raises the cost structure of industry in general and so reduces demand, output and employment. This is the likely result, since protection once granted to certain favoured trades tends to be extended across the board to practically all trades. Because of the interdependence of production (i.e. the input–output structure of industry) protectionism leads to an uneconomic cost structure not only in the sheltered industries, but also in the industries which use as inputs the outputs of protected industries or trades. Free trade is a spur to efficiency in other ways besides acting on costs – it also stimulates development of new products, the adoption of the latest techniques and the search for new, improved methods. Turgot's total commitment to free trade and its benefits puts him at variance with mainstream physiocratic thought. He did not view foreign trade as merely a 'necessary evil' and he, no doubt, did not go along with Adam Smith's exception of *laissez-faire* in the case of defence and shipping. He was also against the monopoly of colonial trade, including colonial preferences. On the international adjustment mechanism Turgot was, of course, familiar with the writings of Locke, Cantillon and Hume and fully agreed with the quantity theory of money and its application to the international economy. Efforts to maintain a favourable balance of trade are doomed to failure, says Turgot, since in an open economy 'sales and purchases are always equal in the long run', i.e. in money value.[58]

LE DOUX COMMERCE

The thinkers of the Enlightenment propagated the remarkable idea – already suggested by Bodin, but almost forgotten until then – that free international trade promotes harmony in international relations and helps prevent wars. Apart from economic gains, the expansion of foreign commerce was also confidently expected to bring in its train beneficial political, social and moral effects. Commerce was a civilising agent, a solvent of national animosities and a bond of friendship between peoples. This is a far cry from the view commonly held only fifty years previously by, for example, Child and Colbert that commerce was the continuation of warfare by other means. Writing in 1734 Jean-François Melon asserted: 'The spirit of conquest and the spirit of commerce are mutually exclusive in a nation.'[59] Actually, at about the time Colbert made his notorious remark 'Commerce is a perpetual combat' another Frenchman, Jacques Savary, discerned a rather more exalted function of commerce:

> '[Divine Providence] has not willed for everything that is needed for life to be found in the same spot. It has dispersed its gifts so that men would trade together and so that the mutual need which they have to help one another would establish ties of friendship among them.'[60]

However, it was Montesquieu who gave the fullest expression to this optimistic line of thought regarding international trade: 'The natural effect of commerce', he affirms, 'is to lead to peace. Two nations that trade together become mutually dependent: if one has an interest in buying, the other has one in selling; and all unions are based on mutual needs.'[61] The pacific nature of trade Montesquieu traces to the fact that it is based on the pursuit of rational, predictable 'interests' in contrast to the unruly, unpredictable 'passions'. The latter often sways rulers in the direction of undertaking costly foreign wars for no other reason than the satisfaction of dynastic ambitions or the passion for conquest. International trade is an antidote to such barbaric urges. Commerce is an intricate network of mutual obligations built up and sustained by the activities of merchants from any lands in pursuit of their money-making interests. By virtue of the reciprocal nature of commerce these interests are interdependent. A relationship thus forged is costly to break. The expansion of commerce further strengthens this web of interdependent relationships among traders of all countries. Just as at the domestic level a harmony of interests prevails when citizens are freely allowed to pursue their interests, so at the international level there prevails a harmony of interests among states.

Montesquieu actually saw the possibility of political freedom as residing in the expansion of foreign trade. The development of trade – the increasing sophistication of commercial practices – attenuates the hold of the ruler over his subjects (at any rate, the business class). Through mechanisms such as the bill of exchange, foreign-exchange operations and commodity arbitrage traders can mobilise their assets at a moment's notice so as to profit from or evade national controls and regulations. In principle, wealth becomes internationally mobile and with this goes the corollary: the sovereign is constrained in the exercise of his powers over his subjects. Since property, assets, wealth of his subjects can be removed from his jurisdiction the sovereign no longer can successfully indulge in what Montesquieu calls *les grands coups d'autorité* (i.e. sudden, arbitrary actions). The expansion of commerce therefore showers a double blessing on mankind: (a) it guarantees freedom domestically, and (b) ensures universal peace. At its best, commerce is a civilising force; it improves manners, enlarges sensibilities and elevates taste. In a word, 'commerce is *doux*'.

Montesquieu's belief in the pacific and moral consequences of commercial expansion was taken up by kindred spirits who belonged to the Scottish Enlightenment. Thus the historical sociologist William Robertson wrote in 1769: 'Commerce tends to wear off those prejudices which maintain distinctions and animosity between nations. It softens and polishes the manners of men.'[62] And Hume expressed similar views both in his *History of England* and *Political Discourses*. The 'rise and progress of commerce' – which Hume attributes to the stimulus provided by foreign trade – brings to the fore men of 'middling rank' whose motives are guided solely by self-interest. Such people being diligent and predictable are the natural supporters of order, peace and freedom both within and among countries. Thus according to Hume, self-interest, money-making, individualism and trading activities go together. These in turn generate political freedom, decentralisation and a cosmopolitan outlook. Sir James Steuart also asserted the Providential basis of trade – the existence of reciprocal needs grounded on the diversity of world resources. Foreign trade, as the vehicle for fulfilling these needs, binds international society together: 'intercourse tends to unite the most distant nations as well as to improve them: and ... their mutual interest leads them to endeavour to become serviceable to one another'.[63]

These arguments for a liberal social order, based on the nature of self-interest or the psychological motivation of man produced the marvellously soothing notion of *le doux commerce*. But however influential these ideas might have been on subsequent generations, they were unsupported by the realities of contemporary trade and international relations. Marx was later to wince in disbelief that notable minds could have seriously entertained such notions. Trade was anything but *doux* and pacific in the eighteenth century. There was the slave trade, and there were commercially aggressive wars. Edmund Burke, rejoicing at the ending of the patriotic and immensely profitable twenty years' warfare against the French (1763), could truthfully claim: 'Commerce has been made to flourish through war.'[64]

AN IDEOLOGICAL SHIFT

Viner argued that the decline of state intervention and regulation in the post-1740 period resulted more from the criticism of the existing order by the *philosophes* of the Age of Reason (including Hume and Smith) than from the strictly economic arguments for a free economy advanced by these and other writers. Ekelund and Tollison, however, disagree with this view, and downgrade the impact of intellectuals on public policy and the process of institutional change. They suggest that Hume, Smith and all the other great free-trade intellectuals were 'bystanders (albeit important by-standers)' in the process that led to the freeing of the economy. So if neither the philosophers nor the economists were primarily responsible for the decline of mercantilism, who or what was? It looks as if we are back to 'circumstances and events', for this is indeed what Ekelund and Tollison suggest in effect. According to these authors, the reason for the demise of mercantilism in England and its entrenchment in France was the earlier shift in the locus of power from the king to Parliament in England. Constitutional changes reduced the net benefit of regulation to merchants and other self-interested parties. Lobbying costs rose and uncertainty increased over the permanence of legislative enactments. These changes weakened the effectiveness of regulation, reduced the demand for controls and thus led ultimately to a situation where *de facto* free trade existed in England.[65]

The rent-seeking paradigm thus supports Hayek's contention that the cause of economic freedom was won in England as an unintended consequence of the struggle for the power to supply legislation. Free trade was thus a by-product of the evolution of English constitutional and legal institutions.[66] This view, which assigns a secondary role to ideas in the development of institutions and policies, was succinctly expressed by Adam Ferguson, a leading light of the Scottish Enlightenment and often quoted by Hayek: 'Nations stumble upon establishments which are indeed the result of human action but not the result of human design.'[67]

However useful and illuminating this interpretation of the decline of mercantilism may be, it does not detract from but adds to the significance of the combined influences we have identified above. Ideas altered perceptions of economic reality and, perhaps more importantly, offered visions of an alternative economic system or the possibility of a different state of affairs. When these prospects corresponded with the interest of influential groups, men acted in a manner that changed institutions, and hence, policies.

Recent work by historians offer some help in constructing this scenario. Joyce Appleby's discovery of the Restoration Liberals in her book *English Thought and Ideology in the Seventeenth Century* (1978) is a case in point. Her research indicates that these seventeenth-century writers came to an awareness of the salient contours of the market economy, saw it in its international dimension and envisaged a situation where it could serve the national interest through the pursuit of supportive policies. According to Appleby, seventeenth-century English economic thought represented an ideological or intellectual shift – 'the imaginative restructuring of economic relations by seventeenth-century thinkers created new truths. ... As men studied the market, they in turn were changed by their studies. ... They ... contributed to ... the modern restructuring of their society.'[68] John Stuart Mill once remarked that a good cause seldom triumphs unless someone's interest is bound up with it. The rent-seeking explanation for the decline of mercantilism purports to be an example of this maxim. As the constraints on wealth-maximisation through rent-seeking increased, business interests felt that it was not worth the candle to continue with the regulatory game. They came to appreciate the virtues of a free economy. The theory of tariff formation is another example of a politically constrained profit-maximising problem. Ever since Taussig's pioneering work on the tariff history of the United States it has been apparent to economists that an important variable in the determination of tariff changes is the success or failure of special-interest groups in obtaining economic rents associated with a protectionist policy. Underneath every protectionist argument nonsensical or otherwise, lies the rational, calculating profit motive! When protection becomes unprofitable (through institutional, political and economic changes) the arguments are reversed, corrected or amended. In this sense the transition to economic liberalism may be viewed as an ideological shift associated with institutional and economic change.

In the realm of policy, though, it must be noted that, while a substantial deregulation of English internal markets was achieved by 1689, protectionist measures actually intensified and remained highly restrictive until well into the early nineteenth century. According to the theory of regulation, then – viewing mercantilism as a system for enriching special-interest groups and as a means of providing the government with funds – protection was presumably privately profitable and publicly necessary.

Part II
Classical Political Economy and Foreign Trade

4 Classical Trade Theory

SMITH ON FOREIGN TRADE

The *Wealth of Nations* (1776) launched the new science of political economy. Its foundation was the maximising behaviour of individuals in free and competitive markets. Its objective was twofold: (i) to explain and interpret the workings of developing capitalism; and (ii) to advise, guide and direct policy according to the sound principles of political economy. Central to its concerns was an interest in economic growth, a topic Adam Smith placed prominently on the agenda of intellectual and political debate right from the start. Another was the role of international trade in the process of economic development. These were, of course, the very concerns of mercantilism; but the approach and perspective of the classical economists were radically different. Like Smith, they rejected blundering mercantilist (or government) regulation and placed their bets on the competitive market as the best mechanism for promoting growth. Foreign trade – which connects the national market with the wider world market – had an important role to play in this process. To be sure, these economists did not all speak with the same voice, but, in general, they had optimistic visions of prosperity and progress based on the potentials of developing capitalism. Classical political economy is associated in the popular mind with domestic *laissez-faire* and international free trade. At least in respect of foreign trade this portrayal of classical orthodoxy is substantially correct. This policy preference was derived from hypotheses purporting to reveal the true nature and benefit of trade for all countries.

To trace this development of the analysis of the causes and consequence of foreign trade we start with the views of the founding father, Adam Smith. We have already referred to his famous polemic against the mercantilist system and would now like to turn to his theory of international trade.

Economists generally do not rate Smith's contribution to international trade theory very highly. Compared with Ricardo's work his theoretical writings on foreign trade are regarded as being neither original nor brilliant. His work as a theorist (not only in matters of trade) is often said to suffer from a fuzziness and eclecticism which obscures the clarity and sharpness of his reasoning.[1] At the same time as a policy analyst he is frequently praised for his devastating attack on mercantilist regulation. Thus modern textbooks on international economics only mention Smith's theory as an example of the meaning of *absolute* advantage and then hurry on to the more interesting case of comparative advantage associated with his successor David Ricardo.

Recently, however, as part of the resurgence of interest in Smith's economics his theorising on foreign trade has come in for closer scrutiny. The result has been a greater appreciation of the value of his work in this area which vindicates it against long-standing criticism. Typical of this rehabilitation is Professor Bloomfield's assessment: 'Smith showed profound insights as to the underlying basis and gains of trade. He analysed in greater detail than any of his predecessors the nature and benefits of international specialisation and the factors affecting them.'[2] As one who repudiated mercantilist fallacies and shifted the focus of economic discourse from exchange to production (like the Physiocrats before him) Smith saw no peculiar virtue in foreign-trade activities. Indeed, viewed from the perspective of the social returns on investment, foreign trade ranks pretty low. In terms of employment-generating effects a given amount of capital has the highest productivity when used in agriculture followed by home trade and the lowest in foreign trade. That is, Smith believes that capital invested in either agriculture or domestic manufacturing support a larger quantity of productive labour and raises national income more than an equal investment in foreign trade. Smith thus reverses the order of investment priorities that prevailed in mercantilist thought.

For him, foreign trade is not essentially different from domestic trade. Although greater distances are normally involved in international trade and hence higher transport costs are incurred which tend to reduce what he calls 'the frequency of returns' (stock turnover) this is not always the case. The English Channel is no great distance, hence the frequency of returns is higher in trade between the southern counties of England and France than it is in domestic trade involving the Home Counties and distant parts of Great Britain. Smith did not differentiate (as did his followers in the classical school) domestic from foreign trade in terms of differing assumptions about the mobility of productive factors. This being the case, Smith finds the basis of international trade in the fact that both foreign and domestic industry have branches where each is more efficient. That is to say, countries have absolute advantages in the production of the goods they export. In each country imports consist of goods made more efficiently abroad (at lower real costs) and exports consist of goods made more efficiently at home (also at lower real costs). We have here an application of the concept of opportunity costs, since it is clear that a country benefits from trade because the exports required to pay for the imports cost less to produce in real terms than it would cost to produce the imports at home. There are thus mutual gains (in production and consumption) from free exchange through trade – a greater abundance and variety of goods. These gains arise from a more efficient allocation of resources in each country (i.e. international specialisation) based on inter-country differences in absolute costs. Smith puts the principle thus:

> It is the maxim of every prudent master of a family, never to attempt to make at home what it will cost him more to make than to buy.... What is prudence in the conduct of every private family, can scarce be folly in that of a great kingdon. If a foreign country can supply us with a commodity cheaper than we ourselves can make it, better buy it of them with some part of the produce of our own industry, employed in a way in which we have some advantage.[3]

This is, of course, the 'eighteenth-century rule' (previously mentioned) for free trade based on static allocative efficiency grounds. But Smith does not stop here; he quickly moves on to a dynamic model and the consideration of benefits provided by trade through the widening of markets and a more intensive division of labour. Applying his dictum: 'Division of labour is limited by the extent of the market' to trade, he shows how it helps to overcome the narrowness of the domestic market.[4] This widening of markets raises the level of productivity of all resources and sets in motion other growth-inducing effects, viz.: (1) economies of scale, (2) activation of idle resources, (3) improvement of workers' skill and dexterity through further divisions of labour, and (4) the adoption of specialised capital equipment, etc.

These are the dynamic benefits of trade which Smith reckons to be of a high order. He also makes reference in several places in connection with the market-widening effect to the fact that trade opens up a market for goods produced in excess of domestic requirements (consumption or demand). Are two themes then implied in Smith's account of the dynamic effects? H. Myint has for a long time maintained that this is in fact the case and is in keeping with the general developmental orientation of Smith's work. He detects two distinct theories implicit in the foregoing ideas: (1) a 'productivity' theory, and (2) a 'vent-for-surplus' theory.[5] Smith's own classical followers, John Stuart Mill and David Ricardo, regarded the 'vent-for-surplus' idea as a weakness in Smith's trade theory. Mill rejected it as a 'surviving relic of the Mercantile Theory' and Ricardo more moderately observed that it was 'at variance with all [Smith's] general doctrines on this subject'.[6] In our own times, trade literature specialists like Haberler, Bloomfield and Hollander find no real distinction between the two ideas which they take to be merely two aspects of the same theory.[7]

The trouble with the vent-for-surplus idea is that while it has some relevance for Third World countries (or developed countries in the past) it obviously conflicts with much of what Smith has to say about the workings of the competitive-market mechanism in Book I of the *Wealth of Nations*. There the whole emphasis is on the clearing of markets, allocative efficiency and the way a fully employed economy adjusts to disequilibrium. How does he square these general market characteristics with the existence of a surplus which can be disposed of through foreign trade? Smith cannot obviously do this, except by making special assumptions relating to demand inelasticity and internal factor immobility. Since there is no unequivocal textual evidence for these special assumptions, Hollander and Bloomfield prefer to see the vent-for-surplus idea as being related to the widening of the market or 'productivity' theory rather than a separate theory in its own right. Hollander's conclusion is that 'in a sense, mere lip-service was paid by Smith to the vent-for-surplus doctrine'.[8]

Smith's analysis of foreign trade is a synthesis and integration of the better type of theorising on the subject current during his time. However, by virtue of his more systematic approach his treatment is richer and more insightful than that of his predecessors (and to some extent even of his successors). Some of the variables he considered crucial for an understanding of the basis and commodity composition of trade, such as differential factor endowments and transport costs, were neglected by several succeeding generations of economists and the trade and growth nexus emphasised by him, though never absent, was not prominent in classical thought. Like Hume, he did not overlook the indirect benefits of trade. Demonstration effects (changes in taste patterns induced by consumption of foreign goods), the impact of these on incentives and the transmission of technology through trade were all recognised by Smith.

On trade policy Smith is a pragmatic free-trader. The question he asks about all institutional barriers to trade is: Do they increase or diminish the benefits derived from foreign trade? Generally, he finds, they tend to diminish the benefits as compared to a regime of unrestricted trade. Trade regulations often stand in the way of self-interest based on the profit motive. Moreover, they are often unnecessary, even when they are designed to stimulate exports. Trade would take place anyway, since there is a natural 'propensity to truck, barter and exchange goods'. And Smith asserts:

> No regulation of commerce can increase the quantity of industry in any society beyond what its capital can maintain. It can only divert a part of it into a direction into which it might not otherwise have gone; and ... the immediate effect of every such regulation is to diminish [the country's] revenue.[9]

Since free-market processes always ensure that a country's entire capital must find a profitable use, the protection of relatively ineffcent industries cannot raise aggregate output. Indeed, it does the opposite; for while the output of the protected industries will be stimulated, the capital that went into such industries would have yielded more if its allocation had not been distorted by trade regulation. But, of course, this argument only holds on the assumption of full employment, at least of capital. Smith did, in fact, make this assumption, as the passage indicates. He warned against the distortions that might arise from the 'clamorous importunity of vested interests' and asserted that:

> every system which endeavours, either, by extraordinary encouragements, to draw towards a particular species of industry a greater share of the capital of the society than what would naturally go to it; or, by extraordinary restraints, to force from a particular species of industry some share of the capital which would otherwise be employed in it; is in reality subversive of the great purpose which it means to promote ... and diminishes, instead of increasing, the real value of the annual produce of its land and labour.[10]

Departures from the free-market outcome need to be examined and justified on grounds of overriding national interest. Thus, he rejects the 'infant industry argument' for protection, but upholds the defence (national security) argument. He allows the continuation of the Navigation Acts and subsidies to defence-related industries (e.g. sailcloth and gunpowder). He advocates free trade in its unilateral form (apart from the special treatment of defence), but makes reservations for the use of retaliatory tariffs as a bargaining counter in trade negotiations. He grants that moderate duties may have to be retained for revenue purposes; on this score the export duty on British wool is justified, even though it has the effect of giving a competitive edge to the domestic textile industry. He recognises, in the case of a domestic industry subject to particularly heavy excise taxation on its product that it would be fair to levy a 'compensating' duty on competing imports so as to equalise the conditions of competition;[11] but the 'countervailing' duty should not be so high as to confer protection on competing home production, neither should this special treatment be extended to other cases of alleged unfair treatment *vis-à-vis* foreign competitors. In other words, Smith wanted to warn against the use of this argument as a facile justification for tariffs to offset the general disabilities from which a country's industry might be said to suffer. Apart from these legitimate exceptions, all protective devices served only to promote the interests of a selfish minority at the expense of the whole community; this included the system of corn duties and bounties, known as the Corn Laws.

He was too much of a practical man to be rushed into a precipitous removal of import duties which he knew would spell ruin for many merchants and manufacturers who had invested skills and capital in formerly prosperous trades. Tariffs must be reduced gradually, he cautioned, so as to give time for domestic traders to make the necessary adjustments. He urged caution in the withdrawal of protection, especially in the case of trades employing 'a great multitude of hands', but was optimistic about the prospects for the reallocation of resources resulting from reform. He pointed to the relative ease with which large numbers of disbanded soldiers (100 000 of them) were redeployed after the Seven Years War and expressed the belief that it was certainly easier 'to change the direction of industry from one sort of labour to another, than to turn idleness and dissipation to any'.[12] Full employment of labour could be maintained after protection was removed if the institutional barriers to free mobility were removed (i.e. corporate privileges and the statute of apprentices).

Like many thinkers of the Enlightenment, Smith believed that commercial rivalry (fostered by the false maxims of mercantilism) was at the root of the wars between England and France during the eighteenth-century. He repudiated the 'malignant jealousy and envy' between nations as a foundation of international economic relations:

> France and England may each of them have some reason to dread the increase of the naval and military power of the other; but for either of them to envy the internal happiness and prosperity of the other, the cultivation of its lands, the advancement of its manufacturers, the increase of its commerce, the security and number of its ports and harbours, its proficiency in all the liberal arts and sciences, is surely beneath the dignity of two such great nations. These are the real improvements of the world we live in. Mankind are benefitted, human nature is ennobled by them.[13]

A reform of foreign economic policy along free-trade lines would be a step in the right direction towards a more harmonious and peaceful world. At the same time he was not a blinkered idealist on the prospect for free trade, even in his own country. Thus he wrote: 'To expect, indeed, that the freedom of trade should ever be entirely restored in Great Britain is as absurd as to expect that an Oceana or Utopia should ever be established in it.'[14]

On the balance-of-payments adjustment process Smith did not have much to say, despite the fact that he was quite familiar with Hume's work. He contented himself with a perfunctory statement of the price-specie-flow mechanism and the natural distribution of specie hypothesis, but the emphasis throughout is on the role of offsetting specie and/ or commodity flows. He played down the role of divergent price-level movements in the equilibrating process.[15] What he seems to have in mind is a 'cash-balance' type mechanism operating in a world where purchasing-power parity and the 'law of one price' prevail. According to Smith, excess money supply causes the 'channels of circulation' to 'overflow' in the form of specie to pay for increased import purchases as domestic residents adjust to the excess supply of money without causing divergent price-level movements as required by a Humean-type adjustment mechanism. With a common price-level in all countries determined by the supply and demand for money in the world as a whole, payments adjustments must come from changing national money holdings (i.e. changes in real expenditures), and it is these adjustments that cause inflows and outflows of specie that alter the balance of payments of the trading countries.

However, it has been claimed that Smith did, in fact, state the adjustment process in terms of price-level changes and that he did not neglect the implications of domestic inflation, as Viner believed.[16] But his discussion on this aspect of the matter centred on disequilibria in the bullion market and did not directly relate to the gold price of commodities. Before jumping to the conclusion that Smith must therefore have rejected the quantity theory of money, as Angell did: 'Smith adopts what seems to be the exact antithesis of the quantity theory view'[17] we must remember that Smith was referring to monetary equilibrium in a closed economy. Humphrey and Keleher observe that 'in discussions relating to the closed economy he [Smith] explicitly adopted a quantity theory view'.[18] Apparently Smith was involved in some inconsistency in his treatment of the equilibrating mechanisms. This probably resulted from the following two suppositions: (a) that Smith realised that the Humean doctrine would have conflicted with other aspects of his monetary theory,[19] and (b) he therefore preferred to avoid the issue rather than engage in a public controversy with his friend.[20]

In the event, however, Smith's analysis which stressed money-stock adjustment as the determinant of spending, trade balance and the direction and volume of international money (specie) flows together with the inference that this process would continue until the equilibrium international distribution of specie was achieved anticipated to a remarkable degree the modern monetary theory of the balance of payments, as Bloomfield noted.[21] In order to rationalise Smith's position fully, however, says T. Wilson, it is necessary to make additional special assumptions such as: (a) no inflation elsewhere in the world, (b) a regime of fixed exchange rates, and (c) the absence of non-tradable goods.[22] But Smith assumed that the foreign exchanges were fixed and that paper currencies were fully convertible into gold. As for the existence of non-traded goods, this was not damaging for Smith's theory so long as there existed a high degree of substitutability between traded and non-traded goods in consumption and production. Equally, inflation in the rest of the world poses no special problem, as this implies the obverse of adjustments that follow from domestic inflation. Stigler's opinion is not that Smith's theory is erroneous, but that it represents 'a retrogression from the generality and predictive power of the monetary theory in Hume's essays'.[23]

RICARDO AND THE DEVELOPMENT OF COMPARATIVE ADVANTAGE

Smith's case for free trade was merely an application of the principle of specialisation and division of labour on a global scale. It was firmly grounded on the 'eighteenth-century rule' concerning the mutual beneficiality of international exchange when each country has an absolute advantage in the production of one or more commodities. Each country gains by specialising in commodities where (with the same quantity of productive resources) a larger output than any rival can be produced.

This was a sound common-sense argument for the free movement of goods across international frontiers. But it offered no guidance for the extreme, though no less interesting and realistic case of a relatively 'backward' country having no lines of production where it is manifestly efficient relative to the rest of the world. What happens when one country is more efficient in the production of *all* commodities, i.e. it can produce all goods in greater amounts with the same resources as compared with its trading partner? Is there any basis for mutually beneficial trade here? Would not trade cease under these circumstances since the backward country would take steps to insulate itself against ruinous competition from its more efficient neighbour?

Smith's analysis was incapable of dealing with the kind of situation indicated by this question. The answer was provided by his early successors in the British classical school in terms of the principle of comparative advantage. David Ricardo, James Mill and Robert Torrens extended Smith's theorising and produced a more general and precise formulation of profitable international trade by showing that a country can gain from trade even if it has no absolute real cost advantage in the production of any commodity. The demonstration runs in terms of a world of two countries, each being capable of producing two commodities using only one factor of production, labour, which is assumed to be completely immobile between the two countries but completely mobile within each country. Thus in each country the costs (and prices or exchange ratios) of both commodities are determined by their relative labour content. The law of comparative costs can be illustrated by adopting Ricardo's example as in Table 4.1:[24]

Table 4.1 Labour requirements per unit of output

	Cloth	*Wine*
England	100	120
Portugal	90	80

According to the data in Table 4.1 Portugal enjoys an absolute advantage in the production of both goods, since it can produce cloth and wine with less amounts of labour than England. Although Portugal is more efficient than England in the production of both goods the extent of Portugal's superiority is greater in wine production since $90/100 > 80/120$. That is, the cost ratio for cloth is greater than the cost ratio for wine in Portugal compared with England. Thus the cost of producing cloth in Portugal is 90 per cent of the cost in England; but for wine production, Portugal's costs are only 67 per cent of England's. Portugal thus has a comparative advantage in producing wine and a comparative cost *disadvantage* in the production of cloth. England has an *absolute* disadvantage in the production of both cloth and wine because $100 > 90$ and $120 > 80$. However, England's disadvantage is *smaller* in the production of cloth than in the production of wine, since 100/90 < 120/80. It costs England approximately 1.1 times as much to make cloth but 1.5 times as much to make wine as Portugal. Thus, it can be said, England has a *comparative advantage* in the production of cloth and a *comparative disadvantage* in the production of wine. Comparative advantage, as opposed to absolute advantage is a *relative* term. Once one country's comparative advantage is identified, the other country's comparative advantage is logically determined. Thus the inequality used to determine England's comparative advantage, 120/80 > 100/90 is mathematically equivalent to the inequality 90/100 > 80/120, which is used to determine Portugal's comparative advantage – since England's cost ratios are simply the inverse of Portugal's cost ratios. Notice also that the inequality expressing Portugal's comparative advantage in wine can be stated either as 90/100 > 80/120 or equivalently 90/80 > 100/120, i.e. it does not matter whether we compare the cost ratios of the different commodities within the same countries or the cost ratios of the same commodities in the different countries.

Such then is the basis of trade which, under these cost conditions, suggest the possibility of gains in efficiency from specialisation rather than national self-sufficiency. As long as the internal cost ratios differ between countries (i.e. whenever the *relative* ability to produce goods differs between countries) specialisation by each country in the commodity in which it has a comparative advantage can increase aggregate world output from the same quantum of labour resources. Thus if England devotes her entire labour supply to the production of cloth and Portugal puts her labour wholly into wine production, the world output of cloth increases from 2 to 2.2 units and that of wine from 2 to 2.125 units. A real goods gain thus materialises from international division of labour which through international exchange can ultimately (or potentially) result in more consumption for both England and Portugal. The extent of the increase in consumption each country obtains after trade depends on the terms of trade or international exchange ratio between the two goods. It is obvious that both countries benefit if each can trade at the pre-trade price ratio prevailing in the other country. Ignoring transport costs, the equilibrium terms of trade must lie somewhere between the two countries comparative cost ratios, 90/80 and 100/120. Suppose, like Ricardo, an equilibrium terms of trade of 1:1. Given the opportunity to trade at this international price ratio, each country (using the same amount of labour) can increase its consumption of at least one commodity without decreasing its consumption of the other commodity through specialisation and exchange.

Thus, if out of her specialised output of 2.125 units of wine Portugal should export 1.125 units to England in exchange for 1.125 units of cloth, the Portuguese would end up with the same amount of wine but a larger amount of cloth compared to the no-trade situation. England is equally better off from trade since upon specialisation trade with Portugal allows her to consume 1.075 units of cloth and 1.125 units of wine – in this case larger amounts of both commodities compared to autarchy.

This is a statement of the principle of comparative advantage – the core of the classical theory of international trade. It has a clear hortatory or persuasive message: free trade, like honesty, is the best policy. With international specialisation, free trade (a) allows each country to consume at least as much of each good as before specialisation or (b) minimises the real cost (in terms of labour time) of obtaining a given income or quantum of consumption for the world as a whole; or what amounts to the same thing, maximises the aggregate level of real income (in terms of a given price ratio) obtainable from a given (full employment) utilisation of labour resources.

Ricardo believed in the general validity of the principle of comparative costs: the division of labour applies as much to individuals as to nations:

> Two men can both make shoes and hats, and one is superior to the other in both employments; but in making hats, he can only exceed his competitor by 1/5 (or 20%), and in making shoes he can excel him by 1/3 (or 33⅓%). Will it not be for the interest of both that the superior man should employ himself exclusively in making shoes, and the inferior man in making hats?[25]

In both cases the results of specialisation and exchange are the same: a saving of labour to both parties. Thus Portugal might find it advantageous to exchange her wine for English cloth, although she may be able to produce those cloths cheaper herself. The principle, moreover, rationalises the mutual beneficiality of free international trade regardless of country sizes, degrees of affluence, absolute levels of economic efficiency or stages of economic development. The only thing that matters is a difference in the relative costs of production in the absence of trade. The hard-headed Ricardo was even moved to echo the sentiments of the eighteenth-century thinkers that were to be repeated later by Cobden and Bright when he declared that international economic relations based on the observance of the law of comparative costs binds together, by one common tie of interest and intercourse, the universal society of nations throughout the civilised world. It is this principle which determines that wine shall be made in France and Portugal, that corn shall be grown in America and Poland, and that hardware and other goods shall be manufactured in England.[26]

The welfare or 'normative' orientation of the early statement of the principle of comparative advantage is well-known – Viner emphasised this often enough. The principle was not meant to explain the forces determining the actual pattern of international specialisation, but rather to demonstrate how countries could gain from such specialisation and exchange. Implicit in the early accounts there were, of course, vague suggestions concerning the sources of comparative advantage, e.g. in Ricardo it was 'climatic' differences and factors connected with location and 'other natural and artificial advantages'. But the arithmetical model which contained these hints was merely an ingenious vehicle for conveying the free-trade policy recommendation. Indeed, the very implausibility of the particular example chosen to illustrate the principle – Portugal (*circa* 1817) portrayed as technologically more advanced and efficient than England – only served to highlight the economic logic of the argument. The idea of comparative cost was precisely to point out that even the least-efficient, highest-cost country in the world could benefit from trade. That every country has, by definition, a comparative advantage is an important point in the argument.

The effect of this principle was to forestall protectionist arguments based on the fear that a more efficient trading rival would be in a position to undersell the producers of one's country in every line of production; or, conversely, from the standpoint of the producers and workers in the rich advanced country, the fear that they would be unable to withstand competition from 'cheap foreign labour' without suffering business bankruptcies and a reduction of wage levels. Unlike some other classical propositions (e.g. the wages fund doctrine) the law of comparative cost has stood the test of time remarkably well. It is, in fact, one of the few propositions in economics that is both true and non-trivial – in the formal logic sense. It has been hailed as one of the truly great discoveries of economic analysis – a triumph of economic logic, perhaps even more significant than the famous law of diminishing returns. For whereas diminishing returns are a phenomenon observable in the physical world and intuitively fairly obvious, comparative cost is not.

The latter requires not only reflection, but some economic sophistication as well. Perhaps it is true today, as some experts ruefully complain, that it cannot be assumed that the principle is fully understood by businessmen or even, for that matter, by all those charged with the conduct of international trade negotiations. To most people, that is, 'industries that have a comparative advantage' usually signify 'industries whose cost compare favourably with the cost of imports', i.e. industries that can produce goods that are cheaper than the equivalent imports. However, 'competitive advantage' is not the same thing as comparative advantage.

Before proceeding to an examination of the development of the classical trade model, it is of some interest to consider the question of the origins of the law of comparative advantage. To whom do we owe the discovery of this principle? – David Ricardo, Robert Torrens or James Mill? It is less common now than it used to be to credit Ricardo with the first precise statement of the principle. From Viner's writings, students of international economics became aware of Torrens's contribution to trade theory generally and his anticipation of the law of comparative advantage in particular.

Torrens's priority has been acknowledged by other scholars besides Viner, including Seligman, J. Hollander, Schumpeter, and, more recently, by the late Lord Robbins in his 1958 study of Torrens.[27] Some writers doubted, however, whether Torrens really understood the implications of the principle, or that what he wrote prior to 1817 (when Ricardo published his *Principles*) constitutes a full and satisfactory statement of the same. Torrens's claim to priority rests on his two publications, *The Economists Refuted* (1808) and the first edition of *An Essay on the External Corn Trade* (1815).[28] In the earlier work, however, Torrens merely enunciated the eighteenth-century rule on the gains from trade in terms of absolute advantage. So while Torrens succeeded in providing a perfectly satisfactory argument for the gains from trade, the argument was not based on comparative advantage since, as Chipman pointed out, Torrens's example was a comparison of the domestic cost ratio (in one country) with the international price ratio. He did not compare the cost ratios between two countries.[29] In *An Essay on the External Corn Trade* (1815) Torrens did succeed, after twice repeating the eighteenth-century rule, in expressing the essence of the law of comparative advantage in a passage which suggested that England would find it advantageous to specialise in, and export manufactures in exchange for, corn, even though England might have an absolute advantage in agriculture:

If England should have acquired such a degree of skill in manufactures, that, with any given portion of her capital, she could prepare a quantity of cloth, for which the Polish cultivator would give a greater quantity of corn, than she England could, with the same portion of capital, raise from her own soil, then, tracts of her territory, though they should be equal, nay, even though they should be superior, to the lands in Poland, will be neglected; and a part of her supply of corn will be imported from that country.[30]

'But', says Lord Robbins, 'as pure analysis it still lacks the final emphasis upon the comparison of ratios which is the ultimate essence of this principle.'[31]

This analytical detail Torrens finally added in 1827 (in the fourth edition of *External Corn Trade*). Its inclusion in the later passage strengthened the logic of the argument and made it, in Robbins's view the most impressive account of the new doctrine ever to be published before Taussig (the early years of this century).

Ricardo's contribution appeared in 1817 when his *Principles* was published, but this was after Torrens had enunciated the 'essence' of the doctrine. Ricardo's first major work, *The Essay on Profits*, appeared coincidentally on the very day that Torrens's book came out – 24 February 1815.[32] Yet there was no hint of the new doctrine, even though his conclusion pointed to the advantage of free trade in corn. In 1815 Ricardo based his case for free trade on the gains stemming from the exploitation of *absolute* advantage. The nearest he came (at that time) to the idea of *comparative* advantage was in a passage where he recognised the advantage of a withdrawal of capital from marginal land (subject to rapidly diminishing returns) and its transfer to manufacturing, the products of which could be exchanged for imported corn. In point of time, therefore, Torrens was 'first in the field'.[33]

But two years later Ricardo achieved what Samuelson called his 'greatest tour de force' with the famous three-paragraph demonstration of comparative advantage in chapter 7 of the *Principles*, complete with the 'four magic numbers that constitute the core of the doctrine'.[34]

Yet the illustration was not the focus of the chapter, nor was it an integral part of his thinking on foreign trade which was concerned with the role free trade in corn could play in averting diminishing returns and its consequences. Sir John Hicks noted: 'Though Ricardo ... stated the "law of comparative cost" it appears no more than incidentally in a chapter ... which is mainly devoted to other matters. ...'[35]

In fact Ricardo's discussion of the barter (as distinct from the monetary) theory of trade is extremely brief and he provides just the bare essentials of the doctrine. Surprisingly for a master analyst that Ricardo was, the page-long discussion is carelessly worded, the logic is ambiguous and conclusions are arrived at which do not immediately follow from the preceding arguments. Thus there are two *non sequiturs* in the first two paragraphs where the conclusion is reached that England should export cloth and Portugal wine – the analysis leading to this conclusion is made in later passages.[36] Also his account of the rationale for making a comparison of relative cost ratios in two countries is weak and unimpressive; the logic, while implicit in his particular example is not explicitly developed and defended. This has led some writers to question whether Ricardo truly understood the doctrine, just as others have queried Torrens's comprehension of it. Perhaps Ricardo did not 'truly understand' the doctrine because he was not an independent discoverer of it. It has been suggested, for instance, that Ricardo borrowed the idea from Torrens since he was apparently much impressed with the latter's *Essay on the External Corn Trade*. This has not been readily accepted by others. Hollander believes it 'unlikely that Ricardo [consciously] derived any benefit from the brief allusion in [Torrens's] *Essay*'. Also, although Torrens continued to press the logic of comparative cost in a vigorous manner, he 'often merely repeated what Ricardo and Mill had already published'.[37] Recently William O. Thweatt in a fresh attempt to unravel the mystery of the origins of comparative advantage traced the doctrine to James Mill.[38] Mill's involvement with the comparative advantage concept began about the same time as that of Torrens's. Both writers independently developed the idea as part of their general attack on a certain conception of Britain's economic destiny advocated by publicists like William Spence and William Cobbett. The physiocratic and underconsumptionist views represented by Spence and Cobbett – and to some extent by Malthus – entertained visions of a self-sufficient, agrarian England. This provoked replies from Mill (*Commerce Defended*, 1808) and Torrens (*The Economists Refuted*). Both writers invoked the eighteenth-century rule regarding the gains from trade, but thereafter Mill's role was crucial for the development of the comparative cost doctrine. In Thweatt's view Mill set the lead; the others followed. Mill influenced Ricardo and was responsible for the insertion of the comparative-cost example in the latter's *Principles*. Shortly afterwards Mill published articles containing the comparison of cost ratios long before Torrens came out with his own extended version of the doctrine in the fourth edition of his *Essay*. There is no doubt that Mill wanted to establish an economic orthodoxy based on what he considered 'sound principles' of political economy. He saw himself as its ideological guardian, and sought canonical status for the 'approved' doctrines of the new social science. In his role of 'taskmaster and press agent' for Ricardo he placed his full weight behind the Ricardian version of political economy. It is therefore understandable why Mill should have been eager to see incorporated in the book bearing the 'true message' (Ricardo's *Principles*) the important doctrine of comparative advantage which, for him, revealed a great truth. Professional opinion, on the whole, seems to have been persuaded by this account of how comparative advantage came to be integrated into classical political economy. However, Samuel Hollander remains unconvinced. His reading of the evidence suggests, to the contrary, that Mill himself 'explicitly attributed the comparative-cost principle to Ricardo'; and continues, 'there certainly seems to be no convincing evidence that Ricardo was in any way dependent on James Mill'.[39] Notice, however, that on Thweatt's own interpretation of the evidence Torrens still has priority for being the first in print with an analytical explanation of the gains from trade that went beyond the eighteenth-century rule.

Perhaps what we have here is simply a case of multiple discovery, evidently fairly common in science. Like the other famous multiple discovery made about this time – diminishing returns – it emerged simultaneously in the minds of different thinkers under the pressure of relentless debate over urgent policy matters. Thus Mill, Torrens and Ricardo, in contact with each other, their minds exercised over the Corn Laws issue and having before them the eighteenth-century rule, came up with essentially the same concept which they each articulated and assessed in their own fashion and for their own purposes (e.g. polemical, ideological or theoretical).

THE LABOUR THEORY OF VALUE AND RICARDO'S TRADE MODEL

Whether at the instigation of James Mill or not, the insertion of the comparative advantage principle in Ricardo's chapter on foreign trade meant that it was through Ricardo and not Torrens that the principle came to be recognised as one of the sound and original doctrines of the early classical school. 'As so often happens in the history of thought', writes Samuelson, referring to the rival claims of Ricardo and Torrens 'the greater name drives out the lesser one'.[40] Torrens's writings on economics never amounted to a systematic, consistent whole. He sometimes reverted to absolute advantage examples in his discussions of trade policy which were often tinged with mercantilist notions and appeals to nationalism and imperial grandeur.

If James Mill had a hand in it, the choice of Ricardo as a vehicle for conveying the doctrine was therefore eminently well-judged. In another sense the choice was justified, for when later much of Ricardo's system was abandoned the comparative cost principle was retained. James Mill himself enhanced the orthodox status of the principle in his *Elements of Political Economy* 'the first textbook in economics'[41] which contained 'a marvellously lucid and succinct early statement of the distinction between absolute and comparative advantage'.[42]

Yet it was from John Stuart Mill with his 'theory of international values' that later economists came to a full understanding and appreciation of the centrality of comparative cost in international trade theory. But because the younger Mill, out of 'filial respect' as Schumpeter put it, played down his own achievement and praised Ricardo for his 'more accurate analysis of the nature of the advantage which nations derive from a mutual interchange of their productions',[43] Ricardo's name became closely associated with comparative costs.

Today, beginning students in international economics come to an understanding of comparative advantage through Ricardo's example as we have just done and the first empirical test ever done on the pure theory of trade was explicitly designed to verify the Ricardian theory of the pattern of trade.

Returning now to the classical trade model, developments after Ricardo were mainly concerned with the elaboration and refinement of its logical structure. Gaps were filled in the original argument and the assumptions underlying the model were explicitly stated. Some of these assumptions were dropped and others generalised without substantially altering the logic or conclusions of the pioneers.

Let us briefly list Ricardo's assumptions:

1. Two commodities, two countries. Each commodity can be produced in both countries.
2. The labour theory of values applies.
3. Production takes place under constant cost conditions.
4. Transport costs are zero both internally and internationally.

5. Labour is perfectly mobile within each country and completely immobile internationally. Perfect competition prevails in all markets.
6. Multilateral convertibility prevails and a specie-flow mechanism exists which ensures that the value of imports is equal to the value of exports for each country. Thus trade takes place effectively on a barter basis.
7. Maximization of aggregate world real income is the desired objective; national gains are determined by the terms of trade.

In his demonstration of the comparative-cost principle, an exercise which is essentially one of comparative statics, Ricardo did assume additionally: no change in the distribution of incomes and no technical change and economic development in the two countries. But he relaxed these extra assumptions when dealing with matters arising from trade and growth. In fact, Ricardo used two trade models which he never managed to integrate: the static comparative-cost theory and a dynamic long-run model. The former model (which Ricardo only ever used once) was concerned with the immediate static gains from a more efficient international allocation of resources while the latter was concerned with the more extensively discussed dynamic gains from trade and, in particular, was applied in the analysis of the effects on the British economy of the repeal of the Corn Laws. Ricardo's trade-growth model will be discussed later.

The late Joan Robinson, a long-time critic of the neoclassical theory of trade, observed a decade ago that 'the development of the theory (of international trade), to this day, runs in the narrow channel that was appropriate to Ricardo's demonstration of the principle of comparative advantage'[44] – something she deplored. What she was referring to was the wide gap that existed between orthodox theory and actual problems of the world economy which she traced to the restrictive and often unrealistic assumptions inherited from the classical past.

At the time when the classical theory was formulated, however, it was a significant breakthrough in the analysis of foreign trade simply because it was grounded in a serviceable theory of value. From the classical and neoclassical perspective, the shortcomings of the mercantilist conception of foreign trade stemmed from their (i.e. the mercantilists') failure to articulate an adequate theory of value or price theory. That is, the earliest economists had no clearly worked out idea of a price system's role in the allocation of resources. And since trade theory is merely one aspect of general allocation theory, i.e. the efficient deployment and use of resources on a global scale, this explains why the microeconomics of trade proved elusive for the mercantilists. Thus Stigler, in his Nobel Lecture, asserted: 'Without a theory of value the economist can have no theory of international trade.'[45] W. R. Allen said exactly the same thing: 'Without price theory, there can be no theory of international trade.'[46] But the contention still remains to be substantiated that mercantilist thought was devoid of valid insights into allocative mechanisms – witness the writings of Petty, Cantillon and before them, the Salamanca jurists. Their value theory was rudimentary (often 'macro' in nature), but they certainly had one which they applied to problem-areas that concerned them – foreign exchange, money and interest. Few of the seventeenth century writers 'after all, were directly concerned to formulate a *theory* of economic activity'.[47]

A regulated foreign trade marked by the absence of competition between foreign and domestic sources of supply was a facet of economic activity that did not encourage speculation about the role of allocative mechanisms. Only later, when free trade became an issue – when economic reality was transformed by dramatic technological and social changes – did the question of how resources should be allocated and valued at the international level, i.e. what should be produced and in what quantities present itself as one requiring economic analysis for an answer.

Adam Smith had a common-sense theory of the role of the relative prices of commodities – the cost of production or 'adding-up' theory. He also understood the workings of the price mechanism and its role in the allocation of resources – insights which led him to provide an answer to the above question and the advocacy of free trade. Yet he failed to advance trade theory beyond the concept of absolute advantage.

Ricardo developed his own version of the labour theory of value in connection with the Corn Law controversy and more precisely in response to what he regarded as the unsatisfactory (mistaken) views of Adam Smith on that subject; and Ricardo grounded his trade model in his labour theory of value. It is interesting to note that 'the only place where Ricardo addressed himself specifically to the allocation problem was in the chapter on foreign trade' and that 'here ... he saw further and deeper than Adam Smith'.[48]

Is this, then, confirmation of the assertion: no price theory, no trade theory? If so, was it further the case that both price theory and trade theory originated in and were motivated by the same cluster of circumstances, intellectual challenges and ideological preconceptions that mark the evolution of social thought?

It is as easy to share Mark Blaug's doubt 'whether Ricardo would have developed his theory of international trade without a strong animus against the landed classes' as it is to agree with the sequel to the sentence 'but this theory survives the removal of his prejudices'.[49]

The role of the ideological element cannot be denied; and if we are convinced of the Millian influence upon Ricardo then the critic who declares that 'the international division of labour associated with the law of comparative advantage has never been "natural" but was manufactured by the very British industrial interests and their overseas allies who then enshrined this division as a supposed natural law'[50] cannot be lightly dismissed as a prejudiced rhetorician. The attitude to foreign trade encapsulated in the principle of comparative costs sprung not only from developments in economic theory but reflected a 'shared vision' among political economists of Britain's economic future. It so happened that this coincided with the interests of the new and rising industrial bourgeoisie. As one writer puts it: 'Ricardo's economics were affected by and eminently suited to an analysis of the issues and problems of early-nineteenth-century British economy' and that Ricardo's advocacy of a free-trade policy 'clearly represents a fusion of the interests of the commercial and industrial bourgeoisie'.

Joan Robinson puts it bluntly: 'When Ricardo set out the case against protection, he was supporting British economic interests.'[51] Fernand Braudel, the eminent French historian, confesses that simple-minded tautologies such as 'growth breeds more growth' or 'a poor country is poor because it is poor' make more sense to him than 'the so-called "irrefutable" pseudo-theorem of David Ricardo'. He finds the picture too reassuring, since 'there is an unasked question here: when did the division of tasks (which Ricardo assumed in 1817 to be part of the natural order) begin and why?'[52] Braudel goes on to argue, drawing on historical examples, that the nineteenth-century distribution of tasks among nations was not the result of natural and spontaneous tendencies or the operation of a set of supra-historical laws, but was the outcome of mercantilist and colonial policies based on the unequal distribution of power among nations. The world division of labour was not arrived at through agreement among equal partners and subject to review, but rather was determined by power politics and other long-standing realities which developed in an irreversible direction. Some countries ended up as primary producers, others continued and advanced further in secondary and tertiary sectors.

According to Ricardo, the ratio in which commodities are exchanged for each other depends on the relative amounts of labour they embody, i.e. prices of goods are determined by their labour content. Actually, Ricardo conceived of production as taking place with inputs of capital and labour combined in fixed proportions, the units of which are qualitatively homogeneous. Changes in either the profit-rate or wage-rate can cause changes in relative prices which diverge over time from the corresponding changes in ratios of embodied labour. Ricardo believed, however, that the magnitude of these divergences were small; and, because of this, Ricardo has been credited with belief in a '93 per cent labour theory of value'.[53] There are, of course, well-known difficulties with the labour theory as a theory of relative prices. Taken together, the assumptions under which the theory is valid amount to a radical oversimplification of reality. Thus labour is not the only factor of production, neither is it homogeneous. In addition there are problems with the time phasing of production and questions about durability and turnover of capital as well as rates of return. For instance, with a positive rate of interest, the average cost of a commodity (and hence its price) would be influenced not merely by the amount of labour involved, but also by the length of time involved in its production. The theory can survive these complications only if, among other things, it can be further assumed (a) that the proportions in which labour is combined with other factors is the same in all industries, or what Marx referred to as 'equal organic composition of capital', and (b) fixed capital is of equal durability in all lines of production and production processes are such that all commodities require the same time to be brought to market.

Ricardo was fully aware of these complications, and clearly recognised the assumptions under which the theory was valid. For Ricardo the labour theory was primarily an explanation of *changes* in relative prices over time and the consequences of these for the distribution of income. This led him into the search for an 'invariable measure of value' (absolute value). For want of a better alternative, he settled on embodied labour and concluded (as we have already indicated) that changes in long-run exchange values corresponded closely with changes in the labour content of commodities.

At any rate, with fixed labour requirements per unit of output, production takes place at constant costs – in modern parlance, the production possibility curve between two commodities is a downward-sloping straight line indicating a constant rate of transformation. Given the fixed coefficients of production, relative prices are technologically determined by the invariant labour productivities. Under these conditions it follows that the supply curves for both commodities are horizontal at the given real-wage level; hence, demand has no role in the determination of relative prices in the closed economy.

This proportionality relationship between prices and labour values in each country ceases to hold once the economies are opened to trade. Ricardo writes: 'The same rule which regulates the relative value of commodities in one country does not regulate the relative value of the commodities exchanged between two or more countries.'[54]

Thus, while according to the law of value, the labour of 100 Englishmen cannot be exchanged for the labour of 80 Englishmen, through international trade England would gladly give up the produce of the labour of 100 men for the produce of 80 foreign labour.[55]

The need for a separate theory of international trade therefore arises because the theory of value appropriate to a closed economy is inadequate to explain values in international trade. This separate treatment of domestic and international trade did not cause Ricardo (as it did later economists) to question the general validity of the labour theory of value. He attributed the difference to the international immobility of capital and labour: 'The difference in this respect, between a single country and many, is easily accounted for, by considering the difficulty with which capital moves from one country to another, to seek a more profitable employment, and the activity with which it invariably passes from one province to another in the same country.'[56]

This assumption implied that the rate of profit, although uniform throughout a given country, could vary as between countries. In addition, because of barriers to international migration, wage differentials caused by productivity differences could persist indefinitely. Even assuming uniform capital–labour ratios in each country, commodities would no longer exchange in proportion to relative labour inputs. The sharing of comparative advantages is thus, for Ricardo, a means of overcoming the segmentation of national markets caused by factor immobilities. Trade in commodities becomes a substitute for the international mobility of labour and capital. It increases 'the mass of commodities, and therefore the sum of enjoyments' in each of the trading countries.[57]

In Ricardo's trade model international prices or the terms of trade are left largely unexplained. He admits that the general rule of cost-price based on the labour theory of value breaks down in the context of foreign trade. This led others to conclude that, however useful the labour theory of value might be as an explanation of domestic price ratios, it could not offer an explanation for international values. A 'subjective' theory of value was therefore necessary to determine relative prices between the two countries' embodied labour ratios. What is recognised here is that value in exchange in international trade is determined not only by production costs (whether limited to labour or not), but also by demand.

The labour theory of value focused attention on supply or the cost side of trade and neglected the role of demand. This did not matter in the analysis of domestic trade, for by the constant-cost and single-factor assumption, domestic prices are determined solely by supply. But if trade is to be generated and neither country is sufficiently 'small' to have its terms of trade determined by the cost ratio of the other, then conditions of demand have to be brought in to fix the ratio of international exchange. The fact is that (a) the actual pattern of specialisation and (b) the division of the gains from trade depend on the equilibrium terms of trade. For instance, the Ricardian model implies complete specialisation by each country in consequence of the assumption of constant-cost conditions. In this case the division of the benefit between them depends solely on the conditions of demand and relative prices are no longer governed by costs of production.

This point is illustrated in modern textbooks through the construction of a world production-possibilities frontier for the constant-costs case.[58] Two countries' production-possibility frontiers are joined together in one diagram. Except for the case of equal-opportunity costs the world frontier so derived is not a straight line, but consists of two straight-line (linear) segments kinked at a specific point. At this point each country specialises completely in producing the commodity in which it has a comparative advantage and world production is also indicated by this vertex point. But at this 'Ricardian point' the slope of the world production-possibilities frontier (and hence the equilibrium terms of trade) is indeterminate. The slope at this point can range from the slope of the first country's production-possibility curve to that of the second country's production frontier as world prices vary parametrically, while remaining common to both countries. The pattern of world demand for the two commodities – usually represented by a world indifference curve – is then needed to determine the equilibrium terms of trade within the range spanned by the production-possibility curves (i.e. cost ratios) of the two countries.

Conditions of world demand can be such that the terms of trade settles at the cost ratio of one of the countries. In such a case partial specialisation results with that country producing both commodities and the other country completely specialised. Thus, in the Ricardian example, if England consumes more wine than Portugal can supply to the English market then world prices will have to reflect English costs so that some English wine production would also take place. Portugal then gains on the terms of trade in respect of all her imports. The pattern of specialisation and trade is reversed if Portugal becomes the country producing both commodities.

The Ricardian result is easily generalized for the case of many countries and two commodities, say X and Y. In this case, we have a 'chain of comparative advantage' determined by inter-country differences in labour-cost ratios (technological differences). The role of demand here is to break the chain and separate the X-exporters from the Y-exporters.

It is obvious, then, that both supply and demand differences contribute to the relationship between pre-trade commodity–price ratios and the equilibrium terms of trade – hence to the pattern of trade. The recognition of the role of demand led to the first break with the labour theory of value. Although he was not the first to take demand conditions into account, John Stuart Mill provides an explicit demonstration of international equilibrium incorporating demand in his account of how 'the inclinations and circumstances of the consumers on both sides' would determine where between the two internal cost ratios the equilibrium terms of trade would lie.[59] Mill's analysis was later developed and given geometric refinement in the offer curves of Edgeworth and Marshall. The development of marginal utility analysis in the 1870s made it an anachronism to work with two theories of value (one for internal and another for external trade) since, as Marshall observed, both blades of the scissors (costs or supply and demand) must cut to determine market-clearing prices whether in domestic or international trade.

Gottfried Haberler later went on to reinterpret the doctrine of comparative costs in opportunity-cost terms. The shift from a labour theory of value to an opportunity-cost theory provided a simpler and more general definition of comparative advantage–more general since it could (unlike the labour theory) handle cases of increasing costs and thereby explain the real-world phenomenon of partial specialisation. But some of the leading trade theorists in the classical tradition (e.g. Taussig and Viner) were reluctant to abandon a 'real cost' approach to international trade related to, but not identical with the classical labour theory – an approach explored earlier by Bastable and Marshall. Viner strenuously defended the classical theory against the charge that it was somehow unsatisfactory because it was cast in terms of an outmoded theory of value. He claims that 'the association of the comparative-cost doctrine with the labour-cost theory of value is a historical accident'. And further, he observes, only Ricardo and James Mill among classical writers on comparative costs were exponents of the labour theory in its strict form.[60]

Despite the shortcomings of the labour theory of value, it served the purpose of bringing out sharply the nature of the international division of labour and the gains from trade. Modern economists employ other definitions of costs to prove exactly what Ricardo did. In Haberler's view the sole purpose of the labour theory of value was to determine the pre-trade price ratios in the two countries. He too claims that Ricardian trade theory is not wedded to a labour theory. The restrictive assumptions of the latter could easily be dispensed with in favour of a more general theory of production 'without having to discard the results obtained from it: these will remain, just as a building remains after the scaffolding, having served its purpose, is removed'.[61]

But this dismantling of the classical gantry of trade theory did not appeal to Viner, mainly on the ground that a real-cost approach was essential for making welfare comparisons. The merit of the classical approach resided in the fact that welfare conclusions followed directly from the analysis of price determination. In this approach imports and exports possess 'real value significance'; for Viner accepts, despite the difficulties involved, the proportionality relationship between real costs and money costs (or market prices). The classical theory then furnishes a simple welfare criterion according to which alternative trade policies (or the gains and losses from free trade) can be assessed. Specifically it shows how, under free-trade conditions a given amount of real income (a given bundle of goods) can potentially be secured by a country at lower real costs.

The labour theory of value was, of course, of fundamental importance in the work of Karl Marx, and writers in the classical Marxian tradition, and the newer Sraffa or neoRicardian theorists continue to use the labour theory in one form or another in their analyses of international trade. Marx, unfortunately, never wrote his projected book on international trade; hence we have no definite statement of his trade theory. The latter has to be pieced together from various comments scattered in his published works. From what he wrote about international value or how the law of value operates in the world market, one gets the impression that his theoretical framework was not very different from the Ricardian theory as modified by Nassau Senior. He did not explicitly reject the concept of comparative advantage. Indeed, he pointed out that, in principle, specialisation according to comparative advantage could be advantageous for backward countries, since such countries 'thereby receive commodities cheaper than they could produce them'.[62] He nevertheless regarded advanced manufacturing countries as 'exploiters' in their trading relations with less-developed countries even when such trade allows both parties to gain. His contention was that poor countries (i.e. countries with low average productivity) gave up more labour in exchange for less of the developed countries' labour – the terms of trade tended to move adversely against agricultural countries. Thus Marx wrote:

> Say, in his notes to Ricardo's book ... makes only one correct remark about foreign trade. Profit can also be made by cheating, one person gaining what the other loses. Loss and gain within a single country cancel each other out. But not so with trade between different countries. And even according to Ricardo's theory, three days of labour of one country can be exchanged against one of another country. ... Here the law of value undergoes essential modification. The relationship between labour days of different countries may be similar to that existing between skilled, complex labour and unskilled, simple labour within a country. In this case, the richer country exploits the poorer one, even where the latter gains by the exchange, as John Stuart Mill explains in his *Some Unsettled Questions*.[63]

Marx postulated that whereas in the domestic market the law of value based on 'socially necessary labour time' rules, in the international market this was not the case:

> The different quantities of commodities of the same kind, produced in different countries in the same working-time, have, therefore, unequal international values, which are expressed in different prices, i.e. in sums of money varying according to international values.[64]

Marx explained this by the use of the concept of the 'average unit of universal labour' as a unit of measurement of a country's average productivity. The average 'intensity of labour' (i.e. labour productivity) varies from country to country. With trade the value of labour is directly related to levels of productivity. But the value of labour (as expressed in monetary terms) in a developed country is higher than its value in a backward, poor country. Thus the transformation of international values into international prices implies the transfer of value (expended labour) from some countries to others. Ricardo would have agreed that inequalities in basic production conditions were the essence of foreign trade; for the source of the gains lay in the discrepancy between local and foreign prices which ultimately reflected international differences in relative labour productivity. But he would not have agreed that this was the source of asymmetric relationships.

In general terms, then, Marx's notion of international value based on some sort of average of national values is not incompatible with the Ricardian principle of comparative advantage. Indeed, the Marxian procedure of ranking countries according to the average productivity of labour in the production of different commodities implies the notion of comparative advantage differences. But the Marxian idea that some countries (underdeveloped countries characterised by low capital intensity and labour productivity) suffer permanent exploitation in their dealings with manufacturing capitalist countries does not correspond with Ricardian reasoning. The underdeveloped country – in fact, every country – gets the equivalent of the labour embodied in its exports, according to the Ricardian principle of comparative advantage. The total gains from trade need not be equally shared, but a net gain still remains for each country. The Marxian notion that a country can simultaneously gain and lose in trade, and also the assumption of exploitation whenever imports do not bring in the equivalent of exported labour certainly challenges the Ricardian hypothesis. Marx's sketchy and unsystematic treatment of foreign trade left scope for the development of widely differing approaches by his followers. One approach which describes exploitation derives from the analysis of capitalist accumulation on a global scale, and stresses the transfer of surplus value from the less-developed countries to the capitalist metropoles. Another approach, which makes use of classical Marxist schemas, further develops the idea of 'unequal exchange'. In the latter type of work exploitation results through a non-equalisation of wages across countries and unchanged patterns of specialised trade, even though profits are equalised internationally.[65] But this is a twentieth-century development, and we must return to Ricardo.

THE GAINS FROM TRADE

Turning now to the results Ricardo derives from his static trade model; these are: (1) Foreign trade increases 'the mass of commodities, and therefore the sum of enjoyments'.[66] (2) The opening of trade or its extension does not increase the rate of profit except where the imported commodities enter the real wage. Foreign trade does not alter the 'value' of the national product.

The first proposition, as we have already indicated, is related to the sharing of comparative advantages and therefore has to do with the welfare consequences or gains from trade. What is involved here is the argument familiar from modern gains-from-trade analysis of the enlargement of consumption possibilities for the same input of labour. Through specialisation and trade a country can consume beyond its production-possibility frontier. The real-income effect produced is the same as if there had been an outward shift in the country's production frontier. Thus, by exploiting gainful trade opportunities England can enjoy more wine with no less cloth than before from its given level of employment. Here, the optimality of free trade is assessed in terms of the maximisation of real income (a given bundle of goods) – each good being weighted by the given world price ratio – from a given input of labour. Equally, we can talk in terms of the minimisation of the real cost of obtaining a given amount of real income. The two concepts of optimality are really equivalent ways of looking at the same thing – at any rate, as long as we are concerned with marginal changes in income or input levels.

There was a rather confusing debate between Ricardo and Malthus on this matter. As we have seen, Ricardo adopted the increase-in-income approach which suggests that the opportunity to trade at relative prices that differ from those in isolation at home must improve domestic real incomes available for domestic consumption – the 'mass of commodities'.

In Malthus's view, the gain from trade consisted of 'the increased value which results from exchanging what is valued less for what is valued more'.[67] Now, this is a perfectly legitimate and satisfactory statement of trade benefits, and one that is compatible with Ricardo's approach. But in an attempt to rebut Ricardo's second proposition mentioned above – foreign trade does not increase domestic value – Malthus misrepresented (or misunderstood) Ricardo's position. He attributed to Ricardo a narrow version of the saving-in-cost approach: 'Mr Ricardo always views foreign trade in the light of means of obtaining cheaper commodities.'[68]

Later, in *Notes on Malthus* Ricardo repeated his increase-in-income criterion: 'The advantage ... to both places is not [that] they have an increase of value, but with the same amount of value they are both able to consume and enjoy an increased quantity of commodities.'[69] Malthus's reformulation of the Ricardian position into the alternative saving-in-cost method posed the interesting question: In what sense are the two welfare criteria equivalent? The issue was raised for the first time in the Ricardo–Malthus debate and was only finally resolved with the invention of the techniques of modern welfare analysis which added greater precision to the concept of the gains from trade. Malthus objected to the saving-in-cost measure – the reduced cost of obtaining imported goods through trade instead of by domestic production – on the ground that this overestimated the gains from trade, e.g. when imported goods (a) could not be produced at home (silk, cotton, indigo) or (b) could be produced only at extremely high costs. In such cases the relevant goods would simply not be imported. More generally the gains from the opportunity to trade cannot be counted as being equivalent to the necessary expansion of labour input if the free-trade bundle of goods is produced domestically.

Malthus's point is that the opening of trade would change relative prices. The country would have more of the imported goods but less of the native commodities. How, then, do we compare the increase with the decrease? Consumers may in fact prefer more of the potential export good if the free-trade equilibrium bundle was produced domestically by an increase in labour input. Since the closed-economy equilibrium combination of goods resulting from an expansion of labour input is preferable in terms of consumer welfare to that produced by free trade, the cost-saving approach would overstate the gains from trade. The correct procedure, therefore, to meet Malthus's criticism is to reckon the saving in cost in terms of the amount of labour needed to produce a closed-economy bundle that is equivalent to the free-trade combination in so far as consumer welfare is concerned.

Having done that there still remains the problem of how to decide whether a given bundle of goods is equivalent or superior to another bundle. A comparison of the quantity index numbers of the two situations will presumably help as would the use of the modern technique of community indifference curves. But in a community not made up of identical individuals some people would be hurt (and others gain) by the opening up of trade. Again, modern welfare analysis suggests ways of dealing with this problem. The classical economists were aware of the welfare question – indeed, it was the paramount issue at stake during the Corn Laws debate. But in a strict sense, since labour is the only factor of production in the classical model trade cannot possibly hurt anyone. Yet the constraints of the model did not blind the classicals to the reality of the income distribution struggle.

This brings us to Ricardo's distributional result. Ricardo writes:

> As the value of all foreign goods is measured by the quantity of the produce of our land and labour, which is given in exchange for them, we should have no greater value, if by the discovery of new markets, we obtained double the quantity of foreign goods in exchange for a given quantity of ours.[70]

And again: 'Foreign trade, then ... has no tendency to raise the profits of stock, unless the commodities imported be of that description on which the wages of labour are expended.'[71]

These propositions follow logically from Ricardo's theory of value and his 'fundamental theorem', i.e. the inverse profit–wage relationship. By value, Ricardo meant the total input of labour in a country and his distributional theorem was that 'profits can be increased only by a fall in wages'. Thus, through international trade, a country may get more use-value but no more labour-value than another. And since the rate of profit depends on the labour-cost of producing the necessary real wage, trade tends to raise the general rate of return only when imports consist of wage goods (especially foodstuffs).

Ricardo thus challenges Smith's suggestion that the diversion of capital from domestic industry consequent upon the opening up of profitable trading opportunities tends to raise the general return on capital. The rate of profit cannot rise, Ricardo holds, because what occurs is merely a change in the composition of final consumers' demand. Smith overlooked the shift in demand to foreign goods which accompanies the deflection of capital from the domestic market, says Ricardo. He argues that since demand for domestic goods is now less, prices at home will not rise; hence higher profits cannot be earned. 'I am of opinion', writes Ricardo, 'that the profits of the favoured trade will speedily subside to the general level.'[72] The implication here is that domestic prices will alter sufficiently to restore equality of the marginal products of capital in all trades and the reallocation of capital will go on until this is accomplished. Ricardo also points out that an expanded money-supply is a *sine qua non* for any general price rise and profit-rate increase arising from any source including the discovery of new markets. It cannot be assumed that the necessary monetary means would automatically be forthcoming. Here, as elsewhere, Ricardo relied on what came to be known later as Say's Law in opposition to Smith's 'competition of capitals' theory.

In an instructive commentary on the Smith–Ricardo differences on foreign trade and the profit rate E. G. West points out that Smith's anticipation of a rise in the profit rate was based on the presumption that capital would be shifted to a controlled foreign trade where capital enjoyed monopoly profits. The reduction in the number of domestic traders would tend to bring about a monopolistic market situation at home which raises the profit rate through a squeeze on the real purchasing power of consumers.[73]

Ricardo considers next the effect on the savings ratio of cheaper imported luxury goods (e.g. wine, silks and velvets). The profit rate will not be directly affected; but to the extent that the importation of such goods increases the purchasing power of profit incomes, it raises the savings capacity of the capitalists. The rate of profit on capital may then be altered through the stimulus to capital accumulation provided by increased savings. He likens the introduction of machines to extensions of foreign trade in so far as the effects on the profit rate and capital accumulation are concerned. Mechanisation which reduces the value of wage-goods tends to raise the rate of profit, saving and the rate of capital accumulation. Similarly, the importation of wage-goods at prices lower than the internal prices have the same effect. On the other hand the introduction of machines which lowers the value of luxury goods and the importation of relatively cheap luxury goods have no direct impact on the rate of profit; but they tend to increase saving and the rate of capital accumulation through enhancement of the purchasing power of capitalists.[74]

Commenting on Ricardo's analysis of the benefit of trade in terms of his England–Portugal example, E. K. Hunt suspects that, despite his labour theory of value, Ricardo's conclusion that free trade would increase the 'sum of enjoyments' of each country implies some sort of utility theory of exchange value, i.e. the theory which tends to equate price and utility; hence, the higher the price the greater the utility or satisfaction to the consumer.[75] Otherwise, Ricardo's conclusion would not follow from his premises. Samuel Hollander seems to lend support to this interpretation when he asserted that 'the "mutual determination" of exchange value by demand and cost considerations was a thoroughly central aspect of Ricardian doctrine'.[76] Logically, then (consistent with utility reasoning), Ricardo had to assume that the import of the relatively more expensive commodity (wine) would increase the 'sum of enjoyments' – landlords and capitalists would prefer to spend their surplus on both cloth and wine. A labour-theory perspective would have suggested that the importation of wine be prohibited until every worker had adequate clothing (the domestically produced good) – workers would prefer to have more clothing and less wine. This would increase 'social welfare' more than the importation of wine which merely pandered to the tastes and monetary demands of capitalists and landlords. Hunt ascribes this contradiction in Ricardo's thought to the fact that although he fully recognised the reality of class conflict, Ricardo was blind to the possibilities of social change and took property relationships, the distribution of wealth and power and class relationships as given, natural and unchanging. Certainly Ricardo did not consider increasing the 'sum of enjoyments' by changing the distribution of power, wealth and privilege – a reflection, no doubt, of Ricardo's class bias. But surely his conclusion on the gains from trade does follow from his labour theory-based model and nothing else. As far as economic analysis is concerned this was achievement enough.

ELABORATION OF THE CLASSICAL MODEL

In the Ricardian model the purpose of the comparative-cost example in terms of barter was to lay bare the principles on which trade is based – principles which showed how to allocate resources for the good of each country. However, trade actually takes place on the basis of money prices, not on the barter ratios used to illustrate the principle. Is mutually advantageous trade still possible when money is brought into the picture?

Ricardo was able to show, on the basis of assumptions about money wages and the rate of exchange, that the introduction of an international medium of exchange made no difference to the barter relations. The natural distribution of specie ensures that the movement of goods across national frontiers corresponds with the trade flow under conditions of barter.

Starting from the obvious fact that traders buy a foreign good only when its price is lower than at home, Ricardo shows how comparative differences in costs can be converted into absolute differences in money prices. The country which has an absolute advantage in every commodity must have a higher money wage-rate. Thus trade is possible between England and Portugal because money-wage and price levels are higher in Portugal than they are in England. If money-wage rates were the same in both countries English cloth would not sell in Portugal and gold would flow from England to Portugal to pay for English imports of Portuguese wine. Eventually, money-wage levels and prices would rise in Portugal and fall in England until absolute differences in money prices are restored which allow profitable two-way commodity traffic. Gold inflows and outflows, therefore, cause adjustments in relative wage and price levels that not only maintain balanced trade, but also ensure that trade takes place according to comparative advantage.

It was, however, William Nassau Senior, writing ten years after Ricardo's work appeared, who first stated the classical theory of international prices in a fairly satisfactory manner. Senior focuses on money-wage differences between countries and shows how these reflect productivity differentials – more precisely, productivity differences in the export sectors. Money-wage rates are linked both to commodity prices and to physical productivities. Senior relates these tendencies to the process whereby silver and/or gold is distributed throughout the world – a process which forges the international linkage of domestic price levels. According to Senior, relative price levels between countries reflect differences 'in the cost of obtaining silver',[77] i.e. money-wage rates. Wage levels, in turn, are determined by differences in physical productivity in the production of exportable commodities. Thus the explanation for higher wages in England compared with India is due to 'the diligence and skill with which English labour is applied enables the English labourer to produce in a year exportable commodities equal in value to those produced in a year by eight Hindoos. ...'[78] Thus, if labour in Portugal is twice as efficient as English labour in wine production, then Portuguese wages at its maximum would be double the English wage-rate. The minimum limit to Portuguese wages is then determined by a comparison between Portuguese and English labour productivities in cloth. Wages in the export sector, according to Senior, determine the general level of wages and money-incomes generally in the economy and hence the level of prices. This relationship is due to the higher value-productivity of labour and capital in the export industries which enables all domestic residents to increase their command over foreign commodities. Englishmen could thus obtain foreign products 'not merely at the expense of less labour than it would cost to produce them in England, but often at the expense of less labour than they cost in the producing countries'.[79] Does this statement go further than Ricardian theory allows? Not really, since all that Senior is claiming is that because of its overall technological superiority England has an absolute advantage over practically the whole range of manufactured products *vis-à-vis* other trading partners. But this does not mean that England does not benefit from trade. There must be some English industries where, although each one of them enjoys an absolute advantage with respect to *imports* within England each holds a comparative advantage over all other domestic industries. For the law of comparative costs this is the only thing that counts. In fact, Senior goes on to argue that the relatively greater efficiency (productivity) of English labour causes money-wages to be higher in England than elsewhere, as already related. It is therefore essential to concentrate this efficiency in branches of production where English superiority is most pronounced, otherwise there is the danger of being undersold in foreign markets since the workers employed in the relatively unproductive jobs must still be paid 'what they might produce if their labour were properly directed'.

Nevertheless, 'to complain of our high wages is to complain that our labour is productive – that our workpeople are diligent and skilful'.[80] Senior, therefore, quite properly, draws attention to the tendency under balanced trade for high output per head to be associated with high money-wages and therefore to high real wages in terms of tradable goods. This means, of course, that such a country also has the relatively higher price level. And such levels of prices which govern trade patterns are determined by gold movements operating on relative money-wages. The upshot of Senior's discussion, then, is that higher wages compensate for higher productivity; hence the more efficient country has no cause to fear competition from low-wage countries, since the low wages merely reflect a low level of productivity. Every country necessarily has a comparative advantage.

In this age of 'positive' empirical economics it is natural to ask the question: Has the classical theory identified with Ricardo's trade model any predictive value? Is there empirical evidence in favour of it?

The theory had been around for over a hundred years before anyone attempted to test it empirically. Surprisingly, perhaps, to most economists it performed exceedingly well in explaining the pattern of international specialisation. The results were unexpected since in the meantime an alternative, more sophisticated neoclassical model of trade (the Heckscher–Ohlin theory) gained widespread acceptance. By the early 1950s the Ricardian theory was regarded as hopelessly naïve because of its allegedly simplistic assumptions, particularly its attachment to the labour theory of value and the single-factor assumption.[81] The theory itself from its inception was not so much concerned with explaining or predicting the pattern of trade as with deriving welfare conclusions from its simple logic. The theory does, however, suggest a testable hypothesis: Given two countries, A and B, A will tend to export to B commodities for which A's productivity ratio relative to B's exceeds the ratio of A's money wage-rate relative to B's. This is the hypothesis Sir Donald MacDougall tested in 1951.[82] In essence the Ricardian theory postulates that comparative-cost differences between countries exist because production function for a given commodity varies from one country to another and the extent of the variation differs for the two commodities. The chain of reasoning is as follows: Inter-country differences in the productivity of labour give rise to differences in relative costs, which in turn produce differences in pre-trade price ratios. The country with the relatively low price for a commodity will tend to be an exporter of it.

MacDougall examined 1937 data on output per worker, wages and exports relating to twenty-five commodities in a comparison of British and American export performance in third-country markets. A direct bilateral test was ruled out because the period covered by the test coincided with the height of the inter-war depression and trade between the United Kingdom and the United States was severely restricted by tariffs and other protectionist devices; however, 95 per cent of the two countries' exports were sold in third-country markets.

The results of the test indicated that there was a tendency for each country to capture a larger share of the exports markets as its comparative advantage (measured in terms of labour productivity) became higher. There were some objections to the procedure adopted by MacDougall, notably by Jagdish Bhagwati, to the effect that MacDougall went from productivity to trade (export shares) without first checking prices. According to Bhagwati, the Ricardian reasoning starts from productivity differences then goes on to costs followed by prices, which finally determine trade flows. Bhagwati himself found, using MacDougall's data, that there was no significant relationship between export-price ratios and labour-productivity ratios.[83] But since pre-trade prices cannot be observed and post-trade prices are necessarily equalised by competition the finding that labour productivity explains market shares must be accepted for what it is worth, i.e. as a verification of the Ricardian hypothesis.[84] The initial work by MacDougall was followed by Balassa, Stern and some further work by MacDougall, all of which tended to confirm the original finding.[85]

As late as the 1920s the classical trade model continued to be used by writers like Edgeworth. Taussig and Viner. By that time the theory had evolved into a general model of production and trade capable of dealing with a wide range of problems. For this development, credit must go to John Stuart Mill principally, but also to a succession of writers after Ricardo who developed the labour-cost basis of the theory into one grounded on real costs.

The Ricardian trade model survived the 'marginal revolution' of the 1870s partly because it was modified through the introduction of more real-world complications. This adaptation kept unimpaired the model's appeal for classical-school followers and made it acceptable to the new band of marginal-utility theorists. Trade theory was enlarged and developed, but within the framework originally established by Ricardo. It is a remarkable fact that even when the utility theory of value gained currency in general economics the labour-costs approach was retained in trade models. This led Ohlin to complain as late as 1933: 'If the classical labour value theory had been discarded as an explanation of prices in the one case, ... why should it be retained in an analysis of pricing in several communicating markets?'[86] In retrospect there is no doubt, however, that the work of Ricardo's successors prepared the way for the transformation of the classical into the neoclassical or modern pure theory of trade.

As we noted previously, the theory of comparative cost as fashioned by Ricardo was incomplete since without introducing demand the theory could not explain on what terms trade would take place. The role of demand and its relevance in the determination of the terms of trade was appreciated by writers such as Torrens, Longfield and Pennington; but it was John Stuart Mill who first explicitly demonstrated how the gain from trade is determined by conditions of demand both at home and abroad.

The mechanism which determined the world price ratio (or terms of trade) is 'reciprocal demand', i.e. 'the amount and extensibility of demand' in each country for the other country's product. This ratio will be stable when 'the equation of international demand' is satisfied, i.e. when the value of each country's exports is just sufficient to pay for its exports.

Mill is justly famous for his work on logic and political science, but in economics he is remembered more for the reputation he enjoyed during his lifetime as an Establishment figure than for his originality. But anyone familiar with his theory of international values would see in it the true mark of genius. Mill outlined his solution to the problem left unanswered by Ricardo in his 1844 essay 'On the Laws of Interchange between Nations'. The argument was developed in chapter 18 'Of International Values', book III of his *Principles* (1848).[87] Edgeworth referred to the latter as Mill's 'great' and 'stupendous' chapter, and Chipman has more recently praised Mill's Law of International Value in these terms: 'In its astonishing simplicity, it must stand as one of the great achievements of the human intellect.' O'Brien calls it one of the greatest performances in the history of economics.[88] Without the benefit of marginal-utility analysis and relying mainly on verbal reasoning Mill was able to develop a rigorous general equilibrium model. Within this analytical framework, he shows how the reciprocal demand mechanism can be generalised to the case of more than two countries and two commodities. He derives the result that the stronger (and more elastic) the foreign demand for a country's exports the more favourable are the terms of trade of that country. He perceives the relationship between total revenue and demand elasticity and distinguishes the three degrees of price elasticity now known as 'elastic, unitary and inelastic'. He makes this deduction in section 5 of his 'great Chapter' when he introduces a cost-reducing technological change in one country (Germany, in his example) and proceeds to analyse the terms of trade effects according to each of the three different demand elasticities. He considers the effects of transport costs and the discrepancy they create between prices of traded commodities in different locales. Every increase in transport costs lessens the gain from foreign trade, but as long as these costs are not sufficient to wipe out the gains from trade trade will still take place on the basis of comparative advantage. Some commodities, however, do not enter international trade because of high transport costs.

Mill was bothered by the problem of multiple equilibria (crisscrossing of offer curves) which arises when either country has an inelastic demand for the other's product and the conditions prescribed in the equations of international demand are satisfied. To deal with the indeterminancy represented by this possibility, Mill added supplementary sections (6–9) to the chapter in the third edition of the *Principles*. The status of these added sections has, however, been the subject of some debate and controversy. Unlike the earlier sections, the new 'superstructure' met with a generally unfavourable response from a succession of economists including Edgeworth, Marshall, Bastable and Viner. Edgeworth, for instance, agreed with Bastable that they were 'laborious and confusing'.[89] Chipman, however, formed a different opinion of the new sections as a result of applying the modern mathematical technique of non-linear programming to Mill's problem. Chipman discovered that Mill did, in fact, succeed in finding a *proof* of the existence of a unique equilibrium price ratio.

In a 1979 paper, Appleyard and Ingram questioned Chipman's interpretation.[90] The new sections, these authors say, make no contribution to the matter of multiple equilibria, except in the case of unitary demand elasticity. But since Mill had already indicated in the earlier sections that a unique exchange ratio would exist when demand elasticities were equal to 1, he failed to achieve his avowed objective, i.e. 'Mill did not really come to grips with the problem of multiple equilibria that he sets out to solve.'[91] The only novelty in the new sections is a statement of the conditions necessary for full specialisation in both countries.

In his reply to Appleyard and Ingram, Chipman maintained his original assessment of the importance of the new sections.[92] Basically, what Chipman's point boils down to is this: Whereas in the early sections Mill assumes that a unique equilibrium exists, in the new sections he actually provides a *proof* of it. Mill succeeds in his proof, says Chapman, by virtue of his hypotheses concerning the utility function (especially constant expenditure proportionality); for these assumptions guarantee a unique world equilibrium no matter how inelastic the countries' offer curves might be. In terms of the modern theory of trade Mill's specification of the demand conditions (a single utility function for the world as a whole) is of a form that guarantees the existence of a world indifference map.

Whatever view one takes of this reassessment of Mill's mature work there is no denying that it was a remarkable achievement. Later neoclassical economists added little of substance to Mill's general law of international values. The offer-curve analysis of Marshall and Edgeworth is, as Viner observed, 'in the main, an exposition and elaboration of Mill's analysis'.[93] Mill also explored the effects of technological change on the terms of trade and analysed the terms-of-trade argument for protection. These aspects of Mill's work will be considered later.

Ricardo's labour theory of value was designed primarily to serve as a fundamental preliminary step towards the ultimate aim, which was the analysis of the distribution of income among social classes within a closed economy. But as an analytical category for examining the distribution of output among countries it was a severe handicap; hence the principle of comparative cost had to be invoked to explain the distribution of tasks in open economies. Nevertheless, for the purpose of evaluating potential output (and national gains) in the open economy the labour theory still possessed considerable explanatory power (in the normative sense). This theoretical dichotomy in value theory – stemming from the obvious fact that what is exchanged between countries is not equal quantities of labour, whereas the law of value holds domestically – created a tension in the minds of political economists faithful to Ricardian orthodoxy (e.g. McCulloch, J. S. Mill). At the same time the schism opened up by those writers (Malthus, Torrens, Bailey, Longfield, Senior) who even before Ricardo's death (1828) refused to go along with the latter's interpretation of the labour theory was extended to the theory of international trade. But the orthodoxy in trade matters was so well-entrenched (thanks largely to J. S. Mill) that the latter group of economists could do little but tinker with the theoretical schema. Yet it was the accretion of these modifications over a hundred years that led to the real-cost approach espoused by such leading theorists as Viner and Taussig.

What was the nature of these modifications? They sprung from the efforts of these writers (the new breed of academic economists at Oxford and Dublin – the so-called 'dissenters' from Ricardianism) to work forward, as it were, from physical labour cost to money costs and to show how these costs related to wages and productivity in a multi-commodity context. Instead of taking as given the output of each commodity in two countries with the labour costs (labour time) different, writers like Longfield and Senior (incidentally, Mill also) assumed a given amount of labour in each country, but differing output. In this form the productivity of labour is given prominence in contrast to Ricardo's emphasis on labour costs or labour time. Ricardo had argued that money costs and prices of commodities would be proportional to the labour time embodied in them and that therefore the pattern of trade was ultimately regulated by the relative amounts of labour expended in the production of various products. But since money costs and hence price differences might reflect productivity differentials rather than differences in labour time, it was misleading to explain trade in terms of labour time. There was no reason to expect a strict proportionality between labour time (physical costs) and money costs or final commodity prices.

We have already referred to Senior's work – the effect of differences in wage-rates on comparative costs. He traced labour's productivity (reflected in money-wages) to the co-operation of capital in production and described the path which adjustments of inter-country differences in wage-rates would take. Longfield extended the Ricardian analysis to the multi-commodity, two-country case.[94] A country's wage level, he held, would be proportional to the average productivity of labour. A ranking of a country's industries according to labour productivity would, therefore, be an ordering according to comparative advantage. Each of a country's exports would have a higher than average labour–productivity ratio and each of its imports would have labour–productivity ratios lower than the average. On the assumption that trade leads to an equalisation of prices for all traded commodities, Longfield deduces that the dividing-line between exports and imports will depend on a comparison of relative money wage-rates at home and abroad. However, he does not discuss the forces which keep the wage levels of the two countries locked together. Neither does he discuss how relative wages change as a consequence of price changes required to clear markets. In effect, he does not consider sufficiently the role of demand in breaking the 'chain of comparative advantage' through operating on relative money wage-rates. The fact is that relative money wage-rates which allow comparative advantage to be manifested in the face of productivity differentials are determined by the condition that the balance of payments must be in equilibrium. Thus, increased foreign demand for the home country's exports leads to an improvement in the terms of trade and an export surplus which, in turn, result in a change in the composition of exports and imports. Fewer commodities will now be cheaper in our country, so that some items will move in the opposite direction in trade and this is what ultimately brings about equilibrium in the balance of payments. Therefore, the precise composition of exports and imports cannot be determined solely on the basis of the cost data; it can be determined only by bringing demand into the model. This omission is rather strange for Longfield, since he was quite familiar with demand-and-supply analysis as applied to value theory, and indeed he was a pioneer of the subjective (utility) theory of value. It is of some interest to note that the Ricardian hypothesis tested by MacDougall was essentially the model initially developed by Senior and Longfield (and later by Mangoldt and Edgeworth). This model continues to draw complimentary plaudits from modern trade theorists – to give one example, Ronald Jones: 'I would argue that for trade issues involving many commodities but only two countries, the Ricardian model represents an ideal vehicle for analysis because it strips production relationships down to a simple expression revealing the invariant resource (labour) cost of producing a unit of a commodity in each country.'[95]

Another related matter that attracted criticism was the assumption of domestic immobility of labour. Here, too, Longfield expressed scepticism. It is obvious, he says, bricklayers do not become barristers or barristers bricklayers. Mill thought this observation worthy of note; but it was John Elliott Cairnes, another Dublin academic economist who developed the idea of a country's labour force being segmented into 'non-competing groups' on account of labour-market imperfections, i.e. an implicit recognition of a multiplicity of primary factors of production. Institutional barriers to the free movement of labour cause wage-rates to differ from industry to industry within a country. Here, again, we have another instance where money-wage costs fail to reflect different relative input requirements reckoned in labour time. Even in the long run, then, prices will diverge from real costs, just as they do under international trade.[96]

Both Senior and Longfield held a subjective (utility) theory of value and identified capital as a separate productive factor. Cairnes, on the other hand, rejected Jevons's marginal utility theory as soon as it was published. Yet from different standpoints, they each made their contribution within the same Ricardian framework. But in a sense it can be argued that by undermining the notion that there was a fundamental difference between international and domestic trade requiring the application of two value theories they unwittingly paved the way for the modern theory of trade. A different approach which arrived at the same conclusion, that there was no essential difference between the laws regulating domestic and international values, was taken by Frank Graham. His work on the extension of the theory of international value to the multi-commodity, multi-country case convinced him that labour cost (or opportunity costs in general) – rather than reciprocal demand – governed values in foreign as well as domestic trade. He played down the role of demand (operating through changes in the terms of trade) as the fundamental means of international adjustment and emphasised instead the transfer of resources (labour) from one commodity to another under constant costs as the method of adjustment to disturbances in each country, i.e. quantity (rather than price) adjustments. Graham believed (wrongly, as it turned out) that demand was highly volatile; but because of 'linked competition' among the industrial countries the equilibrium terms of trade would, in practice, be confined within narrow limits, since only slight movements of the terms of trade were required for countries to change from being exporters to importers of particular commodities. Graham's work was intended as a critique of Mill, but he was mistaken in the belief that demand could be ignored in the analysis of international equilibrium. His own model required the introduction of demand to locate the 'marginal' or intermediate country whose domestic cost ratio sets the equilibrium terms of trade. In addition, if, according to Graham, the equilibrium terms of trade normally coincided with the pre-trade equilibrium price ratio of some intermediate country then one would observe violent fluctuations in production – a situation contradicted by empirical studies.[97]

The finale to the story of the classical theory can be briefly told. Writing in 1927, Frank Taussig surveyed all the amendments, modifications and criticisms of the classical theory up to that time and concluded that the doctrine of comparative advantage was adequately conveyed by Ricardo's model.[98] Non-competing groups, capital charges, cases involving more than two countries, etc., could all be accommodated within the labour-cost doctrine. Basically, Taussig's contention is:

(1) That capital–labour ratios are about the same in every industry and that even when they differ, the cost of capital (interest) tends to be small compared with labour cost.
(2) Inter-industry differences in the structure of wage rates are insignificant across countries, because each country has about the same pattern of non-competing groups. Thus: 'if the groups are in the same relative positions in the exchanging countries as regards wages . . . trade takes place exactly as if it were governed by the strict and simple principle of comparative costs'.
(3) The classical approach does not depend on bilateral comparisons of labour–cost ratios – the theory is equally applicable to multilateral trade.

Ten years later, Taussig's famous pupil, Viner, concurred in this appreciation of the flexibility of the classical approach and stressed its relevance 'as a generally valid rule of policy'.[99]

5 The Economists, the Corn Laws and Commercial Policy

5.1 The Economists and the Corn-Law Debate

BACKGROUND TO THE DEBATE

The repeal of the English Corn Laws on 26 June 1846 was an epoch-making event in the history of international economic policy. The decision was significant, perhaps more because of its symbolic value than for any dramatic impact on international economic relationships.

It was, however, preceded by a momentous and controversial debate in which most of the best minds in classical political economy participated. Nothing comparable to it was seen until a century and a half later, i.e. the protracted debate on Britain's membership of the EEC. As in another famous economic debate – the early seventeenth century controversy on the foreign exchanges and the balance of payments – which engaged the attention of leading economic thinkers, the nineteenth-century discussion was accompanied by a great outpouring of economic writings. The shift in policy leading up to the rescinding of agricultural protection has been hailed as one of the greatest triumphs of enlightened economic reasoning, in particular, the law of comparative cost. But this is pure invention, a caricature of the facts as far as they can be ascertained. The myth does not stand up to scrutiny. Thweatt writes 'it is misleading to say the doctrine of comparative costs was influential in the discussion leading to the repeal of the Corn Laws in 1846'.[1] Surveying public opinion at one of the crucial moments (1820) when the first decision was made in favour of free trade, William D. Grampp could find no trace of comparative advantage in the economic opinion of 1820, i.e. what was said in Parliament, the press and in petitions. 'The arguments for free trade were not drawn from the economic theory of the day',[2] he noted. As one observer remarked at the time, the issues of 'cash and corn' touched on many technical points which were 'intricate and foreign to the taste of country gentlemen'.[3]

Apparently, a taste for the finer points of economic analysis has not changed since then. According to Stigler, tariffs are still with us 'because the theory of comparative cost is beyond the comprehension of ordinary citizens. A recital of Ricardo's three-paragraph statement to a tired factory hand or physician is liable to cause the layman to embrace not the English theory of free trade, but a bottle of Portuguese wine.'[4] Corn and currency were not the only economic and social subjects of the debate: the Poor Laws, emigration, unemployment and the machinery question were all on the agenda. Food riots were frequent (1795, 1799, 1804). The political rows were fierce, the pamphleteering wars unrelenting, the clamour of vested interests noisy and divisive. In the background, behind the drawn battle-lines, the political economists carried on their 'highly technical discussions' in Briggs phrase.[5] These discussions on the Corn Laws and commercial policy in general are the subject of this chapter. First, a few words on the factual and intellectual background.

At the heart of the controversy lay the population problem. During the wars food prices rose. The inflationary situation was further aggravated by heavy wartime expenditures which forced Britain off the gold standard. With an inconvertible pound, the money supply expanded rapidly and overall prices increased by some 93 per cent over the period 1792–1814. Farmers were well-off during the 1790s; their production costs also rose, but the enclosure movement accelerated, and new ploughland was opened up. To many radicals the obvious answer to rapid population growth and rising food prices was a programme of assisted emigration and the abolition or reform of the Corn Laws. Malthus, whose *Essay* came out at this time, refused to countenance these solutions. But contrary to Smith's optimistic vision of high wages, increases in industrial productivity and future economic and social progress, Malthus's prospect hinted at conflict between landowners and the rest of society: 'It threatened to undermine whatever remained of the "moral economy" ...', as one writer recently puts it.[6] Agricultural protection and export bounties on grain exports were required to encourage domestic production, advised Malthus. Smith's doctrine of free trade came under fire; so too was his reliance on a manufacturing economy for creating wealth and improving the standard of living of the poor. Physiocratic notions resurfaced, proclaiming agriculture as the sure foundation of Britain's prosperity. Inevitably the landed interest got its way and agricultural protection was increased in 1791 and 1814.

The issue became truly joined between the contending interests at the end of the war when the fall of food prices led to renewed demand for greater protection. Even before the final end of hostilities a serious economic crisis developed (1810–11), resulting in large-scale unemployment in the manufacturing districts. At this juncture the law of diminishing returns and its corollary, the theory of rent, was discovered jointly by Malthus, West, Torrens and Ricardo. Integrated into the rest of classical theory this discovery suggested that a country with a growing population would face ever-increasing food prices and money wages. Unrelieved by the free importation of foodstuffs, this situation implied reduced profits, decreased exports of manufactured goods and ruin for British industry. At least this was the dreadful scenario as envisaged by merchants and manufacturers. The landowners and spokesmen for the squirearchy retorted that a prosperous agriculture was necessary for England's national defence as well as for the preservation of traditional ways of life. Manufacturing labour was 'unproductive' compared with agricultural labour, and far from contributing to the increase of the 'necessaries and conveniences of life', the expansion of manufacturing by draining workers off the land would actually diminish the available food supply. The great issue at stake then was: Should the country try to maintain its agrarian economy or turn itself into a giant manufactory? The debate resolved itself into a consideration of the following: (1) the place of agriculture in society; (2) the relationship between consumers and producers; and (3) the competing claims and ideologies of the squirearchy and the industrialists.

The point at which Ricardo and the other economists besides Malthus entered the debate on the Corn Laws is usually marked by the appearance of William Spence's tract, *Britain Independent of Commerce* (1807) and the replies it provoked. In 1806 Napoleon launched his Continental System of economic warfare against Britain by the Berlin Decrees which ordered the closure of all continental ports to British trade. At a time of serious food shortage at home, the propaganda value of this action was enormous for Spence and the British Physiocrats. Agriculture not commerce, said Spence, was the basis of England's strength; thus the Napoleonic blockade could have no serious consequence for Great Britain. The expansion of commerce and manufacturing created economic instability and insecurity; only the agricultural sector promoted economic growth, stability and security. Therefore, if the agricultural sector was starved of investment funds because of the diversion of capital to trade and industry, then that vital sector would decline; it would be unable to employ the resources (including new technology) to provide the economic surplus required to sustain a growing population at improved standards of living. Spence emphasised the danger of reduced purchasing power (and the threat to continued prosperity) which stemmed from excessive savings by the niggardly capitalist class. All that was necessary for survival and prosperity was for landlords to spend the social surplus and generate incomes in the rest of the economy. Spence's pamphlet was highly praised by Cobbett in his series of 'Perish Commerce' articles in the *Political Register*.[7] Two critical replies appeared, however, which as we have already indicated were crucially important for the emerging orthodoxy, i.e. James Mill's *Commerce Defended* and Torrens's *The Economists Refuted*.

Mill rejected Spence's allegation that foreign trade was a mere swapping of commodities of equal value which benefits no one but the profiteering merchant. A country can benefit from 'the trade of export and import' because it involves the exchange of less-valuable commodities for more valuable ones. Trade, no less than agriculture, increased Britain's wealth, since imports were purchased 'with a quantity of British goods of less value'. Mill also attacked the 'dangerous doctrine' according to which landlords must spend all their incomes to avoid gluts, invoking for this purpose an early version of Say's 'law of markets' – production equals purchasing power, i.e. a level of income sufficient to purchase all that is produced: 'Whatever be the additional quantity of goods therefore which is at any time created in any country, an additional power of purchasing, exactly equivalent, is at the same instant created.' Therefore there was no possibility of inadequate demand for all goods in an economy, either because of underinvestment or underconsumption. The new industrial system was a harmonious, self-sustaining order which did not entail reliance on foreign trade as an outlet for suplus produce:

> Foreign commerce ... is in all cases a matter of expediency rather than of necessity. The intention of it is not to furnish a vent for the produce of the industry of the country, because that industry always furnishes a vent for itself.

Trade was rather a means of procuring cheap and abundant supplies of commodities which enhanced the British standard of living.[8] Tacitly, Mill's reply to Spence was also a critique of Smith's vent-for-surplus idea. The assertion that a nation could never be without a market was, moreover, a supremely confident belief in the existence of a competitive equilibrium – that the market mechanism was self-regulating, both with and without the benefit of foreign trade.

MALTHUS'S CAUTION

Torrens's reply, while distinctly anti-physiocratic, was a curious mixture of mercantilist reasoning and elements of the new political economy. He attacked Spence's 'idea of agriculture being the only source of wealth' and used the eighteenth-century rule to illustrate the gains from trade. However, his general views on trade and colonies were less enlightened than those of Mill. For instance, he (1) accepted Smith's vent-for-surplus theory; (2) believed that a country's gain from trade was greater when it exchanged perishables (wine, fruit) and necessaries (food, woollen cloth) for durables (hardware) and luxuries (silks, lace); (3) felt that domestic trade was, in some sense, more permanent and beneficial than foreign trade; and (4) favoured restrictions on colonial trade along the lines of the 'old colonial system'.[9] From the side of the new orthodoxy Mill's critique of Spence was the more telling, but combined with that of Torrens's it 'laid the physiocratic ghost to rest'.[10] Shortly after this controversy, first James Mill and then Torrens became acquainted with Ricardo – the three who were to provide the intellectual argument against the Corn Laws. When the debate on the Laws resumed at the end of the war Malthus came out with his two Corn Law pamphlets which greatly disappointed his Whig friends for his 'heresy' in urging restrictions on the importation of grain. The remedy for the stagnation of the British economy, said Malthus, was a continuation of the policy of limited protection of the landed interest from the competition of imported foodstuffs which would sustain agricultural income and investment. He recognised that falling food prices (hence wages) would favour the expansion of British manufactured exports, but felt that it was more necessary to maintain demand at home through a high level of domestic spending. He boldly asserted that a high money-price of corn would benefit workers in the purchase of other commodities. The Corn Laws, he believed, made real wages higher than they would otherwise have been. The assumption was that money-wages moved proportionately with the corn price, but other prices which entered the wage basket either did not move (e.g. prices of imported goods) or moved proportionately less than the price of bread. On the added assumption that workers regularly spent two-fifths of their income on bread and flour and the rest on other commodities (meat, milk, butter, cheese, potatoes, house-rent, linen, soap, etc.) Malthus reasoned that the Corn Laws, by keeping up or increasing the price of corn, thereby advanced workers' real income more than the rise in the cost of living. In addition, of course, dearer food meant fewer children and hence, a higher standard of living for the labouring poor. Francis Horner wrote to a friend on 30 January 1815: 'The most important convert the landlords have got is Malthus, who has now declared himself in favour of their Bill.'[11] Two years later Malthus repeated his objection to dependence on imported food and raw materials. He disagreed with those who wanted to expand foreign trade so as to lower food costs and thereby the wages of labour. If that was the way to capture and hold markets, it was patently not worth the effort; for although extra exports might be secured through low wages, the benefit might be more than counterbalanced by a decline in demand at home. He stressed the need for agricultural self-sufficiency, the balanced development of agriculture, industry and commercial services and the maintenance of a high level of effective demand in the domestic market:

> If food and raw materials were denied to a nation merely manufacturing, it is obvious that it could no longer exist ... its progress in wealth must be almost entirely measured by the progress and demand of the countries which deal with it.[12]

He warned that even if Britain became the workshop of the world and common carrier such an international division of labour could not be relied upon to continue indefinitely – it would be merely 'accidental and temporary, not natural and permanent'. Technological leadership and other competitive advantages must inevitably be eroded as other countries industrialised. On the other hand:

> a country with resources in land ... if its industry, ingenuity and economy increase, its wealth and population will increase, its wealth and population will increase, whatever may be the situation and conduct of the nations with which it trades. When its manufacturing capital becomes redundant, and manufactured commodities are too cheap, it will have no occasion to wait for the increasing raw products of its neighbours. The transfer of its own redundant capital to its own land will raise fresh products, against which its manufactures may be exchanged, and by the double operation of diminishing comparatively the supply, and increasing the demand, enhance their price. ... A country, in which in this manner agriculture, manufactures, and commerce ... act and react upon each other in turn, might evidently go on increasing in riches and strength, although surrounded by Bishop Berkely's wall of brass.[13]

But this could only be achieved if Britain continued to tax imported corn and maintained the system of bounties upon its exportation so that farmers should not be discouraged by low selling prices at home in years of good harvests. Malthus seemed to believe that the ultimate check to population growth was set by the growth of *domestic* food supply. A policy of supporting domestic agriculture would therefore ensure that there would always be sufficient 'funds for the maintenance of labour' which alone could ensure full employment. A predominantly manufacturing nation – without the aid of high-consuming landlords – could not avoid the problem of overproduction ('gluts') and falling prices and profits. Nevertheless, for a country with a sufficiency of home-grown foodstuffs the export of manufactured goods could play an important role in sustaining effective demand:

> It is obvious then that a fall in the value of the precious metals, commencing with a rise in the price of corn, has a strong tendency ... to encourage the cultivation of fresh land and the formation of increased rents.
>
> A similar effect would be produced in a country which continued to feed its own people, by a great and increasing demand for its manufactures. These manfactures, if from such a demand the money value of their amount in foreign countries was greatly to increase, would bring back a great increase of money value in return, which increase could not fail to increase the money price of labour and raw produce. The demand for agricultural as well as manufactured produce would thus be augmented.[14]

And Malthus professed his adherence to the theoretical ideal of universal free trade, but with an important caveat in regard to its practical application – some restriction was desirable to safeguard the staple food of the people:

> According to the general principles of political economy, it cannot be doubted that it is for the interest of the civilised world that each nation should purchase its commodities wherever they can be had the cheapest. ... It is evident, however, that local interests and political relations may modify the application of these general principles; and in a country with a territory fit for the production of corn, an independent, and at the same time a more equable supply of this necessary of life, may be an object of such importance as to warrant a deviation from them.[15]

Malthus took issue with Smith in the 1798 edition of the *Essay on*

Population on the welfare significance of increases in national wealth as conventionally measured. In particular, Malthus maintained that it could not be assumed that every increase of wealth necessarily benefited the labouring poor. A more abundant supply of 'silks, laces, trinkets and expensive furniture' (consequent upon freer importation or expanded domestic manufacture) certainly indicated an increase in national wealth (or 'the revenue of society'), but that could not be considered of the same importance as an increase of food – the principal revenue of the great mass of the people. Investment in manufacturing might, indeed, increase national wealth and nominal wages, but if that occurred as a result of reduced investment in agriculture (accompanied by a movement of labour from agriculture to manufacturing) then the increased costs of domestically produced subsistence goods might more than swallow up all the enhanced nominal wages and leave wage-earners worse off than before.

RICARDO'S CRITIQUE

But what were the consequences of the Corn Laws for the distribution of income and the rate of economic growth? In particular, what would happen to the rate of profit and the accumulation of capital? For Ricardo, this was the crucial question to ask. Until 1813 Ricardo was preoccupied with monetary questions (i.e. the bullion controversy). Thereafter he turned his attention to the Corn-Law question and published his *Essay on Profits* in February 1815 as his contribution to the debate. The subtitle to the pamphlet suggests that this was the motivation for his corn model of profits, i.e. the reference to Malthus's recent pamphlets on the Corn laws.[16] Blaug, Dobb and O'Brien state that the significance of the work can only be understood in the context of the public debate about the proposed restrictions upon the importation of corn. Hollander, however, on the basis of the Ricardo–Malthus correspondence and other evidence, traces the origin of Ricardo's profit theory to the latter's criticism of Smith's view that increases in wage-rates led to general inflation – especially as contained in Smith's chapter on bounties.[17]

At any rate, whether inspired by current controversy or not, Ricardo drew immediately relevant political conclusions from his model. In the *Essay* Ricardo demonstrated that a failure to import more corn would be exceedingly costly to the country – it would lower profits, which, in turn, would mean lower levels of investment, employment, output and income. In an imaginative synthesis Ricardo brought together the fundamental building blocks of contemporary theory and constructed a model which indicated that the profits of the farmer regulated the profits of all other trades. As early as March 1814 Ricardo stated his conclusion in a letter to his stockbroker friend, Hutches Trower:

> that in short, it is the profits of the farmer which regulate the profits of all other trades, – and as the profits of the farmer must necessarily decrease with every augmentation of Capital employed on the land, provided no improvements be at the same time made in husbandry, all other profits must diminish and therefore the rate of interest must fall. To this proposition Mr. Malthus does not agree.[18]

The feeding of a growing population necessitated the cultivation of progressively poorer parcels of land and/or the more intensive use of existing land. In either case, because of diminishing returns and the competition by farmers for the more fertile land, the cost of producing food increases over time. The only beneficiaries in income-distribution terms would be the landlords, with their swollen rent rolls. Himself a landlord by that time (the previous year he had bought Gatcombe Park, Gloucestershire, now a Royal Residence), Ricardo's analysis hinted at class conflict:

> the interest of the landlord is always opposed to the interest of every other class in the community. His situation is never so prosperous, as when food is scarce and dear: whereas, all other persons are greatly benefitted [sic] by procuring food cheap.[19]

The losers, the farmers, would suffer a squeeze on their profits. Moreover, argued Ricardo, the rising cost of producing the subsistence wage would depress the general rate of profit in other industries. The pace of capital accumulation would inevitably slow down and thus act as a brake on economic expansion. Malthus, of course, did not accept the last part of this scenario; but it must have frightened others. As Edwin Cannan remarked a century later: 'As a basis for an argument against the Corn Laws, it would have been difficult to find anything more effective than the Ricardian theory of distribution.'[20] The dismal prospect ahead – diminishing returns, rising real-wage cost and falling profits – could, as a matter of logic, be relieved if additional portions of fertile land could somehow be tacked on to the British Isles. But the more realistic practical alternative was obviously to allow the free importation of grain. Since 'rent never falls without profits of stock rising' it follows that Great Britain will benefit greatly by imports of cheap grain. Wages will be lower (reflecting the falling costs of subsistence) and rents will sink as marginal land is abandoned:

> If by foreign commerce, or the discovery of machinery, the commodities consumed by the labourer should become much cheaper, wages would fall; and this, as we have before observed, would raise the profits of the farmer, and therefore all other profits.[21]

Foreign trade provided the means of escape from the consequences of diminishing returns and a falling rate of profit. 'I never was more convinced of any proposition in Pol: Economy', he wrote to Malthus in June 1814, 'than that restrictions on importation of corn in an importing country have a tendency to lower profits'.[22] Should the Corn Laws be repealed, Britain would be able to draw on low-cost food-supplies from abroad (presumably importing such wage goods at constant terms of trade). Should this 'wise policy' be adopted (i.e. exchanging manufactured goods for low-cost food and raw materials from abroad) Great Britain

> could go on for an indefinite time increasing in wealth and population, for the only obstacle to this increase would be the scarcity, and consequent high value, of food and other raw produce. Let these be supplied from abroad in exchange for manufactured goods, and it is difficult to say where the limit is at which you would cease to accumulate wealth and to derive profit from its employment.[23]

Ricardo left no doubt in his readers' minds about his anti-Corn-Law position when he concluded the *Essay* with this peroration:

> I shall greatly regret that considerations for any particular class, are allowed to check the progress of the wealth and population of the country. If the interests of the landlord be of sufficient consequence, to determine us not to avail ourselves of all the benefits which would follow from importing corn at a cheap price, they should also influence us in rejecting all improvements in agriculture, and in the implements of husbandry; for it is as certain that corn is rendered cheap, rents are lowered, and the ability of the landlord to pay taxes, is for a time, at least, as much impaired by such improvements, as by the importation of corn. To be consistent then, let us by the same act arrest improvement, and prohibit importation.[24]

We shall return to Ricardo presently, but for the moment let us take note of two other critiques.

TORRENS'S POSITION

Torrens's *Essay Upon the External Corn Trade* came out the same day as Ricardo's *Essay*. It was not a pamphlet, but a book of 348 octavo pages. In it Torrens again returned to the attack on those who advocated agricultural self-sufficiency. He called for free trade in corn as a means of securing power and prosperity. The cheapest means of obtaining food-supplies for a growing population was to obtain it from abroad in exchange for manufactured goods. This would further extend Britain's undoubted industrial lead since it would widen the market for manufactures.

Like Ricardo, he argued that restrictions on corn imports would inhibit capital accumulation and stunt economic growth. He derived these results from a model incorporating classical postulates on rent and wages; but in a curious reversal of Ricardo's conclusion held that the rate of profit was held up under the protected system. He did not quite see the link Ricardo forged between wages and profit and, consequently at this stage, the 'fundamental theorem' eluded him; and with it, the proposition of a secular decline in the rate of profit arising from diminishing returns to land. In fact, Torrens went on to argue that, with the Corn Laws repealed, capital accumulation would pick up and result in a lower rate of profit. This was obviously a Smithian-derived theory of profit based on the 'competition of capitals'. At any rate, Torrens held that the lower rate of profit under free trade would somehow prove beneficial to industry and commerce (which he saw as the leading sectors of the economy). The contention was that lower capital costs combined with lower money wages would reduce average costs and prices generally, and thus boost the sales of British manufactured goods abroad.

Later, Torrens made use of the more orthodox Ricardian model to analyse the effect of cheap corn imports on economic growth. Thus in 1819 he wrote:

> Under any given degree of skill and economy in the application of labour, the return upon capital will be determined by the quality of land in cultivation; and as inferior soils are resorted to, the rate of profit will consistently diminish, until that stationary state is attained, in which no additional capital can be employed....[25]

Free trade in corn which allowed Britain to exchange manufactured goods for cheap foreign food would raise the rate of profit and allow the country 'indefinitely to advance in the career of improvement'. Like Ricardo, he reasoned shortly afterwards that free trade between Britain and 'the new and thinly inhabited countries' overseas would throw 'the stationary state to a greater distance' and lead to higher rates of capital accumulation and economic growth.[26] In a perceptive passage in the third edition of the *External Corn Trade* (1826) Torrens suggested that in any event Britain would naturally tend to specialise in manufacturing since, unlike agriculture, the former was characterised by increasing returns to scale. Britain was eminently suited to manufacturing production because of its dense population and large domestic market which permitted the full exploitation of the 'effective powers of manufacturing industry' through division of labour:

> As an increasing population compels us on the one hand to resort to inferior soils, and thus to raise the productive cost of raw produce, so it leads on the other hand to more accurate divisions of employment, and to the use of improved machinery and thus lowers the productive cost of all wrought goods.[27]

Torrens is here referring to the spontaneous (endogenous) factors which, under the influence of the profit motive and the possibility of industrial productivity, determine the composition of national output.

Self-sufficiency in food grains was neither feasible nor desirable for a country like Great Britain. Without participating in the international division of labour, a country could 'never make any very considerable advances in wealth and power'.[28] He repudiated the hope entertained by spokesmen for the agricultural interest that Britain might become a grain exporter once again. A corn-exporting Britain, he said, would be 'bankrupt and depopulated, sunk from her place in Europe, and, perhaps, deprived of her existence as an independent nation'.[29]

The theme that runs through Torrens's work is that of the maximisation of national power and imperial greatness. As an advocate of 'free-trade imperialism', Torrens had visions of a 'trade empire' more reminiscent of those glimpsed by Josiah Tucker as early as 1750 rather than to anything imagined by his contemporaries among the classical economists. Thus he wrote:

> The power that is derived from extended commerce is, perhaps, less unstable than that which is derived from extended territory. . . . The question, as respects England, is not, whether her power would be more independent and stable, if she possessed the extended territory and numerous population of France, or Austria, or Russia;

but, whether, being inferior to those great continental states in natural resources, she should avail herself of the artificial, and even, perhaps, less permanent, advantages placed within her reach, and by the wonders of her commerce, create the means for taking an ascendancy in Europe.... Now, we should never cease to remember, that manufactures and commerce are necessary, not only to compensate for our deficiency in extent and population, but also as the source of that justly cherished naval preponderance, without which an insular empire can take up no position among the nations of the world.[30]

In Torrens's later writings these nationalistic sentiments became more pronounced. Thirty-seven years later, he felt compelled to rebuke the free-traders for neglecting the use of commercial policy to foster Britain's imperial power:

The country is undergoing a process of denationalisation. The power and glory of England find no place in the entries of the ledger. The cosmopolites of the Manchester School would not blush to see the western stars triumphantly floating over St. George's Channel. They would give Jamaica for a hogshead of sugar. They would sell Canada for a bale of cotton. For an additional million of exports they would yield up the trident without a struggle; and transfer from the hand of Victoria the sceptre of Anglo-Saxon empire.[31]

A more orthodox critique of the Corn Laws was made by James Mill some months earlier, in reply to Malthus's first Corn-Law pamphlet. As in his 1808 booklet Mill used the 'eighteenth-century rule' to demonstrate the efficiency gains of foreign trade:

If we import, we must pay for what we import, with the produce of a portion of our labour exported. But why not employ that labour in raising the same portion at home? The answer is, because it will procure more corn by going in the shape of commodities to purchase corn abroad, than if it had been employed in raising it at home. A law, therefore, to prevent the importation of corn, can have only one effect, – to make a greater portion of the labour of the community necessary for the production of its food.[32]

There were practical advantages, too, in a policy of free importation of food. Excessive price fluctuations for food grains could be avoided, and more regular supplies assured if instead of relying only on domestic resources, diversification of sources of supply was made use of through free importation of corn from several countries. The remedy for corn-price instability was to extend international trade. That would tend to smooth out cyclical fluctuations, thereby lessening the effect on prices of any one country's production. Complementary trading relationships would develop between Britain and foreign corn-exporting countries – relationships that would be costly for foreigners to disrupt because of their specialisation in primary production. He referred (as Torrens did, some months earlier) to the example of Holland which had attained unparalleled opulence without reliance on domestic self-sufficiency in foodstuffs. He thus made light of Malthus's misgivings about reliance on imported foodstuffs, but ignored the argument that a nation specialising in manufactures could easily find its advantages eroded by foreign competition; and that such specialisation entailed a strong dependency on the continuous prosperity of the country's trading partners. Implicitly, that is, Mill assumed that the international division of labour so envisaged was going to be maintained permanently in Britain's favour. This, of course, followed from his static mode of reasoning which could not handle the sort of complications raised by Malthus.

RICARDO'S DYNAMIC ARGUMENTS

What about Ricardo's advocacy of repeal? Did he not, as is commonly believed, base his arguments on: (a) the law of comparative cost, and (b) a secularly falling rate of profit in the absence of repeal? The fact is, however, Ricardo never made use of the comparative-cost idea in his attack on the Corn Laws, but relied instead on absolute cost differences between Great Britain (in manufactures) and the rest of the world (in agriculture). In a recent analysis of the dynamic aspects of Ricardo's international trade theory, Andrea Maneschi concluded: 'Ricardo's advocacy of the repeal of the Corn Laws was not based on comparative advantage and did not require it'.[33] The comparative-cost example was irrelevant for Ricardo's argument in favour of repeal of agricultural protection for a manufacturing country like Britain, since that example merely highlighted the mechanism whereby consumers' preferences were satisfied in a context where international resources were optimally allocated. As Joan Robinson observed, a lower cost of procuring wine in England did not directly affect the profit-rate and did not lower the real cost of wage-goods – the whole advantage went to the drinkers of wine. But, as we have already suggested, Ricardo clearly understood that there were two distinct benefits of foreign trade – the static gains in terms of a larger consumption bundle, and the dynamic effect on the growth rates of profits and the wage fund – as the following passage indicates:

> it is quite as important to the happiness of mankind that our enjoyments should be increased by the better distribution of labour, by each country producing those commodities ... for which it is adapted, and by their exchanging them for the commodities of other countries, as that they should be augmented by a rise in the rate of profits.[34]

In his polemical campaign against the Corn Laws it was obviously more impressive to stress the dynamic argument based on absolute advantages. This is what he did in numerous correspondences, parliamentary speeches, two pamphlets and four chapters of his major work.

What, then, about the other supposed string to Ricardo's bow – the prospect of a falling rate of profit? There is a shadow over this as well. Leading authorities on Ricardo since Cannan's time have recognised that the theory of distribution was his most effective weapon against the protectionists – the argument suggesting how cheap imported corn could raise the rate of profit. Yet Hollander's detailed reading of Ricardo's writings and parliamentary speeches leads him to assert 'the case made [by Ricardo] against agricultural protection was not based upon the secular downward trend in the rate of return on capital'.[35] Professor O'Brien takes strong exception to this contentious interpretation of Ricardo saying: 'I find this about the most difficult thing to swallow in the entire book.'[36] The point at issue turns upon the question: Is Ricardo rightly to be regarded as an optimist or as a pessimist in regard to the prospects for British growth? The conventional view labels Ricardo as a pessimist because of his 'prediction' of a falling rate of profit and an inexorable drift towards the stationary state. Blaug did much to modify this traditional opinion of Ricardo, pointing out that the stationary state was Ricardo's 'methodological fiction': 'The alleged "pessimism" of Ricardo was entirely contingent upon the maintenance of the tariff on raw produce ... the notion of an impending stationary state was at most a useful device for frightening the friends of protection.'[37] Hollander goes further in painting an optimistic image of Ricardo. Ricardo was so confident of the dynamism of the British economy, he says, that even the Corn Laws and a protected regime could not prevail against the steadfast march of technical progress both in agriculture and manufacturing.

If Ricardo did not attach much empirical (as distinct from analytical) significance to the stationary state then he also did not believe that the Corn Laws posed serious problems for the profitability of British industry. In this interpretation – a view shared by Maxine Berg in her book *The Machinery Question and the Making of Political Economy* – technical change mattered as much for Ricardo as did free trade.[38] Even after the 80s-a-quarter Corn Law was passed on 10 March 1815 Ricardo continued to speak out against agricultural protection both in Parliament and in his writings (including correspondence). In view of the foregoing reconstitution of Ricardo's basic theory, what then were the grounds for his opposition? It appears he had three objections to the Corn Laws:

(1) They caused the profit rate and the rate of capital accumulation to be lower than would be the case under free trade. While protection in itself was not sufficient to bring about the stationary state, the rate of economic growth was rendered lower than in its absence.
(2) They caused excessive fluctuations in grain prices. Fluctuations in prices initiated by the alteration of good and bad harvests were amplified by the artificial wedge placed between domestic and foreign prices so as to maintain high-cost farming in Britain. Thus in times of good harvests (and excess supply) domestic prices had to fall dramatically to the level of world prices before increased sales could be made abroad. Greater stability in the price of corn would result from repeal since domestic prices would then be determined by the worldwide conditions of supply and demand.
(3) On efficiency or static-allocative grounds the Corn Laws were condemned since they caused domestic grain output to expand at the expense of domestic manufactured goods. On the given assumption that Britain's absolute advantage lay in manufacturing the country's welfare would therefore be increased by repeal independently of any effect on the profit- and growth-rate.

There is some uncertainty as to the relative weight placed by Ricardo on these distinct disadvantages. Consistent with Hollander's interpretation it is suggested that Ricardo did not himself take the first disadvantage too seriously. He was more concerned with the price instability and efficiency problems. It is one thing to suspect that Ricardo in his public utterances had a motivation to exaggerate the prospect of diminished profits for its propaganda value; but it is quite another to suggest that he himself did not believe it. Again, O'Brien disagrees with Hollander's account, alleging that the latter has 'emphasised the secondary at the expense of the primary ...';[39] and his comment on Hollander's restatement on this point is that 'it seems to be characterised more by rhetoric than by reasoned argument'.[40]

On corn-price instability there is no doubt that Ricardo was concerned with this problem, especially after 1820 at the time of agricultural distress. His pamphlet *On Protection to Agriculture* (1822) was partly devoted to this topic and he made several speeches in Parliament attributing grain-price fluctuations to the restrictive tariff policy. But considering Ricardo's anti-Corn-Law writings prior to 1822 (and incidentally a long section in *On Protection to Agriculture*) the bulk of which is concerned with profits and economic growth it cannot be maintained that Ricardo set great store on the price instability argument. Blaug was no doubt stating the correct position when he wrote: 'the matter of price variability was a secondary element in the Ricardian attack on the corn laws'.[41]

If anyone can be said to have been seriously bothered by the price-instability problem it is surely McCulloch. To a much greater extent than Ricardo, he consistently urged repeal on the assumption that it would result in greater stability of corn prices. He also felt that the abandonment of protection would stem the flow of capital abroad caused by a declining profit-rate. Malthus, Torrens and Thomas Tooke also referred to price fluctuations in connection with the debate on protection. Thomas Tooke collected data on harvest cycles and presented his analysis of the associated price fluctuations to the Commons Select Committee on Agriculture in 1821. In contrast to the free-traders expectation that free trade in corn would reduce price fluctuations, Malthus asserted that in fact only protection (regulation) could ensure a modicum of stability to an otherwise (i.e. naturally) unstable business.

We may summarise Ricardo's anti-Corn-Law position as follows: Free trade in corn was needed to offset diminishing returns in agriculture, the consequences of which acted as a drag on a potentially dynamic economy. Free importation of 'basic' commodities which enter into workers' consumption would alter the dynamic path of the economy, pushing it on to a higher trajectory appropriate to a country with an undoubted advantage in manufacturing. Once launched on such a blissful path, wages, profits and growth-rates could be expected to increase indefinitely. In a speech to the House of Commons on May 16 1822 (a year before his death) his optimistic vision was reported as follows:

Of all the evils complained of, he [Ricardo] was still disposed to think the corn laws the worst. He conceived that were the corn laws once got rid of, and our general policy in these subjects thoroughly revised, this would be the cheapest country in the world; and that, instead of our complaining that capital was withdrawn from us, we should find that capital would come hither from all corners of the civilized world ... If the government would pursue a right course of policy as to the corn laws, England would be the cheapest country in which a man could live; and it would rise to a state of prosperity, in regard to population and riches, of which, perhaps, the imaginations of hon. gentlemen could at present form no idea.[42]

Ricardo did not call for immediate and total repeal of the Corn Laws. In 1822 he wrote: 'that is not, under our circumstances, the course which I should recommend'.[43] Like Adam Smith, he was a pragmatic free-trader conscious of the power of vested interests. He wanted the system replaced by a 'countervailing duty' of 20/- a quarter initially, reducing annually over a ten-year period to stand permanently as a flat-rate duty of 10/- a quarter on all imported grain. This would be combined with a corresponding 'drawback upon exportation' (i.e. an export subsidy or refund of the domestic tax) of 7/-. He considered this level of protection adequate compensation for the special tax burdens which fell on agriculturists compared with industrialists (e.g. land tax, contributions to the poor rates, tithes and other direct charges on land). Given the existing tax system, this arrangement would also produce the best allocation of national resources and optimum level of aggregate national output. Ricardo's proposal for moderate protection was, however, turned down by the House of Commons – only twenty-five members supported it.

On free trade in general and commercial policy, Ricardo's position was less than forthright compared with his resolute stand against the Corn Laws. Despite the comparative-cost example, his thought in the direction of free trade apparently stopped short at the juncture where capital, in the form of wage-goods, needed for industrial growth could more readily be obtained at better terms from abroad. It is true, generalised free trade only became a matter of public debate from about 1820, shortly before Ricardo's untimely death; but he was in the House of Commons when the famous Merchants' Petition (1820) calling for freer trade was debated. His performance on this occasion was, however, disappointing. W. D. Grampp writes: 'He supported the petition, of course, but he did not enlarge on the case for free trade and made no mention of his own ideas (which he did do on other issues).'[44]

For Ricardo, the significant contribution of trade to national economic development lay in its impact on agricultural prices. When he thought of free trade it was always in terms of a manufacturing country being able to obtain cheap food and raw materials from other countries better endowed with natural resources. Thus: 'While trade is free and corn cheap, profits will not fall however great the accumulation of capital.'[45]

The crucial test was thus the effect of trade on the rate of profit and hence accumulation. The importation of luxury goods (wine, silks, velvets – 'trinkets for the rich') does not matter on this criterion, since trade in such goods leaves the profit-rate unaffected. In his formal theory he clearly distinguished between national and cosmopolitan gains from trade and changes in trade policy. Thus in his analysis of colonial trade, he agreed with Adam Smith that the colonies were disadvantaged by the regime of regulated trade and would benefit from freer trade. But, he argued that 'the trade of a colony may be so regulated that it shall at the same time be less beneficial to the colony and more beneficial to the mother country than a perfectly free trade'.[46] And, 'a measure which may be greatly hurtful to a colony may be partially beneficial to the mother country'.[47] It was nearly always from the perspective of the metropolitan country that he viewed matters relating to colonial trade, just as in trade policy it was always the interest of Britain which mattered.[48] He did not extend the dynamic implications of his model to the countries that were to supply Britain with foodstuffs. He assumed that an elastic supply of food could be obtained from overseas; and although the implications of world-wide diminishing returns in primary production must have been obvious to him, he relegated that eventuality to the distant future. In the meantime, as far as Britain was concerned, free international trade on that basis could make an important contribution to Britain's economic growth. He considered the static benefits accruing to those countries, i.e. the opportunity, given free trade and the reallocation of resources, of obtaining cheap British manufactures. But he failed to recognise that the pattern of product specialisation determined by free trade might be detrimental to the long-term interests of the food-producing countries and that they would take steps to alter the comparative-advantage bases of their national economies. He believed that the world economy functioned in a setting of reasonable international equilibrium and did not envisage problems associated with a balance-of-payments constraint on growth, cyclical slumps and conditions of price and income inelasticity of demand for primary products. Diminishing agricultural efficiency was the centrepiece of his growth analysis, yet he did not stop to consider that this (combined with free trade) would prove a handicap to the development of primary-producing countries in the absence of massive capital investment to counteract the forces of diminishing returns. He was right in his diagnosis that Britain's comparative advantage lay in manufacturing, and that the implied national specialisation would be further strengthened 'by the improvements in machinery, by the better division and distribution of labour, and by the increasing skill, both in science and art, of the producers'.[49] The remarkable growth he predicted did occur, and free trade, when it came, did produce substantial material benefits for the nation. He supported a commercial policy which led to the intense involvement of Britain in the international economy and tied the country's growth in output and living standards to the vicissitudes of the international environment. 'He espoused more balanced international growth, even though it meant more "unbalanced" domestic growth', as J. M. Letiche summarises it.[50] This orientation of the economy was, as we have seen, much regretted by Malthus. His formal theory left unanswered the question: What would become of the source of comparative advantage if knowledge, skills and technology were to be diffused throughout the world economy?

To be sure, as presented in terms of the pure theory of barter, his model suggested that the distribution of tasks among nations was fixed for all time, i.e. that the world distribution of comparative advantages was something static and permanent. This is the conventional view; but it neglects what Ricardo had to say later on in his trade chapter about the international distribution of specie. Here he discussed cases where comparative advantage could change under the impact of technical change, improvements in the arts and machinery or the discovery of new processes. He supposes a situation where English wine technology improves to such an extent that it becomes profitable for England to export wine in exchange for Portuguese cloth – a reversal of comparative advantages and the emergence of a new pattern of trade: 'If the improvement in making wine were of a very important description, it might become profitable for the two countries to exchange employments; for England to make all the wine, and Portugal all the cloth consumed by them.'[51] The idea was, however, not developed; it remained embedded in the particular hypothetical context designed to show the effects of monetary movements, and it is not clear that the circumstances depicted represents a true trading equilibrium. Moreover, the example does not arise in a dynamic setting in which the efficiency of production may change over time, e.g. due to increasing returns, external economies, etc.

Like his father, John Stuart Mill was a severe critic of the Corn Laws. But when he came to write on the issue (in the late 1820s) the matter – at least in principle – was fairly well rehearsed.[52] The parliamentary debates were still intense and lengthy, but there was general recognition of the impossibility of agricultural self-sufficiency in the face of growing population pressure. In addition, the competitive ability of British manufacturers in foreign markets seemed reasonably secure; and the Tory government was on the verge of conceding the necessity for some modification of the Corn Laws. J. S. Mill felt it unnecessary, therefore, to go over the ground covered by his father twenty years earlier in *Commerce Defended*. He was relieved to say: 'One part of the argument we may safely omit . . . the beneficial tendency of free trade in general.'[53] He repeated Ricardo's charge that only the landowners had a permanent interest in protection. But they were misguided, since the landlord 'if he has an interest opposed to that of the community, he has also an interest in common with them'.[54] Mill then stressed the mutuality of interests: cheap foreign food would mean lower poor rates, which would lighten the burden on agriculturists. He allayed the fears of landowners and farmers by predicting that the price of corn would not fall to such levels that would cause widespread bankruptcies and unrelieved distress and endorsed Ricardo's plan for a compensating duty after the phasing out of protection.

Two years later, exasperated by the temporising attitude of the government, he castigated the 'fury of the band of enraged monopolists', i.e. the landlords, whose obstinacy stood in the way of national progress. Resignedly, he lamented:

> Let those be disappointed who looked for any thing better: we confess that our hopes were never very sanguine. It would argue little experience of human affairs to expect from monopolists the abandonment of a monopoly; from landlords the voluntary abatement of rent.[55]

But Mill did not give up. He continued to support the popular campaign against the Corn Laws, and his last recorded effort in this direction was the drafting of a petition unanimously adopted at a free-trade meeting in Kensington, 15 June 1841. This brings us to a consideration of the classical economists' views on commercial policy in general.

5.2 Commercial Policy

In a book on the rise of modern protectionism, Melvyn Krauss writes: 'the conflict between the economic interests of specific groups within the community and the economic interests of the community as a whole is the essence of the issue of free trade versus protectionism'.[56] The classical economists were only too well aware of this. In a speech to the House of Commons on agricultural distress Ricardo observed that protection 'might be beneficial to a particular trade, but it must be injurious to the rest of the country'.[57] But much as it is today, the nineteenth-century controversy was wider than this. It ranged from matters relating to national security to fears over the export of machinery. Thus apart from the pleas of the lobbyists, the free-traders had to contend with the arguments that free trade would: (a) diminish national power and make the country dependent on foreigners; (b) reduce government revenue and therefore increase the national debt; (c) be a renunciation of the country's ability to improve its bargaining position *vis-à-vis* other countries (i.e. the terms of trade argument); (d) lead to the transfer of technology abroad (through the export of machinery) and therefore to the erosion of national competitive advantages and (e) leave a country without the means of fostering the growth of 'infant industries' against competition from abroad.

On the purely nationalistic, beggar-thy-neighbour and politically inspired arguments some of the economists felt that the fears behind them were exaggerated and minimised the force of the arguments while others supported all or some of them. There were those among them who managed to give free trade a mercantilist twist, as clearly exemplified in the works of Torrens. Free trade was seen as a means of gaining for Britain a monopoly of trade in manufactured goods. This projected economic hegemony could be realised by persuading other countries to adopt free trade.

Even the more orthodox of the early classical economists were not extreme and uncompromising free-traders. Like Adam Smith, they qualified their advocacy of free trade in a number of ways: (1) the defence argument for protecting strategically important industries; (2) the revenue argument and (3) the desirability of imposing a compensatory tax on imports where an excise tax on domestic production existed so as to maintain fair competition between domestic and foreign producers.

As the debate on free trade progressed, the economists became clearer what the purely economic arguments were. As a result of this two major exceptions to international *laissez-faire* were conceded: (1) the 'terms-of-trade' argument and (2) the infant-industry argument. The logic of these arguments had to be admitted, for they met the economists' own criteria of (a) buying in the cheapest market and selling in the highest, and (b) long-run efficiency in the allocation of resources. Reservations relating to the practical application of these devices were made, of course and, in addition, some cosmopolitan-minded economists (particularly later neoclassical writers like Edgeworth and Marshall) objected to the narrowly national self-interest on which the arguments rested.

We shall briefly discuss how these economically defensible arguments for protection came to be accepted, but first a comment on the income-distribution aspect. Ricardo, Torrens and Malthus recognised early in the Corn Laws debate that agricultural protection tended to raise landlords' share in the national income. As noted previously, Malthus (in his two Corn Law pamphlets) explicitly discussed the question in terms of the effect of a rise in the price of corn and other commodities. He concluded that high corn-prices meant high wage-rates and that therefore the Corn Laws benefited labour as well, since the purchasing power of workers' income over non-food commodities were thereby enhanced. But, as we have seen, this was not a deduction from the 'one-factor only' formal model of comparative cost – with a one-factor model, income-distribution changes simply do not arise. Neither was it derived from any generalised concept of marginal productivity. What was clear from the Torrens–Ricardo model, though, was that free trade in corn would maximise Britain's national income as a whole. From this larger total income, landlords who lost out from free trade would ultimately benefit; for they knew for sure that repeal of the Corn Laws would benefit capitalists and injure landlords. Alternatively, they implicitly assumed that the change in income distribution could be compensated for by appropriate changes in taxation. Indeed, Lord Landsdowne, the Whig spokesman on economic affairs in the Lords and later a member of the Political Economy Club made just such a proposal in connection with a specific case: the compensation out of public funds for the losses incurred by silk workers consequent upon the freer entry of French silks into Britain.[58] However, in the absence of an automatic mechanism for compensation, could it still be maintained that the gains from free trade constituted an unambiguous improvement in welfare? Henry Brougham was one who implicitly denied this on the ground that since obviously all individuals were not identical in every relevant respect it was impossible to make interpersonal comparisons of utility (or well-being); hence, 'the destruction of one portion of the community could not be considered a benefit, because another portion gained by it. This was a proposition which no philosopher or political economist had ever attempted to deny or dispute.'[59] Finally, then, those who sought to minimise the adjustment costs of free trade were forced to fall back on the factor-mobility assumption. Taking their cue from Adam Smith, and confident that resources (including labour) would be redeployed speedily, the income-distribution effect did not pose a problem for the free-trade case.

It is of some interest to note in connection with the income-distribution implications of the classical theory the fact that as late as 1929 the classical theory was used by Australian economists to derive important policy results which were later shown to be broadly in conformity with the predictions of the 'modern' Heckscher–Ohlin theory of trade. The case in point refers to the semi-official Brigden Report on the Australian tariff (1929) and the part played by Marion Crawford Samuelson and others. Briefly, the Brigden Report concluded that the tariff operated in Australia's national interest since, without it, Australia would not have been able to maintain its increased population at the relatively high current standard of living. The authors of the Report derived their conclusions from nothing more sophisticated than the simple Ricardian theory of trade and growth, without terms-of-trade effects. In response to criticisms of these findings by free-trade theorists (Haberler, Viner, Anderson) M. C. Samuelson in 1939 showed the Australian economists' findings were analytically consistent with a form of the Heckscher–Ohlin theory incorporating certain classical assumptions – a model that Paul Samuelson has also described as 'precisely the Ricardian model that David Ricardo used in his arguments with Malthus on the Corn Laws'.[60]

Two years later a fully fledged neoclassical model appeared – the Stolper–Samuelson theorem (1941), which thenceforth became the standard treatment of changes in trade and factor shares. What the Australian episode illustrates, however, is the remarkable adaptability of Ricardian-type models for dealing fairly rigorously with a wide range of trade-related issues.

THE TERMS-OF-TRADE ARGUMENT

There was, however, a logical flaw in early statements of the free-trade doctrine. When writers recommended free trade they often gave the impression that it was a choice between free trade and no trade, whereas in reality it was about free trade versus protection. Generally, these writers underestimated the adverse short-run effects likely to be caused by removal of restrictions. In particular, they implicitly might have assumed that the movement from protection to free trade would not alter a country's terms of trade. Of the leading writers, Malthus first faced this issue and Torrens and John Stuart Mill and others analysed the commercial policy implications of the terms of trade. No construct in the pure theory of trade has given rise to greater public controversy and heated debate in international forums than the terms of trade; and the credit (or blame) for initiating the terms-of-trade debate goes to the early classical political economists. Torrens (1852) claimed: 'No questions in political economy are of greater importance than those which relate to the terms of international exchange. ...'[61] One of the doubts Malthus harboured about the benefit of free trade against the enthusiastic supporters of industrial growth through unrestricted international commerce concerned the possibility of adverse repercussions on the terms of trade. If free trade stimulated the cheapening of manufactures (through productivity growth) and no significant expansion of demand took place abroad

> then the increasing ingenuity and exertions of a manufacturing and commercial state (such as Britain) would be lost in continually falling prices. It would not only be obliged, as its skill and capital increased, to give a larger quantity of manufactured produce for the raw produce which it received in return; but it might be unable, even with the temptation of reduced prices, to stimulate its customers to such purchases as would allow of an increasing importation of food and raw materials; and without such an increasing importation, it is quite obvious that the population must become stationary.[62]

In other words, if foreigners did not have anything with which to trade in return for all the goods that British exporters were so keen to sell them, then inevitably there would be a deterioration in Britain's commodity (or net barter) terms of trade. But even with such lower prices British manufacturers might not be able to sell their goods because of deficient demand abroad. The result of this overproduction would be continuously falling prices and profits.

Another source of stagnation might arise from foreign competition. Thus:

When a powerful foreign competition takes place, the exportable commodities of the country in question must soon fall in prices which will essentially reduce profits; and the fall of profits will diminish both the power and the will to save. Under these circumstances the accumulation of capital will be slow, till it comes nearly to a stand.[63]

Malthus worried about the problem of effective demand, i.e. the permanent and persistent tendency for the total supply of goods to outstrip demand. His fears were shared by others (Sismondi, Chalmers, Lord Lauderdale), but brushed aside by James Mill, J. B. Say, Ricardo and McCulloch on the grounds of the adjustability of production and insatiability of demand. 'I consider the wants and tastes of mankind as unlimited'; and 'if there is a glut of one commodity produce less of that and more of another' was Ricardo's reply to Malthus.[64] Nevertheless it was Malthus's belief that specialisation in international trade was the source both of glutted markets and adverse terms of trade. The industrial economy would, no doubt, adjust to disequilibrium in the way suggested by Ricardo, i.e. by the reduction in output of the overproduced and unprofitable commodities. But this would 'throw labourers out of work' and lead to general unemployment. Malthus knew that Sismondi, another critic of industrial capitalism, came to the same conclusion about the effects of overproduction and glutted world markets inherent in unrestricted international competition – falling prices, redundant capital, stagnation, unemployment and crises. Sismondi had reported (1819):

We have seen merchandize of every description, but above all that of England, the great manufacturing power, abounding in all the markets of Italy in a proportion so far exceeding demand, that the merchants, in order to realize even a part of their capital, have been obliged to dispose of them at a loss of a fourth or a third, instead of obtaining any profit.[65]

Say's answer to the problem: 'The quantity of English merchandize offered for sale in Italy and elsewhere is too great, because there is not sufficient Italian or other produce suitable to the English market'[66] did not satisfy Sismondi and Malthus. Equilibrium would, no doubt, be established at market-clearing prices if a counter set of commodities were produced and offered for sale in the glutted market. But that was precisely the problem! As Joan Robinson once remarked on another occasion: 'The hidden hand will always do its work, but it may work by strangulation.'[67] Given the specificity of factors, the existence of inertia, indolence, etc., the adjustment to equilibrium can be a protracted and painful process. Chipman, in his survey article, gave credit to Torrens for his early attempt to prove the existence of competitive equilibrium (via price adjustments) in such case including a statement describing a cobweb path to equilibrium.[68] But a decade later Torrens completely reversed his position on this question when he asserted that 'in a country exporting manufactured goods, and importing raw materials, there may be a general glut of capital, and excess of production, in relation to foreign demand, which cannot be remedied by transferring capital from one branch of manufacturing to another'.[69]

Malthus reverted to the possibility of deteriorating terms of trade (resulting from increased investment in export production) in his 1820 *Principles*. There he outlined the argument in greater detail, hinting also at single-factoral terms of trade losses (where one unit of labour exported bought less foreign goods):

> as capital continued to be accumulated and employed in large quantities on the exportable manufactures, such manufactures, upon the principles of demand and supply, would in all probability fall in price. A larger portion of them must then be exchanged for a given portion of corn ... , more work being necessary to earn the same quantity of corn ...[70]

Sir William G. Sleeman, an anti-Ricardian writer, noting the fall in manufactured goods' prices caused by the efficiency of British industry, said that meant foreign countries 'are continuously giving less and less of the produce of their domestic industry for the same thing, or receiving more and more of our produce for the same portion of theirs'.[71] In 1833 George Poulett Scrope made a case for colonisation based partly on alleged unfavourable terms of trade to Britain when it obtained its food supplies from foreign countries under free-trade conditions. The efficiency of agricultural production in these non-British countries might not keep pace with Britain's own growth, and thus 'we carry on what may be called a losing trade with them; we are continually exchanging larger quantitities of the produce of our industry for less quantities of theirs'. The answer to this adverse trend under generalised free trade was for Britain to develop agricultural resources in the colonies with British capital and labour and thus free itself from dependence 'on the slow increase of the productive capacities of foreigners'.[72] In an earlier article, Poulett Scrope referred to a phenomenon now known in the literature as 'immiserising growth'. This is the case where factor accumulation and the resulting growth in output actually makes an open economy worse off than under autarky. That is, if (a) the growing country is large enough to influence the international terms of trade; (b) demand is inelastic, and (c) the productivity growth is largely experienced in the export industry, then it is possible for the deterioration in the terms of trade to be so large as to outweigh the effect of the physical increase in output and therefore leave the country worse off than before. Scrope contended that deteriorating terms of trade (initiated by faster growth in the home country than elsewhere) would cause wages and profits to fall in England, with the result that 'the general condition of that country must rather deteriorate than improve through its increasing productiveness'.[73] Scrope stated the problem; he did not analyse it. Although one can take his reference to lowered wages and profits as implying a reduction in aggregate national real income, it is not clear how 'immiserising growth' actually arises from his hypothetical example – as Bloomfield recently observed.[74] Torrens frequently wrote about the adverse repercussions on the terms of trade of British growth. In 1837 he observed:

> If in the markets of America, the demand for English goods should remain stationary, while the supply of them should be increased, then, in the American markets, a given quantity of English goods would exchange for a less quantity of American produce than before.[75]

From these writings it was obvious that unfavourable terms-of-trade trends could be arrested or reversed by commercial policy. It was soon realised by imposing a tariff a country could, by restricting the volume of its imports, lower the price of importables relative to its exports – thereby improving the terms of trade. Torrens was one who saw the benefit of a tariff to Britain, and became a firm advocate of 'reciprocity' as the indispensable basis of a country's commercial policy. But here again, although he was the first in print with the terms-of-trade argument, the idea was not original with him; for John Stuart Mill had formulated the argument on the economics of reciprocity since 1829, but only published it in 1844, i.e. the first chapter of Mill's *Essays on Some Unsettled Questions in Political Economy*. Torrens was, of course, always at his best when advocating or attacking specific policies. He had no hesitation in changing or modifying his basic theory to suit the shifts and turns in his practical opinions. He criticised Malthus for abandoning principles firmly held; but he himself was guilty of this charge, for in his early writings Torrens advocated unconditional free trade or unilateral tariffs reductions – he was, after all, a co-discoverer of the comparative-cost principle. As a member of the Political Economy Club he was a signatory of the Merchants' Petition (1820), which he also supported in his newspaper, *The Traveller*. A year later he was still an unequivocal free trader, as his *Essay on the Production of Wealth* attests. But by the 1830s he moved away from free trade. He expressed doubts as to the unilateral reduction of import duties. By the 1840s these fundamental reservations developed into active opposition, to the point where he came close to repudiating his own concept of 'territorial division of labour'. Initially, at any rate, Torrens's defence of reciprocity seems to have rested on fear of deflation and general economic stagnation, as F. W. Fetter pointed out.[76] It was an old mercantilist argument, of course: tariffs are necessary to stem the outflow of specie which would otherwise cause deflation and unemployment. But Torrens soon after coupled this with the more orthodox terms-of-trade argument. The unilateral removal of import duties turned the terms of trade against Britain; therefore the country should not lower its tariffs unilaterally, but only if British tariff cuts were matched by equivalent tariff reductions on the part of other countries. Torrens's recommendations were challenged by, among others, Senior and McCulloch.

Like Frank Graham a century later, Senior seemed to have claimed that demand variations had no practical effect in the long run. An equilibrium price-ratio determined exclusively by reciprocal demand was the exception rather than the rule. The pattern of international specialisation, influenced as it was by productivity differences, was, he held, remarkably stable. Thus, costs of production determine value in international trade. Senior habitually thought of international trade in monetary terms, and was fully conscious that in the real world trade takes place in many commodities among many countries. Given this approach, he faulted Torrens's argument on several grounds:[77]

(1) World prices are comparatively little affected by changes in supply or demand from particular countries, i.e. the elasticity of supply in world trade is infinite. Substitution effects on the supply side exert a stabilising effect.
(2) Tariffs interfere with optimal resource allocation by limiting the division of labour and specialisation. It forces capital and labour into branches of production where their value-productivities as measured by world-market prices were less than fully maximised.
(3) Torrens was misled by his 2×2 model. In a multi-commodity,

multi-country world the diminished efficiency of capital and labour in the tariff-imposing country would lead to a deterioration of the country's international competitive position, both in the domestic market and markets abroad. The gain from tariff restriction is therefore purely illusory, according to Senior; for whatever extra specie is obtained by this policy would rapidly be lost again because of reduced factor productivity and higher unit costs relative to those abroad.

Senior did not deny that there was a valid terms-of-trade argument on purely theoretical grounds, but he doubted that the conditions under which the argument was valid did, in fact, prevail generally in the real world. Most countries were not in a position to practise favourable manipulations of the terms of trade, and it was highly unlikely that cartel-type arrangements among groups of countries (principal suppliers) would prove viable. Special cases of inelastic demand and rigid price structures were conceivable, but it was unrealistic to assume that the supply response of the rest of the world remained the same whether or not tariffs were imposed. Foreign producers might have other outlets for their exports, or they might prefer to shift to other products or simply reduce output.[78]

Like Senior, McCulloch ruled out the practical possibility of rigging the terms of trade on the ground that the elasticity of supply in international trade is infinite.[79] But according to Professor O'Brien, his argument was more convincing than that of Senior's because McCulloch consistently held a cost-of-production theory of trade based squarely on absolute differences in such costs. Costs of production, not demand, govern world prices and these were further constrained within limits set by a competitive international average rate of return. Thus unique among the classical economists, McCulloch was able to reject Torrens's case on theoretical grounds. In addition, because of the certainty of retaliation and the loss from trade diversion, McCulloch dismissed Torrens's case as irrelevant and inconsequential.[80] But surely Torrens was attempting to make a valid point: if a country can monopolistically affect the prices of what it buys and sells on world markets, then free trade would not be the optimal policy. By exploiting its monopoly or monopsony power, the country can turn the terms of trade in its favour at the expense of restricting its trade volume – the optimum position being one where the gain from improved terms of trade exceeds by the greatest possible margin the loss from reduced trade volume. This is what Torrens said. He was hinting at the 'optimum-tariff' argument. However, he did not analyse fully the conditions under which the argument was valid. In his reply to Senior's criticisms, Torrens claimed that if the tariff caused wage-rates in the export sector to be higher than under free trade then, despite the allocative-efficiency losses from a reduced volume of trade, this showed that the country enjoyed a net gain. But aggregate wages (and profits) might fall, and therefore it was not at all clear that total national income (or welfare) would have been augmented with trade restriction. Torrens was misled by his naïve assumption that the efficiency of labour could only be measured by the terms of trade. The issues involved in this argument only became clearer with J. S. Mill's elaboration of reciprocal demand functions, which were, in principle, welfare functions representing net incomes.[81]

Torrens's real aim was the creation of an imperial Zollverein (a free-trade area protected by discriminatory tariffs against the outside world) linked to an active programme of colonisation so that 'England might become a vast industrial metropolis, and the colonies agricultural provinces of unlimited extent. ... By extending our colonial system, and opening new and expanding markets in our trans-marine dependencies, coupled with the rigid enforcement of the principle of reciprocity, we may arm ourselves with accumulating force to break down hostile tariffs, and to establish free trade throughout the world.'[82]

Torrens backed up Wakefield's theory of self-financing colonisation with economic arguments based on his fears of adverse terms of trade (arising from protective tariffs in America and Europe), oversupply of capital and labour in England and the depressive effects these produced on the domestic rate of profit and wages. He evidently sincerely believed in an 'economy of high wages' and sought an escape from Malthusian pessimism (diminishing returns, falling rate of profit and excess population) in emigration. From the late 1820s, therefore, Torrens linked colonisation with British capital redundancy and commercial policy. Thus, after remarking on the tendency towards adverse terms of trade, he continued:

> On these obvious, and universally admitted principles of commerce, we can explain the process by which, in a commercial and manufacturing country, importing raw produce, the increase of commercial and manufacturing capital may lower the wages of the operative class.[83]

This led him to repudiate the Mill–Say law of markets which obviously did not square with observed facts. But, as Chipman reminds us, even as Torrens's thought took a different turn, analytically he did not abandon his previous position on gluts. That is, Torrens always maintained that surplus capital and gluts would not occur in crisis proportions if there was 'a proportional extension of the foreign market'. By the latter he meant a proportional increase in foreign demand or a sufficient increase in the supply of foreign exportables, i.e. the counter-commodity argument. Torrens's diagnosis was substantially correct. There was a crisis in the export sector at that time, and Britain experienced adverse movements in her net barter terms of trade – a combined tendency which acted as a drag on Britain's growth. In these circumstances of sluggish trade in goods, he reasoned, the general economic stagnation could only be relieved by labour and capital movements to the 'empty' lands of the Empire in Canada, Australia and South Africa – a policy he summarised in a parliamentary speech (15 February 1827): 'England had a redundant population, while the colonies had redundant land. Emigration therefore was merely a method of the application of the redundant capital and population of the United Kingdom to the redundant lands of the colonies.'[84]

Commenting on this imperial strategy, a modern historian approvingly observes, 'without a most unlikely restructuring of the economy and society, it does not seem possible that any large part of the resources devoted to supplying the export trade and to overseas investment could have found alternative uses'.[85]

This consciously designed policy was, of course, a breach of strict *laissez-faire* principles – even though under Wakefield's scheme, private companies, not the state, were the principal agents; and one might have queried whether colonisation was indeed the only answer to surplus capital. The rate of return was as high (perhaps even higher) in South America and Europe as it was in the colonies. There was no particular reason why capital should be directed in a certain direction. As early as 1821, one writer pointed out: 'Should capital find no profitable employment in one country it will soon go to seek for it in another ... capital will not lose its uses anywhere, till every corner of the world has acquired as large a share of it as can be productively employed.'[86] Huskisson (at the Board of Trade) also warned that colonisation merely shifted the problem elsewhere 'by causing a glut of population there, and thereby creating a production beyond any demand the emigrants could obtain for it in an advantageous interchange with other countries'.[87] But as far as Torrens was concerned, the case for colonisation did not rest solely on economic considerations; it was part of the plan to enhance Britain's imperial greatness. In the 1827 speech in Parliament he unfolded the grander purpose of emigration:

> In giving effect to extensive and improved plans for colonisation, we are multiplying the British nation; we are rocking the cradles of giant empires; we are cooperating in the schemes of Providence, and are its favoured instruments in causing civilization to cover the earth, as the waters cover the sea.[88]

Besides Torrens, Wakefield's project was also endorsed by J. S. Mill, Poulett Scrope and Bentham.[89]

MILL ON THE TERMS-OF-TRADE ARGUMENT

As far as Mill was concerned, the terms-of-trade argument arose naturally from his work on the market mechanism in international trade. Mill revealed in the preface to the *Essays* that they were actually written much earlier and were published (1844) in response to the writings of Torrens, with whom he disagreed as to the practical application of the argument. Mill's analysis showed that tariffs affect the ratio of interchange between exports and imports, i.e. the reciprocal offers of the trading countries can be altered by exploiting monopolistic/monopsonistic advantages in foreign trade. Writing on British tariffs, Mill noted: 'if the restrictions were removed, we should have to pay rather more for some of the articles which we now import, while the articles which we are now prevented from importing would cost more than might be inferred from their *present* price in the foreign market'.[90] Under certain circumstances, Mill's analysis showed, taxes on imports and exports can be paid entirely by the foreigner. Although he drew too sharp a distinction between revenue and protective duties, he never had any misconception about the benefits which a single country could derive (at the expense of its neighbours) from imposing revenue duties. Recognising this, Mill was a strong supporter of reciprocity:

> A country cannot be expected to renounce the power of taxing foreigners, unless foreigners will in return practise towards itself the same forbearance. The only mode in which a country can save itself from being a loser by the duties imposed by other countries on its commodities, is to impose corresponding duties on theirs.[91]

Equally, however, Mill clearly recognised the theoretical limitations and practical drawbacks of a policy of 'taxing the foreigner'. First, it only applies if the reciprocal demand of the outside world has a low elasticity and the tariff-imposing country's own reciprocal demand a high elasticity. Second, retaliation is likely; this tends to neutralise the initial advantage to the tariff-imposing country. Third, it is a desirable policy strictly from the national point of view. Better terms of trade for one country necessarily implies worse terms of trade for its trading partners. The misallocation of resources (i.e. the distortions in production and consumption) resulting from the pursuit of national gains is a general loss for the world as a whole. If the losses of trading partners exceed the gains of the tariff-imposing country, then such an outcome is patently unjust as well as economically undesirable.

Mill candidly discussed the difficulties which attended a policy of unilateral free trade except for imports that could be classified as 'necessaries of life' or 'materials and instruments of production'. Writing in the aftermath of the crisis of 1825 and the depression which followed, he felt a strong sympathy with the businessmen, who complained about the flood of imports, and criticised the doctrinaire free-traders for their uncritical acceptance of Hume's Law, i.e. that increased imports necessarily and automatically generated more exports. An influx of imports, he wrote,

> is a forced increase, produced by an efflux of money and fall of prices; and this fall of prices being permanent, although it would be no evil at all in a country where credit is unknown, it may be a very serious one where large classes of persons, and the nation itself, are under engagements to pay fixed sums of money of large amount.[92]

Apart from the disruption caused by the rush of imports, Mill also consistently wrote about the adverse shift in the terms of trade that was bound to follow the unilateral abolition of tariffs.

The mere removal of trade restrictions was not sufficient to keep up the domestic rate of profit. Population pressure and excessive capital accumulation called for expanding markets for exports, additional sources of supplies of produce and raw materials and new investment opportunities overseas. In recognition of these needs Mill found in emigration, colonisation and foreign investment solutions to the problems of the British economy. Consequently, at the theoretical level Mill's position moved closer to that taken by Malthus, Sismondi and Torrens. In the second of his early essays, 'On the Influence of

Consumption on Production', he mounted a trenchant refutation of Say's Law:

> Of the capital of a country there is at all times a very large proportion lying idle. The annual produce of a country is never anything approaching in magnitude to what it might be if all the resources devoted to reproduction, if all the capital, in short, of a country were in full employment.[93]

And again:

> This argument [Say's Law] is evidently founded on the supposition of a state of barter. ... If, however, we suppose that money is used, these propositions cease to be exactly true. ... Although he who sells, really sells only to buy, he needs not buy at the same moment when he sells; and he does not therefore necessarily add to the *immediate* demand for one commodity when he adds to the supply of the other.[94]

Mill returned to a more orthodox line in his *Principles* for, although bits and pieces of the earlier analysis are there, the stress in the later work is on the stability of equilibrium. Mill's position on reciprocity in trade relations also rested partly on his belief that

> the richest countries, *caeteris paribus*, gain the least by a given amount of foreign commerce: since, having a greater demand for commodities generally, they are likely to have a greater demand for foreign commodities, and thus modify the terms of interchange to their own disadvantage.[95]

The explanation for 'Mill's paradox', as Edgeworth called it, was, of course, that an expanding industrial economy such as Britain would soon run up against deterioriating terms of trade unless wider export markets for manufactures could be found and a more rapid development of agricultural resources took place. In the short run, reciprocity would ensure a more balanced growth of trade without imposing welfare losses on Britain; but in the long run, the answer lay in the export of British capital and labour to develop the resources of the 'larger community' of the British Empire.

Mill explained the matter as follows:

> It is to the emigration of English capital that we have chiefly to look for keeping a supply of cheap food and cheap materials of

clothing proportional to the increase of our population; thus enabling an increasing capital to find employment in the country, without reduction of profit, in producing manufactured articles with which to pay for this supply of raw produce. Thus, the exportation of capital is an agent of great efficiency in extending the field for that which remains and it may be said truly that up to a certain point the more capital we send away, the more we shall possess and be able to retain at home.[96]

But Mill did not go along with Torrens when the latter claimed that the advantages from trade could only be realised on terms of perfect reciprocity; and that therefore increased British duties were required to force foreign countries to negotiate reciprocal reductions in tariffs on manufactured goods, or as retaliation against the imposition of hostile foreign tariffs. As early as 1829 Mill pointed out that, despite deteriorating net barter terms of trade, Britain still gained substantially from trade:

> On the whole, England probably, of all the countries of Europe, draws to herself the largest share of the gains of international commerce: because her exportable articles are in universal demand, and are of such a kind that the demand increases rapidly as the price falls.[97]

This statement does not confict with 'Mill's paradox', noted above. The latter is a general proposition about the adverse effects of growth (factor accumulation, technical progress or a general increase in productivity) on the growing country's net barter terms of trade. The point he is now making is that trends in the ratio of import and export prices (whether favourable or unfavourable) do not tell the whole story about the total gains from trade. One needs to take into account also trends in the volume of trade, since the actual gains from trade depend on both the terms of trade and the volume of exports and imports. The two are partly interconnected and partly independent. A country may have highly favourable terms of trade, but if this means that its exports are too expensive for foreigners to buy then the country has zero trade volume and makes no gain at all from trade. Just as a firm's success in the market is measured by the extent to which it maximises net revenue from sales (quantity sold times unit price), so a country's total gain from foreign trade is measured by its net proceeds from foreign sales. This is what Mill was referring to in the passage quoted. Britain's gain from international trade was still substantial, for, although export prices were falling (e.g. for cotton goods), the volume of exports were rapidly expanding (relative to other European competitors) because of high income and price elasticity of demand for British manufactures in world markets.

To round off this discussion of the terms-of-trade argument it is of some relevance to consider the claim of a modern historian (Donald N. McCloskey) that free trade lowered the rate of growth of British national income during the period 1841–81.[98] It did this by causing British terms of trade to deteriorate over the period; and in this sense free trade imposed a welfare loss on the British people. This finding challenges the conventional view that trade was for Britain a powerful 'engine of growth', and that the coming of free trade was a significant factor in the explanation of the marked rise in the British growth-rate at mid-century. By implication he attributes the 'grotesque prominence' given to foreign trade as a causal factor in Britain's growth to the uncritical acceptance by historians of free-trade ideology and the free-trade bias of economists from Smith to Marshall whose practical motive 'was in large part the early encouragement and late defense of Britain's policy of free trade'.[99] However, the charge that the early classical economists ignored the risks attached to greater involvement in the international economy cannot be sustained. Malthus and Torrens would not have been surprised by McCloskey's findings, neither would John Stuart Mill, who developed the theoretical tools for dealing with precisely this problem. The popular enthusiasts for free trade (Perronet Thompson, Harriet Martineau, Jane Marcet and, later, the Anti-Corn-Law League) and, perhaps, Ricardo and James Mill were guilty of failure to perceive that free trade would entail terms-of-trade losses for a growing economy like Britain; but the other major economists saw the connection and discussed it in great detail, as we have seen.

Torrens, for one, took a pessimistic view of the course of the terms of trade as it related to Britain and other industrialised countries. He also predicted that as the less-developed countries industrialised (against a background of diminishing returns in agriculture and increasing returns in manufacturing) the relative price of agricultural products would rise to such an extent that the comparative-advantage basis of trade would cease to exist. Hence trade between industrial and agrarian countries, while not ceasing altogether, would be reduced to exchanges based on irreducible absolute cost differences:

As the several nations of the world advance in wealth and

population, the commercial intercourse between them must gradually become less important and beneficial. ... Hence, in all new settlements, the increasing value of raw produce must gradually check its exportation, and the falling value of wrought goods progressively prevent their importation; until at length the commercial intercourse between nations shall be confined to those peculiar articles, in the production of which the immutable circumstances of soil and climate give one country a permanent advantage over another.[100]

Torrens was thus an early exponent of the hypothesis later known as 'das Gesetz der fallenden Export Quota' (law of falling importance of foreign trade) from the writings of Werner Sombart, the German economic historian, and others.[101] Mill and Torrens's defence of reciprocity was partly based on the terms-of-trade argument, as was noted above. Both of them, therefore, had no time for the crude propaganda of the Anti-Corn-Law League. Mill did concede though that Britain still enjoyed a favourable trading relationship (compared with other European countries) owing to high income and price elasticities of demand for its exports in world markets, and that improvements in agricultural technology were likely to slow down (postpone) the inevitable rise in the relative price of agricultural products. Ultimately, then, Mill's case for reciprocity rested on the belief that it was essential to ensure an adequate long-term increase in trade volume to counterbalance the stagnant or downward trend in Britain's net barter terms of trade.

Leading politicians and officials likewise were not remiss in taking seriously the terms-of-trade problem. They repeatedly took action or made threats designed to force reciprocal reductions in other countries' tariffs. In 1825 Huskisson (at the Board of Trade) announced:

> As a stimulus to other countries to adopt principles of reciprocity, I shall think it right to reserve a power of making an addition of one-fifth to the proposed duties upon the productions of those countries which may refuse, upon a tender by us of the like advantages, to place our commerce and navigation upon the footing of the most favoured nation.[102]

These efforts were largely unsuccessful, in so far as trade with Europe was concerned, for as Sir John Clapham observed, 'no amount of tariff manipulation or reciprocity would have opened very much wider the European markets'.[103]

The Economists, the Corn Laws and Commercial Policy 209

To summarise, then, McCloskey is no doubt correct that Britain's free-trade policy arose from the declining importance of tariff revenues in government finance, as well as the triumph of free-trade ideology – 'an economic truth [which] acquired ... the dignity and vitality of a moral law' as the Victorians saw it.[104] But it is misleading to suggest that contemporary economists subscribed to this, or uncritically accepted the popular slogans of the doctrinaire free-traders.

MILL ON THE INFANT-INDUSTRY ARGUMENT

The other exception to the classical case for free-trade – the infant-industry argument – was also legitimised by John Stuart Mill. The argument in a crude form was, of course, of long standing, dating back to Elizabethan times when it was frequently invoked in pleas for the grant of monopolistic privileges; but the later mercantilists made little use of it. Adam Smith noted the possibility of gain from temporary infant-industry protection but expressed considerable scepticism on the ground that even if the infant industry ultimately grew up, the reduction in the value of capital accumulation during the learning period was likely to outweigh the benefits in terms of future growth potential.[105] The argument was reformulated with reference to young and developing countries by Alexander Hamilton, George Washington's Secretary of the Treasury in 1791, and later by the German national economist, Friedrich List (1841).[106]

The majority of English writers dismissed the writings of the national economists as being no more than naïve reversions into a pre-scientific mercantilism; but Mill saw that the arguments of the national developmental economists did not contradict the main propositions of classical trade theory. Accordingly, says Schumpeter, J. S. Mill 'accepted the infant-industry theory, realising that it ran within the free trade logic'.[107] Indeed, Mill provided the clearest formulation of the argument and since his exposition is beautifully concise it is worth quoting in full:

> The only case in which, on mere principles of political economy, protecting duties can be defensible, is when they are imposed temporarily (especially in a young and rising nation) in hopes of naturalizing a foreign industry, in itself perfectly suitable to the circumstances of the country. The superiority of one country over another in a branch of production often arises only from having

begun it sooner. There may be no inherent advantage on one part, or disadvantage on the other, but only a present superiority of acquired skill and experience. A country which has this skill and experience yet to acquire, may in other respects be better adapted to the production than those which were earlier in the field; and besides, it is a just remark of Mr. Rae, that nothing has a greater tendency to promote improvements in any branch of production, than its trial under a new set of conditions. But it cannot be expected that individuals should, at their own risk, or rather to their certain loss, introduce a new manufacture, and bear the burden of carrying it on, until the producers have been educated up to the level of those with whom the processes are traditional. A protecting duty, continued for a reasonable time, will sometimes be the least inconvenient mode in which the nation can tax itself for the support of such an experiment. But the protection should be confined to cases in which there is good ground of assurance that the industry which it fosters will after a time be able to dispense with it; nor should the domestic producers ever be allowed to expect that it will be continued to them beyond the time necessary for a fair trial of what they are capable of accomplishing.[108]

Mill thus rescued the argument from its association with special pleading and economic nationalism and gave it theoretical and practical respectability under one condition: the infant industry must eventually overcome its historical handicap and grow up, able to withstand foreign competition without benefit of further protection – the 'Mill test', as Kemp calls it.[109] Bastable later pointed out that the 'Mill test', though necessary, was not a sufficient condition. He proposed an additional criterion: the protected industry (or firm) must eventually generate sufficient savings in costs to compensate society for the consumption losses incurred during the period of maturation. Mill was, however, disillusioned by the use of his argument at the hands of self-seeking protectionists in the United States and Australia where protection was indiscriminately and permanently extended to a wide range of industries, many without promise; and in later life regretted his endorsement of the use of import duties for the purpose and strongly qualified his statement quoted above. If protection for infant industries were needed at all, he said, it should be in the form of subsidies rather than tariffs. An annual subsidy, being clearly visible to taxpayers, was less likely to be continued on a permanent basis than a protective duty.[110]

Modern economists generally agree with Mill on this. A tariff introduces a consumption distortion without necessarily ensuring the realisation of the social benefit claimed for the policy. The optimal (or 'first-best' policy) is to subsidise directly the acquisition of knowledge by the firm or industry. Moreover, since a domestic not a foreign distortion is involved, some sort of subsidy rather than tariffs is called for. The argument has been subjected to a good deal of analytical scrutiny involving the theory of domestic distortions, economics of knowledge and elements of human capital theory. Thus, Harry Johnson writes: 'What is involved is an investment in a process of acquisition of knowledge which is socially profitable but privately unprofitable because the private investor cannot appropriate the whole of the social return from his investment.'[111] In the contemporary world, the argument has been used by Third World countries to justify their protective duties in the interests of industrialisation. General Agreement on Tariffs and Trade (GATT) rules even allow it for such countries, and the various preferential arrangements for developing countries' manufactured exports in the markets of developed countries are based on an extension of this argument.

Mill must have been familiar with the works of the national economists such as Henry Carey and Friedrich List, but he never recommended the 'infant-stage-of-development' argument favoured by these writers. There were more efficient means of promoting national economic development, not the least important of which is trade itself. Trade, in fact, he held was even more important for less-developed countries than it was for rich ones. In particular, the indirect benefits as they affect growth were of a high order. The opening of foreign trade initiates 'a sort of industrial revolution' in poor countries. More generally, every extension of the market through trade tends to improve the processes of production: 'A country which produces for a larger market than its own, can introduce a more extended division of labour, can make greater use of machinery, and is more likely to make inventions and improvements in the processes of production.'[112]

5.3 The Export of Technology

An important issue in trade policy which exercised the minds of the political economists was the export of machinery and emigration of skilled artisans. Although not comparable in economic and political significance to the Corn-Law controversy, this debate was equally wide ranging and aroused the same sort of intellectual passion. The protagonists in the debate – Torrens, Senior, McCulloch, Hume, etc. – if resurrected, would have been on familiar ground had they witnessed the US Congressional battles in the 1970s over foreign trade and investment where the key question was the regulation of the exportation of technology. The arguments were essentially the same in both cases. In the 1970s US trade unions (AFL/CIO) blamed the export of jobs on 'runaway plants' in Mexico, Hong Kong, Taiwan and Korea, which operated with cheap labour and efficient borrowed American technology. This allegedly jeopardised the traditional living standards of American workers; and there were calls for stringent controls on all US direct investment activities, i.e. export of skills and technology. The only difference was that the economists in the twentieth-century debate had the advantage of sophisticated theories and hypotheses on 'brain-drain', product cycles, multinational corporations and the international diffusion of technology.

The nineteenth-century policy debate presented an agonising challenge to the free-traders. It forced them to think through the practical implications of free trade and, as Maxine Berg shows,[113] it generated new ideas in economic thought, in particular the development of concepts and models for analysing the impact of growth and technological change on comparative advantage and trade patterns. Did free trade apply only to commodities, or must the principle be extended also to capital and labour? Did the restrictions on machinery exports signify protection for one industry only – the capital-goods or machine-making industry – or were they the means whereby all industries were protected? What were the implications for Britain's comparative advantage in manufactures of freer transfer of technology? How did trade patterns alter under the impact of technological change and the international transfer of technology? These were some of the questions suggested by the terms of the debate.

It was widely believed that machinery gave Britain a peculiar advantage over her trading rivals, and that whatever social disadvantages (e.g. technological unemployment, de-skilling of the labour force, etc.) attended its use, nevertheless, international considerations made it imperative to take full advantage of technology embodied in machinery. Ricardo admitted in a parliamentary speech (30 May 1823) that the extensive use of machinery

> must, in some degree, operate prejudicially to the working classes. But still he would not tolerate any law to prevent the use of

machinery. The question was, – if they gave up a system which enabled them to undersell in the foreign market, would other nations refrain from pursuing it? Certainly not. They were therefore bound, for their own interest, to continue it.[114]

In the 1821 edition of his *Principles*, he reaffirmed the advantages of machinery:

> if a capital is not allowed to get the greatest net revenue that the use of machinery will afford here, it will be carried abroad, and this must be a much more serious discouragement to the demand for labour. ... By investing part of a capital in improved machinery, there will be a diminution in the progressive demand for labour; by exporting it to another country, the demand will be wholly annihilated.[115]

Like Adam Smith it appears that Ricardo was against the restrictions on the export of machinery. Sraffa tells us that shortly before his death Ricardo promised Joseph Hume (the leading campaigner for repeal) that he would support his proposed motion for a parliamentary committee of inquiry to look into the matter.[116]

In a debate on tariff reform in 1825 Sir Henry Parnell confidently proclaimed that 'in all cases where we employ machinery, and have the raw material as cheap as foreign nations have it, we have no grounds for apprehending any injury from the most open competition'.[117] On the other hand, there was a growing feeling that British superiority in machine production was only relative, in view of both continental industrialisation and the speed of diffusion of technical knowledge. Malthus, for example, pointed out 'how difficult it is to confine improvements in machinery to a single spot'. Torrens said much the same thing: 'the adoption of the latest improvements in scientific power cannot be confined to a particular country'.[118] McCulloch observed that the processes of knowledge diffusion are such that significant inventions soon become public (free) goods to the world as a whole: 'It is no longer possible to monopolize an invention. The intimate communication that now obtains amongst nations renders any important discovery, wherever it may be made, a common benefit.'[119] McCulloch exaggerated the trade consequences of rapid diffusion: invention is one thing, but innovation or development of the idea into a marketable produce is another thing. Where innovations are the result of basic research freely available (via journals) there need be no connection between the country originating an idea and the country subsequently developing it into a marketable product. The key elements in the process are much more the innovation and marketing stages rather than that of invention. Technological leadership is much more closely associated with ability to innovate and develop – an ability outstandingly characteristic of Britain in the early nineteenth century. The example given by McCulloch – an invention (or technical improvement) spreading from China or Peru to England would appear less plausible had he reversed the direction of the technical diffusion.

As early as 1805 William Playfair sketched the dynamic process whereby technological progress works to confer a temporary monopoly on the innovating country, but which tends to be eroded by imitative production elsewhere. He shows why it is sometimes uneconomic to apply the 'best' technology, and how the imitation of foreign technology can be advantageous (avoidance of the initial costs of acquiring new knowledge):

> As to the difficulties of rivalling a nation in skill, in any mechanical art, there are none. The only difficulties in manufactures are in the inventions and improvements, and these have been overcome by the leading nation, and are no difficulty to that which follows.

Because of short imitation lags and the chance that the imitating country may itself begin to innovate, Playfair argued that to maintain a favourable balance of trade the leading country must continually introduce new and better products and processes. Referring to England, he warned: 'the nation the farthest advanced in invention has only to remain stationary a few years, and it will soon be overtaken, and perhaps surpassed'.[120]

The debate on the pros and cons of lifting the restrictions on the export of technology and emigration of artisans took place between 1824 and 1841. It was conducted in the usual forums: Parliament, the London and provincial press, memorials, petitions, and in the writings of the political economists. Most of the restrictions against machinery export were imposed between 1750 and 1785, and were designed to guard against competition in manufacturing from potential foreign rivals on the Continent – legislation which Adam Smith deplored. The tools, equipment, utensils and machinery used in the cotton, woollen, silk, iron and steel industries were all banned from export. The matter was investigated by three Select Committees of the House of Commons. The ban on the emigration of skilled artisans (imposed by Acts in 1719 and 1750) was lifted in 1824, following the recommendations of the Select Committee on Combination Laws, Artisans and Machinery (mainly because it proved impossible to enforce); but the prohibitions on machinery remained in force until 1843 when they were repealed on the recommendations of the 1841 Select Committee on the Export of Machinery. In the meantime (i.e. from 1825 until 1843) the Board of Trade was vested with discretionary powers to grant licence for the export of machinery. Licences were easy to obtain (although on average a quarter of applications were refused); but the textile manufacturers made sure that the machinery exported was obsolete models or those that did not threaten their current exports.

Leading the campaign for repeal was Joseph Hume on behalf of the machine-makers and other interested parties. When Hume (after much obstruction from Huskisson and Peel) laid his motion for repeal before Parliament in December 1826 Torrens, newly elected MP for Ipswich, true to form, voiced his opposition. Insisting that he was generally a friend of free trade, declared that *laissez-faire* was not a recipe for all seasons, that repeal would mean the surrender of a valuable and exclusive national advantage, and it would injure England to let other countries share in those advantages:

> in every science, there must necessarily be exceptions. There could be no universal principle applicable to all circumstances. Now, it was admitted on all hands, even by the hon. member for Aberdeen [Hume], that we made better machinery than our rivals. ... If such was the case, he would ask, why should we give up our exclusive advantage?[121]

In fact, Torrens later claimed, not enough was being done to forestall foreign competition; he went further and urged a duty of 50 per cent on all British coal exports to Europe, since without cheap British coal French manufacturers would be unable to operate steam-engines efficiently.[122] To an old Marine like Torrens, comments Fetter, the free export of machinery and coal was 'as much folly, as presenting enemy troops with improved weapons'.[123]

This attitude, perhaps in a less extreme form, was shared by many who, on other issues (e.g. the Corn Law), were fond of using *laissez-faire* slogans and free-trade rhetoric, i.e. Baring, Peel, Bright and, surprisingly enough, Nassau Senior.

Senior's argument was more sophisticated. Writing in 1830 he protested that it was idle to pretend that England would not suffer from the enhanced technological capability of its neighbours, for both England and Europe were competitors in the general market of the world. He dissented from the view (held by J. S. Mill) that if, through the acquisition of superior British technology, the Europeans managed to produce cheaper cottons then Britain would benefit from cheaper cotton imports and could put its resources to other, more profitable manufactures. England, he said, 'might find it easier to obtain cottons, but we should find it more difficult to import everything else'. If England, through default, gave up its technological leadership and resigned itself to simple, less skill-intensive manufacturing, 'it is guilty of the same folly as the farmer who should plough with a race-horse'.[124] Briefly, his reasoning was: Wages and living standards in Britain depended on the prosperity of foreign commerce and the country's trade rested on the efficiency of labour in manufacturing. What made British labour comparatively more productive was the combination of higher skill levels and the more intensive use of machinery than elsewhere. Senior made it clear in a footnote that his remarks bore significantly on the question of technology exports. Senior's line of reasoning was adopted by other free-traders who objected to machinery exports in public debate (e.g. Lord King).[125]

The arguments for removal of the restrictions were: (1) they were ineffective in achieving their objective; (2) they were unnecessary, since even with the free availability of British machinery foreigners were unable to rival British manufacturers, and (3) they were, on balance, beneficial to Britain since earnings from machinery exports contributed to Britain's future economic growth. Much like illegal arms traffic today, there was extensive smuggling of machinery – hidden in cotton bales, consigned via distant fishing-ports, etc. The dealer networks were well-organised, and there was even a market for insuring and guaranteeing shipments. Industrial espionage took place, and the patent laws were such that plans, models and patent specifications could easily be acquired by visiting foreigners. The diffusion process was also helped by the rapid dissemination of scientific knowledge through journals, learned societies, etc. Exports of machinery did not materially affect the supply on the domestic market, for when machinery was in short supply, foreign orders (for which licences were granted) were either not accepted or had to wait until domestic requirements were attended to. These facts were referred to by McCulloch and Malthus, the only two economists of note who gave evidence before the 1824 Committee. These circumstances were part of their argument for the lifting of the restrictions. Further, they pointed out, the effect of the restrictions (in so far as they were effective) tended to encourage the growth of machine-making industries on the Continent and in America by raising the price of machines abroad and thereby stimulating production there. British machine-makers lost business without any commensurate benefit to British manufacturers in the long run. Malthus's opinion was that free machinery export would not endanger Britain's trade or its technological leadership. Malthus also sounded his customary caution about the wisdom of the pursuit of further industrialisation on (a) the economic ground of insufficiency of investment funds and aggregate demand, and (b) the technical limits to the division of labour. The restrictions, McCulloch said, deprived Britain of 'an additional branch of manufacture'.[126]

The second point, that prohibition was unnecessary for the reason mentioned above, rested on several premises relating to conditions for the effective international transfer of technology, the role of skills and human capital in the process of technological innovation, and technological leadership and comparative advantage. Thus, it was argued, Britain's technological leadership rested on a complex of factors including a highly skilled and industrious work-force, efficient management and organisational techniques, better division of labour, an intellectual and social environment conducive to enterprise, the application of science to technology and responsiveness to change. . . . These were the sources of Britain's comparative advantage in manufactures, and, since the effects were cumulative, these advantages could not easily be eroded. In the hands of foreigners, machines by themselves were insufficient if they lacked the skilled labour needed to erect, adapt and service the equipment. 'Even when the Belgians employed British machines and skilled workers, they failed to import the English spirit of enterprise and secured only disappointing results.'[127] The Select Committee on Machinery Exports listened to much evidence along these lines, as summarised in the following passage:

> Supposing, indeed, that the same Machinery which is used in England could be diffused on the Continent, it is the opinion of some of the most intelligent of the witnesses that the want of arrangement in foreign manufactories, of division of labour in their work, of skill and perseverance in their workers, and of enterprise in the masters, together with the comparatively low estimation in which the master manufactures are held on the Continent, and with the comparative want of capital, and of many other advantageous circumstances detailed in the evidence, would prevent foreigners from interfering in any great degree by competition with our principal manufacturers.[128]

Those who held the view that skills and 'mental' capital were more important than the machines in which these were embodied suggested that, if machinery were freely exported, then there would be little emigration of mechanics and other skilled artisans. The retention of these skills were necessary if Britain was to keep ahead of foreign competitors in technological development. Against this, it was argued by others, e.g. John Kennedy and the Manchester Chamber of Commerce that there was a complementary relationship between machines and skills, so that the more machinery was exported the greater would be the demand for skilled British artisans and therefore the greater the loss to continental rivals. Kennedy put it this way:

> The exportation of machinery absolutely compels the foreign manufacturer to possess the means of becoming his own machine maker; and the more machines you send abroad, the greater the number of mechanics become necessary to keep their parts in order. Hence again arises a demand for those tools which are necessary to mechanics, the mechanics with their tools are sure to be ultimately employed, not merely in repairing the existing machines, but in the making of new ones.[129]

The third point above was made by John Stuart Mill in terms of an efficient allocation of global resources. It was, he argued, 'in the common interest of all nations that each of them should abstain from every measure by which the aggregate wealth of the commercial world would be diminished'. It was therefore in Britain's interest to promote this by every means including the free export of machinery, since restrictions tended to be generalised, to no country's advantage. Foreign countries would use British machines to produce goods in which they already possessed natural advantages. To the extent that they were successful in that, the demand for British manufactures would fall, but Britain would gain from the greater efficiency of foreign producers in the manufacture of goods sold on the British market. He disputed Senior's point that England would not benefit from cheaper imports consequent upon improvements abroad.[130] William Ellis, a philosphical radical and friend of Mill, made a similar point in favour of free exportation, but based his remark on the observation that exports are only needed to pay for a country's imports, and it was the volume and price of the latter which really measured the benefit from trade. Like McCulloch, he regarded the restrictions as hindering the expansion of a potentially major British industry.[131]

Mill, however, had some reservations; for he conceded that the export of machinery could be a source of disadvantage until all restrictions on trade were done away with, and concluded that until that time came 'the exportation of machinery may be a proper subject for adjustment with other nations, on the principle of reciprocity'.[132]

The restrictions on the export of machinery were lifted three years before the repeal of the Corn Laws and, as in the greater debate on the latter, economic conditions finally dictated the change in policy. The depression of 1841–2 resulted in a slump in the demand for textile machinery following the boom conditions a few years earlier. Export markets were therefore necessary to maintain prosperity, and this added urgency to the machinery manufacturers' demands for repeal. The groups opposed to free exports were divided, and the influential Manchester Chamber of Commerce lost the will to carry on the opposition. One knowledgeable witness revealed to the Select Committee in 1841: 'the master manufacturers are almost desponding as regards the state of our trade, and the general expression of feeling is, that the legislature may do whatever they please, they cannot make things worse'.[133] Commenting on the lifting of the restrictions, a modern historian wrote: 'Manchester had decided that, if it was impossible to kill off the industry of others by restrictions ... , then perhaps Corn Law repeal might do the trick instead.'[134]

6 Gold, Money and Trade

THE GOLD STANDARD AND THE BULLION DEBATE

Free trade and the gold standard are inseparably associated with the nineteenth-century and its classical economists. However, except for Great Britain (from 1816) and Portugal (from 1854) the gold standard was not generally adopted until 1879; hence adherence to the international gold standard lasted only thirty-five years, i.e. until 1914. To later generations it epitomised all that was good and bad in classical *laissez-faire* and its regime of free trade. To those who see the good in it, it stands for monetary order, low interest rates, price stability and high rates of economic growth. To those who see it 'warts and all' the gold standard was a 'fair-weather' system that worked well only so long as the world economy was booming. Memories of the inter-war years are still vivid and for those deeply scarred by the depression it stands for deflation, unemployment and hardship.

The gold-standard system was not consciously designed. It developed in a historical process and took shape through a series of contingencies, *ad hoc* measures and responses to circumstances. The stages in its evolution can be summarised as follows:

1. The fixing of the gold guinea (first minted by Charles II in 1663) at 21 silver shillings in 1717 following the recommendations of Sir Isaac Newton, Master of the Mint. The mint price of an ounce of standard gold in terms of the unit of account, the pound sterling, was set at £3. 17s. 10½d. The gold/silver ratio of 1 : 15.21 thus established overvalued gold, i.e. silver could be exchanged for more gold in the free market. The result was that England attracted gold and for most of the eighteenth century went on exporting silver (to the Netherlands, Russia, the Levant, India and China). Domestically, silver tended to go out of circulation as more and more gold was brought to the mint for coinage – a situation leading to a *de facto* gold standard.
2. The move away from bimetallism (the linkage of the pound sterling to gold) was given further momentum by an Act of 1798 which stopped the free coinage of silver altogether. Silver Coins

were no longer legal tender in full discharge payment for sums over £25 (except by weight).
3. The gold standard was officially proclaimed by the Coinage Act of 1816 which made the pound sterling (20 shillings) equivalent to the gold sovereign. The sovereign was a real gold coin weighing 7.988 grammes, and constituted 11/12 pure metal (i.e. 11 parts of gold to 1 of alloy). Silver became token money (the coins contained less silver than their stated value) and was further restricted in its legal-tender status only to payments up to £2. The gold standard became fully operative in 1823 when convertibility of gold into notes (as well as coin) was established. The paper pound thus became equivalent to the gold sovereign.

Britain's early commitment to gold rather than silver for her monetary standard followed the momentum of events. But the decision to choose gold instead of silver was also influenced by policy decisions at crucial moments. Thus Britain gained access to Brazilian gold through her control of Portuguese trade (which involved large annual payments surpluses with Portugal). The decision to overprice gold led to a 'currency reversal' (the supplanting of silver by gold) through the operation of Gresham's Law.[1] Towards the end of the eighteenth century, as the output of gold from the Brazilian mines fell off drastically while at the same time Mexican silver output increased, another currency reversal threatened – this time pushing gold coins out of circulation. It was to forestall this that the decision was taken to stop the free coinage of silver and base the paper money on gold. When Britain adopted the gold standard, most of Europe and the United States remained officially on bimetallic standards. The shape of world monetary arrangements was undoubtedly influenced by Britain's preponderant role in world trade and investment; but it might never have taken final form without the aid of (a) the Californian and Australian gold discoveries of the 1850s and 1860s, and (b) the absorption of all newly mined silver by India whose currency, based on silver, expanded enormously during 1856–65. These two developments disturbed the equilibrium in the relative value of gold and silver hitherto maintained by the dominance of France's bimetallic system. The market price of silver rose in Europe and this tended to push silver coins out of circulation. The new German Empire adopted gold in 1871 (in anticipation of the French indemnity payment) and by 1879 most of the world, including the United States was on the gold standard. Fortunately for the general acceptance and stability of the system were the gold discoveries in South Africa, Alaska (Klondike–Yukon) and Colorado and improved lower-cost methods of mining and refining gold in the early 1890s. The increased supplies of monetary gold allowed newcomers to the system to build up their gold reserves without subjecting their economies to painful deflationary pressures.

Adherence by national governments to the international gold standard involved compliance with the following:

1. Each country ties its money to gold, i.e. the price of domestic currency is fixed in terms of gold.
2. The convertibility of domestic currency into gold. The central bank in each country stands ready to buy and sell gold freely at the fixed price and allows unrestricted import and export of gold.
3. That each country followed the so-called 'rules of the game' the most important of which required gold flows to exert their full influence on domestic money supplies and price levels through a rule that links domestic money creation to the central bank's holdings of gold.

The first two rules together ensure that exchange rates between countries on the gold standard are fixed within narrow limits. Thus if in the United States the par value (the official fixed price) of an ounce of gold is $20.67 and in Britain it is £4.25 per ounce, then these par values imply a bilateral exchange rate of $4.86 = £1. With arbitrage, deviations from the implicit exchange rate are normally limited by the cost of buying and shipping gold.

Such was the formal arrangement of the gold standard fixed-exchange-rate regime which lasted until the outbreak of the First World War. Later a myth grew up about its rationale and the 'automatic' manner of its workings, as summarised in the Cunliffe Report (1918).[2] Certainly there was a rich heritage of monetary theory which provided a solid basis for this international monetary arrangements, i.e. the Quantity Theory of Money and Hume's price-specie-flow mechanism and natural distribution of specie hypothesis. By the time of the Cunliffe Report these were virtually unquestioned, even by Keynes. But what was then regarded as standard orthodoxy was the subject of heated debate in England, first from 1797 to 1810, known as the Bullionist controversy, and, second, the 1820–45 arguments of the Currency and Banking Schools.

The Quantity Theory and Hume's influential price-specie-flow mechanism might have led logically without further argument and debate to some such arrangement as the gold standard had wartime

Gold, Money and Trade

inflation and inconvertible paper not supervened to open wide the floodgates of dissension. Hume wrote at a time long before there was a gold standard when it was uncertain whether gold or silver would become the dominant medium of international exchange. Hence, his use of the vague term 'specie' to denote either gold or silver. Moreover, his specie-flow mechanism referred to fixed exchange rates under a metallic standard and not to flexible exchange rates under an inconvertible regime. The monetary framework inherited from Hume (and Smith) offered some general guidance, but on the specific monetary problems that troubled England in the decades following the Napoleonic Wars – rapidly expanding money supplies, high inflation, high price of bullion and a depreciating pound – the protagonists in the debate were free to choose their own explanations and, not surprisingly, different remedies were prescribed. As a result, however, some of the best classical works on monetary theory and policy were written. The background to the debate was the same as that touching on the Corn Law issue. In the present context the monetary background will be briefly described before we turn to the two debates over monetary policy: the bullionist controversy, which was followed in the second quarter of the century by the Currency v. Banking School dispute. An understanding of these debates on money, interest rates, prices and the foreign exchanges sheds considerable light on the evolution of the classical monetary theory of international trade and the establishment of orthodoxy relating to the mechanism of international adjustment as institutionalised in the gold standard.

The suspension of gold convertibility of Bank of England notes on 27 February 1797 (intended as a temporary restriction) lasted until the resumption of gold payments in 1821 during which time the country experimented with an irredeemable paper pound. The money-stock (Bank of England and country bank-notes) expanded rapidly. In one year alone (1800) prices rose by 8 per cent and over the period 1792–1814 prices rose by about 94 per cent. Overall price indexes were not available to contemporaries and the only current financial data were on interest rates, exchange rates and the prices of gold and silver bullion. These were often taken by bullionist writers as rough indicators of monetary conditions, and they all pointed to marked increases in the price of bullion, foreign exchange and commodities in term of bank-notes. Domestic bullion prices increased above the official mint price of gold, e.g. in January 1801 the price of gold reached £4. 6s. an ounce – a substantial premium (or *agio*) over the official mint price of £3. 17s. 10½d. As indicated by the premium on foreign bills of exchange (discount on sterling) sterling depreciated against those currencies which had maintained their links with gold at fixed or stable values. The fall in the exchange value of sterling on the Hamburg market – the only regular foreign exchange market then active – was 12 per cent in the second half of 1808; it fell lower by 19.5 per cent in early 1809.[3]

What divided the disputants in the Bullion debate was the fundamental issue of the cause of inflation. Did the exigencies of wartime finance and the suspension of convertibility lead to an overissue of paper currency, rising prices and a fall in the exchanges? According to the bullionist writers the depreciation of the pound, the high price of bullion and rising domestic prices were all the result of currency mismanagement, i.e. the overissue of inconvertible currency through extensive discounting of commercial paper. To the anti-bullionists (people like Charles Bosanquet, Nicholas Vansittart and the directors of the Bank of England) the matter was much more complicated. The various manifestations of inflation were due to military expenditures abroad (including subsidies to allies), outflow of short-term capital attracted by high interest rates in Hamburg and such 'real' factors as bad harvests which necessitated large grain imports from the Baltic (£2.3 million in 1796) and the disruption of trade. They denied that bank-note circulation was excessive and opposed bullionist demands for a prompt return to the gold standard. The Bank of England directors absolved themselves from any responsibility for the depreciation of sterling. It was not within their power, they claimed, to stabilise the exchange rate. Fluctuations were caused by real factors beyond their control. As far as the expansion of note-issue was concerned they saw no connection between that and the state of the exchanges. The anti-bullionists invoked Adam Smith's 'real bills' doctrine according to which the issue of paper money cannot be excessive as long as the bank-notes are created to meet the genuine needs of trade, i.e. for facilitating the production or distribution of goods. Notes issued against bills of exchange relating to real transactions are 'self-liquidating' on completion of the real business transactions. According to this principle, then, output increases by an amount equal in value to the increase in the money supply which implies that changes in the money supply are endogenous, i.e. they respond to changes in the demand for bank money.

The first shot in the bullionist salvo was fired by Walter Boyd in his *Letter to Pitt* (1801) where he wrote: 'The premium on bullion, the low rate of exchange and the high prices of commodities in general, [are] ... symptoms and effects of the superabundance of paper.'[4] This was a straightforward application of Quantity Theory reasoning to the note-issue of the Bank of England – a theme elaborated and developed by other writers in the bullionist camp such as Henry Thornton, Ricardo and other lesser-known figures such as Lord King, Horner and John Wheatley. Boyd was a severe and uncompromising critic of the Bank of England. He contended, quite rightly, that the country bank-issue being convertible into Bank of England notes was closely regulated in its volume by the quantity of Bank of England notes held by the country banks as reserves, and therefore self-regulating. The Bank of England was, therefore, ultimately solely responsible for the inflation and the depreciation of the pound on the foreign-exchange market. Initially, at any rate, Malthus took a contrary view and placed the blame on the country banks by referring to 'the great paper issues of the country banks, in raising the price of commodities, and producing an unfavourable state of exchange with foreigners'.[5] Three years later he deleted this footnote reference, presumably because he came round to the majority opinion after discussing the matter with Thornton. However, it is worth mentioning, from our modern vantage-point, in defence of the Bank that it was powerless to engineer a 'credit crunch' that might have brought the crisis to a speedier end through the expedient of a sharp rise in the rate of interest charged to borrowers. Until 1833 the maximum discount rate the Bank could charge was 5 per cent, according to the last of the usury laws then in force – the Act of 1714.

Like the latter-day macroeconomic controversy between monetarists and Keynesians where theoretical and policy disagreements range over a wide spectrum, so in the bullionist controversy there were hard-line bullionists and moderate bullionists. We focus on the subtle and sophisticated monetarist theories of Henry Thornton whose 1802 classic *The Paper Credit of Great Britain* was praised by Schumpeter as the best contribution to the English bullionist controversy.[6] Although overshadowed by Ricardo's fame, Thornton wrote one of the greatest works on monetary theory and policy and was responsible for a number of new ideas which had to be rediscovered by later generations. He made a careful and balanced analysis of the consequences (domestic and international) of the expansion and contraction of money, and warned of the dangers of excessive monetary restraint. His arguments tracing the monetary roots of inflation were novel and insightful, and some of them are worth noting before turning to his analysis of international monetary equilibrium. His rejection of the 'real bills' doctrine was based on: (a) the difficulties of distinguishing between 'real' and 'fictitious' or 'accommodation' (finance) bills; (b) the fact that when the same goods pass through several merchants' hands, the result is an excessive circulation of real bills or credit, and (c) the application of the doctrine implies that the quantity of money at any moment can never be judged excessive whatever the current rate of inflation. The fallacy of the doctrine was the failure to realise that the nominal quantity of bills offered for discount was itself a consequence of the volume of money and hence the level of prices (assuming full employment). Therefore to link the volume of money to the quantity of bills offered to the banks was to create a positive feedback mechanism which would leave the volume of money and the price level indeterminate. Following this recipe, rising prices would lead to an expansion of the note-issue which would in turn increase the supply of bills offered for discounting and thus to a further round of price increases and more discounting and so on. The supply of discountable bills might, in fact, become infinitely elastic in a situation where the Bank (through law or custom) discounted at an unduly low rate of interest. A chronic excess stock of notes in the circumstances of the Restriction period would have led to a continuous depreciation of sterling on the foreign-exchange market; but after the resumption of gold convertibility it was apparent to even the most diehard believers in the real-bills doctrine that an external drain would put an end to excess money creation. Thornton explicitly noted that under the gold standard an indefinite increase in paper currency was ruled out owing to drains through the foreign exchange market. He did not take a mechanistic view of the impact of monetary growth on levels of prices, income and employment. He recognised the 'liquidity effect' of a change in the quantity of money on the interest rate and hence prices and, accordingly, held that the velocity of circulation varied with the state of business confidence, interest rates and the mix of coin and notes in the total nominal currency stock. Long before Irving Fisher, Thornton distinguished between real and nominal interest rates and observed that interest rates were at one time 20 to 25 per cent in St Petersburg on account of inflationary expectations. He also anticipated Knut Wiksell's cumulative expansion process in which expansionary bank lending takes place when the market rate of interest (the expected rate of profit on capital) is below the 'natural' or equilibrium rate. At such times bankers should not ignore the state of the foreign exchanges when making bank advances.

On external monetary equilibrium, Thornton exposed the fallacy of arguing that the exchange rate falls because of an unfavourable balance of trade or payments. A passage by John Locke expressing the balance-of-trade view comes in for critical scrutiny. Thornton writes:

> The passage implies, that it is the comparative state of our exports and imports which regulates the exchange, and not at all the state of the exchange which regulates the comparative state of our exports and imports. It leads us to suppose, that an unfavourable balance of trade (that is, the excess of the goods imported above those exported) is exclusively the cause, and that the bad state of the exchange is altogether the effect. It appears that the coming and going of gold does not 'depend wholly on the balance of trade'. It depends on the quantity of circulating medium issued; or it depends, as I will allow, on the balance of trade, if that balance is admitted to depend on the quantity of circulating medium issued. Mr. Locke, however, is very far from leading his reader to conceive that the balance of trade depends on the quantity of circulating medium issued; for he describes an unfavourable balance as resulting from a 'losing trade', and from an 'over great consumption of foreign commodities'; terms which seem to imply an unprosperous state of commerce, and a too expensive disposition in the people, and which naturally lead to the conclusion, that the prosperity of the country will effectually secure us against the danger of the exportation of our coin, whatever may be the quantity of our paper.[7]

Both in *Paper Credit* and in his speech of May 1811 Thornton sets forth the PPP theory of exchange-rate determination according to which changes in the exchange rate 'nearly equalize the relative value of our currency and commodities with the relative value of currency and commodities in other countries'.[8] The equilibrium value of the exchange rate is linked to its internal purchasing power. The inflation resulting from excess paper money automatically produces a roughly equivalent depreciation of the exchange rate. Imports increase and exports fall, resulting in an excess supply of pounds which lowers the sterling exchange rate to a new equilibrium consistent with the higher level of British prices. The causal link runs, therefore, from the domestic money stock to the exchange rate through the price level. In Thornton's view, exchange-rate changes do not affect (except temporarily) real variables such as the balance of trade or relative prices. Exchange-rate changes merely serve to offset divergent nominal inflation rates between countries leaving the real (barter) conditions of international trade unaltered. Thus, he argues, higher inflation in Britain relative to the rest of the world cannot reduce British exports, since the offsetting depreciation of the exchange rate will 'prevent the high price of goods in Great Britain from producing that unfavourable balance of trade which for the sake of illustrating the subject was supposed to exist'.[9] Thornton makes explicit reference to Hume's footnote concerning the self-correcting mechanism built into exchange-rate flexibility, but added to Hume's analysis the role played by income changes in balance-of-payments adjustment.

Thornton's general monetarist position differed from that of the strict bullionists in that he accepted several modifications to that position:

1. The self-adjusting mechanism refers to a long-run equilibrium situation which does not necessarily hold at every moment of time, e.g. in the short run.
2. Stressing, as he did, the extreme variability of velocity, he saw that money and exchange-rate changes do not vary in strict proportion in the short run, although they do in the long run.
3. He took notice of real factors affecting the exchange rate and the balance of payments in the short run while holding to the view that monetary factors dominate in the long run. Thus, despite his criticism of the Lockean view that an adverse exchange arose only as a result of trade difficulties, Thornton judged that the depreciation up to 1802 was due to real factors (poor harvests, disruption of exports, etc.) but at the time of the Bullion Committee and the Irish Currency Committee he attributed the Irish and British depreciations to overissue of paper currency. In the earlier period, despite the 1797 restriction, gold coin remained in circulation and was accepted on par with notes. The fall in the exchange rate and the depreciation of notes relative to the mint price of gold drew gold coin out of circulation and from hoards which were then used to finance the balance-of-payments deficit. By the latter period the loss of gold had removed the safeguard against overissue and Thornton therefore in 1811 supported resumption.[10]

Thornton, in contrast to the strict bullionists like Ricardo and Wheatley, fully recognised that real factors could disturb the exchanges mainly because exports and imports could not be speedily adjusted. Ultimately, however, equilibrium in the trade balance would be restored through changes in income and purchasing power. In the case of unilateral transfers (such as affected Britain in the early 1800s) the equilibrating factors were changes in purchasing power and subsequently in the terms of trade. But after the transfer (an extraordinary foreign payment) was accommodated any remaining weakness in the exchange rate must be corrected by monetary restriction roughly in proportion to the depreciation. In such circumstances, where the adverse exchange was clearly due to overissue, his policy prescription corresponded with that of Ricardo, i.e. it was 'to lean to the side of diminution, in the case of gold going abroad, and of the general exchange, continuing long unfavourable'.[11] The Bank of England must use its discretionary power to regulate the volume of bank notes in times of external drains.

Thornton sensed (as most others did not) that the key to resolving the dispute between those who held that the depreciation of sterling was due to British inflation and those who maintained that it was the result of heavy financial transfers lay in a failure to recognise that the pound had depreciated because, with the increased level of extraordinary payments (capital movements) to other countries, prices of actual and potential export goods were too high to make possible a sufficient export surplus at the pre-war exchange rate. Exchange-rate depreciation, therefore, acted as a necessary corrective mechanism which stimulated exports and checked imports. Once the transfer had been effected, however, and the nominal exchange rate continued to depreciate then that was a clear sign that domestic currency had been issued to excess; and corrective measures of a discretionary kind were therefore called for.

In contrast to this moderate monetarist position, Ricardo adhered to rigid versions of the Quantity Theory and price-specie-flow mechanism. He denied that real factors could have any effect on the exchanges, even in the short run. In his view, an adverse exchange was solely the result of an excess issue of domestic currency, and therefore amenable to correction by monetary restraint. Ricardo's old sparring partner, Malthus, challenged him on this point in the columns of the *Edinburgh Review* for February 1811:

> The great fault of Mr. Ricardo's performance is the partial view which he takes of the causes which operate upon the course of Exchange.... He attributes a favourable or unfavourable exchange *exclusively* to a redundant or deficient currency, and overlooks the varying desires and wants of different societies as an original cause of a temporary excess of imports over exports, or exports above imports.... We have already adverted to the error of denying the existence of a balance of trade or of payments, not connected with some original redundancy or deficiency of currency.[12]

Later on, in the review article, Malthus again censured Ricardo

> for considering redundancy or deficiency of currency as the mainspring of all commercial movements. According to this view of the subject, it is certainly not easy to explain an improving exchange under an obviously increasing issue of notes; an event that not infrequently happens.[13]

Malthus's criticism was directed at Ricardo's belief that international transfers could have no significant effect on the exchanges. Such transfers would be fully effected in goods (trade-balance changes) with only negligible changes in relative price levels, exchange rates and specie movements. In some statements of his position Ricardo seemed to have assumed an almost instantaneous adjustment to disequilibrium caused by real shocks (crop failures, foreign subsidies, etc.) to the balance of payments. The long run and the short run were collapsed into one frictionless act of adjustment. In other contexts he adopted a more flexible position. In these, the transfer mechanism was described more realistically in terms of exchange-rate movements, bullion flows and changes in domestic relative prices, albeit at unchanged absolute price levels.

Thus Ricardo sometimes follows Wheatley and offers an account of the transfer process (e.g. in the case of crop failures and emergency food imports) whereby the reduction of domestic real income and purchasing power causes a fall in demand for non-food imports, but at the same time stimulates exports as their domestic prices fall relative to foreign prices. The absolute increase in exports completely offsets the food imports. The process of adjustment can be accomplished with or without exchange-rate movements depending on the severity of the real disturbance.

In all of his exposition Ricardo was concerned to stress the point that a depreciated exchange was solely the result of an excess issue of currency. An exchange-rate movement was purely a monetary phenomenon. Emergency food imports, foreign remittances and war-time trade disruptions only affect the exchange rate and the balance of payments through monetary channels, i.e. the demand for and supply of money. For example, a crop failure which reduces the volume of commodities in circulation and thus the level of real income means that the demand for money also falls. But with an unchanged money stock cash balances are now too high. Domestic residents adjust to monetary disequilibrium by increasing their real expenditures on imports. The result is a depreciated exchange-rate and/or a balance-of-payments deficit. In such circumstances a contraction of the note-issue (or credit in general) is the appropriate policy response, since what causes the depreciation in the first place is not the emergency food import, but the excessive monetary circulation which allows the depreciation to take place in the face of extraordinary foreign payments. This was the policy advice Ricardo wanted to give. He wished people to concentrate their minds on the duty of the Bank of England, as the guardian of the nation's currency, to so regulate the note-issue that external monetary equilibrium was maintained at all times. Thornton's analysis might lend some credence to the Bank's excuse that it had no control over exchange-rate fluctuations, particularly in the case of unilateral transfers.

For Ricardo the natural distribution of specie could not be altered by monetary policy, i.e. control of the circulating medium. Market forces alone dictated what the optimum quantity of money was for each country. Inconvertibility and paper money were liable to be abused by reckless governments or issuers of money. Because of this (although he was not against paper money as such) he wanted a standard to be established which would link paper money to gold. He called for a return to the gold standard which would obviate the need for discretionary policy on the part of the Bank of England in expanding or contracting the supply of money. In Ricardo's opinion the gold standard was an effective barrier against the indefinite issue of paper currency and continually unfavourable exchanges. This was what the 70-page *Bullion Report*[14] recommended in the face of opposition from the majority of those (especially the bankers) who gave evidence before the Committee. The main recommendation, reflecting the views of the bullionists called for a gradual return to gold convertibility (within two years) as the best means of ending the inflation and raising the value of the pound on the foreign-exchange market. The Report was rejected by the government and Parliament; but within a decade the recommendation was put into effect by the Act of Resumption, 1819. This piece of legislation, which ended the bullionist controversy for all practical purposes, obliged the Bank to resume payment on demand in gold for its notes at the old mint parity of 1797 – £3. 17s. 10½d. Except for Thomas Attwood and his followers, opposition to the gold standard ceased; for by that time, all the others agreed that policy must be based on the maintenance of convertibility (external and internal) of Bank of England notes into gold at a fixed price – although some thought the price of gold was set too high and consequently would have preferred a lower exchange value for sterling. However, shortly thereafter, a new row flared up – this time over the causes of and cures for the general trade fluctuations that repeatedly beset the economy.

Neither Ricardo nor the authors of the Bullion Report foresaw the deflation that was bound to follow from a policy that involved the deliberate shrinkage of the money stock so as to lower the market price of gold (which then stood at £4. 0s. 6d.) to its pre-war parity. The process was helped by foreign-exchange speculation in anticipation of resumption. Deflation began in 1814 and ended in the late 1820s. From the first quarter of 1814 to the end of 1816 prices fell by 38 per cent. By 1830 prices had fallen below their level of 1790. The cry of distress was heard throughout the manufacturing and agricultural districts with complaints of falling farm prices, low profits, business bankruptcies and high unemployment. Judged by the numbers on poor-relief, unemployment varied between 6 to 10 per cent of the working population. The distress aroused strong revulsion especially in the depressed towns against the principles and practice of 'sound money' and the gold standard. In Parliament there were calls for alternatives to the gold standard as the basis for the currency. The Prime Minister, Lord Liverpool, expressed his disbelief in the theory that the state of the exchanges were directly related to the note-issue – in other words, repudiation of Ricardian theory.[15] Baring called for a return to a bimetallic standard and claimed that 'the evil of a single [i.e. gold] standard was clearly perceptible'.[16] The spokesman for the hard-pressed manufacturing classes, Thomas Attwood, led the campaign against the supporters of financial orthodoxy and called for a reflationary policy to reduce unemployment and raise profits. For a while the movement (the Birmingham Political Union) was supported by working-class radicalism; but by the time the Chartists withdrew their backing for Attwood's currency plans the contest was already decided in favour of *laissez-faire*, non-discretionary monetary policy with the passing of Peel's Bank Charter Act, 1844. It was a victory of the Currency School over the Banking School, as the earlier bullionist contestants became known in the resumed debate over monetary regulation of the banknote-issue. The details need not detain us long here, for it was simply a replay of the bullion controversy. In the Currency School were ranged Lord Overstone (Samuel Jones Loyd), Horsley Palmer, G. W. Norman, McCulloch and Torrens against those on the other side – the Banking School – Thomas Tooke, John Fullarton, James Wilson and J. B. Gilbart. The controversy generated a sizeable literature urging the merits of an unregulated banking system as the remedy for business cycles. A recent writer, drawing attention to this neglected literature, reinterprets the British currency debates in terms of free-banking–central-banking issue and identifies a third school, the Free Banking School, whose members included Sir Henry Parnell, Samuel Bailey and also Gilbart. They were not simply spokesmen for the country banks; they presented analyses and drew conclusions which challenged the presuppositions of the main contenders over the wider issues of the debate.[17]

THE CURRENCY–BANKING SCHOOLS DEBATE

By the time of the Bank Charter debate the question of convertibility was not a matter of dispute. However, the depression and a series of financial crises and bank failures in the 1820s and 1830s convinced members of the Currency School that the convertibility obligation was not a sufficient guarantee of financial stability and monetary equilibrium. In addition, statutory note-control (compulsory cover for notes) was essential to ensure that the currency conformed to the principle of 'metallic fluctuation', i.e. the mixed currency of paper and coin must be made to function exactly as if it were wholly metallic. The domestic money-supply should automatically expand and contract on a one-to-one basis with inflows and outflows of gold. To bring this about, the Currency School called for a compulsory 100 per cent gold reserve backing for outstanding bank-notes. Since under this rule the volume of notes would vary identically with changes in nationally held monetary gold stocks, the scope for central-bank discretion over the note-issues was eliminated. Statutory note-control was thus seen as the ultimate safeguard against inflationary overissue of paper currency and the attendant threat to convertibility posed by external specie drains and the depletions of gold reserves.

In the view of the Currency School an external drain of specie was at one and the same time both the symptom and proper remedy for an excess stock of domestic currency balances and an excessively high price level. The country banks, in particular, were held responsible for the amplification of cyclical fluctuations through the inflation of the currency stock by their reckless behaviour in expanding their note-issues. To ensure the rapid, even instantaneous, restoration of equilibrium all that was necessary was to pattern the behaviour of the banking system on the idealised image of the automatic price-specie-flow mechanism (i.e. a pure specie-currency system). Thus, for every pound exported to finance an incipient deficit in the balance of payments (external currency drain) the domestic currency stock would fall by one pound, thereby setting up corrective equilibrating forces that work off the excess almost immediately it manifested itself. This rule for regulating the volume of a mixed currency so as to maintain the purchasing power or value of the monetary unit would only operate if it could be assumed that the velocities of circulation of bank notes and specie were identical. But, as Thornton pointed out in criticism of Adam Smith, this assumption was highly dubious.

The rationale for the currency principle was stated by Loyd as follows:

> A metallic currency, I conceive, by virtue of its own intrinsic value, will regulate itself; but a paper currency, having no intrinsic value, requires to be subject to some artificial regulation respecting its amount.... It is important that that paper currency should be made to conform to what a metallic currency would be, and especially that it should be kept at all times of the same amount. Now, the influx and efflux of gold is the only sure test of what would have been the variations of a metallic currency, and therefore, I conceive that that constitutes the only proper rule by which to regulate the fluctuations of a paper currency.[18]

The Currency School favoured the centralisation of control over currency supply in the hands of the Bank of England so as to make it easier to regulate the volume of currency according to the 'currency principle'. This meant, of course, the elimination of the country banks' right of issue. Ricardo went further than most in this direction in his *Plan for the Establishment of a National Bank*, published posthumously in 1824.[19] Here, in flagrant violation of his own *laissez-faire* principles, he made a plea for putting an end to both the Bank of England and the country banks' privilege of issuing paper money. The right of note-issue was to be vested in a state-run National Bank (modelled on the commission for the national sinking fund) that would provide no other banking operations. This arrangement would, he believed, secure for the public the profits from note-issue and involve as well the monetisation of government debt. But Ricardo also regarded the plan as a cheap means of achieving the aims of convertibility and monetary stability through the imposition of automatic control rules on the monetary authority. Critics warned, however, that such an arrangement gave ministers the power to interfere directly with the currency and therefore no rules would be sacrosanct. Earlier, with the same objective in mind, he had proposed his famous 'ingot plan' or gold bullion standard, which meant the convertibility of the paper currency into gold bars rather than into coin. This the Bank of England could not accept, for they had undertaken in 1817 to issue gold coin for £1 and £2 notes under the Suspension Act.

The Currency School claimed too much; like some modern monetarists they fondly (but naïvely) believed that if only a simple automatic rule was followed, fixing the growth rate of the money supply at a certain level, then all would be well in the economy. It was this belief that the Banking School adherents contested. Ayone acquainted with conventional Keynesian monetary thought (or, for that matter, the British Radcliffe Report, 1959)[20] will find the Banking School arguments familiar:

1. The 'quantity of money' is an elusive concept. It is difficult to pin down, let alone attempt to fix in some desired relationship to real magnitudes. It is like a balloon: squeeze on one side and it expands on the other to compensate. The Currency School's preferred analogy was that of the concertina: squeeze the 'monetary base' end and the whole thing contracts, and vice versa. Monetary circulation cannot be controlled through the note-issue alone (the monetary base), because by limiting this, people are encouraged to shift to deposits, bills of exchange and trade acceptances instead (i.e. money substitutes). J. S. Mill expressed the matter very neatly when he wrote:

> The purchasing power of an individual at any moment is not measured by the money actually in his pocket, whether we mean by money the metals, or include bank notes. It consists, first, of the money in his possession; secondly, of the money at his banker's, and all other money due him and payable on demand; thirdly of whatever credit he happens to possess.[21]

The quantity of money is, therefore, an independent endogenous variable, i.e. it is demand-determined.

2. Deficits in the balance of payments (and therefore external specie drains) normally arise from real shocks to the current account and the capital account rather than from domestic price inflation. Banking School writers implicitly recognised the 'law of one price' in international trade (arbitrage), and with this in mind rejected the price-specie-flow mechanism which was supposed to work through divergent movements in general price levels. Thomas Tooke wrote:

> Transmissions of the precious metals might and would take place occasionally between this and other countries to a considerable amount ... without being a cause or a consequence of alteration in general prices ... consequently the doctrine by which it is maintained that every export or import of bullion in a metallic circulation must ... cause a fall or rise of general prices, is essentially incorrect and unsound.[22]

Rather, international equilibrium came about through commodity and money flows. Moreover, since the specie-flows normally come from central bank hoards (idle balances), specie movements do not automatically affect price levels. But, of course, this was precisely what the Currency School wanted to avoid by calling for an institutional/legal arrangement whereby the central bank's reserves were linked directly to the money stock and therefore to domestic prices.

The Banking School's rejection of the opposing side's framework for analysing the balance-of-payments adjustment mechanism stemmed from a different perspective on the causality relationship between money and prices. The price level did not depend on the money supply. In the closed economy, price-level variations arose from non-monetary causes and the note-circulation simply accommodated price movements. In the small open economy under convertibility and an international gold standard the domestic price level and other nominal magnitudes (even in the short run) were determined by the level of world prices and domestic real income and therefore not susceptible to changes in domestically created bank money. Instead, the domestic money stock was determined by the world price level in terms of gold and the desired real-money balances of domestic residents. If this latter was the practical context in which the Banking School understood the relation between prices and money, then they cannot be accused of the nominalist fallacy of confusing nominal with real income. This group, therefore, saw little relevance in the Currency School's objection that, since the prices of all transactions could be halved or doubled without the occurrence of any changes in real wealth, then such happenings must obviously be directly related to changes in the quantity of money. Both Tooke and Fullarton pointed out that since price-level variations could not cause external species drains, then in that sense the mixed currency system in its sef-regulating behaviour already corresponded with a purely metallic currency. They therefore questioned the need for an artificial rule to regulate the currency. A rule making the circulation of bank-notes fluctuate exactly with the Bank of England's specie reserve could, in fact, disrupt credit markets and initiate cyclical fluctuations. Indeed, Tooke argued, strict adherence to the rule was unlikely to achieve the objective of keeping the domestic price level in line with the requirements of external balance in fairly typical circumstances. Thus an adverse trade balance (deficit) could develop because of bad harvests at home or other causes unconnected with the note-issue (e.g. expansion of bank deposits, a flurry of speculative activity in commodity markets or a real shift in the demand and supply for traded goods). Such disequilibria would go on unchecked and no contractionary action would be taken by the Bank until specie began to flow abroad. The rule, therefore, could not cope with all possibilities and, in fact, could be quite destabilising and costly. In recognition of this Tooke maintained that the only reform necessary was a large increase in the Bank's average gold reserve holdings (not less than £10 million). This would enable the Bank to ride out temporary crises leading to external specie drains without recourse to damaging domestic monetary deflation.

Peel's Bank Charter Act, 1844, abated the controversy. The work of the Bank of England was split into two distinct departments: the Issue Department, which issued notes against deposits of coin and bullion above a fixed fiduciary issue (£14 million), and a Banking Department, which made loans and discounts up to a multiple of its reserves consisting of part of the note-issue.

The arrangement was a compromise which allowed both sides to claim victory. Those who wanted to limit the money-supply (the Currency School) got what they wanted, i.e. the legal acceptance of the 'metallic principle'. Except for the small fixed fiduciary issue, supplementary note-issue required a 100 per cent marginal gold reserve. The automatic, non-discretionary adjustment mechanism was thus institutionalised. With notes rigidly tied to gold, bullion flows were to be matched one-for-one by changes in the amount of currency outstanding. Those who were in favour of 'discretion' rather than 'rules' and who wanted to expand the money supply, particularly in the trough of a depression so as to get economic recovery going, lost out in a formal sense. The Banking School's plea for larger Bank of England reserves sufficient to accommodate external gold drains without domestic deflationary consequences went unheeded. But the Banking Department and the failure of the Act to limit deposits as well as currency was a limited victory for the Banking School. Deposit banking and the widening use of cheques which developed after 1844 frustrated the intentions of the Currency School to limit the money supply. The

Banking Department was left free to exercise discretionary control over a growing proportion of the broadly defined money stock through changes in its reserve–deposit ratio. Through the use of the same device the Banking Department was able to affect the money-supply independently of the existing stock of bullion. That is, in the face of external gold drains and payments deficits the Bank's reactions (allowing the reserve–deposit ratio to decline) often resulted in 'sterilisation' of bullion outflows.

The first major test of the new British gold standard system occurred in 1847. The commercial crisis of that year was precipitated by harvest failures in England and most parts of Western Europe. The high level of railway investment prevented a serious slide into deep depression; but the symptoms of crisis were unmistakable: commercial distress and financial panic caused partly by speculative forward purchases of food as British merchants searched the world for grain. Emergency corn imports (much of it from Russia) led to a huge trade deficit and a loss of bullion reserves at the Bank of England. Interest rates as well as prices rose rapidly. In October of that year, as an internal drain (run on the banks) developed, prices slumped and further commercial failures occurred, the government suspended Peel's Act. The crisis subsided when the discount rate was raised to a record high of 8 per cent and the Bank proceeded to issue fiat money (notes without gold backing). In a recent re-examination of the 1847 crisis, Dornbusch and Frenkel show that, contrary to the predictions of the price-specie-flow mechanism, adjustment to the external disequilibrium came about largely through international capital flows and changes in banking policy.[23] Automatic, non-discretionary adjustment played no part in overcoming the crisis. The Bank of England engaged in sterilisation operations (it passively tolerated a large decline in its reserve–deposit ratio), raised its discount rate and attracted short-term funds from abroad, which effectively financed the trade deficit. Some of these funds (over £15 million) came from the sale and repatriation of foreign assets. Specie outflows did not reduce the domestic money-supply. On the contrary, the very substantial inward capital flows reversed the earlier bullion flows and led to monetary expansion which eased the liquidity crisis and restored confidence.

Dornbusch and Frenkel concluded that the Bank therefore acted properly by financing the temporary balance-of-payments deficit (caused by a real disturbance) through the capital account. It would have been inappropriate to rely on the price-specie-flow mechanism which would have operated (if at all) only slowly and painfully through the trade account.[24]

The way in which the Bank reacted to the crisis was an interesting aspect of the 1847 episode. It vindicated the Banking School's criticism of Peel's Act and exposed the fallacy of the Ricardian position that identified every external drain with the process of getting rid of an excess stock of domestic money. The circumstances of the 1847 crisis were precisely what Banking School writers had in mind when they made their plea for the Bank's role as a 'lender of last resort'. In the case of a temporary external drain, this would require the Bank to finance the balance of payments deficit by selling foreign securities abroad or by running down its gold reserves rather than by trying to force a reduction in the deficit through domestic deflation. If the crisis entailed an internal run, then the duty of the Bank should be to maintain financial and real stability by accommodating commercial borrowers. Accommodation could be through the induced capital inflows which would allow monetary expansion to defuse the liquidity crisis. Fortunately, the Bank exercised discretion and did not follow Torrens's advice which called for strict adherence to the currency principle so as to obviate the need for 'the superfluous duty ... of supporting commercial credit'.[25]

Thus, although no formal provision was made in the statute for the Bank's role as a 'lender of last resort' the experience of a series of liquidity crises obliged the Bank to accept an obligation in that respect. By the end of the century, when the gold standard was supposedly at its height, not only did the Bank cushion the domestic economy against the effects of external gold drains, but it also came to recognise that the surest way to halt and reverse an internal drain (confidence or liquidity crisis) was via a policy of liberal lending. In 1873 Bagehot defined the Bank's role as a lender of last resort. Since the Bank was the ultimate guardian of the nation's specie reserve, said Bagehot, 'they will recognise and act on the obligations which this implies; that they will replenish it in times of foreign demand as fully, and lend it in times of internal panic as freely and readily, as plain principles of banking require'.[26]

The 1844 Act enshrined the principles of the gold standard. Despite the straitjacket of rigid note-issue (the Currency School dogma) the system survived several liquidity and commercial crises (1847, 1857, 1866, 1873, 1882 and 1890) until the general breakdown of 1914–18. And during this period the priority objective (both in theory and practice) was the maintenance of convertibility – the fixed gold parity of sterling – and the preservation of the gold standard.

MARX ON INTERNATIONAL MONEY

Karl Marx's views on monetary matters were influenced by his reading of the monetary arguments leading up to Peel's Act. He commented a great deal on the monetary theories of his contemporaries, and it is of some interest to take note of where he stood on these matters. As is well known, Marx was an unswerving defender of the gold standard, but at the same time an implacable opponent of the Quantity Theory of Money which supposedly provided the rationale for the automatic working of the former. Marx himself revealed that it was the economic changes brought about by the Californian and Australian gold discoveries which first led him to a serious study of the nature and dynamics of bourgeois political economy:

> The enormous material on the history of political economy which is accumulated in the British Museum; the favourable view which London offers for the observation of bourgeois society; finally, the new stage of development upon which the latter seemed to have entered with the discovery of gold in California and Australia, led me to the decision to resume my studies from the very beginning and work up critically the new material.[27]

Marx's research armed him with a thorough knowledge of the history of British monetary debates, in particular, the Bullionist and Currency School/Banking School controversy. He provided a brilliant summary of the latter, both in his *Contribution to the Critique of Political Economy* and in *Capital*.[28] Given his dislike of Quantity Theory reasoning, Marx supported the Banking school. In particular he enthusiastically embraced Tooke's 'law of reflux' (the invariance of the total nominal currency stock to changes in the value of bank-notes) and the 'real-bills' doctrine. Despite the respect Marx accords Ricardo in other respects, he curtly dismisses him as a monetary theorist whose 'death occurred in time before the onset of the crisis of 1825 demonstrated the falsehood of his forecast'.[29]

Unlike Keynes who called gold a 'barbarous relic' and referred to the *auri sacra fames* – the detestable greed for gold – Marx (like Davanzati before him, and Jacques Rueff and General de Gaulle afterwards), hailed gold as the ideal, 'universal money'. As a labour-value theorist,

Marx was naturally predisposed to gold, since it was a highly standardised commodity easily divisible. Gold was also extremely durable, and by the middle of the nineteenth century its weight and fineness could be measured with remarkable accuracy. For Marx these natural properties made gold particularly suited to function as the measure of pure exchange value. Its status was enhanced by the fact that the state could not regulate the value of the money commodity itself, i.e. gold. For Marx gold is not only a product of labour, but it is also 'the social incarnation of human labour'. Gold is the 'universal equivalent'. 'Nature', he writes:

> no more produces money than it does bankers or discount rates. But since the capitalist system of production requires the crystallization of wealth as a fetish in the form of a single article, gold and silver appear as its appropriate incarnations. Gold and silver are nót money by nature, but money is by nature gold and silver.[30]

He favoured 'hard money' as against paper money. What he called 'worthless tokens' were signs of value only in so far as they represented gold within the sphere of circulation: 'While gold circulates because it has value, paper has value because it circulates'.

Marx makes a distinction between money as a 'medium of circulation' (it mediates the exchange of commodities) and money as a 'means of payment' (money mediates the relation between debtors and creditors). On this basis he mounts an attack on the Quantity Theory:

> The rapidity of circulation being given, the volume of currency is simply determined by the prices of commodities. Hence, prices are not high or low, because there is more or less money in circulation, but on the contrary, there is more or less money in circulation, because prices are high or low. This is one of the most important laws, whose demonstration in detail by means of the history of prices constitutes perhaps the only merit of the post-Ricardian English Political Economy.[31]

The foregoing is one of the baldest statements of the doctrine of the endogeneity of the domestic money stock ever written. According to Marx, changes in the stock of money – gold or bank-notes – have no predictable effect on price levels, employment or on the real output of goods. The Quantity Theory explanation for inflation had some plausibility during the time of Hume (the depreciation of precious metals in the sixteenth and seventeenth centuries) and Ricardo ('the depreciation of paper money'). But for Marx it clearly had no relevance as an explanation of the commercial crises of the nineteenth century – a time of

> big storms on the world market, in which the antagonism of all elements in the bourgeois process of production explodes; the origin of these storms and the means of defence against them were sought within the sphere of currency, the most superficial and abstract sphere of this process.[32]

Marx's position on money and prices was strengthened by his own historical survey of the Quantity Theory and by Tooke's researches into the history of prices. He was pleased to note that Tooke was

> compelled to recognise that the direct correlation between prices and the quantity of currency ... is purely imaginary, that increases or decreases in the amount of currency ... are always the consequence, never the cause, of price variations ...[33]

The Bank of England or any central bank was therefore powerless to control the stock of money. The gold standard, according to Marx, was nevertheless an ideal system for settling international payments; and his position on how it worked corresponded closely with that of the Banking school, although he felt that they had an incomplete understanding of the nature of gold. In a regime of general convertibility of currencies, Marx holds that gold has a parity *vis-à-vis* each of these currencies, but no price. Since it is the 'universal equivalent' it serves as a physical standard for all other commodities and therefore has no price itself. Thus Marx says, what is known as fixing the price of gold 'is, as Locke correctly remarks, only fixing the name of fractional parts of gold ...'.[34] As international means of payment, money is

> gold in its metallic actuality, a valuable substance in itself, a quantity of value. It is at the same time capital, not capital as commodity-capital, but as money-capital ... (money in the eminent sense of the word ... universal world-market commodity).[35]

As world money, i.e. as the universal means of exchange, gold functions both as 'means of purchase' and 'means of payment'. As a means of payment it is used in the normal settlement of international balances. It functions as international means of purchase when 'the customary equilibrium in the interchange of products between the different nations is suddenly disturbed, i.e. when a bad harvest compels one of them to buy on an extraordinary scale'. Thus, when gold leaves 'the domestic sphere of circulation ... it falls back into its original form as precious metal in the shape of bullion . . . as world money . . . it regains its original natural form in which it played a role in barter originally'.[36]

Marx could extol the virtues of the gold standard because he was writing at a time when new gold supplies kept the world money machine well-oiled and working smoothly and efficiently. It was not an independent cause of disturbances. For Marx the origin of economic crises lay elsewhere – in the sphere of production.

WORKINGS OF THE GOLD STANDARD – DIVERGENT VIEWS

Nevertheless, even during the balmy days of mid-Victorian prosperity there were outcries by provincial industrialists against the gold standard. As British banking and finance became increasingly orientated towards the financing of world trade and investment, provincial businessmen felt that their interests (e.g. in cheap and ready credit) were being sacrificed to international financial considerations.[37]

Criticisms of the gold standard mounted worldwide during the 1880s when world gold supplies virtually dried up, prices fell and trade depression engulfed country after country. The contraction of the world money supply – the rate of growth of monetary gold stocks declined from 4 per cent in 1852 to under 2 per cent by 1880 – came at a time when silver was rapidly being demonetised in many countries (with the exception of India, whose hoarding of silver absorbed part of the overabundant metal). The bimetallist controversy which developed, particularly in the United States, was about the merit or otherwise of increasing the money supply through the monetisation of the rising US silver output – a demand which founded its appeal on Quantity Theory logic. William Jennings Bryan led his Populist crusade for unlimited issue of silver certificates in the US presidential campaign of 1896 under the banner: 'You shall not crucify mankind on a cross of gold'. Whether or not Marx's espousal of the gold standard had anything to do with the lack of labour support for Bryan's cause is a matter for political historians to debate; but Bryan lost and monometallism (and the 'sound money' policies which it entailed) triumphed. The gold standard's victory was consolidated by the passage of the US Gold Standard Act (1900); but, more importantly, it was validated by the fortuitous coming on stream of the Witwatersrand and Alaskan gold.

As we have seen, at the time of the Bank Charter Act there were two quite different versions of the mechanism of international monetary adjustment. One version (the Currency School dogma) became associated with the classical economists and the nineteenth century because of (a) the triumph of classical political economy and *laissez-faire* ideology and (b) the fact that this version was enshrined in Peel's Act. But, as is well known, the gold standard never worked as classical theory would have it. The gold standard became a 'sterling standard' and was 'managed' by Great Britain by virtue of her preponderant role in international trade and investment aided by the political authority of the Pax Britannica. Later writers in the classical tradition (e.g. Taussig) could not see this largely because of the intellectual influence of classical ideology. How the gold standard worked in its heyday was a puzzle for Taussig, writing in the 1920s.[38] Efforts at unravelling the mystery by, among others, Triffin, Bloomfield and Ford, dispelled the myth of the gold standard, i.e. automatic, non-discretionary adjustment according to the putative 'rules of the game'.[39]

The critical empirical literature is well known to students of international economics, the details of which need not concern us here. Bloomfield showed that the principal rule of the gold standard – allowing gold flows to exert their full influence on domestic money supplies and price levels was not followed. Central banks often engaged in sterilisation policies whereby they compensated (either partially or fully) for the external loss of reserves by increasing domestic credit. The central banks of France and Belgium pegged their discount rates at low levels regardless of gold flows, i.e. they relied on variations in their reserves to deal with external imbalances. Yet Taussig and his students found that sizeable balance-of-payments disequilibria were speedily adjusted. Small gold flows and minor relative price changes seemed to be sufficient to restore equilibria. Thus, although the 'rules of the game' were not strictly followed, there was balance-of-payments stability. Why? The missing links in the classical explanation were: (1) the operation of the income-adjustment mechanism and (2) the equilibrating role of international capital movements. The two processes relate to different adjustment periods, but are in fact interrelated. Thus, an outflow of bullion resulting from a balance-of-trade deficit leads to a monetary contraction (in the absence of sterilisation). The monetary contraction (in the face of an initially unchanged demand for money) raises the interest rate which attracts short-term capital from abroad. This stems the fall in the money supply and restores the initial disequilibrium by financing the deficit. But in the meantime the high interest rates result in a decline in aggregate demand, recession and a fall in imports which ultimately removes the cause of the disequilibrium. To the extent that wages (and therefore prices) are sticky downwards, the improvement in the balance of payments on current account improves, not merely through a reduction in domestic money incomes, but also by means of and at the cost of unemployment and a loss of output. It is astonishing how long it took economists to recognise the role of these two equilibrating mechanisms. Ricardo's explanation of the adjustments mechanism took no notice of international capital movements; indeed, his formal theory ruled out capital mobility. Gold flows were activated solely by imbalances on current account, and changes in the terms of trade (relative prices) restored equilibrium. John Stuart Mill was exceptional in recognising the role of capital flows (i.e. the capital account) in the adjustment process:

> it is a fact now beginning to be recognized, that the passage of the precious metals from country to country is determined much more than was formerly supposed by the state of the loan market in different countries and much less by the state of prices.[40]

Gold movements are not necessarily accompanied by shifts in the balance of trade, or changes in the domestic relative to foreign price level are neither necessary nor sufficient to transmit gold from deficit to surplus countries. Yet by the time of Marshall and Pigou this important element of overseas investment – international lending and borrowing – was still overlooked in accounts of the equilibrating mechanism. Joan Robinson often criticised them for their failure to take notice of such obvious phenomena, and their reliance upon adjustments of price levels to keep trade in balance. As she rightly pointed out: 'The operation of the gold standard mechanism was to keep flows of lending in line with income balance.'[41]

As for the income mechanism of adjustment, failure to incorporate this stems from the implicit assumption of classical theory that output and employment are unaffected by international monetary disturbances. Quantity Theory reasoning and the orthodoxy instilled by the Currency School led to the conventional view that changes in money demand affected prices and costs rather than output and employment – the same amount of workers would produce the same volume of real output. The alternative adjustment theory championed by the Banking School, which did not rely on relative price changes, surfaced from time to time; but it was not until the inter-war years of the next century that the adjustment of international payments and receipts through changes in real income and employment won acceptance as a valid hypothesis.

This, of course, arose out of the work of Ohlin, Joan Robinson and Keynes.

How, then, was the system managed? Simply by virtue of the fact that the Bank of England, as the centre of the system, managed and operated the gold standard as if it were a sterling standard system. This control resulted from London's role as the world's principal gold and produce market. Sterling became a 'key currency'. Not only was it widely used as a 'vehicle currency' in the finance of world trade – the 'bill on London' amounted to a world currency – but it was also the principal 'reserve currency'. That is, foreign central banks (mainly, but not exclusively in the British Empire) held their foreign-exchange reserves as deposits with commercial banks in London. The result was that when a deficit arose in the British balance-of-payments gold would not flow out; there was merely a change in the total volume of deposits or in the cash reserves of British commercial banks – hence, no automatic adjustment. The full burden of adjustment fell on the rest of the world, i.e. other central banks had to adjust their policies to those of London. Relationships were therefore asymmetrical, since, besides this, British traders drew no bills in foreign currency, neither did British banks hold balances in other currencies. Drafts in virtually all currencies could be bought and sold for sterling. In the short run the stability of the system was helped by the Bank of England's ability to manage its gold reserve (on average, less than 5 per cent of the aggregate liabilities of the banking system) in a prudent manner when confronted by liquidity crises. In the long run the factors making for stability were those related to Britain's role in international economic relations:

(1) The maintenance, through the policy of free trade, of a relatively open market for the exports of countries in balance-of-payments difficulties.
(2) The provision of counter-cyclical foreign long-term lending, i.e. British overseas lending was closely correlated with cyclical trade deficits in borrowing.
(3) A willingness to act as an international 'lender of last resort' (i.e. to participate in international rescue operations). The Bank of England shared this responsibility with the Bank of France until 1870 when the Franco-Prussian War forced France to drop out of this role.

Until the early 1970s there were then two accounts of the *modus operandi* of the classical gold standard:

(a) That it was a managed system orchestrated by the Bank of England by virtue of the unique role played by Britain in the nineteenth-century world economy. They way in which the international monetary system was guided by London was described by Keynes as follows:

> During the latter half of the nineteenth century the influence of London on credit conditions throughout the world was so predominant that the Bank of England could almost have claimed to be the conductor of the international orchestra. By modifying the terms on which she was prepared to lend, aided by her own readiness to vary the volume of her gold reserves and the unreadiness of other central banks to vary the volume of theirs, she could to a large extent determine the credit conditions prevailing elsewhere.[42]

(b) The Keynesian-type income-expenditure explanation of the working of the gold standard, which placed emphasis on variations in income, employment and output induced by deficits or surpluses as crucial elements in the restoration of equilibrium. With few exceptions, no one took seriously the price-specie-flow mechanism which was supposed to ensure the stability of the system through the medium of relative price-level changes between countries consequent upon gold flows. The empirical evidence was overwhelmingly against this hypothesis. It indicated that prices in the major trading countries moved in a parallel rather than divergent fashion in time periods relevant for the prediction of the theory.

With the resurgence of monetarism came new perceptions on how the gold standard worked. This monetarist perspective was not altogether novel. After all, it derived from insights gained during the course of monetary debates going back to Hume and beyond and reaching forward to the Currency School/Banking School controversy. There are, of course, strict and moderate monetarist interpretations of the gold standard era corresponding to the positions taken by earlier monetary controversialists. More recent models of portfolio balance (which focus on the capital account and explicitly incorporate international capital mobility) come to essentially the same conclusions as general monetarist models. Indeed the trend is towards an integration of both approaches in applied work which go well beyond the original monetarist formulation so that it is difficult to speak of a simple differentiated monetarist explanation.

The latest interpretation of the gold standard starts from Ricardo's premise that under fixed exchange rates a balance-of-payments deficit is the means whereby domestic residents rid themselves of an excess supply of money.[43] By Walras's Law (or some general-equilibrium market-clearing process) the excess stock of money has its counterpart in the excess of the value of imports – goods and assets – over exports. In this way the money stock is reduced in line with the public's desired money holdings. The restoration of monetary equilibrium ensures the re-establishment of external equilibrium. Quantity Theory reasoning is used to offer an explanation for the trend behaviour of global prices, interest rates and nominal incomes. Under a gold standard the world money-supply is determined by world production of gold, i.e. by mining costs. An increase in the demand for money causes the price of gold to rise relative to the price of commodities. A rise in the gold price stimulates gold-mining activity and increases the growth rate of the stock of money. Conversely, a low gold price leads to a contraction of gold-mining and monetary growth. Since gold-mining is subject to increasing marginal costs, if the price of gold remains fixed in the absence of new gold discoveries, the incentive to mine diminishes and the gold stock ceases to grow. Part of the existing stock of gold is also used for non-monetary purposes – in jewellery, dentistry, industrial uses and private hoarding. Gold is the base of the monetary system, and national money stocks consisting of deposits, notes and token coin are backed by gold reserve holdings of the commercial banks and the central bank. A fractional gold reserve system thus economises on the use of gold, i.e. it reduces the real resource costs of the gold standard. The important point is that under the gold standard the world price level is assumed to emerge in the long run out of the interaction of the global demand for money with the money (gold) stock. Thus, in the case of a small open economy the domestic purchasing power of money is given by the world purchasing power of gold. The demand for real currency balances by the domestic public then determines the desired nominal currency stock.

On this view of the matter, central banks and central-bank policy had no control over interest rates, prices or money incomes. All these monetary variables were determined in a global context. Further, it is asserted, the monetary authorities cannot sterilise the effects of reserve (gold) flows on their money-supplies (e.g. by increasing the ratio of notes and deposits to gold holdings), given the assumption of international capital mobility. Attempts at sterilisation only stimulate further gold-flows, and since gold-flows are the means whereby the domestic supply of money is brought into balance with the demand gold-flows will continue until money holdings are reduced to the level consistent with what the public is willing to hold. There is therefore a large, if not perfect, offset to domestic central-bank actions. As a consequence, it is maintained, the money-supply becomes a totally *endogenous* variable. The central bank can control the gold stock by creating or destroying credit – it can change the composition of money as between gold reserves and domestic credit – but it cannot control the domestic money-supply. Except in the case where the country is large enough (i.e. in terms of the ratio of the country's supply of money to the world's supply) to exert an independent influence on the world money-supply. Great Britain, the supposed 'manager' of the system was not in that position according to the monetarists – a 10 per cent increase in British money-supply would only increase world supply by an insignificant 1.4 per cent. Central bankers did, in fact, push levers and pressed many buttons; but all those efforts were futile. The variables over which they thought they had control – prices, interest rates, money-supplies, even employment levels – were determined by external forces. Whether central bankers obeyed the 'rules of the game' or not made no difference to the functioning of the system. When one major country absorbed large amounts of gold, others lost it. In general, since sterilisation was not a viable proposition, gain or loss by one country was offset by loss or gain of another. The equilibrium distribution of the world's gold stock among countries (i.e. the situation when the excess demand for money in each country was zero) could not be affected by monetary policy. As long ago as 1841 a spokesman for the Free Banking School, James William Gilbart, expressed scepticism about the possibility or wisdom of monetary management. No doubt, proponents of the modern monetarist/portfolio-balance approach would echo his sentiments that 'when a few more theories have been tried ... then we may discover that all our attempts to regulate the currency have been productive of mischief, and we shall be willing to let the currency regulate itself'.[44]

The components of this theoretical framework have been mentioned in various parts of this book – in connection with Hume, the Quantity Theory and the nineteenth-century monetary controversies. The essential assumptions and linkages (apart from the ones already indicated above) are:

(1) The 'law of one price' rules. International arbitrage (or the threat of arbitrage) brings national price levels into equality with world price levels when expressed in a common currency. World markets for traded goods are unified so that one price, and only

one price, prevails for each traded good everywhere (except for minor differences caused by transport costs, tariffs and other impediments to trade). The prices of non-traded or home goods are linked to the prices of tradables through the mechanism of high substitutability between tradables and non-tradables in both consumption and production. Hence, within each country, the prices of traded and non-traded goods move together. Under flexible exchange rates, where the focus is on the determination of the exchange rate, this assumption is equivalent to the PPP (purchasing-power-parity) hypothesis.

(2) With the assumption of perfect international capital mobility goes the linkage between the spot and forward exchange rates and, therefore, between domestic interest rates and rates in the rest of the world. When the forward discount is zero (as it is under a rigidly fixed gold standard) then, according to the interest-parity theorem, domestic and foreign interest rates on comparable securities can only differ by a risk factor.

(3) Price flexibility is assumed to prevail in all markets (including the labour market) so that markets always clear – there are no quantity constraints.

(4) Adjustment is costless, arbitrage is costless. In some versions it is further assumed that economic agents efficiently use all available information to make rational forecasts of the likely effects of policy changes on the nominal variables that concern them. Individuals immediately discount purely nominal changes (through the formation of rational expectations) and by so doing bring about a situation where the expected values of the relevant variables are always equal to the actual values. In other words, purely nominal changes (e.g. changes in money-supplies or tax rates) have no effect on real variables (output, employment or real income). It is assumed that economic agents can carry out their transactions almost immediately or with short time lags – e.g. as in Ricardo's contention that any excess money stock is immediately vented in an external drain and an inflow of goods of equal value. Some of the relationships involved in the model are said to exist only in long-run general equilibrium; yet it is assumed that individuals react in a ready and prompt manner.

Although suggestive, the approach gives a highly stylised portrayal of monetary equilibrium under the classical gold standard. It has affinities with the implicit model used by members of the Banking and Free Banking Schools such as Tooke, Fullarton and Gilbart. But it ignores some of the valuable insights of these writers such as recognition of time-lags, the effects of fluctuations of credit conditions on real variables and the effects of real disturbance on the balance of payments – effects which could not be fully anticipated by private market participants. Making the model fit the facts of the gold standard only serves to highlight its weaknesses.[45] A detailed critique will not be given here. It means a plunge into current macroeconomic controversy, and, as such, outside the scope of this book. The following brief critical points must therefore suffice:

1. The law of one price or the assumption of perfect arbitrage is doubtful. If Hicks's distinction between 'flexprice' and 'fixprice' markets are empirically relevant, then the law of one price only holds literally when all commodities are tradable and flexprice (e.g. homogeneous primary commodities traded on organised auction markets). Most manufactured goods, however, are traded in imperfect markets characterised by product differentiation and rigid pricing strategy.
2. The assumption of instantaneous adjustment in all markets is clearly unwarranted. Even if the speed of adjustment in asset markets is swift, goods markets certainly adjust more slowly. In the short run therefore central-bank policy can have effects on the real variables in the system.
3. The assumption of perfect international capital mobility is also questionable. During the gold-standard era interest-rate differentials persisted in different financial centres (despite the absence of exchange controls); these interest-rate differences were particularly marked during crises (not necessarily because of speculative activity primarily). It is not clear that domestic and foreign assets were perfect substitutes in portfolios. James Foreman-Peck quotes a source to the effect that British domestic investment was not a perfect substitute for British foreign investment.[46] Bloomfield mentions several factors that tended to impede the mobility of short-term capital between gold-standard countries.[47] The Bank of England presumably had some leverage in altering the direction of capital flows.
4. Of course, 'sterilisation' was not perfect. We have seen, however, that during the 1847 crisis the Bank of England did successfully

sterilise the effects of bullion losses enough to diffuse the liquidity crisis. In this case, and others like it, banking policy was an important factor in the adjustment process.
5. The monetarist interpretation takes no notice of asymmetries in the system. Keynes's comment on the influence of the Bank of England cannot be controverted. Foreign countries economised on specie by using sterling bills, i.e. these functioned as international money. The Bank of England, through its discount-rate policy, set the rate on these bills and therefore controlled the level of world interest rates. Thus it was, the lead having been set by London, that national interest rates moved up or down together. It was a forced integration of national asset markets, not dictated by non-hegemonic, cosmopolitan market forces. As the main international lender and borrower (both at short and long term) London could contract the whole world's money supply in the short run. Looking only at the ratio of the British money stock to world money-supply gives a misleading impression of the leverage exerted by London, aided and abetted by the effective monetisation of outstanding sterling bills.
6. The monetarist perspective takes too narrow a view of the money-supply process. Like Ricardo and the Currency School, it tends to regard gold as the only or most important regulator of the quantity of money. By contrast the Banking School explained monetary expansion in terms of the extension of domestic credit. What the monetarists overlook is the fact that an increasing portion of the money-supply during the gold-standard days was accounted for by domestic credit creation through an expansion of bank-notes and deposits. The process was related to the boom in deposit banking and banks in general in Germany, Italy, Austria, Spain and France. Apart from innovation and development in banking facilities, there is the question of the behaviour of velocity of circulation over the trade cycle, which casts doubt on the stable demand function for money usually assumed by monetarists. In addition, the monetarist presumption that when one country lost gold another gained it cannot explain the extraordinary synchronisation of cyclical fluctuations observed during the late nineteenth century. How did it happen that central banks seemed to have expanded or contracted their economies simultaneously?

The clash between the two opposing views on the gold standard – on the one hand that it was a managed system (the Keynesian view) and on the other that it was beyond national management and control because of the relentless discipline it imposed (the global monetarist view) carries traces of the Currency School/Banking School controversy. Strangely enough, however, despite the strong monetarist cast of Currency School thinking, the modern global monetarist model has more in common with the Banking School and Free Banking School (perhaps even with Marx) than with the regulated system advocated by Ricardo, Torrens and Samuel Jones Loyd. As one modern writer puts it:

> Free banking thought has little in common with the sort of argument for a pseudo-gold standard that depicts stabilization of the exchange rate between a distinct national currency and gold as the optimal rule for central bank policy. Under a specie standard there is no distinct national currency. Free banking means the elimination and not the redirection of the central bank.[48]

7 Free Trade and the National Economists

CRITICISMS OF CLASSICAL TRADE THEORY

Fifty-five years ago John Henry Williams of Harvard University launched a devastating attack on the English classical theory of international trade.[1] He criticised the static nature of the theory, the unrealism of its assumptions and its neglect of the interrelations of trade and growth. A theory which assumed fixed quantities of productive factors already existent and fully employed and rules out international factor mobility became merely an exercise in 'cross-section value analysis', i.e. a demonstration of static allocative gains. As such it was singularly incapable of dealing with the relation of international trade to 'the development of new resources and productive forces' and hence could not offer an explanation for the glaring facts of persistent inequalities of income and structural imbalances among countries. 'Logically followed through', said Williams, 'the classical doctrine of international trade contradicts itself; its conclusions contradict its premises.'[2] J. S. Mill was criticised for failure to see (a) 'the relation of international trade to national economic development spread over time'[3] and (b) that specialisation according to comparative advantage was in conflict with the internal mobility assumption. Specialisation for foreign markets freezes the domestic industrial structure and heightens the vulnerability of the economy to external shocks. Smith and, to a lesser extent, Marshall were exempted from this criticism. Smith's theory of absolute advantage made no distinction between domestic and international mobility of factors and moreover Smith was 'a close observer of facts'.[4] Marshall fully accepted the assumptions of classical theory, but recognised that comparative costs were liable to change under the impact of shifting reciprocal demands. Right down to the present day, essentially the same criticisms have been made of orthodox trade theory (the classical theory and its neoclassical variants) by writers with perhaps a different perspective from that of Williams – Joan Robinson, Raoul Prebisch, Gunnar Myrdal.[5] From a radically different (i.e. Marxist) perspective, challenges to orthodox doctrine continue to emanate from Emmanuel, Samir Amin, André Gunder Frank, etc.[6] Certainly, what unites the former group of writers is the belief (a) that the equilibrium-theoretic framework of conventional trade theory is inadequate for comprehending issues of trade and development and (b) that free trade may inhibit the growth of 'productive forces' in poor, underdeveloped countries. The expression *'produktionskräfte'* was introduced into the literature by Friedrich List ten years after the publication of Ricardo's comparative-advantage theory.[7] For a time in Germany it eclipsed the bright rays of 'free trade' which were being emitted from Britain by Cobden and Bright. It became the core of the national economic policy which spurred German industrialisation in the mid-nineteenth century. List's ideas went into oblivion, and it was only after the revival of interest in the developmental problems of less-developed countries after the Second World War that they came to animate the debate on these issues. Whether they are conscious of the fact or not, development economists the world over owe a great debt to the memory of Friedrich List, for he was the first champion of their cause against the ideology of free trade and the static-equilibrium theory which underpinned it. Economists concerned with the international dimensions of economic development (Prebisch, Singer, Seers, etc.) stand in a long tradition which started with the so-called 'national economists' (German and American) of the early nineteenth century.

The national economists were protectionists. They denounced free trade and called into question the classical theory on which this policy was based. Britain's commitment to and advocacy of free trade they regarded as a device for maintaining British economic hegemony. The monopoly of industrial production enjoyed by Britain was due to the productive capacities of machinery. Young nations and countries which, for various reasons, had lagged behind in economic development could not hope to compete with the British colossus without a conscious state-directed policy of industrial protection. The alternative was to remain as pastoral economies condemned to a miserable future serving only to feed the British market with food and raw materials. Without a thriving industrial sector a country could not hope to maintain an adequate population, ensure its prosperity and achieve status and influence in the world. In short, they wanted to catch up on Britain and to do it as quickly as possible.

The issues involved in the national economists' concern about the role of trade in development was prefigured in a mid-eighteenth-century debate between Josiah Tucker and David Hume.[8] In his essay 'Of Money', Hume expressed the opinion that the relatively low wage-rates and costs of subsistence in poor countries would attract manufacturing industry from rich countries and, as a consequence, the rich countries would ultimately lose their wealth to formerly underdeveloped countries. In other words, trade and investment would act as 'engines of growth' working to produce an equalisation of income levels throughout a free-trade world economy. Tucker objected to this analysis and contended that the rich country would always maintain its advantages under free trade provided the country's wealth was acquired by 'general industry'. Such a country has

> an established trade and credit, large correspondences, experienced agents and factors, commodious shops, workhouses, magazines, etc., also a great variety of the best tools and implements in the various kinds of manufactures, and engines for abridging labour ...[9]

as well as good transport facilities, skilled workers and a progessive agriculture. With all these advantages, an advanced manufacturing country has nothing to fear from competition with poor countries.

Although wages might be higher in the rich country, average costs (hence prices) would be relatively low because competition in the large domestic market would encourage large-scale production and specialisation (division of labour). The higher level of productivity resulting from these processes implied that the price level would not be proportional to the wage level. Generalising from this, Tucker proposed a general principle: 'it may be laid down as a general proposition which very seldom fails, that operose, or complicated manufactures are cheapest in rich countries; – and raw materials in poor ones'.[10] Hence Tucker was confident that the 'richer manufacturing Nation will maintain its Superiority over the poorer one, notwithstanding this latter may be likewise advancing towards Perfection'.[11] Tucker used the foregoing arguments to attack the mistaken belief that 'trade and manufactures, if left a full liberty, will always descend from a richer to a poorer state; somewhat in the same manner as a stream of water falls from higher to lower grounds ...'.[12] In answer to Hume's objections, Tucker made several observations strikingly similar to the arguments of the later national economists. Hume's main point in rebuttal was that if Tucker's arguments were true, then 'one nation might engross the trade of the whole world and beggar all the rest'.[13] To this Tucker replied that such a monopoly position would be counteracted by the poor countries taking steps by means of legislation and state intervention to promote their own industries wherever conditions of soil, climate and native skills provide such countries with special advantages. Tucker elaborated on this point in private communication to

Hume through their mutual correspondent Lord Kames. Referring to the possibility that poor countries would always be undersold in the international market, Tucker says

> It is true likewise, that all of them have it in their power to load the manufactures of the rich country, upon entering their territories, with such high duties, as shall turn the scale in favour of their own manufactures; or of the manufactures of some other nation, whose progress in trade they have less cause to fear or envy. Thus it is in my poor apprehension, that the rich may be prevented from swallowing up the poor; at the same time, and by the same methods, that the poor are stimulated and excited to emulate the rich.[14]

The force of the Anglican dean's arguments made the great philosopher reconsider his position, as Hume's essay 'On the Jealousy of Trade' indicates. Tucker took comfort from the fact that although Hume never acknowledged his indebtedness to him, he 'made him [i.e. Hume] a convert to the doctrine he now espouses'.[15]

Tucker's message is unmistakable. Backward countries can pull themselves up by their own bootstraps; for the same long-winded process of mutual causation which led to cumulative growth in rich countries can be short-circuited by policy. The conditions for economic prosperity can be duplicated wherever circumstances are favourable by state intervention in matters of commercial and industrial policies.

AMERICAN NATIONAL ECONOMISTS AND PROTECTIONISM

There is no evidence that the national economists in Germany or the United States were aware of this debate and therefore we can safely assume they derived no benefit from it. But the curious blend of mercantilist and free-trade logic underlying Tucker's arguments was fairly common by the early nineteenth century. The equally relevant Spence–Mill–Torrens debate which preceded the Corn Law controversy went largely unnoticed by the national economists. Whenever they used theoretical arguments these were primarily directed against Adam Smith's version of classical economics, in particular their understanding of his free-trade doctrine. But they were essentially economic pragmatists who looked for solutions in the sphere of policy to the problem of getting industrialisation started. One who went to some lengths to formulate an analytical system for dealing with the problem of national economic development in an international context was Friedrich List. Before turning to his work, let us briefly survey the views of the early American economists and statesmen among whom the tenets of modern economic nationalism first took roots.

The origin of American protectionism can be traced to Alexander Hamilton's state papers, in particular the *Report on Manufactures*[16] (already referred to in connection with the infant-industry argument). The goal was industrialisation: the rapid transformation of the newly independent country from the status of an economic dependant to that of a first-rate world power. Indeed, the report has been called the 'charter of American industrialism'.

A programme of government assistance to native manufacturing industry through protective duties, bounties, subsidies and drawbacks was an essential element in the strategy. As the leaders of the revolution saw it, the measures envisaged for achieving the long-term objective of industrialisation were in harmony with other immediate desirable ends: raising Federal revenue from tariff duties, lessening dependence on imports and thus the avoidance of shortages in times of war, stemming the loss of coin caused by excessive imports, strengthening of national unity and regional interdependence through the processing of southern staples in the north. Thus a sound public credit policy, national unity, abundance of national supplies and a healthy balance of payments could all be attained by the development of native manufactures.

In the *Report* submitted to Congress in December 1791 Hamilton outlined the benefits a country derived from manufacturing industry. He evoked visions of factories, mighty machines and large-scale production throughout the land, all offering greater scope for division of labour and increases in labour productivity than could ever be achieved in agriculture. The importation of foreign manufactures checked the progress of native industry and deprived the country of great benefits. An agricultural country producing only a few staples must depend upon foreign outlets for the disposal of its surplus. Such a country (bereft of processing facilities) often traded on disadvantageous terms with manufacturing countries because of the frequent occurrence of glutted markets and depressed prices. Terms-of-trade losses, specie drains and unfavourable trade balances were the common experiences of non-industrialised countries.

Hamilton then turned to the obstacles to be overcome: shortages of skilled mechanics, machinery and capital and lack of adequate transport facilities. Since a country ought to aim at possessing 'all the essentials of national supply'[17] it was the duty of the state to help entrepreneurs cope with the difficulties by offering inducements to invest in manufacturing industry through a government programme of eleven types of aid and protection. Hamilton considered protective tariffs, bounties, patents and infrastructural projects as absolutely essential elements of the planned programme of assistance. Agriculture was not to be neglected. It had a role to play in national economic development. Washington had declared that he 'would not force the introduction of manufactures by extravagant encouragements, ... to the prejudice of agriculture'.[18] Hamilton concurred and pointed out that the best prospect for agriculture lay in the growth of industry which would enlarge the market for produce and raw materials. The demand so generated would be more certain, steady and profitable than reliance on foreign markets. High transport costs across the ocean which reduced farmers' net income from the proceeds of sales would be avoided.[19]

Hamilton's proposals were not put into effect immediately. The early tariffs, designed primarily for the purpose of raising revenue, afforded only incidental protection. The one clear protectionist measure – the Tonnage Act of 1789 – did indeed provide substantial protection to U.S. shipowners and shipbuilders. The Act established uniform tonnage duties of 50 cents a ton on every entry into a U.S. port by foreign vessels and 6 cents a ton on U.S.-owned vessels. Apart from the protective element, the measure was also revenue-raising and could be used as a bargaining weapon in commercial negotiations with foreign countries to secure reciprocal reductions in discriminatory trade practices. But it was not until after the Anglo-American War of 1812 that American trade policy turned massively protectionist. The Tariff Act of 1816, for example, imposed duties of $7\frac{1}{2}$ to 30 per cent *ad valorem* on a wide range of manufactured products; but still the demand grew for more protection.

The manufacturing interests of Pennsylvania, New England and New York state called for higher import duties, and in this they were supported by the early American economists, who also, in their writings, reflected the nationalist aspirations of the political leaders. Daniel Raymond, a Baltimore lawyer, championed the protectionists' cause. In his two books, *Thoughts on Political Economy* (1820) and *Elements of Political Economy* (1823),[20] he disputed Adam Smith's view that the net result of the interactions of individuals pursuing their own interests was the promotion of social welfare and economic growth.

The interests of individuals, Raymond asserted, were always at variance with the national interest. The cotton and tobacco planters in the south were free-traders because it was in their interest to import cheap textiles from England; but the trade was not beneficial to the country as a whole.[21] National wealth was not the sum total of individual exchange values or total expenditure on consumption; rather it was the capacity to produce goods. The pace of national economic development was determined by a country's ability to increase its productive capacity. The latter could be speeded up by an active government policy of intervention, particularly in regard to external trade. What held back U.S. entrepreneurs was the inability to compete on equal terms with the superior skills and technology of the English.[22] It was the duty of the state to remedy this deficiency through a policy of protective tariffs to encourage investment in infant industries and ensure the full employment of labour. Besides, tariffs were the cheapest way of providing such assistance. The same conclusion was reached by John Rae on the basis of his analysis of the role of capital formation in economic development.[23] Because of the social benefits of investment the state must take an active interest in capital formation. The government could positively encourage the growth of industry by subsidising inventions, new technical processes and offering tariff protection to immature industries. John Stuart Mill was apparently impressed by some of Rae's arguments and explicitly mentioned Rae in connection with the infant-industry argument.

Another early protectionist writer worthy of note is Willard Phillips, a Harvard-educated Boston lawyer. He started out as a defender of free trade, but by the time his book, *A Manual of Political Economy* (1828) was published he was already converted to protectionism.[24] He rejected large parts of classical doctrine after careful study of the works of Smith, Malthus, Ricardo, Say and McCulloch. His criticisms of classical writers were often well-substantiated, and his own positive contributions were quite significant. His discussion of international trade was fairly sophisticated for that time (e.g. his analyses of the terms-of-trade argument for protection and international demonstration effect in consumption). Free trade, he argued, was not a rational policy for a country given the existence of national trade barriers. Countries should rather aim for 'perfect reciprocity' whereby the effects of other countries' trade regulations could be neutralised – a policy of 'fair trade', as we should say today. Besides arguing the case for protection, Phillips made noteworthy contributions to general economic theory and method in areas such as value, distribution, location and rent.

Not all early U.S. economists were protectionists, of course; but the free-trade writers, not unnaturally, were mainly to be found in the southern states (Jacob Cardozo, George Tucker and Thomas Cooper). But even these writers, while they upheld the free-trade logic, were severe critics of imported economic doctrines.

During the 1820s – years of ardent nationalism in the United States – the protectionist movement grew steadily, and coalesced in the Pennsylvania Society for the Promotion of Manufactures and the Mechanic Arts founded in 1826 and based in Philadelphia. Leading the agitation was Henry Clay (the politician) and Matthew Carey (the publisher). Carey's son, Henry Charles Carey, later became well-known as the leading theoretical defender of U.S. protectionism.[25] He was well-read in British political economy and declared himself a follower of Adam Smith; but he rejected much of classical doctrine as being inapplicable to a large and young country like the United States. His recipe for national economic development was a combination of domestic *laissez-faire* and protectionism. He went further than Raymond and advocated protection as a permanent feature of national policy. He saw no inconsistency in this position, and for this reason Carey has been widely regarded as the mouthpiece of American business interests at that time. He denounced the British policy of free trade, claiming that its real aim was to secure for England a monopoly of machinery. The 'American system' (the protective tariff policy) sought to break down that monopoly.[26]

But Carey was not simply a propagandist for the industrial lobby. There was a strong physiocratic streak in his economic thought and it can be argued that his ultimate aim was a prosperous agriculture. Like the Physiocrats, he contended that the basis of industrial growth came from the surplus of the agricultural sector. There was a symbiotic relationship between the two sectors. If agricultural expansion was a precondition for industrial take-off, the continued prosperity of agriculture depended on steady growth of the industrial sector. But economic diversification could only come about through a policy of industrial protection. It is in this context of a vision of balanced growth that we must see Carey's protectionism. In his empirical work relating the tariff history of the United States to cyclical fluctuations in the economy during the first half of the nineteenth century Carey observed that each of the three tariff increases were associated with periods of rising prosperity. Depressions, marked by low farm prices and falling demand for industrial goods followed with a lag every time average tariff rates fell. He concluded that industrial protection stimulated the economy since it shifted the terms of trade in favour of the United States, increased domestic industrial production and raised farm prices and incomes. A virtuous circle was put into motion every time tariff levels were increased. Increased protection widened the domestic market for manufactures, offered scope for large-scale production and resulted in low prices, i.e. low relative to the prices of competitive imports taking into account transport costs. Rising levels of urban incomes and activity increased the demand for farm products (food and raw materials) and, as farm incomes and prices rose, so the demand for manufactures was further stimulated.

LIST – THE NATIONAL ECONOMIST

In June 1824, one year before the establishment of the Pennsylvania Society, Friedrich List, the German political exile, arrived in the United States.[27] It was a momentous event in the life of the man who was to be identified both by his own and succeeding generations with the creed of economic nationalism. He was not an ordinary immigrant. He accompanied General Lafayette, who was then making a triumphal return tour of the country and met several prominent Americans including President John Quincy Adams, Henry Clay, Chief Justice Marshall, Daniel Webster, some of whom became personal friends (Andrew Jackson, James Madison). He came to America at a time when the protectionist agitation was at its height. The discussions surrounding the problems and prospects of American economic growth made a strong impression on him. He saw parallels with his native country and these observations, together with his experiences from several business projects, strengthened his earlier beliefs in national unity, protection and the possibilities for accelerated industrial growth through enlightened policies. His doubts deepened concerning the relevance of classical doctrine for countries attempting to get on the threshold of industrialisation; as he noted in his diary, the American experience forcibly brought home to him the fact that countries passed through different stages of economic development and that different policies were required for each stage.[28]

As editor of the *Readinger Adler*, an influential immigrant weekly paper, List gained a national reputation as one of the foremost defenders of the 'American System'. He plunged himself into the propaganda activities of the Pennsylvania Society and wrote a series of letters to Charles Ingersoll, vice-president of the Society, calling for the imposition of high import duties to protect American manufacturers from British competition and thus ensure steady economic growth. He campaigned on behalf of the winning Democratic presidential candidate, Andrew Jackson, and when his letters to Ingersoll were subsequently published as *Outlines of American Political Economy* (1827), copies of this work were circulated to Congressmen. List's literary and political efforts came to fruition a year later when Congress passed the Tariff Bill of 1828. Dubbed the 'Tariff of Abominations', this Act imposed import duties averaging 45 per cent *ad valorem*. Although tariff rates declined somewhat up to the outbreak of the Civil War, they rose again sharply afterwards and remained so for the rest of the century. The United States therefore never adopted free trade in the nineteenth century.

The *Outlines* was List's first attempt at a systematic presentation of his theory on national economy. Here he justified his policy of protective tariffs, criticised the classical economists and discussed how the problems of development could be overcome. In it, all the leading ideas of his later works were foreshadowed, e.g. national economics, productive powers, balanced growth and stages of economic growth. These ideas were further developed and illustrated with a wealth of sociological and historical references in List's next two major works, *The Natural System of Political Economy* (1837) and *The National System of Political Economy* (1841).[29] List's public life, although full of dramatic and tragic turns was all of one piece: all his activities and intellectual efforts were directed towards the realisation of the 'national idea' (*Nationalitätsprinzip*), above all its full realisation in his beloved Fatherland.

Before he left for America, as secretary of the Union of Merchants and Industrialists (*Handels- und Gewerbsverein*) and editor of its journal, List mounted a campaign for the abolition of internal tolls and duties and the establishment of an all-German external tariff to protect German manufacturers from foreign (British) competition. Thenceforth he became the driving force behind the Zollverein. He had visions of an integrated German economy, with its national railway network and national merchant marine supporting industrialisation and the realisation of the country's full economic potential. When he returned to Germany he resumed with unflagging zeal his work on all matters concerned with the promotion of German industrialisation until he took his own life in 1846.

List set up his own system of national economics in opposition to what he regarded as the erroneous teachings of the classical economists on the subject of trade and development. He habitually refers to the classical writers as 'the School', suggesting a greater uniformity of doctrine than was in fact the case. When he mentions names, those most often cited are Adam Smith and J. B. Say. There is no indication that he was ever familiar with Ricardo's principle of comparative advantage or of the writings of Torrens and James Mill. He excluded from consideration large areas of classical thought such as the theories of value, money and distribution and concentrated his attacks on the theory of trade policy, orthodox methodology and growth theory.

List considered the analytical method an appropriate procedure in understanding economic phenomena; but abstract economic doctrines have no universal validity. Changing contingent factors (sociological, political, historical and institutional) require that the axiomatic approach be complemented by inductive, empirical and historical studies; otherwise theory degenerates into vague generalisations, liable to be contradicted by divergent facts. Since theory is only as good as its assumptions would allow it, List makes a plea not only for contextual flexibility in theory construction, but also for the realism of assumptions. Thus he criticises classical theory for its ahistorical, individualistic, cosmopolitan and natural-law concepts. In particular, he indicts the theory for its 'groundless cosmopolitanism', 'deadly materialism' and 'disorganising particularism'.[30] The erroneous policy proposals of the classical school stem from these theoretical shortcomings. Adam Smith and his followers had discussed 'individual economics' and 'cosmopolitan economics' but had lost sight of the nation, and failed to develop a theory of national economics. They reduced all economic activity, including international trade to the free play of competitive acquisitive behaviour in the market-place (worldwide as well as domestic). But, says List, the world is divided into sovereign states. Welfare-maximising individuals are also citizens, and the special interests of individuals do not necessarily coincide with the general interest of the nation. Moreover, the market is not merely a meeting-place for the exchange of commodities into money-equivalents, but is also an outlet for human relationships, i.e. social interchange. The division of labour fostered by the free-market economy certainly promotes efficiency, but it only works because it is a social, co-operative system in the production process. The nation is the link between the individual and mankind. An economic theory which ignores the social and economic significance of this link is bound to be trivial and inconsequential. A relevant political economy, for List, must be one which seriously analyses the infrangible nexus between market economics and politics.[31]

Adam Smith had, quite properly, defined political economy as a branch of statecraft, the principal aim of which was to discover the causes of the wealth of nations; but Smith deviated from his purpose and his quest ended in a blind-alley. His analysis offered little guidance to backward countries which nevertheless possessed all the potentialities for economic growth. List conceives his national economics as an inquiry into the *real* causes of wealth in such countries. Uppermost in his mind, of course, is the case of Germany. The key concepts in List's reconstruction of trade and development theory are 'productive forces' and 'economic stages'. These are essentially dynamic constructs (in contrast to much of classical reasoning), and List handles them skilfully to show the relativity of economic doctrines and the organic nature of development.

For List, the wealth of a nation consists, not as Adam Smith would have it, in the sum total of its exchange-values, but in the full use of its productive powers. These powers of production are not the same as actual production or current income. They are the means whereby further wealth can be created in the future. By productive forces, List means not only a country's private capital equipment, natural and human resources, but also its social overhead capital (especially transport facilities), advances in science and technology, educational facilities, administrative and managerial skills, progressive political and social institutions, etc.[32] In short, all the attributes of a developed country. A nation achieves the optimum utilisation of its resources when it has fully developed all the productive powers of manufacturing, commerce and agriculture in an evenly balanced fashion. It was the duty of the state to act as a catalyst in the release of productive forces that generate the industrialisation process. Once the modernisation process is under way, private enterprise and the market mechanism can be relied upon to continue the momentum. He agrees with J. B. Say that 'laws cannot create wealth', but asserts that laws can 'create productive power, which is more important than riches, i.e. than the actual possession of values in exchange'.[33] One of the most potent and readily available devices for activating dormant productive forces is a protective tariff. The full power of manufacturing can only be developed behind a tariff wall which creates the conditions (a secure home market, adequate return on investment, etc.) for thriving industries. In conditions of economic backwardness, a protective tariff is not only a sure means of bringing unused resources into production, it also 'imparts industrial instruction' (education) to the nation: entrepreneurs gain industrial, business and organisation experience, a work-force is trained and equipped with industrial skills – in short, all the economic success associated with 'learning by doing'. The development of industry is vital, for without it there can be no viable, prosperous agriculture and commerce. The *Normalnation* is one in which there is a harmonious balance between agriculture, manufacturing and commerce – 'in the absence of this harmony, a nation is never powerful and wealthy'.[34] Hence it is absolutely essential that domestic manufacturers be protected against foreign competition, for what is good for manufacturing is good for all other sectors.

List buttresses his developmental programme with a theory of the stages of economic growth. The object of this excursion into historical sociology is to make the point that different economic policies are required for each stage in a nation's development. Indeed, wise policy should aim by all possible means to ease the transition from one stage to another. At least for nations in the temperate zone the ultimate goal of economic maturity will be industrialisation. In the early stages of growth, when the economy is predominantly agricultural, the country should pursue a liberal (i.e. free-trade) commercial policy. As capital accumulates and craft industries make their appearance a protectionist policy must be introduced, but only moderate rates of duty should be imposed since the country will need to import machinery, tools, etc., from the more advanced countries in order to acquire the skills and learn the techniques of manufacturing production. At the second stage of industrial development when the industrial structure of the country is being built up but domestic industries are still unable to withstand competition from more advanced countries tariff policy should become severely restrictive and additional help provided by way of subsidies to manufacturers. The aim of policy here is to nourish and support the development of home industries, since at this stage the only available market is the national one. Only when the country has successfully surmounted all the obstacles to industrial growth and has a complement of well-established industries should commercial policy gradually revert to one of free trade 'to stop farmers, manufacturers and merchants, from falling into idle habits and to encourage them to maintain the supremacy that they have achieved'.[35]

PROTECTION AND INDUSTRIALISATION

List the patriot and nationalist wanted to hasten German unity and industrialisation. All his economic theorising was motivated by this ambition. He wished Germany to 'strive to attain to the same degree of commercial and industrial development to which other nations have attained by means of their commercial policy'.[36] The biggest obstacle to the realisation of this aim was the ideology of free trade that was spreading to Germany. Free trade might be good for England, but it spelt disaster for countries like Germany and the United States. A few German industries managed to get off the ground and even thrived for a brief period under the shelter of Napoleon's Continental System. But when peace came and the ports of Europe were thrown open cheap manufactured goods from British factories flooded the German market and these industries were ruined. The slump that ensued resulted in widespread unemployment, pauperism, vagabondage and drove thousands of destitute Germans to the United States and Canada. List was deeply distressed by this experience and saw it as a British attempt to stifle the birth of German industry. When later, in the United States, he heard that a similar throttling of industry occurred there owing to ruinous British competition, List's reaction was hostile and bitter:

> English national economy has for its object to manufacture for the whole world, to monopolize all manufacturing power, even at the expense of the lives of her citizens, to keep the world, and especially her own colonies, in a state of infancy and vassalage by political management as well as by the superiority of her capital, her skill, and her navy.[37]

This outburst against British economic dominance cannot be lightly dismissed as the emotional outpourings of a frustrated patriot and nationalist devoid of substance. List's grievances were not fanciful or exaggerated. He knew from his American friends that Henry Brougham (an influential Liberal MP who later became Lord Chancellor) had called for a policy of dumping British goods on the U.S. market so as 'to stifle in the cradles those rising manufactures in the United States which the war had forced into existence contrary to the natural course of things'.[38] List's denunciation of British economic hegemony was based on a thorough study of British commercial policy. British political economists and publicists now called for free trade because it chimed in well with British national interests. But it was not always so. The British Industrial Revolution was born and nurtured not on free trade but on protection. But alas, says List: 'It was one of the vulgar tricks of history that when one nation reaches the pinnacle of its development it should attempt to remove the ladder by which it had mounted in order to prevent others from following.'[39] He praised English mercantilist policy, for whatever else might be said of it the policy certainly fostered British commercial and industrial supremacy. Whenever and wherever sufficient political pressure could be exerted, English ministers sought to wrest trade advantages for their merchants and manufacturers. He gave examples: the 1703 Methuen Treaty with Portugal, the suppression of the Indian textile industry in order to safeguard the Lancashire cotton industry; the 1713 Asiento Treaty with Spain and the Eden Treaty, which gave British manufacturers a foothold in South America and France; the prohibition of certain lines of manufacturing in the U.S. colonies which forced on the colonists British imports that they were perfectly capable of making for themselves. All this suggested, said List, that

> England's ministers obeyed the theory of productive power when they determined upon their industrial policy ... by the power which she pursued, [England] acquired power, and by her political power gained productive power, and by her productive power gained wealth.[40]

The fault with the classical theory of trade, List asserted, was that it ignored the possibility of commercial manipulation through the exercise of political influence. It evaded the whole real-world issue of dominance and dependency and sought to elevate free trade to the status of an unassailable principle of universality validity. The failing lay in the premises of orthodox theory, i.e. the assumption that trade takes place between countries of equal economic strength and at the same level of economic development and hence, equality of bargaining power. Remove these unrealistic assumptions and the way is cleared for a theory that can relate more meaningfully both in terms of analysis and policy to conditions of economic backwardness, unequal development and the universal desire for industrialisation. For List, free trade in industrial goods can only be a distant goal to be attained when all suitably endowed countries reach the same level of industrial development and thus in a position to engage in genuine international competition. Until that time countries cannot dispense with tariff protection for they must themselves pass gradually through all the stages which Britain had undergone. Even at the time he was writing, List noted, Britain had not fully departed from protection. The Corn Laws remained in force and although Huskisson had lowered some industrial duties the average tariff level was still high enough to provide adequate shelter to British manufacturers.

List was a hasty writer who sometimes exaggerated to strengthen his arguments. He was also dogmatic, yet he was often correct in his general assessment of the motivations and consequences of British mercantilist policy, as modern research indicates. List's discussion of the Methuen Treaty is a case in point. He disputed Adam Smith's claim that the treaty was not particularly beneficial to England and that Portugal got the better of the bargain. Smith was alone in this opinion, said List, for 'all the merchants and political economists, as well as the statesmen of England have ever since eulogised this treaty as the masterpiece of British commercial policy'.[41] Under the terms of the treaty, in return for British naval support, the Portuguese government accepted conditions of trade which wiped out the Portuguese textile industry, arrested economic development and made Portugal more dependent than ever on Britain. Portuguese trade was henceforth carried on by British merchants and German and Dutch exports were virtually excluded from Portuguese and Brazilian markets – 'Portugal was deluged with English manufactures and the first result of this inundation was the sudden and complete ruin of the Portuguese manufactories.'[42] List did not exaggerate. According to recent research the result of the treaty was

> a strong dependence of Portugal on England. ... The large and chronic deficit created by the type of international division of labour in the Portuguese balance of payments caused Brazilian gold to outflow entirely from Portugal and to be directed mainly to England, where given the different conditions it contributed to the industrialization of that country much more than it had done in Portugal whose manufacturing sector had been sacrified to the production of wine.[43]

List is generally regarded as an arch-protectionist, a neo-mercantilist; others, a minority (e.g. Charles Gide, Eduard Heiman, Rudolph Hilferding), see him as essentially an economic liberal whose ultimate goal was free trade.[44] One can obviously assess List's thought from different perspectives and each would give a different answer to this question. List specifically excluded agriculture from protection. He believed that the growth of industry was a sufficient guarantee of agricultural expansion. The inevitable spread of industrial techniques to agriculture would increase its productivity; together with the growth of urban demand this would ensure the prosperity of domestic agriculture. Protection was not central to List's argument; hence his justification of 'educational tariffs' was not simply an 'exception' to the free-trade principle, as some neoclassical writers make out in order to emasculate List's case by subsuming it under the rubric of mainstream economic theorising. List was concerned with the development of productive powers and its role in propelling economic growth. What mattered for him was whether free trade was an inhibiting or liberating force in the release of productive potential. The adoption of a free-trade policy was a matter of choice conditioned by particular historical circumstances. When free trade was a liberating factor in economic growth it should be adopted; when it was a hindrance it was folly to continue with it.

List gave no indication that he was aware of the principle of comparative cost. He understood Smith's absolute advantage theory, but his application of it was selective to say the least. Thus he said if Smith's doctrine was followed the United States would buy all its cloth from England, but this would ruin the manufacture of cloth in the United States and although U.S. consumers would benefit from cheap clothing there is no guarantee that they would not have to pay higher prices later when British manufacturers felt they had a monopoly position in the U.S. market. Americans would suffer a double loss: high prices and no domestic industry. On the other hand, List thought that the principle applied with particular relevance to trade between the tropics and the temperate countries of Europe and North America. Those who see List as a champion of industrialisation in underdeveloped countries forget that he saw no future for many of these countries along that road. Thus he did not recommend the use of educational tariffs by countries not destined to participate in the historic march towards industrialisation because of their limited, specialised resources (i.e. primary producers).

> A country of the torrid zone would make a very fatal mistake, should it try to become a manufacturing country. Having received no invitation to that vocation from nature, it will progress more rapidly in riches and civilization if it continues to exchange its agricultural productions for the manufactured products of the temperate zone.[45]

List envisaged that the future pattern of world trade would be marked by a complementary relationship between the tropics on the one side and industrial Europe and America on the other. List must have realised, although he did not mention it, that the industrial countries would experience more rapid rate of growth than the tropics since manufacturing took place at decreasing costs. However, List felt that the dependency (exploitative) element in this otherwise unequal relationship would be reduced to the extent that many developed countries (not just one) would be competing for primary products. List's hopes on both these counts have not been fulfilled. The bulk of world trade in the modern world takes place among the industrial countries themselves, not between them and the tropics and dependency is a real complaint often made by Third World representatives.

In other respects List showed some analytical insights still worthy of note. Thus he clearly saw that one of the main advantages of manufacturing was that it afforded opportunities for obtaining increasing returns through enlargement of the scale of production. Long before Marshall, List recognised in 'external economies' an important source of the benefits of industrialisation. These dynamic gains fostered by high growth of demand through protection outweighed, in List's view, the inefficiencies of protection. He was not ignorant of the static allocative-efficiency losses from protection, but maintained they were a small price to pay for the long-run economic, social, cultural and political blessings of industrialisation.

The development of productive forces under protective cover means that the interests of particular individuals would be thwarted, some current income would have to be sacrificed and consumers at large would face increased prices. Unprofitable industries or branches of manufacturing would have to be set up where productivity is lower than abroad at the initial stage. They are unprofitable in terms of the cost of current output valued at world prices or the private return on capital. The nation would therefore lose a part of its exchange values, but gain immensely in the long run when the social benefits are reaped. Lord Robbins saw much evidence of 'misrepresentation and exaggeration' in List's work, but gave him credit for the early analysis of external economies and the growth of productive forces, an analysis which justified the fostering of certain industries in particular historical contexts.[46]

List was a foremost critic of free trade and an advocate of state intervention to promote economic development, but he firmly believed that the capitalist entrepreneur had a vital role to play in the process of industrialisation. He agrees with Adam Smith that free competition within a country leads to an optimum allocation of resources. But the maximum stimulation of a nation's productive powers (industrialisation potential) requires the guiding hand of the state in the absence of an entrepreneurial bourgeois class. The policies he called for were designed to provide the essential economic structure to make a market economy work more effectively. Thus under protection, he believed that competition would prevent monopoly and ensure that prices are kept down – he did not realise that a protected market and increasing returns were ideal conditions for the emergence of monopoly and cartellisation. But his insistence on the active role of the state as a stimulator and an organiser of productive activity led E. H. Carr to say 'on the theoretical side, the father of economic planning belongs rather to Friedrich List than to Karl Marx'.[47]

It is remarkable how quite similar were Williams's criticisms of classical trade theory to those made by List a hundred years earlier; and, for that matter, the close resemblance of List's arguments to those of Joan Robinson, Gunnar Myrdal and others. The fact of the matter is, however, that although the classical model is static the theory is dynamic. This anomaly, often overlooked, was noticed by Joan Robinson in respect of Ricardo's theory of profits and his foreign-trade model.[48] It is this dynamic interpretation of Ricardo that explains his opposition to the Corn Laws, as we have previously indicated. Hla Myint has pointed to dynamic elements in Smith's trade theory and shows how closely interwoven Smith's trade analysis was with his theory of economic development.[49] Mill and Marshall retained the static model, but argued for free trade as an 'engine of growth' in a framework of reasoning which emphasised technical progress and the diffusion of knowledge. The neoclassical trade model, however, remained stuck in the static mould which emphasised allocative efficiency. Some attempts have been made to deal with the sort of questions raised by Williams and List, but the main effort has been put, not in the direction of a modification of the assumptions, but in testing the implications of the assumptions. For List, this would have been a wasteful effort. Like Keynes, he believed that a theory was useless unless it offered sensible advice on urgent policy problems – in List's case, how to get industrialisation going in a backward but potentially powerful nation. List had no use for a theory which by its very assumptions ruled out the most important matters that cried out for investigation. He would have heartily endorsed Joan Robinson's verdict: 'the classical model for the analysis of international trade is reduced to wreckage ... and, for better or worse, international trade must be directed by conscious policy'.[50]

It is a valid point, however, that List misunderstood and misrepresented Adam Smith. He failed to see the dynamic elements in Smith's theory and concentrated on Smith's espousal of free trade which he rejected. List attacked Smith's 'cosmopolitan economics', but did not appreciate that the classical economists (Smith in particular) were patriots first and foremost, as Lord Robbins remarked.[51] List did, in fact, appreciate this; but he felt that others (e.g. the bourgeois class in Germany) did not sufficiently realise it. He saw clearly that the classical economists merely provided a theoretical underpinning for a British 'imperialism of free trade' and he wanted to warn his German readers about the dangers of that.

He agreed with the reservations Smith made to the free-trade case on the grounds of national interests; in some cases he felt Smith went too far, in others not far enough. Thus List favoured bilateral commercial treaties whereas Smith was pessimistic, had a poor opinion of them and considered that they were all based on groundless fears and served the interests of a selfish minority. List saw national safeguards in bilateral (or multilateral) treaties and thought they were 'the most effective means of gradually diminishing the respective restrictions on trade, and of leading the nations of the world gradually to freedom of international intercourse'.[52] (How right he was! and how wrong Smith proved to be!) List was more prophetic, in that he saw that they were the means whereby 'the reciprocal exchange of manufactured products is promoted'.[53] Since the end of the Second World War progress in dismantling tariff barriers has come from hard-bargaining multilateral trade negotiations and not from mere exhortations to national leaders about the cosmospolitan benefits of generalised free trade.

Smith had recognised in a discussion on the external corn trade that in a 'second best' world of trade barriers it might be undesirable for some countries to follow a free-trade policy: 'The very bad policy of one country may thus render it in some measure dangerous and imprudent to establish what would otherwise be the best policy in another.'[54] List agreed, pointing out that it was precisely because Britain had not adopted a free-trade policy after the Napoleonic Wars ended that agrarian countries were forced to develop their own industries. Because of the restrictive British Corn Laws they could not sell enough of their agricultural products to pay for the British manufactured goods which swamped their markets after 1815.

Smith did not believe that tariffs would help to increase the amount of employment available in the country as a whole or the level of its economic activity. The extent of industry was determined by the size of its capital stock; consequently trade controls would merely push some of this capital into socially less advantageous channels where it would not go of its own accord. Yet Smith would allow the imposition of 'countervailing duties' to equalise the conditions of competition between home and foreign products in cases where the foreign products were taxed at a lower rate than domestic products. Why not then, asked List, extend this logic to cover other disabling factors (apart from differential taxation) which discriminate against domestic production?:

> if the burden of taxation to which our productions are subjected, affords a just ground for imposing protective duties on the less taxed products of foreign countries, why should not also the other disadvantages to which our manufacturing industry is subjected in comparison with that of the foreigner afford just grounds for protecting our native industry against the overwhelming competition of foreign industry.[55]

Smith's categorical denial that tariffs could increase aggregate employment or output rested on the implicit assumption of full employment of all resources as the normal state of affairs. But if this condition was not fulfilled, as it was in the German states after 1815, then might not tariffs contribute to the activation of idle productive capacity? asked List.

For List, Smith was at his most vulnerable when he turned from the purely national interest to a cosmopolitan perspective. How splendid it would be, said Smith, if all the countries of Europe were to adopt 'the liberal system of free exportation and free importation' and the world came to 'resemble the different provinces of a great empire'. This was indeed a grand vision, one shared by List. But, first of all, the industrially backward countries must develop their productive forces and reach the same level of development as Britain. Before that time came – an event welcomed by List – those countries must safeguard and advance their industries. The adoption of a free-trade policy would merely confirm the 'insular supremacy of Britain'. It is true Smith referred to this vision in connection with agricultural trade, but if extended to trade in industrial goods (as the followers of Smith were advocating) then that was the result List foresaw. List's basic objection to Smith's mode of reasoning was that Smith saw everything from 'a shopkeeper's point of view'.[56] He was fond of illustrating economic phenomena by taking examples from the behaviour of individual families. He simply lost sight of the total dimension of economic decision-making, of the independent existence of group, social and national actions. He was so obsessed with the shortsighted policies of the interfering mercantilist state and so enamoured of his own system of 'natural liberty' that the release of productive potential through the organising and supportive role of the state receded from his ken. His preference was for the minimal, *laissez-faire*, 'nightwatchman' state; but such a state, however admirably suited to early nineteenth-century British conditions was thoroughly ill-designed and ill-equipped for the task of lifting backward peoples to nationhood and industrial status.

Writing in 1929, the year of Williams's article, Viner declared that List's arguments were 'really a plea for urbanisation' and that he reinforced his infant-industry argument with 'most of the protectionist fallacies current in his time in both America and Europe'. And further that List's references to the doctrines of the free-traders, especially Adam Smith, were 'so unfair as to be caricatures' not deserving of serious consideration 'as objective scientific analysis'. Viner felt, however, that List was 'entitled to praise as a pioneer of the historical point of view in economics'.[57] It is true List was no great analyst of abstract economic phenomena, neither was he a Karl Marx who probed into the inner dynamics of capitalist production. Yet the founders of Marxism (Marx and Engels) nevertheless regarded him as the most outstanding German economist of his day 'despite the bourgeois apologetic nature of his teachings'.[58]

List used Adam Smith as a whipping-boy in his attack on the ideology of free trade, but he missed some of the subtleties of Smith's arguments. He was concerned with a narrow field of inquiry, albeit an important one: how can economic relations between nations be fruitfully analysed to throw light on economic backwardness and international income inequalities? The policies suggested for dealing with this problem were associated with protectionism and nationalism; and for this reason List's concerns were chiefly seen as a reaction to the negative aspects of foreign trade liberalism and not as a 'research programme' in its own right – to use a modern phrase.

Not unnaturally, List's ideas were not well received in the home of classical political economy. British populisers of political economy and publicists of free trade were hostile towards him and all he stood for (including the Zollverein). *The Times*, as well as the two great current affairs periodicals – the *Edinburgh Review* and the *Westminster Review* – carried deprecatory articles on him. The denigration of List ran in terms very similar to those echoed later by Viner: List's views were unworthy of notice; he had departed from the 'true' principles of political economy; he was an unscrupulous propagandist; he misrepresented and distorted both the teachings of political economy and the policies of Great Britain to serve unworthy nationalist ends. Thus in

1842 John Austin, a Benthamite and friend of James Mill, wrote in the *Edinburgh Review* that List's treatise *The National System* was unworthy of notice 'considered as a system of international trade' and that it was obviously 'the work of a zealous and unscrupulous advocate striving to establish a given practical conclusion, and not the production of a dispassionate enquirer, seeking to promote the improvement of a science ...'.[59] *The Times* in 1847 considered List's doctrines as 'extravagant fictions' and rebuked him for spreading 'the most erroneous and absurd notion of the policy of this country'.[60] Sir Travers Twiss, a successor to Senior in the Drummond Chair of Political Economy at Oxford, dismissed List's work as being 'too extravagant to require any serious discussion, motivated as it was by the narrowest and most shortsighted of selfishness'. This too was the opinion of J. R. McCulloch.[61]

J. S. Mill's qualified endorsement of the infant-industry thesis redeemed somewhat List's reputation among British economists, but it also served to obscure List's central message. Now that List's arguments were interpreted as constituting nothing more than mere 'exceptions' to conventional doctrine – exceptions adequately accommodated within the confines of established theory – his call for a radically new approach to the problems of economic development could be studiously ignored.

Perhaps the greatest tribute to List came late in the century (1890) from an unlikely source. 'The brilliant genius and national enthusiasm of List', wrote Alfred Marshall, 'stands in contrast to the insular narrowness and self-confidence of the Ricardian school ... he showed that in Germany and still more in America, many of its indirect effects [Free Trade] were evils. ... Many of his arguments were invalid, but many were not'.[62] Schumpeter said List had 'vision' – a characteristic he shared with Keynes. It is the gift for asking the right economic questions in any given historical age, or in other words, ideological perspective. 'As a scientific economist', said Schumpeter, 'List had one of the elements of greatness, namely, the grand vision of a national situation. ... Nor was List deficient in the specifically scientific requisites that must come in to implement vision if it is to bear scientific fruits.'[63]

In Germany, of course, List enjoyed an enormous reputation; not during his lifetime, but after, and especially during Bismarck's Second Reich when Germany emerged as the industrial giant which List had wanted. Joseph Dorfman noted that not long after List's death 'he was worshipped in Germany as the greatest German economist, the source of the new and supposedly unique German political economy of national power'.[64] He was called 'a great German without Germany', 'Germany's *verhinderten* [handicapped] Colbert', 'an economic genius' who made 'the first real advance' in economics since Adam Smith. List also had an influence on other European protagonists of industrial protection, including Eugen Dühring, the Austrian trade theorist Richard Schueller and the twentieth-century Romanian economist Mihail Manoilesco.[65] There was a less acceptable, even menacing side to List's nationalist vision. In Hans Kohn's words, List was not only the father of German economic nationalism, but also 'one of the most extreme of Pan-German imperialists'.[66] List claimed that overpopulated Germany needed *Ergänzungsgebiete* (additional territories) to give it breathing-space – shades of Hitler's *Lebensraum*! His plans for Greater Germany included the acquisition of overseas colonies, a powerful navy, control of the seaports from the mouths of the Rhine to the Elbe, and the domination of *Mitteleuropa*. In his last year List personally tried unsuccessfully to bring about an Anglo-German alliance which would allow Germany to colonise the Balkans, dominate the Near East, allow England to preserve her global hegemony and act as a bulwark against the rising power of Russia and the United States.

Recently List has been hailed as a precursor of the European Economic Community (EEC) and of a politically united Europe; but as Louis Snyder reminds us 'as a zealous German patriot List looked forward to European economic unification eventually under German auspices'.[67]

Classical trade theory failed to provide adequate explanations for (a) the asymmetries in the world trading system and (b) the observed fact that specialisation among countries was largely a result of historical accidents. The national economists perceived that and started a debate that was bound to occur. List, the visionary and prophet, articulated their intellectual response with a cogency and relevance that today continues to inspire many concerned with these matters. That the message of List and the other national economists should have this perennial appeal was well-expressed by Gustav Schmoller:

> All protective movements are closely connected with national sentiments, strivings after international authority, efforts towards the balance of power, and therefore will continue to exist so long as amongst the fully developed states there are others striving after economic development, and so long as the people for economic purposes have need of every weapon that stands ready for their use.[68]

Notes and References

1 The Age of Mercantilism

1. Quoted by Lionel Casson, 'Where Did Ancient Traders Sail?', in Lionel Casson et al. (eds) *Mysteries of the Past* (London: Mitchell Beazley, 1977) p. 160.
2. Jacob Viner, 'Mercantilist Thought' in *International Encyclopedia of the Social Sciences* (London: Macmillan) vols 3 and 4, p. 435.
3. G. Schmoller, *The Mercantile System and Its Historical Significance* (London: Macmillan, 1897) p. 50. This essay is a translation of Schmoller's introduction to his 1884 work, *Studien über die wirtschaftliche Politik Friedrichs des Grossen*. Schmoller (professor at Berlin University) was critical of abstract economic theorising as practised by Menger and the Marginal Utility School and became associated with *Kathedersozialismus* (German academic socialism).
4. W. Cunningham, *Growth of English Industry and Commerce*, 2nd ed. (London: Cambridge U.P. 1892), vol. II, p. 16. Cunningham, a contemporary of Schmoller, was a nationalist sympathetic to state intervention. According to him, writers on economics before Adam Smith focused on the power of the state: 'Economic history must trace out the conscious efforts ... to develop the resources and expand the commerce of the realm.' Ibid. 5th ed. (Cambridge, 1922) vol. I, pp. 21–2.
5. Eli F. Heckscher, *Mercantilism*, 2nd ed. (London: Allen & Unwin, 1955).
6. See D. C. Coleman (ed.) *Revisions in Mercantilism* (London: Methuen, 1969). J. N. Ball (1977) observes that most attempts to prove that state policy during the early mercantilist era was dominated by mercantilist ideas propagated by merchants have been unsuccessful. J. N. Ball, *Merchants and Merchandise* (London: Croom Helm, 1977) p. 44.
7. That the difference between relativist and absolutist approaches to doctrinal history reflects disagreements about the nature of economics has been aptly summarised by Fetter: 'The more closely one associates economic thought with technical analysis ... the greater is one likely to consider the effect of economic thought on history, and the less the effect of history on thought.' Frank Fetter, 'The Relation of the History of Economic Thought to Economic History', *American Economic Review*, vol. 55 (May 1965) pp. 136–42.
8. Harry Johnson, 'Mercantilism: Past, Present and Future', *Manchester School*, no. 1 (Mar 1974) p. 1.
9. Adam Smith, *The Wealth of Nations* (Everyman ed., vol. II) p. 156.
10. Robert B. Ekelund Jr and Robert D. Tollison, *Mercantilism as a Rent-seeking Society: Economic Regulation in Historical Perspective* (Texas A & M U.P., 1981) p. 155.
11. H. Myint: review of Ekelund and Tollison, *Economica* (Feb 1983) p. 100.
12. J. Schumpeter, *History of Economic Analysis* (London: Allen & Unwin, 1954) p. 337 n. 6.

Notes and References

13. Jacob Viner, *Studies in the Theory of International Trade* (1937) (London: Allen & Unwin, 1955) pp. 109, 115.
14. Mark Blaug, *Economic Theory in Retrospect*, 2nd ed. (London: Heinemann, 1968) p. 18.
15. Revised and enlarged edition Princeton University, 1961, p. 6.
16. Published by Macmillan New York, 1964. Chipman's work, 'A Survey of The Theory of International Trade: Part 1, The Classical Theory', was published in *Econometrica*, vol. 33, no. 3 (July 1965) pp. 477-519.
17. In 1938 M. Beer wrote that English mercantilist doctrine 'grew quite naturally, that is, with necessity, out of the commercial, political, and ethical conditions of the realm'. M. Beer, *Early British Economics* (London: Allen & Unwin, 1938) p. 62. Recently Kubalkova and Cruickshank declared that mercantilism was a logical adjustment of the times, and that it was explicitly based on the recognition of inequalities in political power among states. See V. Kubalkova and A. A. Cruickshank, *International Inequality* (London: Croom Helm, 1981).
18. The historical background is well covered in the following texts: E. E. Rich and C. H. Wilson (eds) *Cambridge Economic History of Europe*, vols IV and V (Cambridge U.P., 1977); R. Davis, *The Rise of the Atlantic Economies* (London: Weidenfeld & Nicolson, 1973); Charles Wilson, *England's Apprenticeship 1603-1763*, (London: Longman, 1965); *The Fontana Economic History of Europe*, ed. C. M. Cipolla, vol. II (London, 1974); Fernand Braudel, *Civilization and Capitalism 15th-18th Century*, vols 2 and 3 (London: Collins, 1982, 1984).
19. Michael Howard, *War in European History* (London: Oxford U.P., 1976) p. 41.
20. Thomas Hobbes, *Leviathan* (1651) (Everyman ed., London, 1940) p. 65.
21. F. Guicciardini, *Opere Inedite* (Florence: Barbera, Bianchi & Co., 1857) vol. I, pp. 61-2.
22. Fernand Braudel, *The Mediterranean in the Reign of Philip II* (London: Collins, 1963, 1967) vol. I, p. 284.
23. D. Defoe, *A Plan of the English Commerce* (London, 1728) p. 75.
24. See Woodruff D. Smith, 'The Function of Commercial Centres in the Modernization of European Capitalism: Amsterdam as an Information Exchange in the Seventeenth Century', *Journal of Economic History*, vol. XLIV (Dec 1984) pp. 985-1005.
25. E.g. Wilson, *England's Apprenticeship*, op. cit.
26. See Richard T. Rapp, 'The Unmaking of the Mediterranean Trade Hegemony: International Trade Rivalry and the Commercial Revolution', *Journal of Economic History*, vol. 35, no. 3 (Sep 1975) pp. 499-525.
27. The colonists were able to obtain many commodities from the Dutch for a third less. See Lawrence A. Harper, *The English Navigation Acts* (New York (1939) 1964) p. 243.
28. See Curtis Nettels, 'England and the Spanish American Trade 1680-1715', *Journal of Modern History*, vol. 3 (Mar 1931) p. 8.
29. Quoted in Robin Reilly, *Pitt The Younger* (London: Cassell, 1978) p. 8: see also J. H. Plumb, *England in the Eighteenth Century: 1714-1815* (Cambridge U.P., 1950) p. 71.

2 Mercantilist Thought on Foreign Trade

1. Paul A. Samuelson, 'Welfare Economics and International Trade', *American Economic Review*, vol. 28 (June 1938) p. 261. Note also John Chipman's observation (1984): 'The emergence of economic science in Great Britain in the seventeenth to nineteenth centuries was to some extent an offshoot of the development of the theory of adjustment of the balance of payments': J. S. Chipman, 'Balance of Payments Theory', in J. Creedy and D. P. O'Brien (eds) *Economic Analysis in Historical Perspective* (London: Butterworths, 1984) p. 186.
2. Paul A. Samuelson, 'Bertil Ohlin 1899–1979', *Journal of International Economics*, vol. 11 (1981) p. 150.
3. Donald N. McCloskey, 'Magnanimous Albion: Free Trade and British National Income, 1841–1881', *Explorations in Economic History*, vol. 17, no. 3 (July 1980) p. 304.
4. Richard Jones, 'Primitive Political Economy of England' (1847), reprinted in W. Whewell (ed.) *Literary Remains* (London: John Murray, 1859) pp. 291–335.
5. J. M. Keyenes, *The General Theory of Employment, Interest and Money* (London: Macmillan, 1936) ch. 23, pp. 333, 339. Keynes was not a reactionary mercantilist, neither was he a protectionist. His position on tariffs was pragmatic: they were 'second-best' measures appropriate when international monetary and other arrangements fail to provide a satisfactory framework for full-employment policies.
6. K. Marx, *Theories of Surplus Value* (Moscow: Progress Publishers, 1975) vol. I, p. 174.
7. A. Serra, *Brief Treatise on the Causes Which can Make Gold and Silver Plentiful in Kingdoms Where There are no Mines* (Naples, 1613); reprinted in A. E. Monroe (ed.) *Early Economic Thought* (Harvard U.P., 1924) pp. 143–67. Serra's work had no influence on contemporaries and was only discovered in 1780.
8. *Discourse* (Lamond ed.) p. 63. The *Discourse* (written in 1549) was originally published in 1581. The edition by Elizabeth Lamond (Cambridge U.P., 1893) attributed the work to John Hales. However, modern historians are inclined to the view that it was the work of Sir Thomas Smith, one of the two Secretaries of State of Elizabeth I. See D. M. Pallister, *The Age of Elizabeth: England Under the Later Tudors 1547–1602* (New York: Longmans, 1983); app. II: The Authorship of the 'Discourse of the Common Weal', pp. 388–9.
9. Quoted in H. W. Spiegel, *The Growth of Economic Thought* (Durham, N.C.: Duke U.P., 1971) p. 99.
10. For a good analytical discussion of the controversy, see Marian Bowley, 'Some Seventeenth Century Contributions to the Theory of Value', *Economica*, vol. 30 (May 1963) pp. 122–39. See also B. E. Supple, *Commercial Crisis and Change in England, 1600–1642* (Cambridge U.P., 1959) ch. 9, pp. 197–221, and J. D. Gould, 'The Trade Crisis of the early 1620s and English Economic Thought', *Journal of Economic History*, vol. 15 (1955) pp. 121–33. A useful supplement to Viner on the

development of the balance-of-trade doctrine is Bruno Suviranta, *The Theory of the Balance of Trade in England, A Study in Mercantilism* (Helsingfors, 1923), reprinted and published by A. M. Kelley, N.Y., 1967.

11. Long before the English controversy, Spanish theologians and jurists of the School of Salamanca had applied supply-and-demand analysis to money, including the determination of foreign-exchange rates. That is, from the middle of the sixteenth century these writers developed rudimentary notions of the quantity theory and the purchasing-power theory of exchange rates. See Murray N. Rothbard, 'New Light on the Prehistory of the Austrian School', in Edwin G. Dolan, *The Foundations of Modern Austrian Economics* (London: Sheed & Ward, 1976) pp. 55–7.
12. G. Malynes, *A Treatise of the Canker of England's Commonwealth* (London, 1602).
13. Malynes, op. cit. pp. 97–8.
14. Malynes, *The Maintenance of Free Trade* (London, 1622) p. 62.
15. Ibid. pp. 84–5.
16. 'This overbalancing consisteth properly in the price of commodities and not in the quantity or quality', Malynes, *A Treatise of the Canker*, op. cit. p. 12.
17. Schumpeter, op. cit. p. 344.
18. Viner, *Studies*, op cit. p. 76.
19. G. J. Kalamotousakis, 'Exchange Rates and Prices', *Journal of International Economics*, vol. 8 (1978) p. 163.
20. Malynes, *A Treatise of the Canker*, op. cit. p. 106.
21. Writing from the standpoint of modern international trade theory, W. R. Allen criticises Malynes, Mun and, more pointedly, modern defenders of mercantilist theory. William R. Allen, 'Modern Defenders of Mercantilist Theory', *History of Political Economy*, vol. 2 (Fall 1970) pp. 381–97. See also Allen, 'The Position of Mercantilism and the Early Development of International Trade Theory', in Robert V. Eagly (ed.) *Events, Ideology and Economic Theory* (Detroit: Wayne U.P., 1968) pp. 65–106. Allen adopts a position similar to that of Viner's. For a critique of Allen's interpretation of the mercantilist literature, see A. W. Coats, 'The Interpretation of Mercantilist Economics: Some Historiographical Problems', *History of Political Economy*, vol. 5 (1973) pp. 483–98. Incidentally, Coats considers Allen's attack on the modern commentators to be 'somewhat overstated and misdirected'.
22. Schumpeter, op. cit. p. 345; also J. D. Gould, op. cit. pp. 124–6, 128.
23. E.g. Gould, op. cit. pp. 128–30; Supple, op. cit. pp. 203–4. Rudolph C. Blitz, 'Mercantilist Policies and the Pattern of World Trade 1500–1750', *Journal of Economic History*, vol. 27 (Mar 1967) pp. 44–7 suggests that the inelasticity argument was behind the mercantilists' rejection of the specie-flow mechanism.
24. Allen, 'Modern Defenders', op. cit. pp. 387–90. See also the comments by Lynn Muchmore, 'Gerrard de Malynes and Mercantile Economics', *History of Political Economy*, vol. 1 (1969) pp. 344–5.
25. Supple, op. cit. p. 211.

26. Malynes, *Maintenance of Free Trade*, op. cit. p. 37.
27. Misselden, *Free Trade: Or the Means to Make Trade Flourish* (London: Waterson, 1622) p. 18.
28. Edward Misselden, *The Circle of Commerce: Or, the Balance of Trade, in Defence of Free Trade* (London: Dawson, 1623) p. 93.
29. Ibid. p. 29.
30. Ibid. p. 116.
31. Ibid. p. 129.
32. T. Mun, *England's Treasure by Forraign Trade* (1664) (Oxford: Blackwell, 1959) ch. 2.
33. Mun, *England's Treasure* (1755 ed.) p. 76.
34. Mun, *England's Treasure* pp. 218–19. Mun denied that there was any sort of conspiracy by exchange dealers to drain England of its bullion: 'In Italy where the greatest Banks and Bankers of Christendom do trade, yet I could never see nor hear, that they did, or were able to rule the price of Exchange by confederacie, but still the plenty or scarcity of money in the course of trade did always overrule them. . . .', p. 20.
35. Mun, op. cit. p. 52.
36. Ibid. p. 17.
37. Ibid. p. 51.
38. Ibid. p. 60.
39. Nun, *The Petition and Remonstrance of the Governor and Company of Merchants of London trading to the East Indies* (1628) p. 21.
40. Mun, *England's Treasure*, p. 92.
41. Blaug, op. cit. p. 19.
42. See George W. Wilson, 'Thomas Mun and Specie Flows', *Journal of Economic History*, vol. 28 (Mar 1958) pp. 62–3; Allen, 'Modern Defenders', op. cit. p. 390. Gould notes the logic of the automatic mechanism would have been quite 'uncongenial to mercantilist preconceptions', *Journal of Economic History* (Mar 1958) 'Rejoinder', p. 63.
43. David Hume, *Writings on Economics*, ed. Eugene Rotwein, (London: Nelson, 1955) pp. 39–40.
44. Mun, *England's Treasure*, op. cit. 84.
45. Joyce Oldham Appleby, *Economic Thought and Ideology in Seventeenth-Century England* (Princeton U.P., 1978) p. 41.
46. William J. Barber, *British Economic Thought and India 1600–1858: A Study in the History of Development Economics* (Oxford U.P., 1975) p. 21.
47. Matthew Decker, *Essay on the Causes of the Decline of the Foreign Trade* (London, 1749) p. 7.
48. Jean Bodin, *Les Six Livres de la République* (1576) p. 876. On Bodin's mercantilism see C. W. Cole, *French Mercantilist Doctrines before Colbert* (Dallas, Texas: Taylor, 1931) pp. 47–62.
49. Bodin, *Discours de Jean Bodin, etc.* (Paris, 1568) p. 59.
50. B. de Laffemas, *Source de plusiers abus, etc.*, p. 2. See pp. 63–112 in Cole, op. cit., on Laffemas.
51. Antoyne de Montchrétien, *Traicté de l'oeconomie politique, dédié en 1615 au roy et la reyne mère du roy*, with introduction and notes by Th

Funck-Brentano (Paris, 1889) p. 241. For selections on Montchrétien see Cole, op. cit. pp. 113–61.
52. Montchrétien, pp. 141–2. For an interpretation of Montchrétien as an early theorist of economic development see M. P. Rudloff, 'A. de Montchrétien et les problemes du developpement economique', *Revue d'Histoire économique et Sociale*, vol. 11, no. 2 (1962) pp. 152–74. For a different interpretation see A. D. Lublinskaya, *French Absolutism: The Crucial Phase 1620–1629*. trans. Brian Pearce (Cambridge U.P., 1968) pp. 104–37.
53. For good analyses of Spanish trade and monetary problems during the mercantilist period see E. J. Hamilton, *Spanish Mercantilism before 1700*, in A. H. Cole et al. (eds) *Facts and Factors in Economic History* (Harvard U.P., 1933); José Larraz, *La época del mercantilismo en Castilla*, (Madrid: 1963); R. Trevor Davies, *Spain in Decline 1621–1700* (London: Macmillan, 1961, ch. v, pp. 92–108.
54. Luis Ortiz, *Memorial Against the Flight of Money From These Realms* (1588). See Larraz, op. cit. pp. 106–10.
55. Quoted in J. Perez, *La Révolution des Comunidades de Castille* (Bourdeaux, 1970) p. 103.
56. S. de Moncada, *Restauracion Politica de Espana* (1619) (Madrid, 1746). See Larraz, op. cit. pp. 168–74.
57. Uztáriz *Teoría y Practica de Commercio y de Marina* (1724) 3rd ed. (Madrid, 1757). Translated by J. Kippax (London, 1757). For good commentaries see Andres V. Castillo, *Spanish Mercantilism. Gerónimo de Uztáriz-Economist* (New York: Columbia Univ. Studies, 1930), and Earl J. Hamilton, 'The Mercantilism of Gerónimo de Uztáriz: A Reexamination', in Norman E. Himes (ed.) *Economics, Sociology and the Modern World* (Harvard U.P., 1935).
58. Giovanni Botero, *The Reason of State* (1589) book VII, p. 141. See the translation by P. J. and D. P. Waley (New Haven: Yale U.P., 1956).
59. Philipp W. von Hornick, *Oesterreich über Alles, Wann Es Nur Will* (1684) (Regensburg, 1717). See selections from Hornick in Arthur E. Monroe, *Early Economic Thought* (Harvard U.P., 1924) pp. 221–44.
60. Sir Francis Brewster, *New Essays on Trade* (London, 1702), title of Essay v, p. 45.
61. Edward Misselden, *The Circle of Commerce* (1623) (New York: Kelley, 1968) p. 137.
62. Mun, *England's Treasure*, op. cit. in J. R. McCulloch (ed.) *Early English Tracts* (1856) (Cambridge: Cambridge U.P., 1954) p. 132.
63. William D. Grampp, 'The Liberal Elements in English Mercantilism', *Quarterly Journal of Economics* (1952), reprinted in J. J. Spengler and W. R. Allen, *Essays in Economic Thought* (1960) pp. 61–91.
64. Quoted in E. A. J. Johnson, *Predecessors of Adam Smith* (Englewood Cliffs N.J.: Prentice-Hall, 1937) p. 308.
65. Quoted in Viner, *Studies*, op. cit. p. 54 n.
66. V. de Forbonnais, *Eléments du Commerce*, vol. I, p. 78.
67. Although the 'infant-industry' case for protection was known to mercantilists, they rarely invoked the argument. The argument, of course, is

premised on production for the domestic market until the industry achieves such economies of scale and other 'learning effects' that it is able to withstand foreign competition in the open market without tariff support. Mercantilist writers rarely considered the potential of the home market, and perhaps this is why the argument was so little employed. Forbonnais was one writer who discussed it in the above sense, see Forbonnais, op. cit. p. 251.

68. Sir Josiah Child, *A New Discourse of Trade* (London, 1696); John Cary, *Essay on the State of England* (1695).
69. Josiah Tucker, *Four Tracts Together with Two Sermons on Political and Commercial Subjects* (Gloucester, 1774), p. 12.
70. Richard Cantillon, *Essai sur la Nature du Commerce en Général* (1755) ed. H. Higgs (London: Macmillan, 1931); 'Of Foreign Trade', part III, ch. 1, p. 233.
71. Central State Archives, Moscow, 35/6, p. 765. Quoted in F. Braudel, *Civilization and Capitalism 15th–18th Century*, vol. 2 (London: Collins, 1982) p. 207.
72. W. Petty, *Treatise of Taxes* (1662) in C. H. Hull (ed.) *The Economic Writings of Sir William Petty* (Cambridge U.P. 1899) vol. 1 p. 41.
73. Mandeville, *Fable of the Bees*, vol. 1, p. 465.
74. Viner, *Studies*, op. cit. p. 55.
75. Edgar S. Furniss, *The Position of the Laborer in a System of Nationalism* (Boston, Mass.: Houghton Mifflin, 1930) p. 31. For the quotations that follow see Furniss, op. cit. p. 22 n., Tucker, op. cit. p. 19, and *Britannia Languens* (1980) in McCulloch (ed.) op. cit. p. 176.
76. [William Petyt], *Britannia Languens* (1680), op. cit. p. 291.
77. Viner, op. cit. pp. 51 f.
78. Misselden, *Free Trade*, op. cit. p. 118.
79. Quoted in Charles Wilson, *Economic History and the Historian: Collected Essays* (London: Weidenfeld & Nicolson, 1966) p. 77.
80. Daniel Defoe, *A Plan of the English Commerce*, op. cit. p. 60.
81. John Cary, *Essay on the State of England* (1695) op. cit. 145–6.
82. Some modern historians take a sympathetic view of this preoccupation with foreign trade as the generator of economic growth and employment – certainly for the early mercantilist period. Barry Supple, for instance, refers to the key role of overseas trade in an economy prone to instability and monetary crises. It touched on the prosperity of England's largest industry and sharply affected the supply of cash and capital in the economy. See Supple, *Commercial Crisis*, op. cit. p. 14.
83. *Certain Considerations Relating to the Royal African Company of England* (London, 1680) p. 1.
84. Samuel Fortrey, *England's Interest and Improvement* (Cambridge: Fiel J, 1663) p. 29.
85. D. C. Coleman, 'Labour in the English Economy of the Seventeenth Century', *Economic History Review*, 2nd series vol. 8 (1955–6).
86. [Humphrey Mackworth], *England's Glory* (1694) pp. 20–1.
87. *The History of the Reign of King Henry the Seventh*, quoted in Heckscher, op. cit. vol. II, p. 16.

88. J. Viner, 'Power versus Plenty as Objectives of Foreign Policy in the Seventeenth and Eighteenth Centuries', first published in *World Politics*, vol. 1 (1948) reprinted in Coleman (ed.) *Revisions in Mercantilism*, op. cit. p. 78.
89. Viner, ibid. p. 76.
90. R. Waddington, *La Guerre de Sept Ans* (Paris, 1899) vol. III, p. 445.
91. Malachy Postlethwayt, *Great Britain's Commercial Interest* (London, 1759) vol. II, p. 551.
92. Francis Bacon, 'Of Seditions and Troubles', in *Essays* (Everyman ed., London, 1936) p. 45.
93. Adam Smith, *Wealth of Nations*, ed. Cannan (London, 1937) p. 579.
94. [Daniel Defoe], *The Evident Approach of a War*, 2nd ed. (London, 1729) pp. 13, 30.
95. In William Cobbett, *The Parliamentary History of England* (London: Hansard, 1812) vol. VI, col. 598.
96. *The Petition and Remonstrance of the Governour and Company of Merchants trading to the East Indies* (London, 1641) p. 16.
97. Andrew Yarrenton, *England's Improvement by Sea and Land* (London, 1677) p. 1 'The Epistle to the Reader'.
98. Nicholas Barbon, *A Discourse of Trade* (1690), ed. J. H. Hollander (Baltimore: Johns Hopkins U.P., 1905) p. 35.
99. D. C. Coleman, 'Politics and Economics in the Age of Anne: the Case of the Anglo-French Trade Treaty of 1713', in D. C. Coleman and A. H. John (eds) *Trade, Government and the Economy in Pre-Industrial England* (London: Weidenfeld & Nicolson, 1976) p. 206.
100. R. Edwards, 'Economic Sophistication in Nineteenth-Century Congressional Tariff Debates', *Journal of Economic History* (Dec 1970) p. 823.
101. D. M. Pallister describes how Tudor foreign policy (1490–1570) was 'dictated more by the pattern of British cloth exports than by considerations of religion or the balance of power'. Pallister, *The Age of Elizabeth*, op. cit. p. 278.
102. *Gentlemen's Magazine*, no. XVIII (1748) p. 66. For other merchants' statements deploring peace with Spain and France in 1745 see Richard Pares, *War and Trade in the West Indies 1739–63* (Oxford, 1936) pp. 62–3.
103. Cobbett, *Parliamentary History*, op. cit. vol. XV, col. 181.
104. The French ambassador in Madrid, the Duc de Duras, reported in 1756 that the English 'have attracted the whole trade of Brazil and India; they have destroyed the manufactures . . . of Portugal and have bought all its produce in order to introduce their own goods.' France, *Archives Nationales*, Archives de la Marine, B^7, 400, 'Mémoire sur le Portugal' (1756).
105. British Library, Add. MS. 11.411, ff. 11–12.
106. See Thomas C. Barrow, *Trade and Empire: The British Customs Service in Colonial America 1660–1775* (Cambridge U.P., 1967) pp. 134–7.
107. In regard to the colonies, Child stressed the need for mercantilist regulation of the trade: 'All Colonies and foreign Plantations do endamage their Mother Kingdom, whereof the Trades of such Plan-

tations are not confined to their said Mother Kingdom, by good Laws and severe Execution of those Laws.' *A New Discourse of Trade* (London, 1693) p. 183.
108. On the eighteenth-century orthodoxy that Britain's imperial commercial system was the foundation of the country's wealth, modern historians remain sceptical (as Adam Smith was). Thomas and McCloskey, for instance, synthesising recent research show that British mercantilism could hardly be described as a system which maximised the wealth of Britain. Rather (as Smith suggested) it promoted the self-seeking interests of special groups and also provided revenue for the government. Taking into account the social costs, the net benefits of the imperial trading system to the British economy was slight or even negative. Trade itself was not 'an engine of growth'. See R. P. Thomas and D. N. McCloskey, 'Overseas Trade and Empire 1700–1860', in Donald McCloskey and Roderick Floud (eds) *The Economic History of Britain Since 1700*, vol. 1, 1700–1860 (Cambridge U.P., 1981) pp. 87–102.
109. Smith, *Wealth of Nations*, ed. Campbell and Skinner (Oxford: Clarendon Press, 1976) pp. 464–5, 518, 522–3.
110. See Viner, 'Power versus Plenty', op. cit. Note, however, Joyce Appleby's observation (based on a detailed analysis of British economic thought and policy during the seventeenth century) that mercantilism in its public-policy aspects, emerged in England only at the beginning of the eighteenth century; and further, that it was only in the eighteenth century that national power was regularly evoked as one of the major benefits of trade – in the previous century, the emphasis was decidedly on 'plenty'. Landlords and manufacturers, in her opinion, not the merchants, were behind the shift in the later period. See Joyce Oldham Appleby, *Economic Thought and Ideology in Seventeenth-Century England*, op. cit. pp. 250–1.
111. Alexander Gerschenkron, 'History of Economic Doctrines and Economic Thought', *American Economic Review*, vol. 59 (1969) pp. 1–17; and *Europe in the Russian Mirror* (Cambridge U.P., 1970) pp. 62–96 where he supports his proposition with a discussion of the Russian experience with mercantilism. Frederick himself was an exponent of classical mercantilism, as his writings indicate. Thus in his *Essay on the Forms of Government and the Duties of Sovereigns* (1777) we read: 'If a country is to remain prosperous, it is absolutely necessary for it to have a favourable balance of trade; if it pays more for imports than it earns by exports, it must necessarily grow poorer year by year. . . .' *Œuvres de Frédéric le Grand*, ed. J. D. E. Preuss (Berlin, 1846–56), vol. IX, p. 206. But it was on national economic development (state capitalism) that he relied for power and wealth, not foreign trade, as his *Political Testament* of 1752 indicates – and his remark: 'I remain firmly on the side of industry, for at all costs I must give my people work, and it is clear that a manufacturer can employ 2000 hands when a trader can barely employ 20.' See K. Hinze, *Die Arbeiterfrage zu Beginn des Modernen Kapitalismus in Brandenburg-Preussen*, 2nd ed. (Berlin, 1963) p. 74.
112. Viner, 'Power versus Plenty', op. cit. p. 68.
113. Smith, *Wealth of Nations*, Modern Library ed. (New York: 1937, p. 441).

114. Quoted in Lewis Samuel Feuer, *Spinoza and the Rise of Liberalism* (Boston: Beacon Press, 1958) p. 275.
115. Thus, 'when business interests were threatened, as in 1645, 1657 and 1668 ... the powerful city [Amsterdam] no longer remained passive, but advocated a policy that was forceful and aggressive'. See M. A. M. Franken, 'The General Tendencies and Structural Aspects of the Foreign Policy and Diplomacy of the Dutch Republic in the Latter Half of the 17th Century', *Acta Historiae Neerlandica*, vol. III (1968) pp. 6–7.
116. Smith, *Wealth of Nations*, 4th ed. p. 220.
117. See, for example, the complaint by Sir George Downing in a letter to Lord Clarendon, 20 Nov 1663: 'It is *mare liberum* in the British seas, but *mare clausum* on the coast of Africa and in the East Indies.' Quoted in Pieter Geyl, *The Netherlands in the Seventeenth Century*, vol. II: *1648–1715* (London: Benn, 1964) p. 85.

3 The Decline of Mercantilist Trade Doctrines

1. Pierre le Pesant Boisguillebert, *Traité des grains*, p. 405.
2. See Eugene Daire (ed.) *Economistes-Financiers du XVIIIe Siècle* (Paris: Guillaumin Libraire, 1843) p. 409.
3. Quoted in C. B. A. Behrens, *The Ancien Régime* (London: Thames & Hudson, 1967) p. 123.
4. Quoted in John Marks, *Science and the Modern World* (London: Heinemann, 1983) p. 106.
5. N. Barbon, *A Discourse of Trade* (London, 1690) p. 32. Mandeville, meanwhile, still urged the authorities 'above all ... keep a watchful Eye over the Balance of Trade in general and never suffer that the Foreign Commodities together, that are imported in one year, shall exceed in value what of their own growth or manufacture is in the same exported to others'. B. Mandeville, *The Fable of the Bees*, ed. F. B. Kaye, op. cit. vol. 1, p. 116.
6. North, in McCulloch (ed.) *Early English Tracts*, op. cit. pp. 513, 543.
7. C. Davenant, *An Essay on the East India Trade* (1697), in C. Davenant, *Political and Commercial Works*, ed. C. Whitworth (London, 1771) vol. I, pp. 98, 99.
8. Davenant, op. cit. vol. V, p. 378.
9. [Henry Martin] *Considerations on the East India Trade*, in McCulloch (ed.) *op. cit.* p. 583.
10. Johnson, *Predecessors of Adam Smith*, op. cit. p. 144. Earlier (1897) Sir William Ashley drew attention to the Tory affiliations of North, Child, Davenant and Barbon and suggested that their politics explained their free-trade opinions: 'Tory writers on trade, however sensible we may suppose them, could hardly fail to have a partisan bias in favour of liberty of commerce ... they were likely to have their insight sharpened by party prejudice.' W. J. Ashley, 'The Tory Origins of Free Trade Policy', *Quarterly Journal of Economics*, vol. 2, p. 338.
11. Leslie Stephen, *English Thought in the Eighteenth Century* (London: Macmillan, 1902 ed.) vol. II, p. 297.
12. Schumpeter, *History of Economic Analysis*, op. cit. pp. 239, 373, 374.

Viner was equally impressed. Martin's work, he said, revealed 'almost no trace of the mercantilist or protectionist fallacies', Viner, op. cit. p. 104. But Martin was no free-trader (at least in regard to Anglo-French trade) as indicated in the text. Ricardo's disciple, J. R. McCulloch, called North 'an Achilles without a heel' and also praised Martin for his understanding of true economic principles. McCulloch, op. cit. pp. xii–xiv.

13. Viner, *Studies*, op. cit. pp. 439–40.
14. Schumpeter, op. cit. p. 376.
15. J. Bodin, 'Reply to the Paradoxes of M. Malestroit', in Monroe (ed.) *Early Economic Thought*, op. cit. p. 127.
16. See Hugo Hegeland, *The Quantity Theory of Money* (Göteborg, 1951) p. 14.
17. Martin de Azpilcueta [Navarro], *Comentario Resolutorio de Usuras* (1556), in Marjorie Grice-Hutchinson, *The School of Salamanca: Readings in Monetary Theory, 1544–1605* (Oxford, 1952) pp. 94–5. See also Peter Bernholz, 'Flexible Exchange Rates in Historical Perspective', *Princeton Studies in International Finance*, no. 49 (July 1982) pp. 4–5. Three years earlier another Salamancan theologian, Domingo de Soto, had applied supply-and-demand analysis to the determination of exchange rates; see Rothbard, op. cit.
18. Mun, *England's Treasure*, op. cit. p. 17.
19. J. Locke, *Some Considerations of the Consequences of the Lowering of Interest and Raising the Value of Money* (London, 1691) reprinted in *The Works of John Locke* (London, 1823) vol. v. For an analysis of Locke's interpretation of the quantity theory, see Arthur Leigh, 'John Locke and the Quantity Theory of Money', *History of Political Economy*, vol. 6 (Summer 1974) pp. 204–10.
20. D. North in McCulloch (ed.) op. cit. p. 538. Locke does, indeed, hint at the automaticity of specie distribution in the following passage: 'Nature has bestowed mines on several parts of the world; but their riches are only for the industrious and frugal. Whomsoever else they visit, it is with the diligent and sober only they stay.' Locke, *Some Considerations*, op. cit. p. 117.
21. Locke, *Some Considerations*, op. cit. pp. 16–17.
22. Jacob Vanderlint, *Money Answers All Things* (1734) in a *Reprint of Economic Tracts* with an Introduction by J. Hollander (Baltimore: Johns Hopkins U.P., 1914).
23. Cantillon, op. cit. ed. Henry Higgs (London: Macmillan, 1931). The *Essai* (which may have been originally written in English – Cantillon was an Irish banker in Paris) was not published until 1755. Large portions of the English original were incorporated in Postlethwayt's writings (1749, 1751–5) and the latter may have been known to Hume.
24. To illustrate the point about non-traded goods, Cantillon gives the example of corn and cattle in England. Corn was freely traded, but cattle imports were banned (i.e. cattle were non-tradables). However great the increase in English money-supply, the price of corn could not rise above the world level, allowing for transport costs and risk. The price of cattle, however, would be determined solely by English market conditions. See Cantillon, op. cit. (original English trans. 1755) p. 179.

Notes and References

25. Cantillon, op. cit. p. 184.
26. Isaac Gervaise, *The System or Theory of the Trade of the World* (1720) in *Reprint of Economic Tracts* with a foreword by J. Viner and introduction by J. M. Letiche (Baltimore: Johns Hopkins U.P., 1954). For a detailed commentary on Gervaise see J. M. Letiche, 'Isaac Gervaise on the International Mechanism of Adjustment', *Journal of Political Economy*, vol. 60 (Feb 1952) pp. 34–43.
27. Johnson, 'Mercantilism: Past, Present and Future', op. cit. p. 4.
28. Frank W. Fetter, *Development of British Monetary Orthodoxy 1797–1875* Harvard U.P., 1965) p. 4.
29. Gervaise, op. cit. pp. 9, 12. This is a composite or reconstruction of several passages in Gervaise's pamphlet. See also Viner's Foreword and Thomas M. Humphrey and Robert E. Keleher (eds) *The Monetary Approach to the Balance of Payments, Exchange Rates and World Inflation* (New York: Praeger, 1982) pp. 122–3. Gervaise extends the specie-distribution process to bank credit, thus asserting that the natural proportion applies to the total money-stock.
30. Gervaise, op. cit. p. 15. Notice that in Gervaise's account of the adjustment process there is no role for changes in relative price levels.
31. Gervaise, op. cit. p. 12.
32. For Hayek's comment see F. A. von Hayek, *Prices and Production* (London: Routledge & Kegan Paul, 1931) p. 9. Marx and Engels's suspicion of plagiarism against Hume is contained in Karl Marx, vol. I of *Capital* (Moscow: Foreign Languages Pub. House, 1977) p. 124 n. and Marx and Engels, *Anti-Dühring* (Moscow: Progress Publishers, 1969) pp. 280–6. For a good summary of the contributions of Vanderlint, Cantillon, Gervaise and Hume see Thomas T. Sekine, 'The Discovery of International Monetary Equilibrium by Vanderlint, Cantillon, Gervaise and Hume', *Economia Internazionale*, vol. 26 (1973) pp. 262–82.
33. David Hume, 'Hume to Montesquieu' (letter 10 Apr 1749), in Eugene Rotwein (ed.) *David Hume: Writings on Economics* (London: Nelson 1955) p. 189.
34. 'Hume to Turgot' in *Writings on Economics*, ed. Rotwein, op. cit. p. 208.
35. Rotwein, op. cit. p. 65.
36. Ibid. 'Hume to Oswald', p. 197. See also Oswald's letter dated 10 October 1749: 'Oswald to Hume', pp. 191–2.
37. Viner, *Studies*, op. cit. p. 319, also pp. 316–18.
38. Rotwein, op. cit. 'Hume to Turgot', p. 209.
39. Paul A. Samuelson, 'A Corrected Version of Hume's Equilibrating Mechanisms for International Trade', in John S. Chipman and Charles P. Kindleberger (eds) *Flexible Exchange Rates and the Balance of Payments: Essays in Memory of Egon Sohmen* (Amsterdam: North-Holland, 1980) pp. 141–57. See also Paul A. Samuelson, 'An Exact Hume–Ricardo–Marshall Model of International Trade', *Journal of International Economics*, vol. 1 (Feb 1971) pp. 1–18.
40. Samuelson, 'A Corrected Version', p. 155. Commenting on Samuelson's version of Hume's mechanism Ronald Jones feels that Samuelson (in his two articles) was a bit harsh on previous interpreters of Hume, e.g.

Haberler and Viner. A correct analysis, says Jones, must incorporate *both* the direct impact at unchanged prices of changes in spending as well as subsequent changes in prices induced by these expenditure changes – as in the transfer problem. See Ronald W. Jones, 'International Trade Theory', in E. Cary Brown and Robert M. Solow (eds) *Paul Samuelson and Modern Economic Theory* (New York: McGraw-Hill, 1983) p. 97 n. 57. John Chipman, in support of Hume, takes a similar position. He points out that Samuelson's main model assumes zero transport costs; but even on this assumption, the only signal merchants will respond to is a price differential. Chipman, therefore, finds that Hume's approach was not unreasonable. He however questions an asymmetry in Hume's account, i.e. Hume only discusses the fall in British merchandise prices after severe monetary contraction, but does not consider the equibrating role of the rise in British gold price relative to gold prices abroad. See Chipman, 'Balance of Payments Theory', op. cit. pp. 190–1.
41. On this alternative interpretation of Hume's mechanism see Charles E. Staley, 'Hume and Viner on the International Adjustment Mechanism', *History of Political Economy*, vol. 8, no. 2 (1976) pp. 252–65.
42. Rotwein, op. cit. p. 74 n. 1. Two interesting articles on Hume and modern monetarism and the monetary approach to balance-of-payments theory are Thomas Meyer, 'David Hume and Monetarism', *Quarterly Journal of Economics* (Aug 1980) pp. 89–101, and Dietrich K. Fausten, 'The Humean Origin of the Contemporary Monetary Approach to the Balance of Payments', *Quarterly Journal of Economics* (Nov 1979) pp. 655–73.
43. Blaug, op. cit. p. 23.
44. Rotwein, op. cit. p. 63.
45. Ibid. pp. 39–40. Although each monetary inflow had only transitory effects on output expansion and employment – there was no long run 'trade-off' between unemployment and inflation – Hume obviously believed that periodic injections of this kind had favourable cumulative effects on economic development. The transitory effects depended on the assumption that when 'a quantity of money is imported into a nation ... it must first quicken the diligence of every individual, before it encreases the price of labour'. (ibid. p. 38). Regular increases in the money-supply were therefore the means to lift the economy to higher levels of output and employment – given, as Hume implicitly recognised, the existence of unused resources.
46. Viner, *Studies*, p. 99.
47. Keynes, *General Theory*, op. cit. p. 343 n.
48. Rotwein, op. cit. p. 76.
49. Ibid. p. 78.
50. Ibid. p. 84.
51. Ibid. pp. 66, 75, 78–81.
52. F. Quesnay, 'Grains', in Eugene Daire, *Physiocrates* (Paris, 1846); (Geneva: Slatkine Reprints, 1971) p. 295. See also A. Sauvy (ed.) *François Quesnay et la Physiocratie* (Paris: Institut National d'Etudes Demographiques, 1958) p. 964.
53. Quesnay, 'The second edition of the tableau', in R. L. Meek, *The Economics of Physiocracy: Essays and Translations* (London: Allen &

Unwin, 1962) p. 124. A similar statement appears in Quesnay, 'Maximes generales du gouvernement', *Physiocratie* (1767).
54. There is evidence for such optimism, e.g. Ralph Davis's observation that 'the years 1730–70 saw a big advance in the productivity of French agriculture'. Davis, *The Rise of the Atlantic Economies*, op. cit. p. 291.
55. By Professor Peter Groenewegen, in 'Turgot's place in the history of economic thought: a bicentenary estimate', *History of Political Economy*, vol. 15, no. 4 (1983) pp. 590, 593. Samuel Hollander says that in Turgot's work, 'we do find some dazzling demonstrations of the organizing function of the competitive price mechanism'. S. Hollander, *The Economics of Adam Smith* (London: Heinemann, 1973) p. 50.
56. Turgot, 'Letter on the Marque des fers', quoted in Groenewegen, op. cit. p. 591.
57. Quoted by Groenewegen, op. cit. p. 591.
58. See G. Schelle, *Œuvres de Turgot* (Paris, 1913–23), vol. 2 p. 510.
59. J.-F. Melon, *Essai politique sur le commerce* (1734), quoted in E. Daire, *Economistes français du 17ᵉ siècle* (Paris, 1843) p. 733.
60. Jacques Savary, *Le parfait négociant, ou Instruction générale de tout ce qui regarde le commerce* (Paris, 1675) (1713 ed.) p. 1.
61. Montesquieu, *Espirt des Lois*, book xx, p. 2 quoted by Albert O. Hirschman, *The Passions and the Interests* (Princeton UP, 1977) p. 80. Hirschman gives an interesting review of writings on the pacific nature of trade.
62. In 'View of the Progress of Society in Europe' (1769); preface to William Robertson, *History of the Reign of the Emperor Charles V*, ed. Felix Gilbert (Univ. of Chicago Press, 1972) p. 67.
63. Sir James Steuart, *An Inquiry into the Principles of Political Economy* (1767) ed. Andrew S. Skinner (Edinburgh: Oliver & Boyd, 1966) vol. 2, p. 217, and vol. 1, lxxiii.
64. Quoted in James L. Clifford (ed.) *Man Versus Society in Eighteenth-Century Britain: Six Points of View* (Cambridge U.P., 1968) p. 14.
65. Ekelund and Tollison, *Mercantilism as a Rent-seeking Society*, op. cit.
66. F. A. von Hayek, *The Constitution of Liberty* (Chicago U.P., 1960) p. 163.
67. Adam Ferguson, *An Essay on the History of Civil Society* (Edinburgh, 1767) p. 187, quoted in F. A. Hayek, *New Studies in Philosophy, Politics, Economics and the History of Ideas* (London: Routledge & Kegan Paul, 1978) p. 264 n. 56. See also Hayek, *Individualism and Economic Order* (London: Routledge & Kegan Paul, 1948) p. 7.
68. Appleby, op. cit.pp. 22–3.

4 Classical Trade Theory

1. Typical of the complaints against Smith are: 'we cannot say that there is any special contribution to the theory of foreign trade in the *Wealth of Nations*' (Bastable); 'all the important elements in Smith's free-trade doctrine had been presented prior to the *Wealth of Nations*' (Viner); and Robbins's remark that Smith's foreign-trade doctrines have 'very little analytical edge'. See C. F. Bastable, *The Theory of International Trade*

(London, 1903) pp. 168–9. Viner, *Studies*, op. cit. p. 108–9. L. Robbins, *Money, Trade and International Relations* (London: Macmillan, 1971) p. 191.
2. Arthur I. Bloomfield, 'Adam Smith and the Theory of International Trade', in A. Skinner and T. Wilson (eds) *Essays on Adam Smith* (Oxford U.P., 1975) p. 481.
3. Adam Smith, *The Wealth of Nations*, ed. E. Cannan (New York: Random House, Modern Library Edition, 1937) book IV. ii. 12.
4. Smith summarises the widening of the market through foreign trade as follows: 'By opening a more extensive market for whatever part of the produce of their labour may exceed the home consumption, it encourages them to improve its productive powers, and to augment its annual produce to the utmost, and thereby to increase the real revenue and wealth of the society.' *Wealth of Nations*, book IV. i. 31.
5. H. Myint, 'The "Classical Theory" of International Trade and the Underdeveloped Countries', *Economic Journal*, vol. 68 (June 1958) pp. 317–37. And 'Adam Smith's Theory of International Trade in the Perspective of Economic Development', *Economica*, vol. 44 (Sep 1977) pp. 231–48.
6. See J. S. Mill, *Principles of Political Economy*, ed. W. J. Ashley (London: Longman, 1923) p. 581. David Ricardo, *The Works and Correspondence of David Ricardo*, ed. Piero Sraffa with the collaboration of M. H. Dobb (Cambridge U.P., 1951–5) vol. 1, pp. 291 n, 294–5.
7. See Gottfried Haberler, 'International Trade and Economic Development', The Cairo Lectures (1959) reprinted in R. S. Weckstein (ed.) *Expansion of World Trade and the Growth of National Economies* (New York: Harper & Row, 1968) pp. 103–4 n. 6. Haberler writes: 'This distinction I find unconvincing. The "vent-of-surprise" (if it is not part and parcel of the productivity theory) seems to me simply an extreme case of differences in comparative cost – a country exporting things for which it has no use.' Bloomfield, op. cit. p. 472. Samuel Hollander, *The Economics of Adam Smith* (London: Heinemann, 1973) pp. 268–76. For a brief, useful survey of the various interpretations of Smith on this issue, see E. G. West, 'Scotland's Resurgent Economist: A Survey of the New Literature on Adam Smith', *Southern Economic Journal*, vol. 45, no. 2 (Oct 1978) pp. 359–61. West suggests that what Myint is really saying is that the subsequent development of trade theory represented 'a degenerating problem shift' in terms of Lakatos's discourse on methodology. Ricardian and neoclassical models of trade shifted the emphasis from development and disequilibrium states (the focus of Smith's thought) to one concerned with the analysis of static general disequilibrium situations. For this reason, later neoclassical writers were bound to find fault with Smith's trade analysis – West, p. 361. Another good discussion is C. E. Staley 'A Note on Adam Smith's Version of the Vent for Surplus Model', *History of Political Economy* (Fall 1973) pp. 438–48. For an analysis of general 'surplus' models of trade and growth see Richard E. Caves, 'Vent for Surplus Models of Trade and Growth', in Robert E. Baldwin *et al.*, *Trade, Growth and the Balance of Payments: Essays in*

Honor of Gottfried Haberler (Amsterdam: North-Holland, 1965) pp. 95–115.
8. Hollander, op. cit. p. 276.
9. *Wealth of Nations*, book IV, ii. 3, 13.
10. *Wealth of Nations*, ed. Campbell and Skinner (1976) p. 687.
11. This exception to the general optimality of a free-trade policy was accepted by later classical and neoclassical economists. Harry Johnson noted a few years ago, however, that recent theorising has shown this exception to be problematical, i.e. the compensating duty restores efficiency in production, but introduces inefficiency in consumption choices. See Harry G. Johnson, 'Commercial Policy and Industrialization', *Economica*, vol. 39 (Aug 1972) p. 265.
12. *Wealth of Nations*, ed. Campbell and Skinner, p. 470.
13. Adam Smith, *The Theory of Moral Sentiments* (New York: Kelley, 1966) pp. 266–7.
14. *Wealth of Nations*, ed. Campbell and Skinner, p. 471.
15. W. L. Taylor records that 'Smith was intimately acquainted with Hume and his works'. W. L. Taylor, *Francis Hutcheson and David Hume as Predecessors of Adam Smith* (Durham, N.C.: Duke U.P., 1965) p. 131. It was therefore a 'mystery' to Viner that Smith 'should have made no reference in the *Wealth of Nations* to the self-regulating mechanism in terms of price levels and trade balances, and should have been content with an exposition of the international distribution of specie in the already obsolete terms of the requirement by each country, without specific reference to its relative price level, of a definite amount of money to circulate trade'. Viner, *Studies*, op. cit. p. 87. O'Brien also remarked on this ' "puzzle" in the history of economic thought'. See D. P. O'Brien, *The Classical Economists* (Oxford: Clarendon Press, 1975) p. 146. However, in the earlier *Lectures on Justice, Police, Revenue and Arms*, ed. Edwin Cannan (New York: Kelley & Millman, 1956) p. 197, Smith wrote approvingly of Hume's theory.
16. See R.V. Eagly, 'Adam Smith and the Specie-Flow Doctrine', *Scottish Journal of Political Economy* (Feb 1970) pp. 61–8.
17. James W. Angell, *The Theory of International Prices* (New York: Kelley, 1965) p. 34.
18. Humphrey and Keleher, op. cit. p. 139.
19. For this resolution of Viner's puzzle see F. Petrella, 'Adam Smith's Rejection of Hume's Price-Specie-Flow Mechanism: A Minor Mystery Resolved', *Southern Economic Journal* (Jan 1968) pp. 365–74.
20. This is O'Brien's conjecture; see O'Brien, op. cit. p. 147.
21. Bloomfield, op. cit. p. 480.
22. See T. Wilson, 'Some Concluding Reflections', in Skinner and Wilson (eds) op. cit. pp. 605–6 n. 1.
23. See G. J. Stigler, 'The Successes and Failures of Professor Smith', *Journal of Political Economy*, vol. 84, no. 6 (1976) p. 1208. Stigler counts Smith's monetary theory as one of his 'proper failures' mitigated, however, by the fact that the theory is tenable as a first approximation. He recognises that Smith's theory is implicitly a simple purchasing-power-parity theory. If

so, as we have suggested, it contains much that passes for conventional wisdom in the modern 'global monetarist' theory.
24. All the leading intermediate texts on international economics discuss Ricardo's theory. The model is analysed well in Akira Takayama, *International Trade* (New York: Holt, Rinehart & Winston, 1972) ch. 4; R. E. Caves and R. W. Jones, *World Trade and Payments* (New York: Little Brown & Co. 3rd ed. 1981) ch. 5, and M. Chacholiades, *International Trade Theory and Policy* (New York: McGraw-Hill, 1978) ch. 2. Ricardo's own statement of the principle of comparative cost is contained in his *Principles of Political Economy and Taxation*, vol. I of *The Works and Correspondence of David Ricardo*, op. cit. Hereafter cited as Ricardo, *Works*.
25. Ricardo, *Works*, vol. I, p. 136.
26. Ricardo, ibid. p. 145.
27. E. R. A. Seligman and J. H. Hollander, 'Ricardo and Torrens', *Economic Journal*, vol. 2 (1911) pp. 448–68; Schumpeter, op. cit. p. 607; L. Robbins, *Robert Torrens and the Evolution of Classical Economics* (London: Macmillan, 1958) pp. 22–3.
28. For *The Economists Refuted* see the reprint in R. Torrens, *The Principles and Practical Operation of Sir Robert Peel's Act of 1844 Explained and Defended*, 2nd ed. (London: Longman, 1857).
29. See the first of Chipman's classic survey, Chipman, op. cit. p. 480.
30. Torrens, *External Corn Trade*, pp. 263–4.
31. Robbins, op. cit. p. 23.
32. Ricardo, *Works*, vol. IV.
33. Robbins, op. cit. p. 23.
34. P. A. Samuelson, 'Economists and the History of Ideas' and 'The Way of an Economist' reprinted in *The Collected Scientific Papers of Paul A. Samuelson*, ed. R. C. Merton (Cambridge, Mass.: MIT Press, 1972) vol. 2, p. 1507, and vol. 3, p. 678.
35. Sir John Hicks, *Classics and Moderns: Collected Essays on Economic Theory*, vol. III (Oxford: Blackwell, 1983) p. 61. Sir John continues: 'its consequences were not fully worked out, and could easily be misunderstood, as did in fact happen'.
36. Chipman, op. cit. pp. 479–80.
37. Hollander, *The Economics of David Ricardo*, op. cit. p. 462.
38. William O Thweatt, 'James Mill and the Early Development of Comparative Advantage', *History of Political Economy*, vol. 8, no. 2 (1976) pp. 207–34.
39. Hollander, op. cit. p. 462.
40. P. A. Samuelson, 'The Way of an Economist', in Paul Samuelson (ed.) *International Economic Relations* (London: Macmillan, 1969) p. 4.
41. Henry William Spiegel, *The Growth of Economic Thought* (Durham, N.C.: Duke U.P., 1971) p. 344.
42. Dennis R. Appleyard and James C. Ingram, 'A Reconsideration of the Additions to Mill's "Great Chapter" ', *History of Political Economy*, vol. 11, no. 4 (Winter 1979) p. 503. Thus Mill writes: 'When both countries can produce both commodities, it is not greater absolute, but greater relative facility, that induces one of them to confine itself to the production of one

of the commodities, and to import the other.' James Mill, *Elements of Political Economy*, 3rd ed. (London: Baldwin, Cradock & Joy, 1826) p. 123.
43. Schumpeter, op. cit. p. 529. J. S. Mill, *Essays on Some Unsettled Questions on Political Economy* (London, 1877) (originally published 1844) p. 1.
44. Joan Robinson, 'Reflections on the Theory of International Trade' in her *Collected Economic Papers*, vol. 5 (Oxford: Blackwell, 1979) p. 130.
45. Stigler, 'Nobel Lecture: The Process and Progress of Economics', *Journal of Political Economy*, vol. 91, no. 4 (1982) p. 534.
46. Allen, op. cit. p. 75.
47. Ronald L. Meek, *Studies in the Labour Theory of Value* (London: Laurence & Wishart, 1965), p. 21.
48. Mark Blaug, *Economic Theory in Retrospect*, 3rd ed. (London: Heinemann, 1978) p. 140.
49. Ibid. p. 6.
50. André Gunder Frank, *Dependent Accumulation*, vol. 1 (London: Macmillan, 1979) pp. 94–5.
51. R. Ballance, J. Ansari and H. Singer (eds) *The International Economy and Industrial Development: Trade and Investment in the Third World* (London: Wheatsheaf Books, 1982) pp. 14, 15. For Robinson's comment see 'What are the Questions?' *Journal of Economic Literature*, vol. xv, no. 4 (Dec 1977) p. 1336. She referred to the ruin of Portuguese industry by free trade following the Methuen Treaty (1703).
52. Fernand Braudel, *Civilization and Capitalism, 15th–18th Century*, vol. III, *The Perspective of the World* (London: Collins, 1984) p. 48.
53. See G. J. Stigler, 'Ricardo and the 93 Per Cent Labour Theory of Value', *American Economic Review*, vol. 48 (1958) pp. 357–67. Hollander, op. cit. p. 469, asserts: 'Ricardo's trade model is a dual-factor model'. Ricardo's analysis of the effects of the Corn Laws certainly required a multifactor model.
54. Ricardo, *Works*, op. cit. vol. I, p. 128.
55. Ibid. p. 135.
56. Ibid. pp. 135–6. If not in Ricardo's time, certainly by the middle of the century, this assumption was patently untenable. The export of British capital, the peopling of North America, the gold rush to the mines of California, South Africa, Alaska and Australia belied the international immobility assumption. As early as 1817 McCulloch criticised Ricardo for denying 'the equilibrium of profit in different countries' resulting from international capital movements. See O'Brien, op. cit. p. 194.
57. Ricardo, *Works*, p. 128.
58. For the construction and properties of a world production-possibilities frontier see any good intermediate text on international economics, e.g. Chacholiades, op. cit. pp. 34–5.
59. J. S. Mill, *Principles of Political Economy* (ed. W. J. Ashley) (London: Longman, 1920) p. 587.
60. Viner, *Studies*, op. cit. p. 490.
61. Gottfried Haberler, *The Theory of International Trade, with Its Applications to Commercial Policy* (London: Hodge, 1936) p. 126. For a survey

of the various interpretations of 'real costs' as well as a trenchant critique of the use of the labour theory in the classical trade model see Edward S. Mason, 'The Doctrine of Comparative Cost', *Quarterly Journal of Economics*, vol. 38 (Aug 1926) pp. 582–606.
62. Karl Marx, *Capital*, vol. III (Moscow, 1971) p. 238. In the introduction to his *Critique of Political Economy* Marx stated that he intended to deal with external economic relations, but never got round to it. It is known, however, that Marx's voluminous notes (24 volumes) – not yet fully published – contain a discourse on international trade. For an analysis of Marx's foreign-trade doctrines, pieced together from his published writings see G. Kohlmey, 'Karl Marx Theorie von den Internationalen Werten', *Jahrbuch des Instituts für Wirtschaftswissenschaften*, no. 5 (1962) pp. 18–122.
63. Marx, *Theories of Surplus Value*, part III (Moscow: Progress Publishers, 1975) pp. 105–6.
64. Marx, *Capital*, vol. I (Moscow: Foreign Languages Publishing House, 1977) p. 525.
65. One well-known work of this type is A. Emmanuel, *Unequal Exchange: A Study of the Imperialism of Trade* (New York: Monthly Review Press, 1972). For criticisms of Emmanuel see Leslie Stein, *Trade and Structural Change* (London: Croom-Helm, 1984) pp. 143–62; David Evans, 'A Critical Assessment of Some Neo-Marxian Trade Theories', *Journal of Development Studies*, vol. 20, no. 2 (Jan 1984) pp. 202–26; P. A. Samuelson, 'Illogic of Neo-Marxian doctrine of Unequal Exchange', in D. A. Belsley *et al.* (eds) *Inflation, Trade and Taxes: Essays in Honor of Alice Bourneuf* (Columbus Ohio: Ohio Univ. Press, 1976) In an appendix to Emmanuel's book, C. Bettelheim declares that 'Emmanuel's critique constitutes an extremely important contribution to the overturning of what might be called the dogma of the theory of comparative costs.' Ibid. p. 274.
66. Ricardo, *Works*, vol. I, p. 128.
67. T. R. Malthus, *Principles of Political Economy*, 1st ed. (London: John Murray, 1820) pp. 460–1.
68. Ibid. p. 462.
69. Ricardo, *Notes on Malthus* (1820) p. 215. For an evaluation of the Ricardo–Malthus debate on this point see Viner, *Studies*, op. cit. ch. IX, pp. 527–32.
70. Ricardo, *Works*, vol. I, p. 128.
71. Ibid. pp. 132–3.
72. Ibid. p. 129.
73. See E. G. West, 'Ricardo in Historical Perspective', *Canadian Journal of Economics*, vol. XV, no. 2 (May 1982) pp. 314–16.
74. See Ricardo, *Works*, vol. I, pp. 131–2. Ricardo's explicit assumption is that savings and capital accumulation depend on the income of capitalists expressed in terms of luxury goods – what Sraffa calls 'non-basic' commodities as distinct from 'basic' commodities. A basic commodity is one which enters directly or indirectly in the production of all other goods.
75. E. K. Hunt, *History of Economic Thought* (Belmont, Calif.: Wadsworth, 1979) p. 107.

76. Hollander, 'On the Substantive Identity of the Ricardian and Neoclassical Conceptions of Economic Organization: The French Connection in British Classicism', *Canadian Journal of Economics*, vol. xv, no. 4 (Nov 1982) p. 591 n. 7.
77. N. Senior, *Three Lectures on the Cost of Obtaining Money* (1830) (LSE Reprints of Scarce Tracts, etc., 1931) p. 1. For an authoritative account of Senior's contribution to trade theory and policy see Marian Bowley, *Nassau Senior and Classical Economics* (London: Allen & Unwin, 1937) ch. 6, pp. 201–34.
78. Senior, *Three Lectures*, op. cit p. 11.
79. Ibid. p. 20.
80. Ibid. p. 28. Senior was not the first to develop a productivity theory of wages linked to the price of internationally traded goods. In 1820 John Clay did much the same in his book *A Free Trade Essential to the Welfare of Great Britain* (London, 1820) in which he contrasted this theory of manufacturing wages with the usual classical treatment in terms of the domestic price of food (i.e. the population and wage-fund theory of wages).
81. The late Bertil Ohlin, the principal originator of the Heckscher–Ohlin model regarded his new theory as the first decisive break with Ricardo's law of comparative costs. In his keenness to emphasise the novelty of his approach he even refused to use the phrase 'comparative advantage'. His strong criticism of the classical theory was partly explained by his dislike of the labour theory of value. See appendix III of his book, *Interregional and International Trade* (Harvard U.P., 1933). Of course, his theory was not a rejection of comparative advantage, but merely a restatement of it along neoclassical lines as part of a more general theory of the causes of trade.
82. G. D. A. MacDougall, 'British and American Exports: A Study Suggested by the Theory of Comparative Costs', *Economic Journal*, vol. 61 (Dec 1951) pp. 697–724; also ibid. vol. 62 (Sep 1952) pp. 487–521.
83. J. Bhagwati, 'The Pure Theory of International Trade: A Survey', *Economic Journal* (1964) reprinted in his book *Trade, Tariffs and Growth* (London: Weidenfeld & Nicholson, 1969) pp. 14–22. Bhagwati found that linear regressions of export price ratios on labour productivity ratios as well as unit labour costs on export price ratios yielded no significant relationships. Hence a puzzle: labour productivity does not determine prices, but it does explain trade!
84. This is the opinion of Caves and Jones, op. cit. p. 191.
85. For a good analysis of the empirical work surrounding the Ricardian hypothesis see Ronald Findlay, *Trade and Specialization* (Harmondsworth, Middx: Penguin Books, 1970) ch. 5. Stein, op. cit. pp. 23–5 shares Bhagwati's scepticism and implicitly challenges the contention that post-trade prices are equalized, and he recalls Caves's earlier recognition that MacDougall's test took place in an environment of imperfect markets.
86. Ohlin, op. cit. p. 563.
87. J. S. Mill, *Principles of Political Economy* (1848) (W. J. Ashley ed. reprint, New York, 1965).
88. F. Y. Edgeworth, 'Theory of International Values', *Economic Journal*

(Dec 1894) p. 610. Chipman, op. cit. p. 484. D. P. O'Brien, *The Classical Economists*, op. cit. p. 183.
89. Edgeworth, op. cit. p. 609. See Chipman, op. cit. pp. 183–4, for the comments of the economists mentioned.
90. Dennis R. Appleyard and James C. Ingram, op. cit. pp. 459–76.
91. Appleyard and Ingram, op. cit. p. 475.
92. John S. Chipman, 'Mill's "Superstructure": How Well does it Stand up?', *History of Political Economy*, vol. 11, no. 4 (Winter 1979) pp. 477–500.
93. Viner, op. cit. p. 536. More recently Sir John Hicks referred to Mill's work on international values as 'an epoch-making discovery' and traced later developments (Marshall, Meade and Johnson) 'back to that essay of Mill's'. Hicks, op. cit. p. 61.
94. M. Longfield, *Three Lectures on Commerce and Absenteeism* (Dublin, 1845) (LSE reprint 1938) pp. 55–6.
95. Ronald W. Jones, 'International Trade Theory', in E. Cary Brown and Robert M. Solow (eds) *Paul Samuelson and Modern Economic Theory* (New York: McGraw-Hill, 1983) p. 82.
96. J. E. Cairnes, *Some Leading Principles of Political Economy Newly Expounded* (London: Macmillan, 1874) ch. III part 1, pp. 66–8.
97. Graham summarised his work on international values, begun since 1923 in F. D. Graham, *The Theory of International Values* (Princeton U.P., 1948). For criticisms of Graham see Chipman, op. cit. pp. 493–5.
98. F. W. Taussig, *International Trade* (New York: Macmillan, 1927), esp. chs 7, 9 and 10. The quotation is on p. 48.
99. Viner, op. cit. p. 512.

5 The Economists, the Corn Laws and Commercial Policy

1. Thweatt, op. cit. p. 208.
2. William D. Grampp, 'Economic Opinion when Britain turned to Free Trade', *History of Political Economy*, vol. 14, no. 4 (1982) p. 508.
3. Sir James Graham, M.P., *Corn and Currency: in an Address to the Landowners* (London: Ridgway, 1826) p. 21. The attitude of one of these landowners, Lord Sheffield: 'I know nothing of Ricardo, nor of Hume, nor of any of the other writers, nor of their works' was fairly typical. Remark quoted in Boyd Hilton, *Corn, Cash and Commerce: The Economic Policies of the Tory Governments, 1815–1830* (Oxford: Oxford U.P., 1977) p. 9.
4. G. J. Stigler, 'Do Economists Matter?' *Southern Economic Journal*, vol. 42, no. 3 (Jan 1976) pp. 347–8.
5. Asa Briggs, *The Age of Improvement* (London: Longmans, 1959) p. 201.
6. Gertrude Himmelfarb, *The Idea of Poverty: England in the Early Industrial Age* (London: Faber & Faber, 1984) p. 101.
7. Cobbett's *Political Register*, issues for November and December 1807.
8. See Mill's review of Spence's pamphlet in *Eclectic Review* 3 (Dec 1807) p. 1056 and *Commerce Defended* in D. Winch (ed.) *James Mill: Selected Economic Writings* (Edinburgh, 1966) pp. 23–35. The quoted passages are from *Commerce Defended*, 2nd ed. pp. 81 and 86. Earlier than

Spence, John Wheatley (1803) asserted that 'an exchange of equivalents is the foundation of all commerce'. Both Huskisson (1810) and Brougham (1803) took him up on this. Huskisson asked: 'if commerce is nothing more than an exchange of *equivalents*, and, the *Balance of Trade* ... only the measure of our foreign expenditure, in what way is a country enriched by trade?' (*The Question of the Depreciation of our Currency stated and examined* (London, 1810). Huskisson went on to answer with some suggestive thoughts on the gains from trade. Chipman suggests that Huskisson's remarks must have been a great stimulus to both Torrens and Ricardo (particularly Torrens) in their development of the law of comparative advantage. See J. S. Chipman, 'Balance of Payments Theory', in J. Creedy and D. P. O'Brien (eds) *Economic Analysis in Historical Perspective* (London: Butterworths, 1984) pp. 209–10.

9. Torrens, *The Economists Refuted*, pp. 15–26, 30–1, 50–1.
10. Spiegel, op. cit. p. 199.
11. Leonard Horner (ed.) *Memoirs and Correspondence of Francis Horner, M.P.* 2 vols. (London, 1843) vol. II, p. 227. The letter was to the publisher John Murray. Malthus's first Corn Law pamphlet (1814) was entitled *Observations on the Effects of the Corn Laws, and of a Rise or Fall in the Price of Corn on the Agriculture and General Wealth of the Country* (44 pages). The second pamphlet came out on 10 Feb 1815 – *Grounds of an Opinion on the Policy of Restricting the Importation of Foreign Corn* (48 pages).
12. Malthus, *Essay on Population*, 5th ed. pp. 408–9.
13. Ibid. pp. 426–7.
14. Malthus, *Essay on Population*, 2nd ed., p. 166.
15. Idem. 3rd ed. (1806) vol. II, p. 237.
16. The full title of Ricardo's pamphlet is *An Essay on the Influence of a low Price of Corn on the Profits of Stock; shewing the Inexpediency of Restrictions on Importations: with Remarks on Mr Malthus's two last Publications*
17. Hollander's interpretation is contained in his *The Economics of David Ricardo*, op. cit. pp. 599–642, and 'Ricardo and the Corn Laws: A Revision', *History of Political Economy*, vol. 9, no. 1 (Spring 1977) pp. 1–47. For the traditional view that Ricardo's profit theory originated in concern over the Corn Laws see Blaug, *Ricardian Economics: A Historical Study* (New Haven, Conn.: Yale U.P. 1958) pp. 31–2; Maurice Dobb, *Theories of Production and Distribution Since Adam Smith* (Cambridg U.P., 1973) pp. 89–90; D. P. O'Brien, *J. R. McCulloch: A Study in Classical Economics* (London, 1970) p. 296. O'Brien maintains 'Secular stagnation resulting from the Corn Laws is the core, indeed the purpose, of the Ricardian model.'
18. Ricardo, *Works*, vol. VI, p. 104.
19. Ibid. p. 21. Note, however, Ronald Meek's comment on the social neutrality of Ricardo's position: 'Ricardo was never particularly concerned to defend the interests of any single social class.' R. L. Meek, 'The Decline of Ricardian Economics in England', *Economica*, vol. 17 (1950) p. 50. Ricardo's reputation as an anti-landlord theorist dies hard, though. A recent writer refers to 'a dark hue to Ricardo's economic

theory' and maintains that 'Ricardo gave the attempt to create a class alliance to campaign against the Corn Laws a sound theoretical basis'. See Anthony Arblaster, *The Rise and Decline of Western Liberalism* (Oxford: Blackwell, 1984) p. 249.
20. Edwin Cannan, *History of the Theories of Production and Distribution in English Political Economy from 1776 to 1848*, 3rd ed. (London: Staples Press, 1953) p. 391.
21. Ricardo, *Works*, vol. IV, p. 26 n.
22. Ibid. vol. VI, p. 109.
23. Ibid. vol. IV, p. 179.
24. Ibid. vol. IV, p. 41.
25. 'Mr Owen's Plans for Relieving the National Distress', *Edinburgh Review*, 32 (Oct 1819) p. 459. All articles in the *Edinburgh* were unsigned, but the work has been attributed to Torrens although McCulloch is sometimes mentioned as being the author.
26. Torrens, *Essay on the Production of Wealth* (London: Longman, Hurst, Rees, Orme & Brown, 1821) pp. 252–60.
27. Ibid. p. 119.
28. Torrens, *Essay Upon the External Corn Trade*, p. 257.
29. Ibid. p. 256.
30. Ibid. p. 235, 331–2.
31. Torrens, *Tracts on Trade and Finance*, no. II (London, 1852) pp. 48–9.
32. *Eclectic Review*, n.s. 2 (July 1814) pp. 4–5.
33. Andrea Maneschi, 'Dynamic Aspects of Ricardo's International Trade Theory', *Oxford Economic Papers*, vol. 35, no. 1 (Mar 1983) p. 79. See also the article by Vivian Walsh, 'Ricardian Foreign Trade Theory in the Light of the Classical Revival', *Eastern Economic Journal*, vol. 5, no. 3 (Oct 1979) pp. 421–7, which plays down the role of comparative costs in Ricardo's model of trade and development. But as Maneschi points out, the static theory (absolute or comparative advantage comparisons) cannot be entirely ignored in dynamic analysis since, for trade to take place at all, there must be a difference in pretrade price ratios.
34. Ricardo, *Works*, vol. I, p. 132.
35. Hollander, *Economics of Ricardo*, op. cit. p. 604.
36. D. P. O'Brien, 'Ricardian Economics and the Economics of David Ricardo', *Oxford Economic Papers*, vol. 33, no. 3 (Nov 1981) p. 376.
37. Blaug, *Ricardian Economics*, op. cit. pp. 31–2. Joan Robinson said: 'He used it as a horror story.' Robinson, op. cit. vol. V, p. 141.
38. Published by Cambridge University Press 1980. See part II, pp. 43–58, esp. pp. 47–9. For a critique of Berg's interpretation see the review of her book by Gregory Claeys and Prue Kerr, 'Mechanical Political Economy', *Cambridge Journal of Economics*, vol. 5 (1981) pp. 251–72.
39. O'Brien, 'Ricardian Economics ...' (1981) op. cit. p. 381.
40. Ibid. p. 251.
41. Blaug, *Ricardian Economics*, op. cit. p. 211.
42. Ricardo, *Works*, vol. V, pp. 187–8.
43. Ibid. vol. IV, p. 243. See also idem, Ricardo to McCulloch (Mar 1821) vol. VIII, pp. 355–60.

44. William D. Grampp, 'Economic Opinion and Free Trade', op. cit. p. 510.
45. Ricardo, *Works*, vol. VIII, p. 208.
46. Ibid. vol. I, p. 343.
47. Ibid. p. 340.
48. Ricardo was frequently lampooned by nationalist writers and popular journalists like Cobbett, who classified him, along with 'the Jews, Scots and subversives' as unpatriotic cosmopolites, caring little for the welfare of Great Britain. Yet Ricardo was anything but 'unpatriotic'. He preferred capital to be invested at home and regarded the Corn Law as being responsible for the export of capital through its depressive effect on the rate of profit (speech, 16 May 1822). See the interesting paper by William Grampp, 'Scots, Jews, and Subversives among the Dismal Scientists', *Journal of Economic History* vol. 36, no. 3 (Sep 1976) pp. 543–71, on the lampooning of the classical economists at the hands of popular, xenophobic writers.
49. Ricardo, *Works*, vol. I, p. 94.
50. J. M. Letiche, 'Adam Smith and David Ricardo on Economic Growth', in Bert F. Hoselitz, J. J. Spengler *et al.*, *Theories of Economic Growth* (Glenco, Ill.: The Free Press of Glencoe, 1960) p. 80.
51. Ricardo, *Works*, vol. I, pp. 137–8.
52. J. S. Mill commented on the issue in two articles for the *Westminster Review* – 'The Corn Laws', Apr 1825 and 'The New Corn Law', January 1827 reprinted in *Collected Works*, op. cit.
53. Mill, *Collected Works*, op. cit. vol. IV, p. 47.
54. Ibid. p. 64.
55. Ibid. p. 143. For an excellent account of the arguments used in the parliamentary debates on the Corn Laws during 1824–30 see Barry Gordon, *Economic Doctrine and Tory Liberalism 1824–30* (London, Macmillan: 1979) pp. 52–66.
56. Melvyn Krauss, *The New Protectionism* (New York, 1979) p. xxiii, also p. 6.
57. *Parliamentary Debates* (Hansard) 1: col. 673 (30 May 1820).
58. See the reference in Grampp, 'Scots, Jews, and Subversives', op. cit. p. 565.
59. *Annual Register, 1820* (London, 1822) vol. I, p. 70.
60. For a revealing discussion of the analytical issues and personalities involved in the Australian case for protection see the exchanges between Paul A. Samuelson and Gary J. Manger in *Quarterly Journal of Economics*, vol. 96, no. 1 (Feb 1981) pp. 147–70.
61. Torrens, *Tracts on Finance and Trade*, vol II (London: Chapman & Hall, 1852) p. 32.
62. Malthus, *Essay on Population*, 5th ed. ii, pp. 409–10.
63. Ibid. pp. 403–4.
64. Ricardo to Malthus, 16 Sep 1814, *Works*, vol. VI, p. 134, and *Works*, vol. VIII, p. 22.
65. J. C. L. Simonde de Sismondi, *Nouveau Principes d'Economie politique* (1819) (Paris: Calman-Levy, 1971 pp. 265–6.

66. Jean-Baptiste Say, *Letter to Mr Malthus on Several Subjects of Political Economy, and on the Cause of the Stagnation of Commerce*, trans. John Richter (London: Sherwood, Neely & Jones, 1821) p. 8. Say also quotes the passage by Sismondi mentioned in the text.
67. Robinson, op. cit. vol. I, p. 189.
68. Chipman, op. cit. pp. 711 and 713. Part 2 'The Neo-Classical Theory'.
69. R. Torrens, A Letter to the Right Honourable Lord John Russell, (London: Longman, Rees, Orme, Brown & Green, 1837) p. 143.
70. Malthus, *Principles of Political Economy* (London: John Murray, 1820) p. 329.
71. Sir W. Sleeman, *On Taxes, or Public Revenue* (London: Elder & Co., 1829) p. 198.
72. G. Poulett Scrope, *Principles of Political Economy* (London: Longman, Rees, 1833) pp. 378–82.
73. G. Poulett Scrope, 'The Political Economists', *Quarterly Review*, vol. 44 (1831) p. 24.
74. Arthur I. Bloomfield, 'Effect of Growth on the Terms of Trade: Some Earlier Views', *Economica*, vol. 51 (May 1984). Bloomfield's article corrects the conventional view that the analysis of growth and the terms of trade started with Mill.
75. Torrens, *Letter to Lord John Russell*, op. cit. pp. 132–3.
76. Frank Whitson Fetter, 'Robbins on Torrens', *Economica* (Nov 1958) p. 346.
77. For Senior's criticism see his article 'Free Trade and Retaliation', *Edinburgh Review*, vol. LXXVIII (July 1843) pp. 1–47.
78. Ibid. p. 42.
79. McCulloch's critique is to be found on pp. 166–8 of the 1849 ed. of his *Principles*.
80. McCulloch, *Principles* (1849) p. 166 and pp. 151–2. O'Brien's comments are in *J. R. McCulloch: A Study in Classical Economics*, op. cit. pp. 227–8.
81. For a good discussion of the controversy between Senior and Torrens, see Marian Bowley, op. cit. pp. 225–8.
82. Torrens, *The Budget*, op. cit. pp. 177 and 66.
83. Torrens, *A Letter to Lord John Russell*, op. cit. p. 133.
84. Colonel Torrens, *Speech in the House of Commons on the Motion for a Reappointment of a Select Committee on Emigration, February 15 1827* (London: Longman, Rees, Orme, Brown & Green, 1828). Quoted in S. A. Meenai, 'Robert Torrens 1780–1864', *Economica* (Feb 1956) p. 55.
85. R. Davis, *The Industrial Revolution and British Overseas Trade* (Leicester: Leicester U.P., 1979) p. 75.
86. John Craig, *Remarks on Some Fundamental Doctrines of Political Economy* (Edinburgh, 1821) pp. 101–2.
87. Hansard, n.s. 18 (1828) cols 1553–5.
88. Torrens's speech 15 Feb 1827 quoted in F. W. Fetter, op. cit. p. 163.
89. On colonisation schemes and the economists' involvement in the debate, see R. N. Ghosh, *Classical Macroeconomics and the Case for Colonies* (Calcutta: New Age, 1967) pp. 25–38 and 228–45.

90. J. S. Mill, *Collected Works*, op. cit. vol. IV, p. 258.
91. Ibid. p. 251.
92. Ibid. p. 258.
93. Ibid. p. 55.
94. Ibid. p. 70.
95. J. S. Mill, *Principles* (1852) 5th ed. vol II, p. 163.
96. Mill, *Principles* (W. J. Ashley ed.) p. 739.
97. Mill, *Some Unsettled Questions*, op. cit. p. 45.
98. Donald N. McCloskey, 'Magnanimous Albion: Free Trade and British National Income, 1841–1881', *Explorations in Economic History*, vol. 17 (1980) pp. 303–20. See also criticisms of McCloskey by P. J. Nain in *Explorations in Economic History*, vol. 19, pp. 201–7, and McCloskey's reply, ibid. pp. 208–10.
99. McCloskey, op. cit. p. 305. Kindleberger expresses a similar view, i.e. that the movement to free trade was due to the ideology of the political economists, 'aided by the potato famine'. See C. P. Kindleberger, *Comparative Studies in Trade, Finance and Growth* (Cambridge, Mass.: Harvard U.P. 1978) p. 53.
100. Torrens, *An Essay on the Production of Wealth* (1821) pp. 288–9.
101. W. Sombart, *Die deutsche Volkswirtschaft im neunzehnten Jahrhundert* (Berlin, 1913) ch. 14. Empirical research has revealed no clear evidence of any tendency for the ratio of trade to national income to fall over time. If anything the ratio has actually increased for most countries since the Second World War.
102. Hansard, n.s. 12 (1825) col. 1213. When the U.S. Congress increased tariffs sharply in 1828 Huskisson called for retaliation. See Hansard, n.s. 19 (1828) cols 1768–70.
103. J. H. Clapham, *An Economic History of Modern Britain*, vol. 1 (Cambridge U.P., 1939) p. 479.
104. Lord Welby, *Cobden's Work and Opinions*, p. 18, quoted in J. A. Hobson, *Richard Cobden: The International Man* (London, 1919) p. 20.
105. *Wealth of Nations*, ed. Cannan vol. i, pp. 422–3.
106. Hamilton's argument was presented in his *Report on the Subject of Manufactures* (1791) and List's in *The National System of Political Economy* (1841) (London: Longman, 1928). In his recent book, *Profit and Crises*, Arghiri Emmanuel points out that 'List only systematised the infant-industry argument' – apart from Hamilton and List, various other eighteenth- and nineteenth-century writers such as Andrew Yarranton, William Wood, Forbonnais and Sismondi constructed protectionist arguments based on infant-industry considerations. Thus Emmanuel recalls, Forbonnais in *Eléments du Commerce*, vol. I, p. 251 estimated that a tariff of 15 per cent should give adequate protection to a viable young industry, since with the inclusion of transport costs, commission, etc., the effective protective margin worked out at between 18 to 20 per cent. See A. Emmanuel, *Profit and Crises* (London: Heinemann, 1984) p. 3 n. 4. List was rather vague about the maximum tariff level necessary to protect infant industries, but it appears he favoured tariffs of between 20–25 per cent.

107. Schumpeter, *History of Economic Analysis*, op. cit. p. 505.
108. Mill, *Principles* (W. J. Ashley ed.) (London: Longmans Green, 1909) p. 922.
109. M. C. Kemp, 'The Mill-Bastable Infant-Industry Dogma', *Journal of Political Economy*, vol. 68 (Feb 1960), pp. 65–7.
110. Cobden Club Pamphlet, *John Stuart Mill on the Protection of Infant Industries* (London, 1911) pp. 11, 13–15, 17. See also J. S. Mill, *Collected Works*, vol. 16, ed. F. E. Mineka and D. W. Lindley (Toronto U.P., 1972) pp. 1043–4, 1150–1, 1419–20 and 1520–1.
111. Harry Johnson, 'A New View of the Infant Industry Argument', in I. A. McDougall and Richard H. Snape (eds) *Studies in International Economics: Monash Conference Papers* (Amsterdam: North-Holland, 1970) p. 60.
112. Mill, *Principles* (1848) (W. J. Ashley ed.) p. 581.
113. Maxine Berg, *The Machinery Question* (1980) op. cit. pp. 203–25. For a good summary of writings on this and other nineteenth-century issues about trade, technology and growth see Arthur I. Bloomfield, 'The Impact of Growth and Technology on Trade in Nineteenth-century British Thought', *History of Political Economy*, vol. 10, no. 4 (1978) pp. 608–35.
114. Ricardo, *Works*, vol. v, pp. 302–3.
115. Ibid. vol. I, pp. 396–7.
116. Ibid. vol. v, p. xx.
117. Hansard, n.s. 13 (1825) col. 1233.
118. Malthus, *Additions to the Fourth and Former Editions of Essay on Population* (London: John Murray, 1817) p. 108; Torrens, *The Budget* (1844) op. cit. p. 235.
119. J. R. McCulloch, *On Commerce* (London, 1833) p. 9.
120. William Playfair, *An Inquiry into the Permanent Causes of the Decline and Fall of Powerful and Wealthy Nations* (London, 1805) pp. 212, 203.
121. *Parliamentary Debates* (Hansard) Second Series, vol. xvi, (6 Dec 1826) cols 294–5. Alexander Baring (the banker), who introduced Torrens to the House, congratulated him afterwards on his speech: 'It had been for so long a time the habit to look upon any man as a Goth who dissented from the modern doctrine of political economy', that it was indeed a pleasure to welcome Torrens to the House. Ibid. col. 296.
122. *Parliamentary Debates* (Hansard) Third Series, vol. xxiv, 2 July 1834, col. 1088; vol. xxv, (2 Aug 1834) col. 908.
123. F. W. Fetter, 'Robert Torrens: Colonel of Marines and Political Economist', *Economica* (May 1962) p. 165.
124. Nassau Senior, *Three Lectures on the Cost of Obtaining Money and Some Effects of Private and Government Paper Money* (1830) op. cit. pp. 25–6, 30.
125. Lord King's Speech, *Parliamentary Debates* (Hansard) n.s. vol. xxiii (29 Mar 1830) cols 969–70, 969–70, 973–4.
126. For McCulloch's and Malthus's testimony before the Committee see Select Committee on Combination Laws, Artisans and Machinery, *Parliamentary Papers* (1824) vol. v, cols, 592, 596 and 598.

Notes and References 305

127. H. R. C. Wright, *Free Trade and Protection in the Netherlands, 1816–39; A Study of the First Benelux* (Cambridge U.P., 1955) p. 130.
128. Report of the Select Committee on the Laws Relating to the Export of Tools and Machinery (30 June 1825) no. 504, p. 15.
129. J. Kennedy, *On the Exportation of Machinery* (London, 1824) p. 17.
130. J. S. Mill, 'Of the Laws of Interchange Between Nations' in *Essays on Some Unsettled Questions* (London: John Parker, 1844) op. cit. pp. 31–2.
131. 'Exportation of Machinery', *Westminster Review*, III (Apr 1825) pp. 386–94.
132. Mill, op. cit. p. 32.
133. *Parliamentary Papers* (1841) vol. VII. Testimony of Holland Hooke, p. 52.
134. P. J. Cain, *Economic Foundations of British Overseas Expansion 1815–1914* (London: Macmillan, 1980) p. 20. For a detailed account of the restrictions and the role of Manchester manufacturers see A. E. Musson, 'The "Manchester School" and Exportation of Machinery', *Business History* (Jan 1972) pp. 17–50.

6 Gold, Money and Trade

1. The process whereby 'good money drives out bad money'. Although associated with Sir Thomas Gresham, counsellor to Elizabeth I, the principle was understood at least from the early fourteenth century. The process is clearly observed in a bimetallic system. If, for instance, the free-market price of gold in terms of silver is higher than the government mint price, then the overvalued metal (gold) will be melted down and replaced by silver coins (the undervalued metal). Thus, 'bad' money (in this case silver, the metal less favoured in the free market) drives out 'good' money (gold, the metal more favoured in the free market). Similarly, worn, clipped or debased coins tend to drive out of circulation good, full-bodied, mint-condition coins.
2. *Report of the Committee on Currency and Foreign Exchanges after the War, 1918–19*, Cmnd 9182. This Report – the *locus classicus* of the pre-1914 gold standard – painted an idealised picture of its workings on the basis of the Currency School dogma. It discussed the steps that were to be taken for the restoration of the gold standard in the U.K., and influenced the policies of successive British governments up to 1931. The Cunliffe Report is reprinted in T. S. Ashton and R. S. Sayers (eds) *Papers in English Monetary History* (Oxford: Clarendon Press, 1953). (There is also a 1979 reprint by Arno Press, New York.)
3. Data and indices of monetary phenomena for this period are contained in Norman J. Silberling, 'British Prices and Business Cycles, 1779–1850', *Review of Economic Statistics*, vol. V (Oct 1923) (supplement) pp. 232 and 255. See also Robert V. Eagly, 'The Swedish and English Bullionist Controversies', diagram II, p. 23 in Eagly (ed.) *Events, Ideology and Economic Theory*, op. cit.
4. Walter Boyd, *A Letter to the Right Honourable William Pitt, on the*

Influence of the Stoppage of Issues in Specie at the Bank of England; on the Prices of Provisions, and Other Commodities (London: J. Wright, 1801) preface, p. xxxi.
5. Malthus, *Population* (1803 ed.) p. 404.
6. Henry Thornton, *An Enquiry into the Nature and Effects of the Paper Credit of Great Britain*, ed. F. A. Hayek (New York, 1962). Schumpeter, op. cit. p. 689 comments: 'No other performance of the period will bear comparison with it, though, several, among them Ricardo's met with much greater success at the time as well as later.'
7. Thornton, *Paper Credit* (1802) op. cit. p. 246.
8. Ibid. p. 198.
9. Ibid. p. 199.
10. On Thornton's change of attitude between 1802 and 1811 see John Hicks, *Critics Essays in Monetary Theory* (Oxford U.P., 1967) pp. 185–6; also Charles F. Peake, 'Henry Thornton: An Accurate Perspective', *History of Political Economy*, vol. 14, no. 1 (1982) pp. 116–18.
11. Thornton, *Paper Credit*, op. cit. p. 143.
12. Malthus, *Edinburgh Review* (Feb 1811) vol. XVII, pp. 342–3.
13. Ibid. p. 359.
14. For the *Report* see the edition by Edwin Cannan, *The Paper Pound of 1797–1821: A Reprint of the Bullion Report* (London: King, 1919).
15. See Hansard, n.s. 14 (1826) cols 450–66.
16. Ibid. col. 80.
17. See the excellent study of the Free Banking literature by Lawrence H. White, *Free Banking in Britain: Theory, Experience* (Cambridge U.P., 1984). The literature on nineteenth-century British monetary controversies is vast. The following are helpful guides: D. P. O'Brien, *The Classical Economists* (1975) op. cit. ch. 6; Marion R. Daugherty, 'The Currency-Banking Controversy', parts I and II, *Southern Economic Journal* (1942–3) vol. 9, pp. 140–55, 241–51; Lloyd Mints, *A History of Banking Theory* (Chicago U.P., 1945).
18. *Parliamentary Papers* (House of Commons) *Report from the Select Committee on Banks of Issue* (1840) vol. IV, Q. 2654.
19. Ricardo, *Works*, op. cit. vol. IV pp. 276–85. James Mill supported the principle behind Ricardo's plan: 'The issuing of notes', he said, 'is one of that small number of businesses which it suits a government to conduct. ...' *Elements of Political Economy* (1821) op. cit. p. 113.
20. The Radcliffe Report, Cmnd 827, endorsed what became known as 'hydraulic Keynesianism' and rejected the Quantity Theory of Money.
21. J. S. Mill in *Westminster Review*, no. 41 (1844) pp. 590–1.
22. Thomas Tooke, *An Inquiry into the Currency Principle*, 2nd ed. (London: Longman, 1844) p. 121.
23. Rudiger Dornbusch and Jacob A. Frenkel, 'The Gold Standard Crisis of 1847', *Journal of International Economics*, vol. 16, no. 1/2 (Feb 1984) pp. 1–27.
24. Ibid. p. 22.
25. Robert Torrens, *A Letter to the Right Honourable Lord Viscount Melbourne on the Causes of the Recent Derangement in the Money Market, and on Bank Reform* (London: Longman, 1837) p. 44.

Notes and References

26. Walter Bagehot, *Lombard Street: A Description of the Money Market* (London: King, 1873) p.71.
27. Karl Marx, *A Contribution to the Critique of Political Economy*, Introduction by Maurice Dobb (London: Lawrence & Wishart, 1971) p. 14.
28. E.g. *A Contribution*, pp. 56 ff., 215 ff.; *Capital*, vol. I, pp. 94 ff., vol. III, chs 28 and 34.
29. Marx, *A Contribution*, op. cit. p. 179.
30. Marx, *Capital*, vol. I, p. 94.
31. Marx, *A Contribution*, op. cit. pp. 105–6.
32. Ibid. p. 182.
33. Ibid. p. 186.
34. Marx, *Grundrisse*, p. 791.
35. Marx, *Capital*, vol. I, p. 242.
36. Marx, *A Contribution*, op. cit. p. 149; *Grundrisse* (German ed.) p. 881.
37. For an account of business complaints against the international complications of the gold standard, see Frank W. Fetter, *The Development of British Monetary Orthodoxy 1797–1875* (Cambridge, Mass.: Harvard U.P. 1965) p. 237–9.
38. Taussig, *International Trade* (1927) op. cit. pp. 239, 261.
39. Robert Triffin, *The Evolution of the International Monetary System: Historical Reappraisal and Future Perspectives* (Princeton U.P., 1964); Arthur I. Bloomfield, *Monetary Policy under the International Gold Standard, 1880–1914* (Federal Reserve Bank of New York, 1959); A. G. Ford, *The Gold Standard 1880–1914: Britain and Argentina* (Oxford: Clarendon Press, 1960; Idem, 'The Truth About Gold', *Lloyds Bank Review*, no. 77 (July 1965); Marcello de Cecco, *Gold and Empire* (Oxford: Blackwell, 1974).
40. Mill, *Principles*, 7th ed. (London: Parker & Co., 1871) book IV, ch. VIII, sec. 4.
41. J. Robinson, 'The Need for a Reconsideration of the Theory of International Trade' (1973) reprinted in *Collected Economic Essays*, vol. IV, op. cit. p. 20.
42. J. M. Keynes, *A Treatise on Money*, vol. II (London: Macmillan, 1930) pp. 306–7.
43. A well-known early version of this monetarist interpretation is Donald N. McCloskey and J. Richard Zecher, 'How the Gold Standard Worked, 1880–1913', in *The Monetary Approach to the Balance of Payments*, ed. J. Frenkel and H. G. Johnson (London: Allen & Unwin, 1976); reprinted in McCloskey, *Enterprise and Trade in Victorian Britain* (London: Allen & Unwin, 1981) pp. 184–208. For a recent interpretation along these lines which highlights international capital mobility and portfolio adjustment see John E. Floyd, *World Monetary Equilibrium*, (London: Allan, 1985) ch. 4.
44. J. G. Gilbart, 'The Currency: Banking', *Westminster Review* (1841) no. 35, p. 67.
45. For some comments on the weaknesses of the monetarist interpretation and an affirmation of the view that the classical gold standard was, indeed, a sterling system, see Charles P. Kindleberger, *A Financial History of Western Europe* (London: Allen & Unwin, 1984) pp. 68–70.

308	*Notes and References*

46. In his book, *History of the World Economy: International Relations Since 1850* (London: Wheatsheaf Books, 1983) p. 181.
47. A. I. Bloomfield, *Short-term Capital Movements Under the Pre-1914 Gold Standard* (Princeton U.P., 1963) pp. 90–1.
48. White, op. cit. p. 149.

7 Free Trade and the National Economists

1. John H. Williams, 'The Theory of International Trade Reconsidered', *Economic Journal* (June 1929) (reprinted in American Economic Association, *Readings in the Theory of International Trade* ed. H. S. Ellis and L. A. Metzler (Philadelphia: Blakisten, 1949)). He referred to List as one of the writers among others (Cournot, Nogaro and Schüller) who refused to accept either the premises or the conclusions of classical theory. Williams later became a senior executive of the Federal Reserve Bank of New York.
2. Williams, op. cit. p. 263.
3. Idem, p. 265. Haberler admitted that the classical theory was static, but pointed out that Mill was 'not oblivious of the indirect, dynamic benefits which less developed countries in particular can derive from international trade'. See Gottfried Haberler, 'International Trade and Economic Development' – The Cairo Lectures, reprinted in Richard S. Weckstein (ed.) *Expansion of World Trade and the Growth of National Economies* (New York: Harper & Row, 1968) p. 103.
4. Williams, op. cit. p. 267.
5. Prebisch, the Argentinian economist, played a leading role in the setting up of UNCTAD and other international organisations concerned with the trade problems of Third World Countries. His writings date back to the early 1950s. For his latest views see R. Prebisch, *The Crisis of Capitalism and International Trade*, CEPAL Review, no. 23 (20 Aug 1983) pp. 51–74. Joan Robinson began her critique of trade theory as early as 1946 – see *The Pure Theory of International Trade*, followed later by *The Need for a Reconsideration of the Theory of International Trade* (1973) and *Reflections on the Theory of International Trade* (1974). All are reprinted in J. Robinson, *Collected Economic Papers*, vols 1–5 (Oxford: Blackwell, 1951–79). Myrdal's early critique is contained in his book *An International Economy* (New York, 1956). Haberler finds it strange that Myrdal 'fails to mention List, to whose theory his own bears a most striking similarity'. G. Haberler, op. cit. p. 102, n. 4.
6. A. Emmanuel, *Unequal Exchange: The Imperialism of Trade* (London: New Left Books, 1972); S. Amin, *Imperialism and Unequal Development* (New York: Monthly Review Press, 1977). André Gunder Frank, *Dependent Accumulation and Underdevelopment* (London: Macmillan, 1978).
7. The expression 'productive powers' was used by Hamilton as well as by later French writers such as Jean-Antoine Chaptal, Charles Dupin and Louis Say. List adopted the concept from these French economists and acknowledged his indebtedness, but List's application of the idea was wider than theirs.

8. The debate is discussed in Bernard Semmell, op. cit. pp. 14–18, who first pointed out its relevance to the national economists' claims: 'Tucker anticipated the program put forward by economists of less-developed countries who sought to challenge British industrial predominance, men such as Hamilton, List and Carey, p. 18. See also George Shelton, *Dean Tucker and Eighteenth Century Economic and Political Thought* (London: Macmillan, 1981) pp. 126–132, and J. M. Low, 'An Eighteenth Century Controversy in the Theory of Economic Progress', *Manchester School of Economic and Social Studies*, vol. II, no. 3 (Sep 1952).
9. Josiah Tucker, *Four Tracts together with Two Sermons on Political and Commercial Subjects* (Gloucester, 1774) Tract 1, p. 30.
10. Tucker, *Four Tracts*, op. cit. p. 28.
11. Idem, p. 47.
12. Idem, p. 14.
13. Idem, p. 49.
14. Scottish Record Office, Kames Collection – Tucker to Kames, 6 July 1758.
15. Tucker, *Four Tracts*, op. cit., 3rd ed. (Gloucester, 1776) p. vii. Also British Library Add. MS. 4319, Tucker to Dr Birch, 19 May 1760.
16. See Samuel McKee Jr (ed.) *Papers on Public Credit, Commerce and Finance by Alexander Hamilton* (New York: Columbia U.P., 1934). For analyses of the *Report* see Joseph Dorfman, *The Economic Mind in American Civilization 1606–1865* (New York: Viking Press, 1946) vol. 1, pp. 408–11, and Louis M. Hacker, *Alexander Hamilton in the American Tradition* (New York: McGraw-Hill, 1957) pp. 171–83, 132–37, 147–54, 162–4.
17. Samuel McKee Jr (ed.) Hamilton's, *Papers*, op. cit. p. 227.
18. George C. Fitzpatrick (ed.) *The Writings of George Washington* (Washington, D.C.: 1931–44) vol. 30, p. 186.
19. Hamilton's *Papers*, pp. 197–8, 228–9.
20. The *Thoughts on Political Economy* was the first systematic treatise on economics by an American writer. *The Elements* was an enlarged second edition of this work.
21. Raymond, *Elements of Political Economy* (Baltimore: Johns Hopkins U.P., 1823) vol. II, pp. 225–6, 231–2.
22. Ibid. pp. 245–6.
23. John Rae (1796–1872) was born in Scotland, but lived most of his adult life in Canada and the United States. Rae's protectionism stemmed from his original theory of capital and interest which was outlined in his rambling but remarkably perceptive book, *Statement of Some New Principles on the Subject of Political Economy: Exposing the Fallacies of the System of Free Trade, and of Some other Doctrines Maintained in the 'Wealth of Nations'* (1834). Besides J. S. Mill, Irving Fisher was also impressed with Rae's work and dedicated his *Rate of Interest* (1907) to the memory of Rae. For Rae's writings see the reprint in R. Warren James, *John Rae: Political Economist*, 2 vols (Toronto: Univ. of Toronto Press, 1965).
24. For a recent appreciative reassessment of Phillips's work see James H. Thompson, 'Willard Phillips: A Neglected American Economist', *History*

of Political Economy, vol. 16, no. 3 (Fall 1984) pp. 405–21. In Thompson's judgement Phillips was 'one of the best economists to appear in the United States prior to the Civil War'. (p. 420).
25. Henry Carey (1793–1879) wrote extensively on economics. His major work (in 3 vols) was *Principles of Social Science* (Philadelphia, 1858–9). His protectionist ideas were first developed in *Past, Present and Future* (1848) and further elaborated in *The Harmony of Interests, Agricultural, Manufacturing and Commercial* (Philadelphia, 1851).
26. Carey, *Harmony of Interests*, p. 72.
27. Friedrich List (1789–1846) was born in the town of Reutlingen in Württemberg (south Germany) just a few days before the French Revolution broke out. He worked as a civil servant for twelve years in his native state of Württemberg until he was appointed at the age of 28 to a newly created Chair in Public Administration at the University of Tübingen. He was forced to resign his professorship on account of his political activities and involvement with the *Hendels- und Gewerbsverein*. In 1819 he was elected to the lower chamber of the Württemberg Diet as a representative of Reutlingen. But again, his liberal reforming agitation antagonised the reactionary ruling authorities and List was expelled from the Assembly and sentenced to ten months' hard labour. This led to his voluntary exile, first in Paris and later in the United States until his return to Germany in 1830 and the continuation of his work on behalf of German economic unity.
28. To what extent was List influenced by American protectionist writers? The answer to this question has given rise to a long-running debate among Listian scholars. In 1897 C. P. Neill made a detailed textual comparison of Raymond's *Elements* with List's *National System*. He found remarkable similarities, and concluded that although List must have read Raymond's work, the coincidences were 'not sufficient to warrant the conclusion that List took his ideas bodily from Raymond'. See Charles Patrick Neill, *Daniel Raymond, an early Chapter in the History of Economic Theory in the United States* (Baltimore: Johns Hopkins U.P., 1897) p. 57. Margaret Hirst found equally striking similarities between Hamilton's *Report* and List's writings and suggested that List was undoubtedly influenced by Hamilton. Margaret E. Hirst, *Life of Friedrich List* (New York, 1909) pp. 114–15. An early denial of any U.S. intellectual influence on List was made by K. Th. Eheberg in his Introduction to *Friedrich List: Das Nationale System der Politischen Oekonomie* (Stuttgart, 1853): 'The beneficial influence exerted on List by his stay in America arose from practical circumstances and not from printed books.' (p. 149). List's latest biographer, Dr W. O. Henderson, points out that List was already a critic of classical economics before he arrived in the United States, and that he was not therefore 'converted to protectionism by studying the works of American writers'. (W. O. Henderson, *Friedrich List: Economist and Visionary 1789–1846* (London: Frank Cass, 1983) p. 155. But Henderson also believes that List's involvement in the U.S. tariff controversy broadened his views, and that when he wrote his letters to Ingersoll he was influenced by the writings of U.S. protectionists such as Hamilton and Matthew Carey. William Notz, in his study on 'List in America' came to essentially the same conclusion.

See William Notz, 'Friedrich List in America', *American Economic Review*, vol. 16, no. 2 (June 1926) pp. 248–65.
29. The three titles cited in the text are included in List's collected works published in 10 vols. under the auspices of the Friedrich List-Gesellschaft: *Friedrich List: Schriften, Reden, Briefe*, ed. Erwin von Beckerath, Edgar Salin et al. (Berlin: Hobbing, 1927–36) – hereafter cited as List, *Werke*. References to List's basic work, *The National System of Political Economy*, are taken from the English translation by Sampson S. Lloyd (London, 1885 and 1966). Hereafter cited as List, *National System*. For details of List's life and work see the recent biography by Henderson, op. cit., which also contains (ch. IV) an excellent summary of List's writings on economics with extensive bibliography and references. See also Edgar Salin and Rene Frey, 'Friedrich List' in *Encyclopedia of the Social Sciences*, vol. 9 (New York: Collier-Macmillan, 1968) pp. 409–12, and ch. 1, 'Economic Nationalism: Friedrich List, Germany's Handicapped Colbert' in Louis L. Snyder, *Roots of German Nationalism* (Bloomington, Ind. U.P., 1978) pp. 1–34.
30. List, *Werke*, vol. VI, pp. 153–4.
31. List, *National System*, pp. 124–6.
32. Ibid. pp. 138–9.
33. Ibid. p. 139 n.
34. List, *Outlines of American Political Economy* (1827) in *Werke*, vol. II p. 105.
35. List, *National System*, p. 158.
36. Ibid, p. x.
37. List, *Outlines* (1827) Letter II.
38. Quoted in K. W. Rowe, *Matthew Carey: A Study in American Economic Development* (Baltimore: Johns Hopkins U.P., 1933) p. 48.
39. List, *Werke*, vol. VI p. 366. List's discussion at this point and elsewhere suggests the hypothesis that dominant countries would always support an open liberal world-trading system, while laggards would prefer a controlled system. The evidence indicates that this is indeed the case.
40. List, *National System*, p. 46.
41. Ibid. p. 61.
42. Ibid. p. 61.
43. S. Sideri, *Trade and Power: Informal Colonialism in Anglo-Portuguese Relations* (Rotterdam: Rotterdam U.P. 1970) p. 13.
44. See Charles Gide, *Cours d'économie politique* (Paris: Sirey, 1931) part II p. 47; Eduard Heiman, *History of Economic Doctrines* (London: Oxford U.P., 1945) p. 132; Rudolph Hilferding, *The Economic Policy of Finance Capital edited with an Introduction by Tom Bottomore* (London: Routledge & Kegan Paul, 1981) p. 304.
45. List, *National System*, p. 75.
46. Lionel Robbins, *The Theory of Economic Development in the History of Economic Thought* (London: Macmillan, 1968) p. 116.
47. E. H. Carr, *The Soviet Impact on the Western World* (London, 1946) p. 23.
48. Joan Robinson, *Collected Economic Papers* (Oxford: Basil Blackwell) vol. V, p. 134.
49. Myint, *Economica* op. cit. (Sep 1977).

50. *Collected Economic Papers*, vol. I, p. 205.
51. Lionel Robbins, *The Theory of Economic Policy in English Political Economy* (London: Macmillan, 1952) p. 10.
52. List, *National System*, p. 323.
53. Ibid. p. 324.
54. *Wealth of Nations* (ed.) R. H. Campbell and A. S. Skinner (Oxford: Clarendon Press, 1976) p. 539.
55. List, *National System*, p. 319.
56. Ibid. p. 350.
57. Viner's review of vol. IV of List's collected works in *Journal of Political Economy* (June 1929), reprinted in J. Viner, *The Long View and the Short, Studies in Economic Theory and Policy* (Glencoe Ill.: The Free Press of Glencoe, 1958) pp. 389–91.
58. A. Anikin, *A Science in its Youth (Pre-Marxian Political Economy)*. (Moscow: Progress Publishers, 1975) p. 334.
59. 'List on the Principles of the German Customs Union. Dangers to British Industry and Commerce', *Edinburgh Review* no. CLII (July 1842) pp. 521–2.
60. *The Times*, 16 Jan 1847, p. 4.
61. Travers Twiss, *View of the Progress of Political Economy Since the 16th Century* (London, 1847) p. 248. McCulloch's opinion is in his *Literature of Political Economy* (London, 1846).
62. Marshall, *Principles*, 8th ed. (London, 1936) p. 727. Marshall did, in fact, make a special trip to the United States to study the practical effects of the theories of Carey and the other American protectionists.
63. Schumpeter, *History of Economic Analysis*, op. cit., p. 504.
64. Dorfman, op. cit. p. 584.
65. Dühring combined List's national economics with elements from Carey's system in his courses at the University of Berlin. Schüller (one of the critics of classical trade theory mentioned by Williams) interpreted List's concept of productive forces as an 'employment argument' for protection. According to Schüller, List's use of the concept implied the existence of unused national resources (particularly labour) which could be brought into production through the use of protective tariffs. Manoilesco was deeply impressed with List's remark that a country which was engaged in agriculture only was like a man with one arm, and developed an argument for industrial protection based on the notion that industry was superior in 'productive power' to agriculture. Tariff protection for industry was necessary to shift workers out of agriculture into manufacturing. Manoilesco's protectionism differed in important respects from both Carey's and List's. For the latter, agriculture was necessary for the maintenance of balanced growth; and List desired industrialisation not primarily or only for its economic benefits (i.e. higher productivity), but also for the cultural and social ethos associated with it.

For Schüller see *Schutzoll und Freihandel* (1905); *Die Klassische Nationaloekonomie und ihre Gegner* (1895). For Manoilesco see *The Theory of Protection and International Trade* (London: King, 1931); *La Theorie du Protectionisme* (Paris, 1929) and *Die Nationalen Produktivkräfte und der Aussenhandel* (Berlin, 1937). Finally, of course, List's approach to econ-

omics makes him a forerunner of the German Historical School of Political Economy.
66. Kohn was one of the pioneer investigators of nationalism. The remark is contained in his book *The Idea of Nationalism* (New York, 1944) p. 322.
67. Snyder, op. cit. p. 34. For an image of List as 'the only truly cosmopolitan German citizen of his age' who foresaw and welcomed a united Europe see E. N. Roussakis, *Friedrich List, the Zollverein and the Unity of Europe* (Bruges, 1968) p. 147.
68. Gustav Schmoller, in 'Verhandlungen des Vereins für Sozialpolitik', *Schriften des Vereins für Sozialpolitik* (Berlin, 1902) p. 270.

Index

absolute advantage 102, 119, 130–1, 136, 137–8, 141–2, 145, 160, 162, 186, 200, 207, 254, 270, 294
Africa, West 18, 19, 32, 33
agriculture 62–3, 79, 96, 116, 118–19, 130, 141, 172–3, 187, 197, 207
 in Physiocratic thought 116–19, 173
 protection of 93, 171–2, 175, 177, 180–1, 185, 187, 191
Allen, William R. 47, 147, 281, 295
Amboyna, massacre of 93
America 14, 18, 21, 22, 30, 33–4, 37, 86, 104, 216
 British trade with 33–5
 colonists 18, 33–5, 37, 84–5, 86, 279
 Spanish 21, 22, 63
Amsterdam 14, 16, 20, 26, 28–9, 35, 66, 287
 entrepôt 26, 28, 29, 35, 66
 Exchange Bank of 28
 golden age of 27–30
Antwerp 26, 27, 28
Appleby, Joyce Oldham 58, 125, 282, 286, 291
arbitrage, commodity 105, 111–12, 122, 235, 249, 251
 see also law of one price; purchasing-power parity
arbitristas 63–5
armaments 16, 24
Attwood, Thomas 231, 232
Australian case for protection 194, 301

Bacon, Francis 17, 41, 78, 80, 285
Bagehot, Walter 239, 307
Baltic trade 14, 19, 20–1, 28, 90
balance of payments 6, 12, 20, 38, 40–1, 44, 46, 50, 56–7, 63–4, 68–9, 108–9, 112, 135, 168, 228, 230, 233–4, 235, 244
 adjustment mechanism 46, 54–7, 103–13, 225–32, 135–6, 233–40
 monetary approach 107, 110, 136, 247–9, 251, 252, 290, 294, 307
 price-specie-flow mechanism 45–6, 56, 110, 229, 233, 235
 real factors and equilibrium in 44, 228, 229, 251
 under gold standard 243–7
balance of power 23, 26, 80–2

balance of trade 5, 10, 39, 40–1, 48, 50–2, 60, 64, 66–7, 69, 71–2, 82, 100, 107
 doctrine: origins of 40–1
 English debate on (1620s) 41–50, 171
 'general' and 'particular' balances 52, 82
 money and 6, 38–41, 68
bankers 4, 26, 27, 246
banking 26, 27, 28, 35, 95
banknotes 95, 225, 226, 228, 231–2, 234
 convertibility 221, 223–4, 231, 233–4, 235
 issue and circulation 95, 224, 231, 233, 237
 over-issue of 224, 227–8, 233
Banking school 222, 233, 235–6, 237, 239, 240, 242, 245
 and Currency school debate 233–40
 arguments 235–7
 plea for larger reserves 237
 see also Currency school
Bank Charter Act (1844) 232, 237–8, 239, 243
 debate on 232
 suspension of 238
Bank of England 223–6, 231, 234, 236–9, 246, 247, 251–2
 crisis of 1847 238–9, 251
 notes 223–5, 231–2, 237
 reserve-deposit ratio 233, 238
Barbon, Nicholas 74, 81, 98, 102, 285, 287
Baring, Alexander (1st Baron Ashburton) 215, 232
Bhagwati, Jagdish N. 163, 297
bills of exchange 4, 28, 30, 35, 44–5, 223–4, 235
bimetallism 220–1, 243, 305
 and Gresham's law 305
Blaug, Mark 11, 55, 113, 148, 178, 185, 187, 279, 282, 295, 300
Bodin, Jean 60–1, 88, 104–5, 121, 282, 288
Boisguilbert, Pierre le Pesant 96, 287
Botero, Giovanni 67, 283
Boyd, Walter 224–5, 305
Bloomfield, Arthur I. 130, 132, 136, 198, 244, 251, 292, 302, 304, 307
Braudel, Fernand 25, 148, 279, 295

314

Index

Brazil 13, 15, 32
  Dutch in 32
  gold 84, 221
  Portuguese repossession of 32
Briggs, Asa (Lord) 172, 298
Brougham, Henry (1st Baron Brougham) 193–4, 267, 299
bullion 12, 20, 21, 30, 33, 42, 44–6, 48, 50, 100, 223–4
Bullion Report (1810) 231, 232
Bullionist controversy 222–32, 240
Bryan, William Jennings 243
Burgos, Pedro de 64
Burke, Edmund 123

Cairnes, John Elliot 169, 298
Cantillon, Richard 72, 99, 106, 108, 110, 121, 284, 288
  monetary disequilibrium theory 108
  on law of one price 108, 288
  on self-regulating specie flows 99, 108
capital 19, 20, 22, 59, 76, 90, 133, 158, 173, 196, 201, 205
  accumulation 19, 22, 59, 159, 178, 179, 181, 186, 204
  movements 106, 238–9, 244–5, 248, 251
capitalism 6, 22, 29, 96, 129, 196
Carey, Henry Charles 211, 261, 309–10, 312
  defence of American protectionism 261–2
Cary, John 71–2, 76–7, 284
Child, Sir Josiah 71–2, 75, 79, 88, 102, 122, 284, 285
Chipman, John S. 10, 141, 165, 166, 197, 201, 279, 280, 290, 294, 298–9
Choiseul, Duc de 79
Clapham, Sir John 208, 303
classical economists 6, 11, 39, 103, 129, 137, 139, 182, 207, 220
  and Corn-Law debate 137–91
  commercial policy 38, 132, 172, 183, 188, 192–4
  machinery export 213–19
  trade policy 171–219 *passim*
classical trade model 103, 141, 145–70 *passim*, 245, 277, 308
  criticisms of 254
  empirical test of 145, 163, 297
  elaboration of 161–70
  see also Ricardo; comparative advantage
Cobden, Richard 61, 139, 255
Cockayne's Project 41, 92

Colbert, Jean-Baptiste 36, 60, 66, 88–91, 96, 119, 122
  mercantilism of 60, 88–91
  programme 90–1, 96
Coleman, D.C. 77, 82, 278, 284
colonisation 32, 197, 201–3
commercial policy 5, 38, 183, 188–90, 192–4, 198, 200, 201, 266
  classical economists and 132, 192–4
  under mercantilism 5, 6, 39, 61–2, 71–2, 78, 82–3
  see also free trade
comparative advantage 58, 100, 115, 130, 137, 138, 140–2, 144, 153–4, 160, 162, 168, 171, 190, 207, 212, 217, 270
  development of doctrine 137, 141–3
  'Eighteenth-century rule' and 102, 103, 141, 143
  empirical tests of Ricardian theory 145, 163, 297
  gains from trade and 138–9, 151, 165, 185
  sources of 140, 190, 217
  technology and 190, 217
  wages, prices and 160–3
  see also comparative costs; 'Eighteenth-century rule'
comparative costs 38, 143, 145, 148, 164, 172, 270, 292
  classical theory of 145–53, 164, 171–2
  law of 100, 137, 140–1, 143–4, 148, 171, 184–5, 297
Condorcet, Marie-Jean (Marquis de) 97
consumption 58–9, 77, 96, 131, 139
Corn Laws (English) 134, 144, 171–3, 175, 183, 184, 186, 188, 191, 193, 219, 268, 272, 301
  background to debate on 171–4, 301
  James Mill's attack on 183–4
  John Stuart Mill as critic of 191
  McCulloch on 187
  Malthus on 175–8
  Ricardo's critique of 178–80, 184–8
  Torrens's case for repeal of 181–3
Cromwell, Oliver 13, 87
Cunliffe Report (1918) 222, 305
Cunningham, William (Archdeacon) 6, 278
currencies 42–4, 49, 221, 222, 242, 246
  devaluation/depreciation of 42–5, 47, 48, 224, 225, 229–30
Currency school 222, 232–3, 235, 252–3
  and Banking school controversy 233–40, 247, 253

Currency school – *cont.*
and principle of 'metallic fluctuation' 233–4
see also Banking school

Davenant, Charles 69, 100, 102, 287
Davis, Ralph 291
Defoe, Daniel 29, 75, 76, 81, 94, 279, 284–5
demand 16, 20, 34, 44, 46–7, 50–1, 54, 60, 158, 164–5, 169, 195–6, 200
domestic market 46, 58–9, 158
elasticity of 16, 44–7, 51, 54–5, 60–1, 165, 200, 207
diplomacy, birth of modern 25–6
division of labour 19, 100, 102, 138–9, 148, 176, 182, 184, 199, 217
and principle of comparative advantage 138–9, 148
Dutch Republic (United Provinces of the) 12, 18, 22–3, 27, 30, 62, 66, 89, 90, 91, 184, 287
Amsterdam entrepôt 14, 29, 30
and commercial diplomacy 92
commercial empire 26, 37
commercial policy 66, 92, 93
Dutch mercantilism 66, 88, 91–3
East India Company 14–15, 16, 21, 32
in Brazil 32
in North America 33
in West Africa 32
struggle with Spain 15–16, 27
West India Company 15–16, 32–3

East India Company (Dutch) 14–16, 21, 32
East India Company (English) 14, 33, 36, 48–9, 81
East Indies 14, 21, 93, 287
economic growth 17–19, 22, 31, 58–9, 68, 115, 117, 119, 129, 187, 197–8, 206–7, 220, 284
and free trade in Britain 207–9
and trade 18–19, 31, 119, 197–8, 284
in early modern Europe 18–19
economic welfare 6, 9, 121, 153, 201, 207
economies of scale 23, 29, 131, 284
Edgeworth, Francis Ysidro 165, 193, 205, 298
'Eighteenth-century rule' 102–3, 120, 131, 136, 141, 175, 183
Ekelund, Robert 9, 10, 124, 278, 291

England (Great Britain) 5, 9, 12, 15, 17–18, 22–3, 25–6, 30–7 *passim*, 48, 94, 124, 172, 173, 214, 217–18, 220–1
commercial empire 26, 30–7, 286
free trade and British national income 207–9
Navigation Acts 30, 32–3, 35, 84–6, 87, 92, 133
penetration of the Mediterranean 31–2, 34
protectionist measures 82, 85–6
re-export trade 30, 95
Enlightenment thinkers 37, 97, 98, 119, 121, 124
equilibrium 50, 108, 112, 114, 152, 165–6, 170, 174, 189–90, 196–7
in international trade 152, 165–6, 170, 174
Mill on 152, 165–6
Ricardo on 152
uniqueness of 165–6
exchange rates 5, 40–8, 49, 50–2, 54, 65, 95, 105, 136, 160, 222–3, 227, 229–30
and Bullionist controversy 224, 227
control of 40–1, 46–7, 52
English mercantilist writers on 42–8, 49–50, 52
money supply and 49–50, 52, 65, 105, 228
Ricardo *v.* Malthus on 229–30
see also purchasing-power parity
exports 5, 54–5, 57, 59, 66, 68, 70, 79, 203–4, 218, 228
of machinery 211, 213–14, 216

fairs 5
Fetter, Frank W. 215, 278, 289, 302, 304, 307
fish, fisheries 28, 50
Forbonnais, François Véron de 71, 303
foreign exchange 5, 38, 40–4, 49, 136, 223
1620s' English debate on 41–50
see also exchange rates
foreign exchange market 42–3, 46, 49–50, 223–4, 226
France 9, 12, 15, 18, 22, 25, 60–2, 73, 96, 115, 124, 252
French mercantilism 88–91
mercantilist thought 60–3
Frederick II, King of Prussia (the Great) 25, 87–8, 286
free trade 37, 40, 94, 97, 99, 100–1, 113, 115–16, 118, 120–1, 124, 129, 133, 136, 139, 142, 177, 188–9, 195, 197,

201, 204, 209, 220, 246, 255–7, 260, 267, 272–3, 275
and efficient allocation of resources 136, 139, 186, 189
classical economists and 100, 115, 129, 143, 209
development of free-trade ideas 94, 97, 98–103
ideology of 144, 148–9, 207, 209, 303
national economists' objections to 255–6, 257–9, 260–2, 265–74
Physiocrats and 117–18, 120–1

gains from trade 57, 100–2, 119, 121, 130–1, 139–41, 144, 146, 151, 155, 156–60, 163, 165, 206–7
comparative advantage and 144, 146, 151, 164–5
Malthus *v.* Ricardo on 156–7
sources of 131, 139, 156
Germany 17, 31, 115, 221, 263, 276–7, 310–11
German Historical School 6, 313
Gerschenkron, Alexander 87, 286
Gervaise, Isaac 106, 108–9, 113, 289
on international adjustment mechanism 108–9, 113
Gilbert, James William 232, 249, 251
gold 18, 19, 66, 220–3, 228, 233, 240, 248
Australian discoveries 221, 240
Californian discoveries 221, 240
points 113, 222
production 19, 248
Gold standard 172, 220–1, 223, 236, 239–40, 243–4, 246–7, 250, 252
abandonment in 1914 220
and Bullion debate 220–33
classical views of 244
divergent views on workings of 243–9, 253
establishment in Great Britain 220–1
international adjustment mechanisms and 237, 244–7, 248, 250
liquidity crises and 238–9, 252
requirements for existence of 222
'rules of the game' 222, 244, 249
stylised facts of 222, 244
government regulation 5, 9, 10, 52, 62, 94–5, 97–8, 120, 124, 129, 132
reasons for decline in 94, 96, 124
under mercantilism 9, 47, 62, 94, 99, 116, 129, 133
see also laissez-faire
Graham, Frank D. 169–70, 199, 298

and theory of international values 169–70, 199, 298
Grampp, William D. 171, 188, 283, 298, 301
Gresham's law 221, 305
Grotius, Hugo 66, 93
Guicciardini, Francesco 24, 279

Haberler, Gottfried von 11, 132, 153, 194, 292, 295, 308
Hamburg 224
Hamilton, Alexander 209, 258–9, 303, 309–10
and infant-industry argument 209, 258, 303
and origins of American protectionism 258–9
Hayek, Friedrich August von 110, 124, 289, 291
Heckscher, Eli F. 6, 8, 9, 70, 78, 278
criticism of Keynes's interpretation 70
on mercantilism 6, 8, 78
Heckscher–Ohlin theory 162, 194, 297
Hicks, Sir John 142, 294, 298
Hobbes, Thomas 22, 24, 279
Holland *see* Dutch Republic
Hollander, Samuel 132, 143, 144, 159, 178, 185, 187, 294, 299
Hornick, Philipp von 67, 283
Hume, David 12, 55–6, 98, 106–7, 111–14, 120–1, 123–4, 132, 135, 222, 241, 247, 249, 255–7, 282, 289–90
and law of one price 110, 112
and natural distribution of specie hypothesis 110, 111
and price-specie-flow mechanism 110–11, 113, 222–3, 289–90
debate with Josiah Tucker 255–6
Keynes on 114–15
on 'jealousy of trade' 115–16
on virtues of moderate inflation 113–14, 290
Samuelson's reformulation of Hume's model 111–12
variations in exchange rates 113, 228
Hume, Joseph, MP 213, 215

imports 5, 51, 54, 57, 59, 66, 162, 203–4
import-substitution policies 39, 61, 78, 82
India 30, 33, 36, 220–1, 243
cottons 30, 33, 100, 102
Industrial Revolution 17, 34, 37

infant-industry argument 133, 209–11, 260, 284–5, 303
  Hamilton on 209, 303
  Mill on 209–11
inflation 19, 20, 22, 42–3, 46, 49, 54–7, 63, 104, 113, 135–6, 223–4, 227, 229, 231, 235
  and exchange rates 43, 46, 49, 54, 63, 224, 227, 229–30
  in Bullionist debate 224, 231
interest rates 6, 19, 68–70, 225–6, 245, 248, 250, 252
  and capital flows 244, 250–1
international adjustment mechanisms 12, 45–7, 54–5, 94, 104–13, 121, 223
  see also balance of payments
international economics 38, 141, 145, 244
international relations 16, 22–3, 26, 38, 61, 79–80, 89, 103, 121, 122, 171, 246
  and conflict 16, 17
  as zero-sum game 6, 17, 79, 80, 89, 121, 134
  pacific influence of trade on 61, 121–3, 134, 135, 139–40
  trade and 61, 121–2, 134–5
  under mercantilism 16, 17
international trade 3, 5, 16, 18, 19, 23–4, 29, 38–9, 80, 95, 99–100, 102, 107, 121, 129, 130, 139, 152, 158, 165, 169, 174, 199, 211
  and the balance of power 80–2
  as solvent of international animosities 61, 121–3, 139–40
  as zero-sum game 16, 17, 57, 100, 103, 117
  colonial trade 13, 33–4, 37, 62, 84, 121, 189, 285
  embargoes 5, 14, 36, 83, 89
  Eastern trade and spices 13–15, 20
  finance of 4, 18, 19, 20–1
  in ancient times 3
  triangular trade 35
international trade policy *see* free trade, protection, commercial policy
international trade theory 11, 38–9, 103, 117, 120, 129, 145–8, 167, 184
  and development 131, 139
  and national economists 254–77 *passim*
  and price theory 146–7
  classical trade model 103, 137–41, 145–54

elaboration of classical model 160–70
  real-cost approach 153–4, 167, 295–6
Italy 5, 17, 24, 25, 26–7, 252
  Italian mercantilist thought 67

Jackson, Andrew 262–3
'jealousy of trade' 12, 115, 134
Johnson, Harry Gordon 109, 211, 278, 289, 293, 304
Jones, Ronald W. 168, 289, 298

Keynes, John Maynard (Lord Keynes of Tilton) 12, 39, 70, 114–15, 221, 246, 247, 252, 272, 280, 290, 307
  on gold 240
  on Hume 114
  on mercantilism 39, 70

labour 69, 70–2, 74–6, 77, 100, 130, 137–8, 149–50, 154, 168–9
  mercantilist views on 69–73, 74–7
labour theory of value 149–50, 152–4, 164, 166–7
  and Ricardo's trade model 145–54, 166
Laffemas, Barthélemy de 60–1, 88–9
  mercantilist programme of 61
laissez-faire 6, 96, 97, 98, 101, 114, 117–18, 129, 202, 215, 220, 244
  emergence of ideas in eighteenth century 96, 102
  origin of slogan 96, 97
Law, John 95
law of one price 110–12, 135, 235, 249, 251
  and arbitrage 105, 111–12, 235, 249, 251
  and purchasing-power parity 106, 110, 135, 250
  as assumption in modern monetary approach 249–50
  Cantillon on 108, 288
  criticisms of 251
  Hume on 110–12
  traded *v.* non-traded goods 108, 111, 136, 249–50
lender-of-last resort 239, 246
List, Friedrich 209, 211, 255, 258, 261–77 *passim*, 308–9, 310–11
  and German expansionism 277
  attack on classical theory 263, 268, 273, 310
  criticisms of 275–6
  on external economies 271

Index

on methodology 264–5
on protection and
  industrialisation 263, 267–72, 312
on stages of development 266
'productive forces' and
  development 255
the national economist 262–6
tributes to 276–7
Locke, John 91, 98, 106–7, 113, 227, 242, 288
  adherence to balance-of-trade
    doctrine 106–7
  and law of one price 106
  on exchange rates 106
  on Quantity Theory 106
Longfield, Mountifort 164, 167–9, 298
Loyd, Samuel Jones (1st Baron
  Overstone) 232, 234, 253

McCloskey, Donald N. 38, 207, 209, 280, 286, 303, 307
McCulloch, John Ramsay 167, 187, 196, 200, 212–13, 216, 218, 232, 260, 288, 295, 304
  on technology diffusion 213
  on terms-of-trade argument 200
Machiavelli, Niccolò 4, 24, 25
machinery 211–12, 214–19 *passim*
  see also technology
Malthus, Thomas Robert 167, 172–3, 176–7, 179–80, 184, 187, 190, 193, 195–7, 204, 207, 260, 296, 299, 301
  and free trade 175–6, 178
  and Ricardo on gains from
    trade 156–7, 296
  criticism of Ricardo on exchange-rate
    determination 229–30
  on dangers of industrialisation 176–8
  on gluts 195–6
  on the Corn Laws 175–8
  on terms of trade 195–6
  on technology exports 213, 217
Malynes, Gerard de 12, 41, 43–8, 49, 55, 71, 105, 281
  controversy with Misselden and
    Mun 44, 49–54
  on exchange control 42–3, 46
  on exchange depreciation and the
    terms of trade 43–5
  on exchange rates and balance of
    payments 43–5
  on international adjustment
    mechanism 45–8
Mandeville, Bernard de 72–3, 98–9, 284, 287

markets 6, 18, 31, 36, 37, 76, 80, 99, 129, 131, 200, 219
  domestic 6, 31, 34, 58, 76–7, 200
  foreign 18, 79, 154, 200, 202, 205, 207
Marshall, Alfred 152, 245, 254, 271–2, 276, 312
Marshall–Lerner condition 46, 47
Martin, Henry 99, 101–2, 287
  and 'Eighteenth-century rule' 102–3
  *Considerations on the East-India
    Trade* 99, 102, 287
Marx, Karl 110, 123, 149, 153–5, 243, 253, 275, 289, 296, 307
  and unequal exchange 154–5
  law of value and trade theory 154–5, 368
  on gold discoveries 240
  on international money 240–3
  on mercantilists 39
  on Quantity Theory 240–2
Melon, Jean-François 122, 291
mercantilism 5, 6, 8, 9, 16–17, 37–9, 67, 70, 78, 81, 88–9, 91, 94, 107, 113–14, 117, 124, 129, 209, 279, 286
  and unemployment 68–73, 100, 105, 114
  definitions of 5–7
  Dutch 66, 88, 91–3
  French 88–91
  historical background 12–27
  interpretations of 5–12
  Prussian 87–8
  Russian 87–8
  Smith's criticisms of 6, 9, 39, 78, 80
mercantilist doctrine 5–12, 13, 38–41, 51–9, 60–7, 68–70, 73–7, 94, 106
  and employment 68–73, 105, 114
  decline of 94–125 *passim*
  English 42–77 *passim*
  French 60–3
  labour and wages in 74–6
  neglect of home market 76–7, 284
  on foreign trade 38–93 *passim*
  Spanish 63–6
mercantilist policy 8–13, 36, 68–77, 78–89
  and employment 68–73
  goals: 'power and plenty' 8, 39, 78–88, 285
  instruments of 82–8
  interpretations of 5, 6
  trade and the balance of power 80–2
merchants 5, 9, 22–4, 26, 31, 35, 51, 58, 124, 278

metallic principle   233–4, 236–7
middle passage   34
Mill, James   137, 141, 143–5, 153, 174–5, 183, 196, 207, 264, 306
   and origin of comparative advantage   137, 143–4
   and orthodoxy   144–5
   critique of Corn Laws   183–4
   refutation of English physiocrats   174–5
   use of Say's law   174
Mill, John Stuart   6, 125, 131, 145, 152, 164–7, 169, 191, 195, 198, 203–9, 254, 260, 272, 292, 295, 301, 306
   and determination of terms of trade   164–6
   and multiple equilibria   165–6
   attack on Corn Laws   191
   on endogeneity of money supply   235
   on free export of machinery   218
   on infant-industry argument   209–11
   on international capital flows   245
   on reciprocal demand   152, 164–5, 201, 204
   on terms-of-trade argument   203–7
Misselden, Edward   12, 41–2, 44, 47, 49, 53, 68, 75, 105, 282
monetary approach to balance-of-payments theory   107, 110, 136, 248–50, 252, 290
   assumptions and linkages   249–50
   criticisms of   251–3
monetary policy   68, 223, 225, 231–2
   under gold standard   222, 232
money   6, 19, 40, 45, 48, 52–3, 55–6, 64, 71, 95, 104–5, 113, 222, 226, 235–6, 238, 241, 252
   demand for   110, 135, 230, 236, 252
   paper money   95, 221, 224, 231, 233–5
money supply   19, 20, 40–2, 45, 48, 65, 95, 104, 109, 111, 113–15, 135–6, 223–4, 227, 233, 235–7, 241, 244, 249
   and balance of payments   45, 48, 54–5, 65, 68, 70, 108–9, 247
   and exchange rates   41–3, 52, 224, 227, 230
   and inflation   19, 20, 43, 49, 53–4, 56, 65, 104–6, 108, 114, 236–7, 241
   and mercantilist thought   39, 51–4, 55–8, 61, 68, 105–6, 113
   Hume on   113–14, 290
   see also Quantity Theory of Money
Montchrétien, Antoyne de   60–2, 88, 283

Montesquieu, Charles de Secondat (Baron de)   122–3
multilateral settlements   21, 35, 94
Mun, Thomas   47–9, 51–9, 67–8, 70, 72, 94, 105, 282–3
   and international adjustment mechanism   54–7
   and relief of unemployment   69
   model of trade and growth   57–9
   neglect of home market   58–9
   on balance-of-trade doctrine   51–4
   on price-elasticity of demand   54
Myint, Hla   10, 131, 272, 278, 292, 311

nation-state   4, 5, 10, 17, 22, 24–6, 38, 40
   growth of   4, 17, 22–6
National Economists   119, 209, 255, 277, 309
   American   257–62, 312
   and free trade   257–62, 265–75
   criticisms of classical trade theory   254–5, 257–62, 267–76
natural law   119, 120
Navarro (Martin de Azpilcueta)   104–5, 288
Navigation Acts (English)   30, 32–3, 35, 84–6, 87, 92, 133
   Adam Smith's opinion on   87, 133
   provisions of   85
New World   4, 13, 15, 18, 20
   see also America, United States
new draperies   30–1, 91
North, Sir Dudley   99, 100, 102, 106

O'Brien, Denis P.   178, 185, 200, 293, 300, 306
Ohlin, Bertil   12, 38, 164, 246, 280, 297
opportunity costs   59, 100–1, 102, 131, 152, 169
optimum tariff   200
Ortiz, Luis   64, 283
overissue of banknotes   224, 231, 233

Parnell, Sir Henry (1st Baron Congleton)   213, 233
Petty, Sir William   69, 72, 284
Phillips, Willard   260, 309
Physiocrats   96, 116–19, 130, 173
   and foreign trade   116–22
   and rejection of mercantilism   117–18

on agriculture as source of
   surplus   117–19
on free trade in agricultural
   products   96, 118
on free trade in manufactures   119
Pitt, William (1st Earl of Chatham)   37
Portugal   13, 14, 16, 19, 23, 32, 83–4,
   86, 93, 139, 140, 161, 221, 269, 285
British trade with   83–4, 221, 269, 285
cloth industry   84
conflict with Dutch   14, 32
control of Eastern trade   13, 14
Methuen Treaty and   83–4, 268–9
Portuguese in Brazil   32
price level   18, 19, 46, 53, 55–6, 65, 106, 233
and money supply   53, 55–6, 104–7
changes in, and adjustment
   mechanism   55–6, 107–8, 110, 227, 236
effect of gold flows on   45–7, 111–12, 233, 236, 247
see also inflation
price revolution (sixteenth century)   18, 19, 20, 104
price-specie-flow mechanism   38, 45–6, 56, 107–8, 113, 135, 222–3, 229, 233, 235, 238, 247, 281
and mercantilist writers   45–8, 55–7, 107–10, 281
Hume on   110–13, 222, 293
prices, international   45, 105, 108, 161, 249, 250
production-possibility frontier   151
productivity (labour)   76, 77, 100, 154–5, 161, 163
differences, and comparative
   costs   161–3, 168
profit   19, 57, 72, 99, 100, 149, 158, 179, 184–5
protection   6, 10, 24, 37, 61–2, 65, 76, 89, 92–3, 121, 125, 132–3, 140, 193, 194, 195, 267–71
and income distribution   158, 179–80, 191–4
and industrialisation   37, 211, 267–72
Australian case for   194
employment argument for   69
in United States   312
National economists and case
   for   209, 255, 257–9, 260–2, 263–6
see also Corn Laws; free trade;
   infant-industry argument
public law of Europe   23, 45–6

purchasing-power parity doctrine
   (PPP)   12, 105–6, 110, 135, 227, 250, 293
and commodity arbitrage   105, 111, 112, 250–1
and exchange rates   45–6, 227–8, 250
Salamanca School and   105, 288
see also law of one price

Quantity Theory of Money   53, 55, 94, 99, 104–13 passim, 121, 135, 222, 225, 241, 243, 248–9, 281
and international adjustment
   mechanism   104–13, 135
and Salamanca School   65, 104–5, 281, 288
Quesnay, François   116, 118–19, 290
see also Physiocrats

Raymond, Daniel   259, 309, 310
Report on Manufactures
   (Hamilton)   258, 303, 310
resource allocation   6, 94, 99, 100, 115, 119, 131, 146, 147, 160, 184, 186, 188, 199, 201, 204, 218
Ricardo, David   6, 11, 102, 105, 130, 137, 139–43, 146, 155, 173, 184–90, 225, 228–32, 245, 252, 253, 294
and changes in comparative
   advantage   190
and class conflict   160, 179, 299, 300
and inverse profit–wage
   relationship   158, 179, 180, 185
and origins of comparative advantage
   doctrine   141–4
critique of Corn Laws   178–80, 184–8, 194, 299, 301
distributional effect of trade   158–9, 179–80, 193–4
dynamic trade model   146, 184, 272, 300
labour theory and trade
   model   144–51, 160, 162, 166
on balance-of-payments adjustment
   mechanism   160–1, 229–31, 245, 247, 248, 250
on gains from trade   156–60
on gold as the standard   231, 234
on machinery   212–13
proposals for monetary reform   234–5
statement of comparative advantage
   principle   137–9, 140, 294
Richelieu, Armand Jean de Plessis
   (Cardinal)   60, 88

Robbins, Lionel (Lord Robbins of Claremarket) 141–2, 271, 273, 291, 294, 312
Robertson, William 123
Robinson, Joan 146, 148, 184, 196, 245, 246, 254, 272, 295, 300, 307, 308
'rules of the game' *see* Gold standard

Salamanca school 65, 104, 105, 281, 288
Samuelson, Marion Crawford 194
Samuelson, Paul A. 11, 38, 111, 142, 145, 194, 280, 289, 290, 294, 301
Savary, Jacques 122, 291
Say, Jean-Baptiste 196, 260, 264, 265, 302
Say's law 70, 159, 174, 201, 205
Schmoller, Gustav 6, 277, 278, 313
  interpretation of mercantilism 6
  on appeal of protectionism 277
Schumpeter, Joseph A. 9, 10, 12, 45, 102, 103, 141, 209, 276, 279, 288
self-interest 94, 98, 123, 132, 193
Senior, Nassau William 154, 161, 162, 167–9, 199–201, 212, 218, 276, 297
  and classical trade theory 154, 161
  and international prices 161–2, 167, 297
Serra, Antonio 40–1, 67, 280
shipbuilding 3, 18, 24, 27, 28, 29, 34, 49, 91
shipping 4, 13, 18, 21, 28, 29, 32, 36, 80
ships 28, 29, 31, 49, 51, 59
silver 14, 18, 19, 20, 21, 33, 42, 61, 63, 104, 107, 221, 223
  drain to East 20, 48, 57, 63
  European production 19
Sismondi, J. C. L. Simonde de 196, 204, 301, 303
  on over-production and gluts 196
slave trade 13, 32, 34, 123
Smith, Adam 6, 9, 11, 12, 16, 37, 39, 78, 80, 82, 87, 93, 99, 103, 113, 121, 124, 129–36, 147, 159, 172, 178, 188, 189, 194, 209, 214, 254, 258, 264, 269, 272–4
  and infant-industry argument 209
  criticisms of mercantilism 6, 9, 39, 78, 80
  on absolute advantage 130–1, 147, 254
  on Anglo–French trade 90
  on balance-of-payments adjustment 135–6
  on foreign trade 129–33, 291
  on free trade 132–5, 147
  on trade policy 132–5
  productivity theory 131, 132
  'real bills' doctrine 224
  'vent-for-surplus' theory 131, 132, 175, 292
Smith, Sir Thomas 41, 70, 280
South Sea Bubble 36
Spain 13–16, 17, 19, 20, 22, 27, 63–6, 252
  balance of payments 56, 64–6
  economic decline 63
  mercantilist thought 63–6
  silver 63
  Spanish mercantilism 63–6
  trade problems 63, 64, 66
specialisation and exchange 58, 130, 139, 140, 154, 196
specie accumulation 5, 39, 41, 51–5, 68, 107
  and balance-of-trade doctrine 54–5, 39–40, 48, 56
  and inflation 55–6, 45–6, 49, 68, 107
Spence, William 143, 173–5
Spice Islands 13, 14, 93
spice trade 13, 14, 21
sterilisation of specie flows 56, 108, 238, 244, 248, 249, 251
Steuart, Sir James 70, 123, 291
Stigler, George J. 136, 147, 172, 293, 295, 298
Supple, Barry E. 48, 281, 284

tariffs 5, 23, 24, 28, 36–7, 66, 86, 89, 90, 92, 115, 133, 194, 198–200, 201, 203, 206, 210, 259, 262, 270, 303
  British 37, 85, 90
  Dutch 93
  US 125, 263, 310
Taussig, Frank W. 125, 142, 152, 163, 167, 170, 244, 307
  and classical theory 170
taxation 24, 25, 37, 65, 95, 96, 117, 133
technology 70, 76, 132, 211–19 *passim*
  debate on export of 211–19
terms of trade 45, 46, 112, 138–9, 152, 164–7, 169, 170, 194–203, 206, 207, 228
  and role of demand 152, 164, 205
  argument in classical economics 166, 194–203, 203–8
  determination of 138, 151, 152, 164
  equilibrium 138, 152, 164–6

indeterminacy of 165
limits of 138, 169
Mill on 152, 203–8
reciprocal demand and 152, 164, 169
textiles 5, 32, 64, 91
Thornton, Henry 225–9, 231, 234, 306
  on balance-of-payments adjustment mechanism 227–9
  on conflict between external and internal policy goals 229
  on external monetary equilibrium 227–9
  on gold standard 226
  Paper Credit of Great Britain (1802) 225, 306
  rejection of 'real bills' doctrine 225–6
Thweatt, William O. 143, 144, 171, 294, 298
Tollison, Robert 9, 10, 124, 278, 291
Tooke, Thomas 187, 232, 235, 237, 306
Torrens, Robert 6, 137, 141–5, 167, 173, 181–3, 187, 192, 193, 197, 198–202, 207, 213, 232, 239, 253, 264
  and free-trade imperialism 182, 183, 201–3
  and law of falling importance of trade 208
  and origins of comparative advantage principle 137, 141–4, 199
  and reciprocity 192, 198, 199
  case for repeal of Corn Laws 181–4
  on existence of competitive equilibrium 197, 201, 202
  on colonization 201–3
  v. Senior on terms-of-trade argument 199, 200
transfer problem 12, 228, 230, 289–90
treasure *see* money
treaties, bilateral commercial 79, 80, 83, 84, 273
Treaties
  Alcobaça (1479) 13
  American (1670) 23
  Breda (1667) 33, 92
  Methuen (1703) 83, 84, 268, 269
  Paris (1763) 36
  Peace of Westphalia (1648) 15, 22, 23
  Tordesillas (1494) 13
  Utrecht (1713) 23, 73, 82, 102
  Zaragoza (1529) 14
Trower, Hutches 179
Tucker, Josiah (Dean) 72, 74, 182, 255–7, 284, 309
Turgot, Anne-Robert Jacques (Baron de l'Aulne) 116, 117, 120–1, 291

United States 210, 221, 222, 257–62, 267, 268, 270, 303, 310
  adoption of gold standard 243
  American colonists 18, 33–4, 34–7, 84, 86, 279
  colonial trade 33–7, 85, 86
  national economists 258, 259–62
  protectionist movement 82, 259–62, 303, 310
  Tariff of Abominations (1828) 263
  Tonnage Act (1789) 259
Uztáriz, Gerónimo de 64, 66, 283

value, labour theory of 149–54, 162, 164, 167
  and international value 153–5, 165, 166, 169, 298
Vanderlint, Jacob 106, 107, 110, 113, 288
  on international adjustment mechanism 107
Venice 13, 26, 27, 31
vent-for-surplus theory 132, 174, 292
Vereenigde Oost-Indische Compagnie (VOC)
  see East India Company (Dutch)
Viner, Jacob 5, 9, 10, 45, 75, 79, 88, 102, 109, 111, 114, 124, 135, 140, 163, 167, 170, 275, 278
Voltaire, François 97, 120

wages 6, 19, 74–6, 160, 161, 167, 168, 175, 201
  comparative advantage and 161–2, 167–8
war and trade 13, 15, 16, 17, 26, 80–1, 87, 90, 92, 122, 123
wars
  Anglo–Dutch 32, 87, 90
  Seven Years' 13, 37, 119
  Thirty Years' 16, 22
wealth and power 38, 78–88
West Indies 13, 15, 33, 34, 35, 86, 93, 285
'Westphalian System' 22
Wicksell, Knut 226
Williams, John Henry 254, 272, 275, 308
  critique of classical trade theory 254, 272
Wilson, Charles 279, 284
wool trade 5, 36, 58, 63, 64

Zollverein 263, 275
  List and 263